# Smart Charging Infrastructures

**Scrivener Publishing**
100 Cummings Center, Suite 541J
Beverly, MA 01915-6106

*Publishers at Scrivener*
Martin Scrivener (martin@scrivenerpublishing.com)
Phillip Carmical (pcarmical@scrivenerpublishing.com)

# Smart Charging Infrastructures

Edited by

**A. Chitra**

**W. Razia Sultana**

and

**V. Indragandhi**

Scrivener Publishing

WILEY

**2 Innovating EV Charging Infrastructure: A Hybrid Energy Storage System Approach for Solar Powered-Based DC Microgrid** **29**
*Sandeep S. D., Satyajit Mohanty and Shashi Bhushan*
2.1 Introduction 29
2.2 System Architecture 30
2.2.1 Modeling of PV System 30
2.2.2 Battery Storage System 32
2.2.3 Supercapacitor 33
2.3 Power Management System 33
2.4 Results and Discussion 36
2.5 Conclusion 39
References 39

**3 Design of Intermediate Charging Facilitated Port Configuration of Charging Station with Consideration of Reliability and Cost** **41**
*K. Vaishali and D. Rama Prabha*
3.1 Introduction 42
3.2 Methodology for Estimating the Reliability Probability of Charging Ports 43
3.3 Introduced Pattern Identical and Non-Identical Configuration 46
3.4 Results and Discussions 49
3.4.1 Identical Port Configuration 49
3.5 Conclusion 54
References 55

**4 AI-Based Smart Charging Infrastructures: Revolutionizing Electric Vehicle Integration** **57**
*V. Bagyaveereswaran, S.L. Arun, M. Manimozhi and B. Jaganatha Pandian*
4.1 Introduction 58
4.2 Fundamentals of Smart Charging 59
4.2.1 Benefits of Smart-Charging Infrastructure 61
4.2.2 Deployment Factors for Smart Charging 62
4.3 Role of AI in Smart Charging 64
4.3.1 Understanding Artificial Intelligence in Charging Infrastructures 64
4.3.2 Machine Learning Algorithms for Predictive Charging 66
4.3.2.1 Benefits of ML-Powered Predictive Charging 69

4.3.3 Real-Time Data Analytics and Optimization Techniques 70
4.3.3.1 Real-Time Data Analytics 71
4.3.3.2 Optimization Techniques 71
4.3.4 AI-Based Demand Response Management 72
4.3.4.1 Understanding Demand Response Management 73
4.3.4.2 Benefits of AI-Based DRM for Charging Stations 74
4.4 Components of AI-Based Smart Charging Systems 74
4.4.1 Sensors and IoT Devices for Data Collection 75
4.4.2 Cloud Computing and Edge Computing Platforms 77
4.4.2.1 Cloud Computing Platforms 78
4.4.2.2 Edge Computing Platforms 78
4.4.3 Communication Protocols and Network Infrastructure 79
4.4.4 Control Algorithms for Dynamic Charging Control 81
4.5 Challenges and Future Directions 83
4.5.1 Security and Privacy Concerns in AI-Driven Infrastructures 84
4.5.2 Scalability and Interoperability Issues 84
4.5.3 Regulatory and Policy Implications 86
4.5.4 Emerging Technologies and Trends in Smart Charging 86
Bibliography 87

**5 EV Smart Charging Using RES—Challenges 91**
***Sowmya Ramachandradurai, Joylin Mary J. and D.F. Jingle Jabha***
Acronyms 91
5.1 Introduction 92
5.2 System Description 92
5.2.1 Description of Photovoltaic (PV) Source 93
5.2.2 Description of Wind Energy 93
5.2.3 Description of EV 94
5.2.4 Objective Function 95
5.2.5 Constraint Conditions 95
5.2.5.1 Equality Constraint 95
5.2.5.2 Generator Constraint 96
5.2.6 Framework of Optimization Algorithm 96
5.3 Results and Discussion 98
5.4 Conclusion 99
References 101

6 **Green Energy-Based Active Grid Optimization Using Deep Learning for EV Charging Infrastructure** **105**
*D. Shruthi, R. Raja Singh, S. L. Arun and R. Rengaraj*
6.1 Introduction 106
6.2 Active Grid and Edge Computing 107
6.3 Modeling of Standalone Hybrid System 109
6.3.1 Solar PV Cell Model 109
6.3.2 Wind Turbine Model 112
6.3.3 EV Battery Model 114
6.4 Deep Learning and Its Implementation 115
6.4.1 Energy Demand Pattern 117
6.4.2 Wind Speed 120
6.4.3 Solar Irradiation 121
6.5 Micro-Grid and Control Mechanism 123
6.5.1 Microgrid Functioning in Different Modes 124
6.5.1.1 Islanded Mode 125
6.5.1.2 Multiple Microgrid Control with Centralized Energy Storage System 125
6.5.2 Energy Storage System Simulation 126
6.5.3 Wind Energy Storage System Simulation 127
6.5.4 EV Battery Control Mechanism 129
6.6 Results and Discussion 130
6.6.1 Deep Learning 130
6.6.2 Matlab/Simulink Model 132
6.7 Conclusion 134
References 135

7 **Bearing Fault Diagnosis in Permanent Magnet Synchronous Motor Using Deep Neural Network** **137**
*Geetha G., Shanthini C., Geethanjali P. and Yokkeshwaran K.*
7.1 Introduction 138
7.2 Methodology 141
7.2.1 Discrete Wavelet Transform 142
7.2.2 Kurtogram 144
7.2.3 Deep Neural Network-VGG 146
7.3 Results and Discussion 148
7.3.1 Case 1: Using DWT 148
7.3.2 Case 2: Using Kurtogram 148
7.4 Conclusion 152
References 152

**8 Enhancing Efficiency in Bidirectional CLLC Resonant Converters: A Hybrid Control Approach** **157**
*Aryan Chaturvedi, M. Rajalakshmi and Razia Sultana W.*
8.1 Introduction 158
8.2 Bidirectional CLLC Resonant Converter 159
8.3 Working by Controlling Conversion of Frequency 160
8.4 How the Inductance Factor (k) Affects Voltage Gain (M) 162
8.5 How the Quality Factor (Q) Influences Voltage Gain (M) 163
8.6 Understanding Frequency-Conversion Control 164
8.7 Combining Frequency Conversion and Phase Shifting with a Hybrid Control Strategy 165
8.8 Simulation Results and Discussion 168
8.9 Conclusion 173
References 173

**9 IoT-Based Smart Charging Systems** **175**
*Tanmay Sharma, Pramatha S. Vasishtha and Razia Sultana W.*
Abbreviation 175
9.1 Introduction 176
9.2 Remote Monitoring and Telematics 176
9.3 Infrastructure Connectivity for Charging 177
9.4 Autonomous Driving and Advanced Driver Assistance Systems (ADAS) 178
9.5 Logistics and Fleet Management 178
9.6 Sustainability and Energy Management 179
9.7 Services and User Experience 180
9.8 Algorithms for Shortest Path Finding 180
9.8.1 Dijkstra's Algorithm 180
9.8.2 Bellman–Ford Algorithm 182
9.8.3 A* Search Algorithm 182
9.8.4 Floyd–Warshall Algorithm 183
9.8.5 Bidirectional Search Algorithm 184
9.8.6 Rapidly Exploring Random Tree Algorithm 185
9.8.7 Probabilistic Roadmap Algorithm 187
9.8.8 Hybrid RRT-PRM Model 189
9.9 Advantages 192
9.10 Conclusion 193
References 193

**10 Embedded Control of Power Converters in E-Mobility** **195**
*Yeddula Pedda Obulesu and Pallamkuppam Vinodh Kumar*
10.1 Introduction 196
10.1.1 Key Components of EV 198
10.2 Evolution of Digital Control in Power Converters 199
10.2.1 Key Functions of Embedded Control of Power Converters 200
10.2.2 Components of Embedded Control Systems 201
10.2.3 Control Strategies 201
10.2.4 Challenges and Innovations 201
10.3 Embedded Systems and Digital Control 202
10.4 Tools and Technologies for Digital Control Systems 202
10.5 Implementation of Embedded Digital Control Based on DSPs 203
10.6 Key Components in Embedded Digital Controllers 205
10.7 Signal Generation for Power Converter Devices 207
10.7.1 Operating Frequency and Resolution 207
10.7.2 Modes of Operation 207
10.8 Field Programmable Gate Arrays (FPGAs) 208
10.9 Code Composer Studio and JTAG 212
10.9.1 Functional Requirements of a Non-Inverting Buck-Boost Converter 217
10.10 Software Development Environment (SDE): Compiler, Linker, Assembler, and Downloader 219
10.11 STM-Based Embedded Controllers 226
10.12 Main Traction Inverter 227
10.13 On-Board Charger 228
10.14 Battery Management System (BMS) 229
Acknowledgement 230

**11 Solar Piezo Hybrid Power Charging System** **231**
*Vedanth S., Varun Baalaji S., Shairahul Gautam S., Sharan Vikash, Ashwini K. and R. Resmi*
11.1 Introduction 231
11.2 Methodology 233
11.2.1 Simulation Modelling in MATLAB/Simulink 233
11.2.2 Brief Description of Various Parts 234
11.2.3 Block Diagram and Working 235
11.3 Operating Modes 236
11.4 Result and Discussion 237
11.4.1 Simulation Results in MATLAB/Simulink 237

11.4.2 Hardware Implementation 238
11.4.3 IoT Integration 239
11.5 Conclusion 240
Acknowledgments 240
References 240

**12 EV Power Train Performance with DC Motor 243**
***Nithya Chandran and R. Resmi***
12.1 Introduction 243
12.2 Methodology 244
12.2.1 Architecture of Battery EV Power Train 244
12.2.2 Requirements of Electric Traction Motors 245
12.2.3 Machine Topologies 246
12.2.4 Vehicle Dynamics and Estimation of Output Parameters 247
12.3 Results and Discussion 249
12.3.1 Simulation Results 249
12.3.2 Cost–Benefit Analysis 250
12.4 Conclusion 251
Acknowledgment 251
References 252

**13 RC Vehicle for Delivery 255**
***Vemulapati Dhanunjaya Reddy, Mallireddy Jayanthi Reddy, Manoj Kumar S., R. Resmi and Y. N. V. Ganesh***
13.1 Introduction 256
13.1.1 Description of the RC Vehicle 256
13.1.1.1 Functioning of L298N Motor Driver 256
13.1.1.2 The Functioning of ESP32 Camera Module 256
13.2 Literature Review 257
13.2.1 Research Gap 259
13.3 Methodology 259
13.3.1 Radio-Controlled (RC) Vehicle 259
13.3.2 Camera System 260
13.3.3 Pan-Tilt Mechanism 260
13.3.4 Anti-Theft Locking System 260
13.3.5 Mobile-Application Interface 261
13.4 Result and Discussions 262
13.5 Conclusion 263
References 264

**14 Aerodynamic Drag Reduction in Heavy Vehicles** **267**
*Amutha Prabha N., Abhishek Gudipalli, Dyuti Ranjan Acharya, Indragandhi V. and Manee Sangaran Diagarajan*
14.1 Introduction 267
14.2 Literature Survey 268
14.3 Methodology 269
14.3.1 Geometry and Meshing 270
14.3.2 Inlet, Outlet, and Boundary Conditions 272
14.3.3 Computational Procedure 272
14.4 Results and Discussion 273
14.4.1 Pressure Contour Comparison 274
14.4.2 Velocity Contour Comparison 275
14.4.3 Streamline Profile 276
14.4.4 VelocityVector Profile 277
14.5 Analysis Comparison 277
14.5.1 Streamline Comparison at Rear to Understand Flow Characteristics 277
14.5.2 Drag Force Comparison 278
14.6 Conclusion 279
References 279

**15 Review of Optimization-Based Sensor Fault Detection for Lithium-Ion Batteries in Electric Vehicles** **281**
*Mohana Devi S. and V. Bagyaveereswaran*
15.1 Introduction 282
15.2 Gestalt of Battery Sensors 284
15.3 Utilization of Battery Sensors in Electric Vehicles 287
15.3.1 Significance of Sensor Fault Identification in Li-Ion Batteries 290
15.3.2 Sensor Fault Modeling 293
15.4 Optimization in Sensor Fault Detection 293
15.5 Advantages and Category of Metaheuristic Algorithm 297
15.5.1 Applications of Metaheuristic Approach for Sensor Fault Detection in Lithium-Ion Batteries 298
15.5.2 Challenges in Fault Detection 303
15.6 Result and Discussion 305
15.7 Conclusion 306
References 306

**16 Development of a Hybrid Foot-Stamping Bicycle with Dynamic Electric Support: A Sustainable Alternative to Traditional Pedal and Electric Bicycles** **313**
*Sumant Shyam, Jahnavi Gayatri D., Anushka and Abhishek Gudpalli*
16.1 Introduction 314
16.2 Background and Motivation 314
16.2.1 Limitations of Traditional Pedal-Based Bicycles 315
16.2.2 The Rise of Electric Bicycles (E-Bikes) 315
16.2.3 The Need for a Hybrid Solution 316
16.2.4 Innovative Foot-Powered System 317
16.2.5 Electric Dynamic Support 317
16.2.6 Motivation for the Proposed Design 318
16.2.7 Design Concepts 318
16.3 Study Objectives 322
16.3.1 Design and Development of the Foot-Stamping Mechanism 323
16.3.2 Integration of Dynamic Electric Support 323
16.3.3 Performance Evaluation and Efficiency Analysis 324
16.3.4 Sustainability and Environmental Impact 324
16.3.5 User Experience and Accessibility 325
16.3.6 Prototype Development and Testing 325
16.4 Scope of Study 326
16.4.1 Design and Engineering Focus 326
16.4.2 Prototyping and System Testing 327
16.4.3 Energy Efficiency and Sustainability Assessment 327
16.4.4 User Experience and Practical Application 328
16.4.5 Technical and Financial Feasibility 328
16.4.6 Limitations and Constraints 329
16.5 Conclusion 329
References 330

**17 A Novel Multilevel Inverter with Reduced Switch for Electric Vehicle Applications** **337**
*Vijaya Sambhavi Y. and Vijayapriya R.*
17.1 Introduction 337
17.2 Proposed MLI 340
17.2.1 Description and Analysis of Proposed MLI Circuit 341
17.3 Control Strategy and Simulation Outcomes 342
17.4 Conclusion 346
References 347

**Index** **349**

# Preface

This book, *Smart Charging Infrastructures*, aims to provide a comprehensive perspective on the emerging landscape of EV charging systems. It explores the evolution of charging technologies from conventional plug-in chargers to wireless and ultra-fast solutions, while addressing the challenges of interoperability, standardization, and cybersecurity. The text emphasizes the role of smart electrical systems, artificial intelligence, machine learning, deep learning, and Internet of Things (IoT) technologies in enabling intelligent decision-making and real-time energy management for sustainable transportation.

The work is designed for researchers, engineers, industry professionals, policymakers, and graduate students who seek both foundational knowledge and insights into cutting-edge advancements. Each chapter has been carefully structured to bridge theory and practice, drawing on recent research findings, reviews, case studies, and global best practices. Our intention is not only to capture the current state of the art but also to inspire new directions for research, innovation, and policy development in this rapidly growing field.

We extend our gratitude to our collaborators, students, and colleagues whose contributions and insights enriched the depth and scope of this book. We also thank the editorial team at Wiley for their support and commitment in bringing this project to fruition.

It is our hope that this book will serve as a valuable reference for advancing the design and deployment of smart charging infrastructures, ultimately contributing to the realization of a cleaner, smarter, and more sustainable energy and mobility ecosystem.

# 1

# Towards Sustainable Mobility: An Autonomous Electric Vehicle Charging Station Powered by Multifaceted Renewable Energy Sources

**K. Kathiravan[1] and P. N. Rajnarayanan[2*]**

*[1]Department of Electrical and Electronics Engineering, Mother Theresa Institute of Engineering & Technology, Palamaner, Andhra Pradesh, India*
*[2]Department of Electrical and Electronics Engineering, Theni Kammavar Sangam College of Technology, Koduvilarpatti, Tamil Nadu, India*

## *Abstract*
The rapid expansion of electric vehicles (EVs) has resulted in an urgent requirement for an effective, eco-friendly, and long-lasting charging infrastructure. This study investigated the development of an autonomous EV charging station that integrates the advantages of various renewable energy sources, including solar panels, wind turbines, hydrogen fuel cells (HFCs), and battery energy storage (BES) systems. This study was motivated by the fact that electric vehicles (EVs) have a lower environmental impact, require less maintenance, and have higher energy efficiency. The ever-growing fleet of electric vehicles poses a challenge to the current charging infrastructure, placing heavy energy demand on the power system network. To mitigate this, this study suggests integrating several renewable energy sources to power the EVCS, which will lessen its dependence on the traditional grid. The design process is elaborated upon with a comprehensive set of equations for each renewable energy component. Different combinations were examined to determine the potential of these sources of synergy. A detailed model and simulation are created within the Matlab–Simulink environment to gain a thorough understanding of the autonomous EVCS's behavior. The simulation results validated the most efficient use of a blend of renewable energy sources, confirming the practicality and effectiveness of this autonomous charging station.

**Corresponding author*: pnrajnarayanan@gmail.com

A. Chitra, W. Razia Sultana and V. Indragandhi (eds.) Smart Charging Infrastructures, (1–28)

The findings of this study represent a substantial contribution to the field of electric vehicle charging systems because they have the potential to advance sustainability and lessen the burden on current infrastructure.

***Keywords***: Energy optimization, autonomous electric vehicle charging station, hybrid renewable energy configuration, sustainable transportation, photovoltaic, wind, hydrogen fuel cells, battery energy storage system

## 1.1 Introduction

Undoubtedly, road travel is the dominant mode of transportation for most people worldwide. Conventional vehicles depend on fossil fuels [1]. Fossil fuel consumption in the transportation sector has harmed the total amount of greenhouse gas and as other gaseous and particulate emissions to the environment [2]. Currently, the electric vehicle (EV) market has grown significantly, leading to a dramatic rise in global EV adoption [3]. EVs are essential for sustainable and efficient transportation [4]. EVs produce almost no pollution, are more energy-efficient and quieter, and require less maintenance [5].

EVs must be connected to the electrical distribution network for charging. However, a significant increase in EVs can impair the distribution network by causing power losses and affecting voltage profiles and overloads, which can compromise the quality of the electric supply [6]. Consequently, the distribution network must be ready for EV-specific demands and requirements. Enhancing the electrical system is one solution to these issues, although it is costly. A preferable alternative is to use battery energy storage (BES) between electric vehicle charging stations (EVCS) and distribution networks [7]. However, the use of BES will only minimally reduce the strain on the distribution network, although accommodating a high volume of EVCS remains difficult [8]. The environmental benefits of electric vehicles (EVs) depend heavily on the sources of electricity-powered charging stations. Integrating renewable energy sources into EVCS is crucial to maximize their positive impact [9].

Photovoltaic (PV) systems are typically employed as renewable energy sources in EVCS. It is the most extensively researched renewable energy source because of its affordability, accessibility, and easy maintenance [10]. Several studies [11–13] have been conducted on PV-based EVCS. Solar irradiation is intermittent; hence, the power injected into the grid relies on the amount of solar irradiation available [14]. Wind energy is another common form of renewable energy. Wind energy is a limitless, cost-free, and sustainable resource. Wind turbines are a low-carbon method for harnessing the kinetic energy of wind. Wind-energy-powered EVCS have been reported in the literature [15–17].

The weather affects the amount of energy produced by renewable energy sources. The efficiency of PV depends on solar radiation, and the wind energy depends on the direction of the wind and its velocity. As a result, different sources of energy must be identified to supply electrical energy, because the same amount of energy cannot be delivered continuously. Electrical energy may be produced using fuel cells, regardless of weather conditions. In a fuel cell system, hydrogen is employed as the fuel and can be produced through electrolysis [18]. The integration of PV and fuel-cell systems was reviewed in [19].

Most earlier publications have concentrated on integrating two renewable energy sources: solar and fuel cells [18], and solar and wind [20, 21]. This study is inspired by the development of an autonomous EVCS that integrates various renewable energy resources.

The uniqueness of this study can be summarized as follows:

- Establishment of novel and cutting-edge autonomous charging infrastructure for EVCS.
- The focus is on combining various renewable energy sources, such as wind, solar, and hydrogen fuel cells, to develop an all-encompassing Battery Energy Storage (BES) system for EVCS.
- Deployment of a BES unit array in parallel to guarantee EVCS operation even in the event of primary energy source failure.
- Utilization of a BES equipped with a unidirectional buck converter as a single EVCS terminal; this arrangement may be expanded to support multiple terminal ports at different voltage levels.
- To improve the primary energy supply, a PI-based unidirectional boost converter for wind and photovoltaic energy sources was proposed.
- Integrating wind and photovoltaic energy as EVCS's main energy sources.
- Integrating a fuel cell with a unidirectional variable DC voltage regulator to supply backup or reserve.

## 1.2 Description of the Proposed Charging Station

Figure 1.1 illustrates the potential structure of the autonomous EVCS system. An autonomous EVCS system is an off-grid design that uses renewable energy as its source of power. The primary renewable energy sources, PV and wind, supply energy to the EVCS. The terminals of the PV and the wind were connected to the boost converter. This system optimizes the efficiency of the solar panel and wind turbine by ensuring their maximum power point tracking (MPPT) conditions are met. This is achieved by matching the voltage levels from these primary sources with the DC bus voltage. The generated energy varies according to the solar irradiation level and wind velocity, and it is volatile. To overcome this, the BES bank and hydrogen-powered fuel cell are connected to the DC bus through a DC-DC converter. The charge controller is a one-quadrant converter, whereas the DC-DC converter has two quadrants.

Upon closing switch 1, the autonomous EVCS is propelled by the primary renewable energy sources. When switch 2 is engaged, the BES bank becomes fully connected to the DC bus, thereby becoming available to

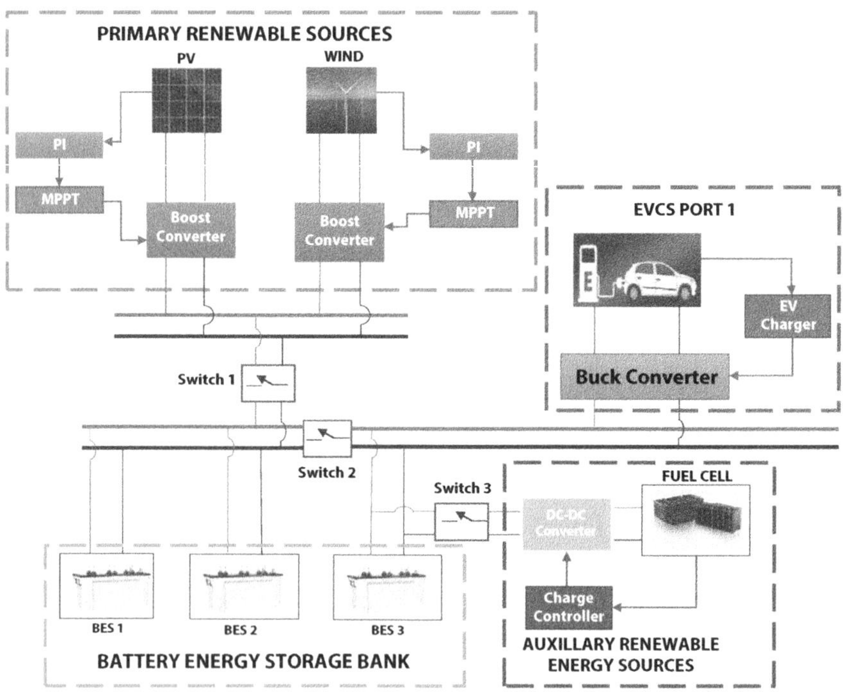


**Figure 1.1** Proposed autonomous system.

supplement the power supply from the primary sources. If the primary renewable energy sources are either unavailable or inadequate to satisfy the energy demand, the autonomous EVCS seamlessly switches to draw power from BES 3, which is connected to an auxiliary renewable source in the form of a hydrogen-powered fuel cell. In this mode, the fuel cell acts as a reserve power source for the EVCS.

To facilitate the energization of the fuel cell by BES 3 of the BES bank, switch 3 is closed. However, this requires that switches 1 and 2 be opened to disconnect the primary sources, BES 1 and BES 2, of the BES bank. Consequently, under such circumstances, energization is not possible for the BES bank. because all switches are open. However, it is noteworthy that BES 3 of the BES bank can still supply energy to the EVCS to the extent of its capacity. In the alternate scenario, when switch 2 is engaged, the entire BES bank becomes available to supply the required energy to the EVCS up to its full capacity.

The proposed off-grid design does not depend on a single charging energy source. Hence, the proposed design acts as an autonomous system for charging the EVCS. If required, the EVCS port can be extended to multiple ports.

The operational configurations of the autonomous EVCS system described above, along with the corresponding energy-supply flexibility, testify to the innovative layout of this state-of-the-art technology. This system's skillful integration and exploitation of primary and auxiliary renewable energy sources is extremely amazing, and serves as a model for sustainable energy solutions.

## 1.3 Design and Analysis of the System

### 1.3.1 PV System

The electrical design of the system includes the design of renewable energy sources, PV, wind, fuel cells, BES, and converters. First, it is necessary to explore the relationship between input energy, power delivered to EVs, and stored energy in the BES.

The assumptions made in this study are [22]:

- The BES initial energy is $E_i$ $W^{-h}$
- The EV station's output power $P_{EV}$ is constant
- The PV panel's solar power "$P_{PV}$" fluctuates over time

$$P_{PV} = \frac{P_m}{36}(36 - t^2) \tag{1.1}$$

where $P_m$ represents the maximum PV power, and t is the time in hours.

Based on the concept of power balance,

$$P_{EV} = P_{PV} - P_{BES} \tag{1.2}$$

Solar photovoltaic cells can be fabricated using various models. This study uses the simplest and most efficient equivalent solar cell circuit, which consists of a shunt resistor, diode, and current source linked in parallel. Figure 1.2 depicts the PV module's equivalent circuit [23].

The load current is

$$I = I_{PV} - I_d - I_{sh} \tag{1.3}$$

where $I_{PV}$ is the PV panel current, $I_d$ is the diode current, and $I_{sh}$ is the shunt current.

The shunt voltage

$$V_{sh} = V + IR_s \tag{1.4}$$

where $R_s$ represents the series resistance.

Current passing across the shunt resistor is,

$$I_{sh} = \frac{V + IR_s}{R_{sh}} \tag{1.5}$$

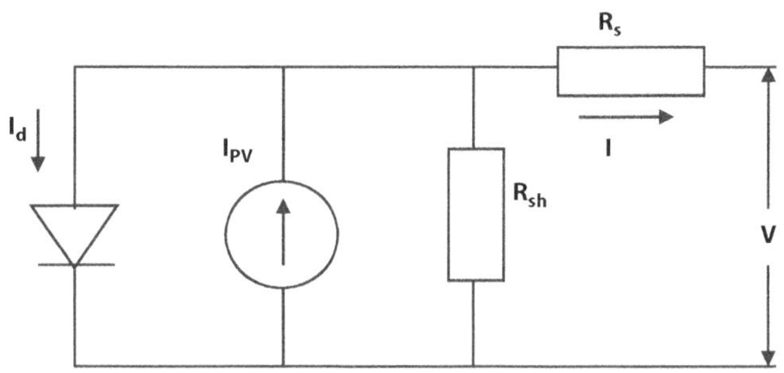


**Figure 1.2** Equivalent circuit of PV system.

In Shockley's equation, the current flowing through the diode is expressed.

$$I_d = I_o\left[e^{\frac{V_{sh}}{nVT}} - 1\right] \tag{1.6}$$

where $I_o$ represents the saturation current, n is the number of solar cells, and T is the solar cell temperature.

$$V_T = \frac{kT}{q} \tag{1.7}$$

where k is the Boltzmann constant, T is the solar cell temperature, and q is the electron charge.

The characteristic equation is

$$I = I_{PV} - I_o\left[e^{\frac{V_{sh}}{nVT}} - 1\right] - \frac{V + IR_s}{R_{sh}} \tag{1.8}$$

where $R_{sh}$ represents the shunt resistance.

Eq. (1.8) can be used to quickly calculate the open circuit voltage and short circuit current at their respective limits. When there is an open circuit, the current is zero, and Eq. (1.8) becomes:

$$0 = I_{PV} - I_O\left[e^{\frac{V_{OC}}{nVT}} - 1\right] - \frac{V_{OC}}{R_{sh}} \tag{1.9}$$

The final term can be disregarded because, in most cases, shunt resistance is high relative to the open circuit voltage. Rearranging the equation while ignoring the term results in:

$$V_{OC} \approx nVT \ln\left[\frac{I_{PV}}{I_O} + 1\right] \tag{1.10}$$

Assigning a zero-output voltage to the short circuit current, results in:

$$I_{SC} = I_{PV} - I_O\left[e^{\frac{I_{SC}R_S}{nVT}} - 1\right] - \frac{I_{SC}R_s}{R_{sh}} \tag{1.11}$$

The size of the PV cell influences its electrical characteristics. Larger cells typically exhibit a higher reverse saturation current ($I_o$) owing to their larger diode junction area. However, they also tend to have lower series and shunt resistances. A solar cell's performance is determined by its fill factor.

$$\text{Fill Factor} = \frac{\text{Maximum Power}}{\text{Open Circuit voltage} \times \text{Short Circuit current}} = \frac{P_{max}}{V_{OC} \times I_{SC}} \tag{1.12}$$

### 1.3.2 Wind

The wind turbine and DC bus are connected *via* a unidirectional DC/DC converter, and the MPPT controller focuses on the WECS's MPP. The DC-link voltage was utilized as a point of reference by the MPPT controller to track the MPP.

The Tip Speed Ratio is a nondimensional quantity that describes how the wind speed and the rotor's rate of rotation interact [24]. It is given by

$$\lambda = \frac{R\omega}{v_w} \tag{1.13}$$

where R is the radius of the turbine, Ω is the angular velocity of the speed, and $v_w$ is the wind speed.

The turbine's output mechanical power $P_m$ is

$$P_m = C_p(\lambda)\, P_w \tag{1.14}$$

where $C_p$ is the power coefficient and $P_w$ is the wind power.

### 1.3.3 Fuel Cell

The chemical energy of the hydrogen fuel stores is converted into electricity by a hydrogen fuel cell. Energy is chemically produced in hydrogen fuel cells. A positive cathode and a negative anode were the two electrodes found in each fuel cell. These electrodes are the sites of the electrical response, accelerated by a catalyst, and in the presence of an electrolyte that transports particles with electric charges between them [25].

Although hydrogen fuels the reaction within a hydrogen fuel cell, oxygen is also necessary for the process to function. A key advantage of these cells is their cleanliness. They require only hydrogen and oxygen to generate electricity, with water vapor as the sole byproduct. Fuel cells powered by pure hydrogen were fully carbon-free.

The anode of the fuel cell was supplied with hydrogen gas. Platinum, a catalyst that facilitates splitting of hydrogen atoms into protons and electrons, was applied to the anode. When the anode and cathode create a circuit, electrons can move across them to power any load connected to them.

Oxidation reaction at the anode

$$H_2 \rightarrow 2H^+ + 2e^- \tag{1.15}$$

Protons created when hydrogen is formed at the anode are transferred to the cathode by the fuel cell's electrolyte. Heat and water are produced by the fuel cell and released when the oxygen supplied to the cathode combines with hydrogen ions and electrons from the external circuit.

Reduction reaction at the cathode

$$O_2 + 2H^+ + 2e^- \rightarrow H_2O \tag{1.16}$$

### 1.3.4 Boost Converter with MPPT

Using a DC-DC boost converter to control and stabilize the DC bus voltage in conjunction with the MPPT algorithm is a practical method for optimizing the PV power output [26]. Although the Perturb and Observe (P&O) method has several drawbacks, such as sluggish response time and frequent oscillations around the MPP, in this work, P&O is used for its effectiveness and simplicity [27]. The number of PV panels set up in parallel and series is considered in the electrical design of the boost converter.

The MPPT block function is primarily excited by repeating sequences of increasing and decreasing climatic variations, resulting in the generation

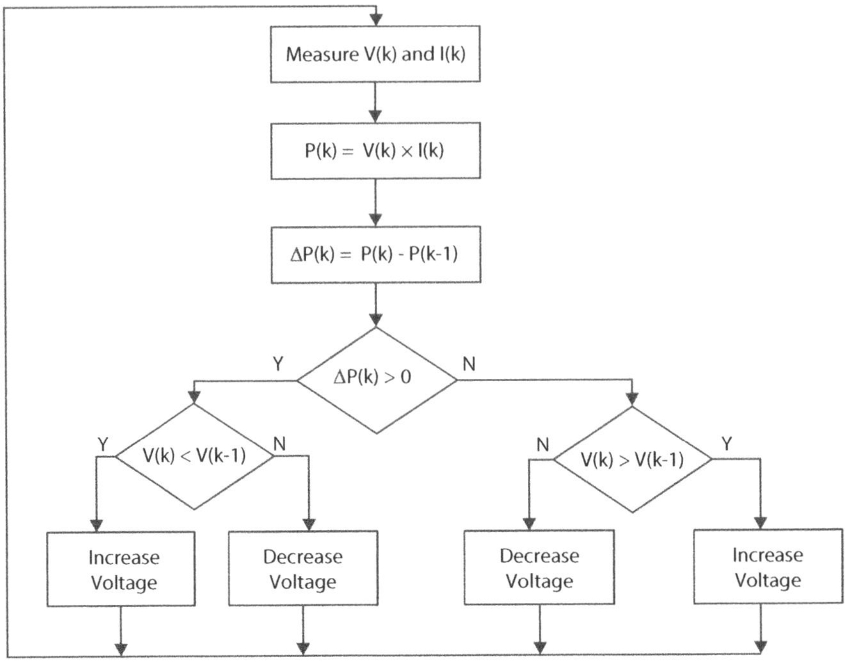


**Figure 1.3** P&O MPPT algorithm.

of a proper duty cycle for transistor control. Hence, the output power is fixed at the maximum point. The circuit's purpose is to energize the BES for use with electric vehicles. The Figure 1.3 shows the algorithm of P&O technique.

### 1.3.5 Buck Converter

Numerous studies have found that the majority of EV batteries require medium voltage. In this situation, a buck converter is required to adjust the voltage rate; however, the duty cycle of the chopper control is set to a steady value to guarantee the required output voltage. The PV panel power is initially stored in the inductor when the boost converter is turned on, and then it is transferred to the load through the capacitor when it is turned off [22].

### 1.3.6 EV Charge Controller

This controller's objective is to control the speed of EV charges. There are many different control methods including pulse, constant voltage (CV), constant current (CC), and constant current/constant voltage (CC/CV) methods. The (CC and CC/CV) approaches are frequently chosen owing to their quick charging times. The (CC/CV) approach was applied in this study. Here, a straightforward PI controller was used. The Ziegler–Nichols method was used to adjust the proportional and integral gains of the PI controller [22].

Simple summaries of the Ziegler–Nichols tuning algorithm are as follows. First, the proportional gain section of the PI controller was reduced to its bare minimum. Consequently, the controller was set to zero to delete integral operations. Note that the controller should not reach its limits at the time the oscillations occur. It may be necessary to introduce a disturbance by altering the setpoint after each gain increment to determine whether the loop oscillates. These oscillations have an oscillation period ($T_o$) and occur at a critical proportional gain ($K_{pc}$). The gains, proportional ($K_p$), and integral ($K_i$) of the PI controller are modified as follows by evaluating the parameters $K_{pc}$ and $T_o$:

$$K_p = 0.35\, K_{pc} \tag{1.17}$$

$$K_i = \frac{0.8 K_p}{T_o} \tag{1.18}$$

## 1.4 System Design Calculations

The proposed autonomous design was designed using the MATLAB–Simulink platform. Figures 1.4, 1.5, 1.6, and 1.7 depict the boost converter, buck converter, EV charge controller models, respectively, and the proposed autonomous system Simulink model.

### 1.4.1 PV System

The Apollo Solar Energy ASEC-120G6M model was considered for the PV calculations. The maximum power was 120 W at a maximum voltage of 17.33 V and a maximum current of 6.93 A. The PV current–voltage characteristics are shown in Figure 1.8.

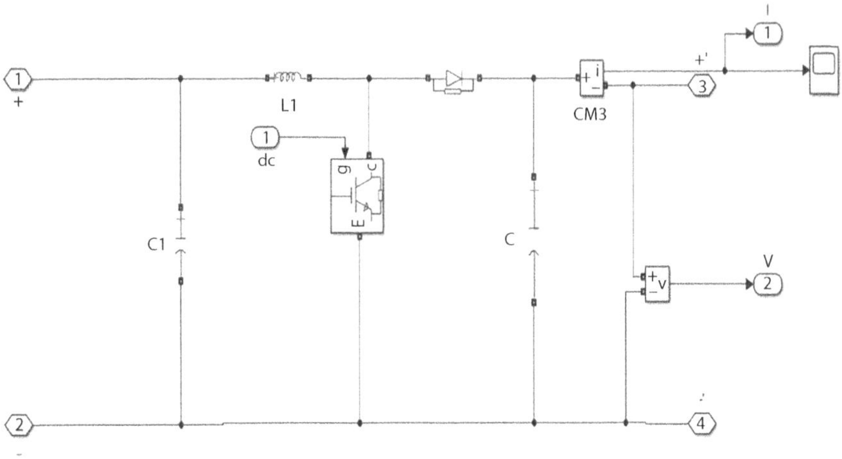


**Figure 1.4** Boost converter model.

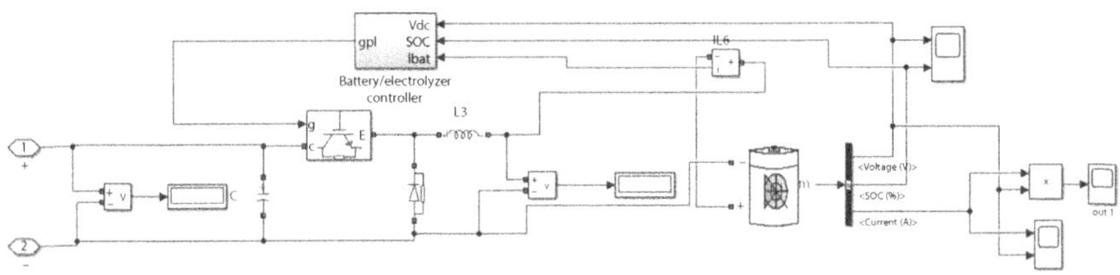


**Figure 1.5** Buck converter model.

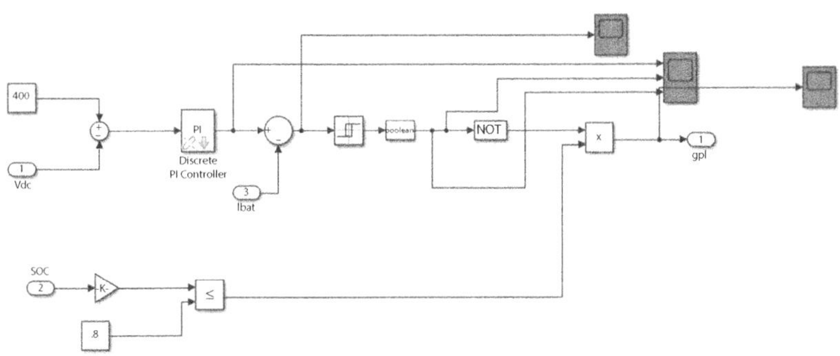


**Figure 1.6** EV charge controller model.

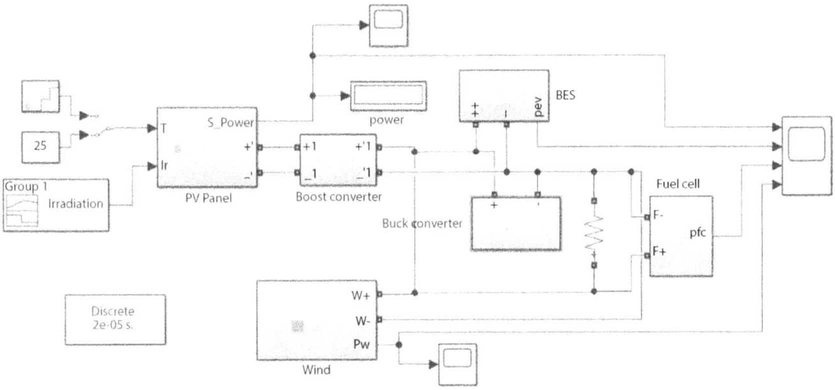


**Figure 1.7** Proposed autonomous system Simulink model.

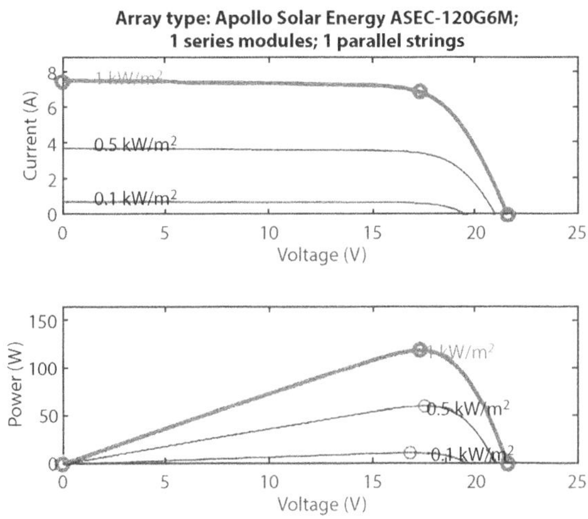


**Figure 1.8** I–V characteristics of PV system.

### 1.4.2 Wind Turbine

The nominal mechanical output power is 100 W. The power characteristics of the wind turbine are displayed in Figure 1.9.

### 1.4.3 Fuel Cell

For the fuel cell, the Solid Oxide Fuel Cell (SOFC) type is considered. The maximum power is 3.4 kW. The V–I characteristics of the fuel cell are shown in Figure 1.10.

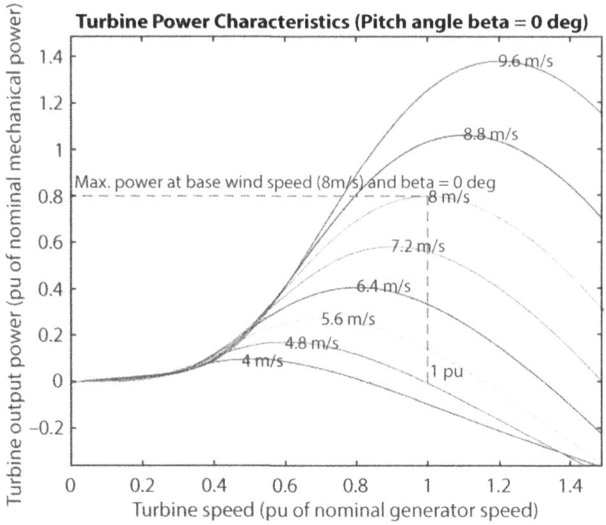


**Figure 1.9** Wind turbine power characteristics.

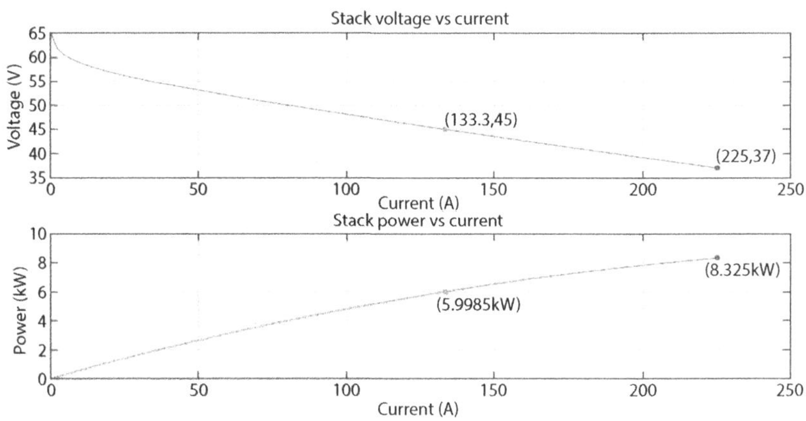


**Figure 1.10** Fuel cell V–I characteristics.

### 1.4.4 Battery Energy Storage System

A Lithium-Ion battery setup was considered for vehicle battery systems. The battery had a rated capacity of 65 Ah and nominal voltage of 12 V. The battery-discharge characteristics are shown in Figure 1.11.

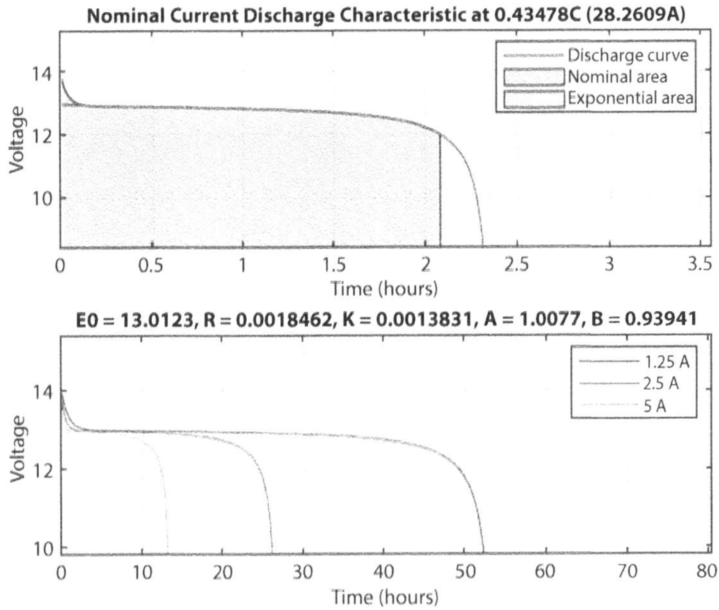


**Figure 1.11** Battery discharge characteristics.

## 1.5 Result Analysis

For the analysis, the following different cases are considered:

Case 1: PV BES Setup
Case 2: PV BES Wind Setup
Case 3: PV BES FC setup
Case 4: BES Wind setup
Case 5: BES FC setup
Case 6: BES Wind FC setup
Case 7: PV BES Wind FC Setup

For the PV-based cases, the solar irradiation level is shown in Figure 1.12. Similarly, for the wind-based cases, wind input is shown in Figure 1.13. The EV voltage and current characteristics are shown in Figures 1.14, 1.15.

### 1.5.1 Case 1: PV BES Setup

For the PV BES setup, the output power characteristics and state of charge (SoC) are shown in Figures 1.16, 1.17.

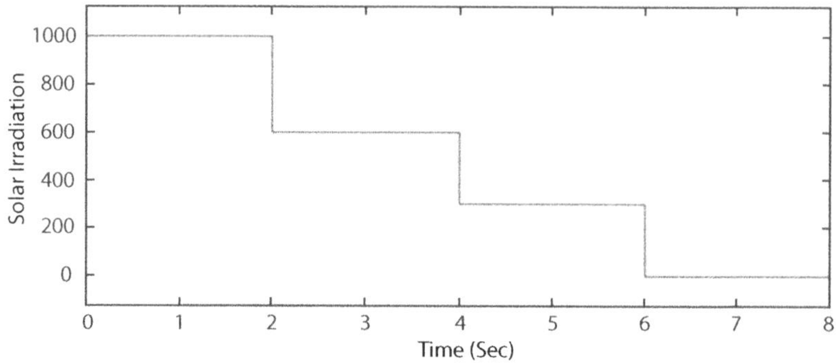


**Figure 1.12** Solar irradiation level.

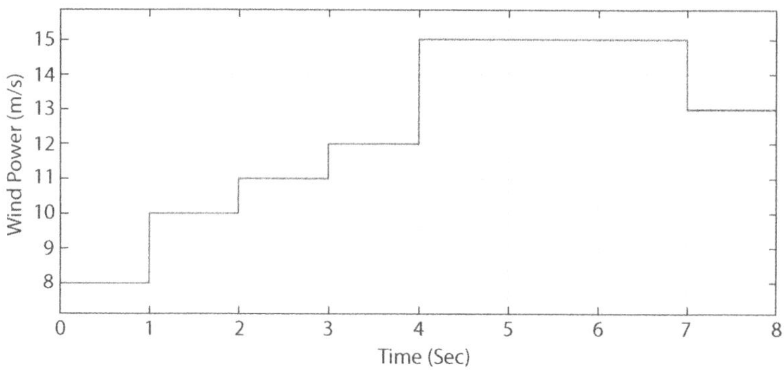


**Figure 1.13** Wind input.

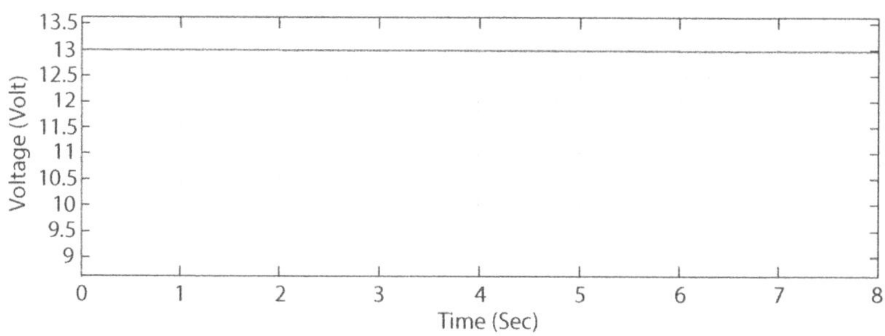


**Figure 1.14** EV voltage.

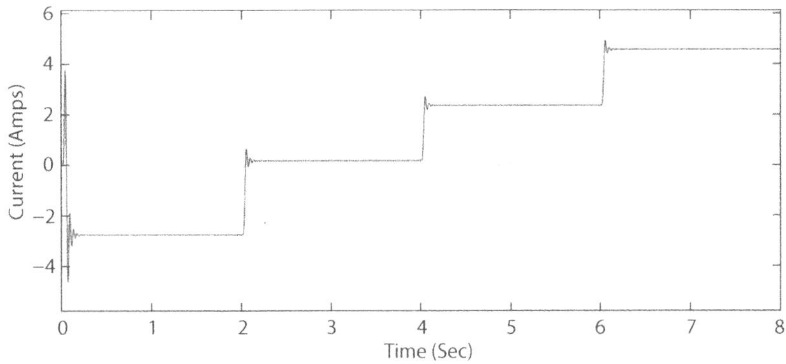


**Figure 1.15** EV current.

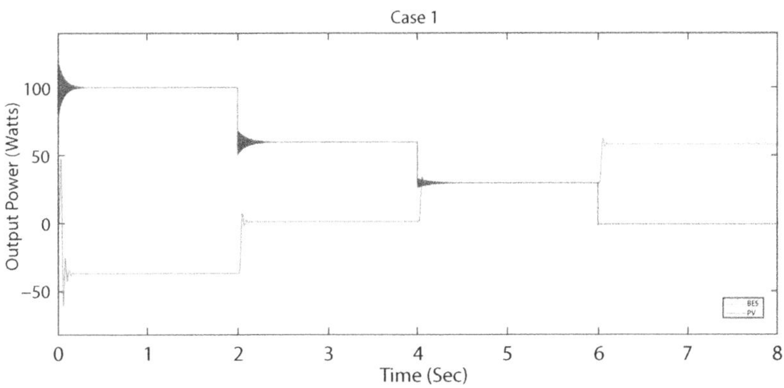


**Figure 1.16** PV BES power.

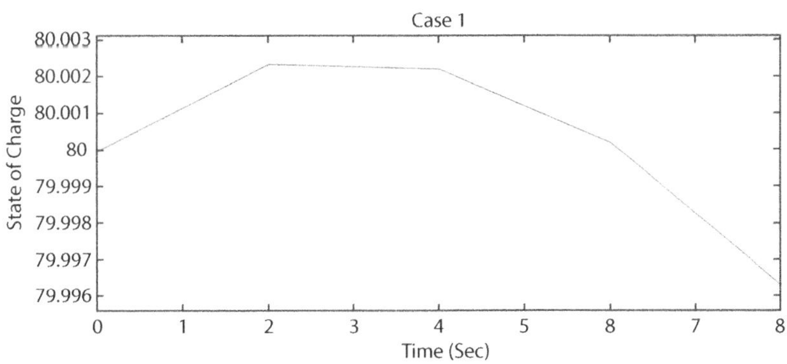


**Figure 1.17** PV BES SoC.

During the initial 2 s, the irradiation level of the PV system reached its maximum (1,000). The generated power reached its peak (100 W) during this time frame, and the SoC of the BES system commenced an upward trend. From 2 s to 4 s, the irradiation level decreased to 600. The power generated from the PV setup was reduced to 70 W and the SoC of the BES system remained constant.

However, as the level of irradiation further decreased to 300 from 4 s to 6 s, the power generated from the PV setup decreased to 35 W. Consequently, the SoC of the BES system started to decrease. This reduction in the generated output from the PV setup makes it challenging for the BES system to obtain the required aid from the PV setup. In this state, the station BES capacity is solely utilized to deliver power to electric vehicles.

From 6 s to 8 s, no irradiation was observed. Consequently, no power was generated from the PV setup, and the SoC of the BES system decreased steeply. This shows that the generated output from the PV setup was entirely shut down, leading to the disconnection of the BES setup from the PV setup. Under these circumstances, the stored capacity of the BES system is utilized exclusively to provide energy to electric vehicles.

### 1.5.2 Case 2: PV BES Wind Setup

For the Case 2 setup, the output power characteristics and SoC are given in Figures 1.18, 1.19.

From 0 s to 7 s, the wind energy was considered to increase from 8 m/s to 15 m/s. At the same time, the duration of the integrated power generated from the PV and wind setup is utilized to energize the station BES, and the SoC of the station BES setup starts increasing from its initial state.

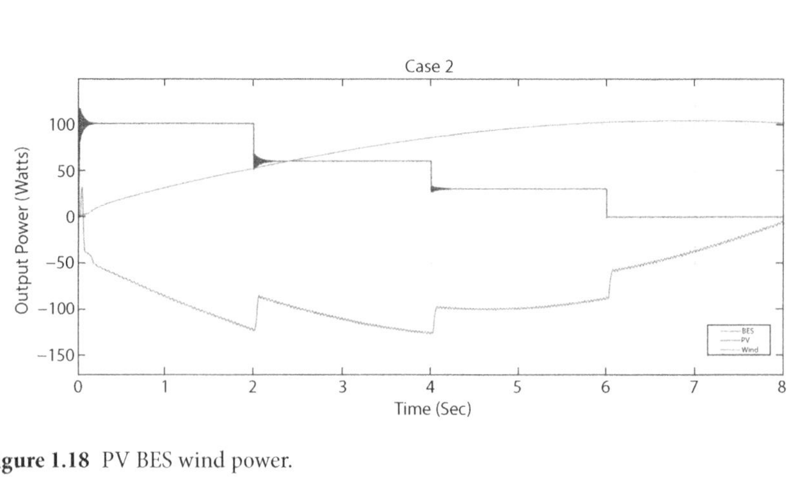


**Figure 1.18** PV BES wind power.

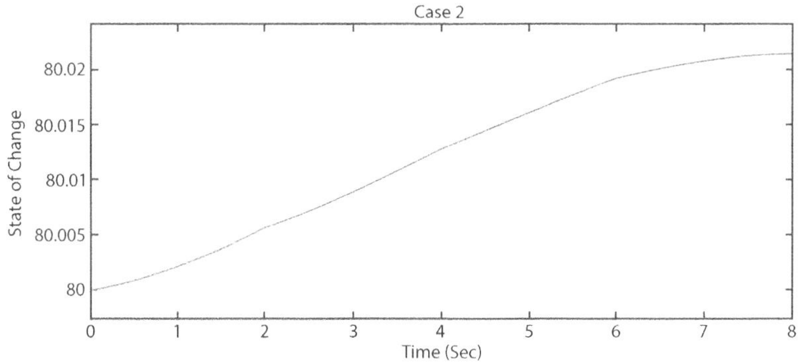


**Figure 1.19** PV BES wind SoC.

This shows that generated output from the integrated setup of a PV and wind system is fully satisfied to maintain the requirement of a station BES to deliver power to EVs.

From 7 s to 8 s, the wind energy was reduced from 15 m/s to 13 m/s. for the same time duration, the PV system is shut down. Now, the wind energy is used to energize the station BES, and the SoC of the station BES setup is maintained, and vice versa. Nevertheless, the SoC of the BES remains stable, signifying that the wind turbine can meet the power requirements of EVs without auxiliary assistance. Overall, the hybrid renewable energy system can fulfil the power requirements of EVs while effectively harnessing both solar and wind energy sources. The BES serves as a crucial mediator for maintaining a dependable and consistent power supply, even amidst fluctuations in the output of the solar and wind sources.

### 1.5.3 Case 3: PV BES FC Setup

For the Case 3 setup, the output power characteristics and SoC are shown in Figures 1.20, 1.21.

The fuel cell's power output of 12 W is designated as a reserved power source for the BES station, which augments the system's energy output and storage capacity.

During the initial 4-second interval, the SoC of the BES station ascended from its initial state. Throughout this period, the integrated power generation from the fuel cell and PV system was utilized to energize the BES station. Consequently, the SoC of the station was effectively maintained. The hybrid system operated comparably throughout this phase.

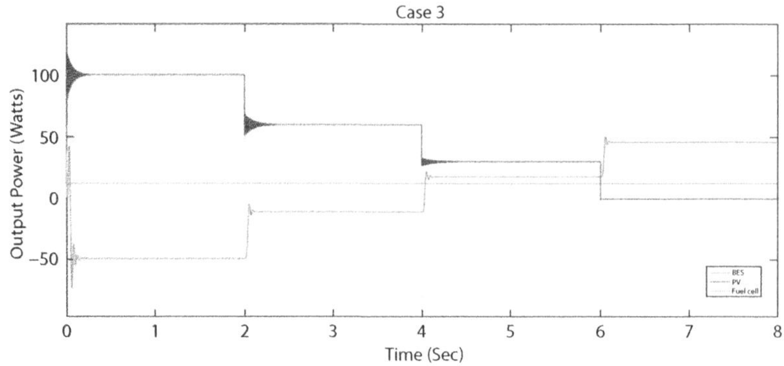


**Figure 1.20** PV BES FC power.

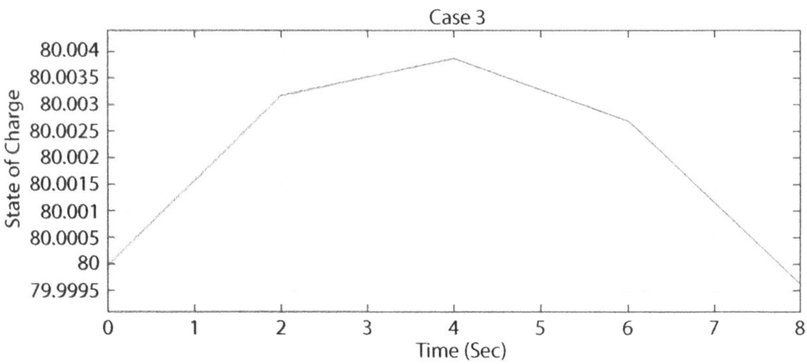


**Figure 1.21** PV BES FC SoC.

However, from 4 s to 8 s, the SoC of the BES station began to decline owing to a dearth of sufficient generated power to meet the energy demands of the station. During this period, the PV system produced 35 W from 4 s to 6 s before being deactivated from 6 s to 8 s. As a result, the station's stored BES capacity is the sole source of power to deliver the requisite energy to EVs.

The integration of the fuel cell and PV system provides a hybrid system with greater flexibility and resilience in coping with variations in energy output. The reserved power of the fuel cell mitigates the impact of temporary energy fluctuations and ensures dependable and stable power supply for the BES station. Nevertheless, certain instances may necessitate the utilization of stored BES energy to satisfy the energy demands of EVs.

### 1.5.4 Case 4: BES Wind Setup

For the Case 4 setup, the output power characteristics and SoC are shown in Figures 1.22, 1.23.

The integration of a battery energy storage (BES) station with wind turbines represents a judicious strategy for augmenting a system's aggregate energy output and storage capacity. Notably, the SoC of the BES station initially experienced a decline but subsequently manifested a steady increase between the first and eighth seconds. This phenomenon is attributable to the progressive linear upsurge in wind power output during the same period, commencing at 8 m/s during the first second and culminating in a value of 13 m/s from the seventh to the eighth second. After the first second, the EV charging station's energy needs are met by the wind system's generated output, which continues for the duration of the simulation.

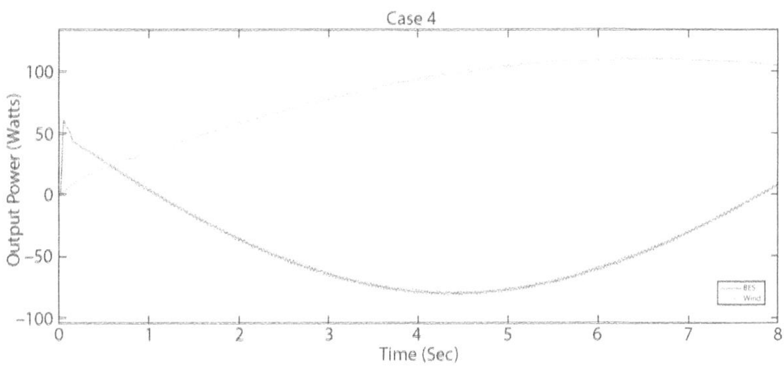


**Figure 1.22** EV wind power.

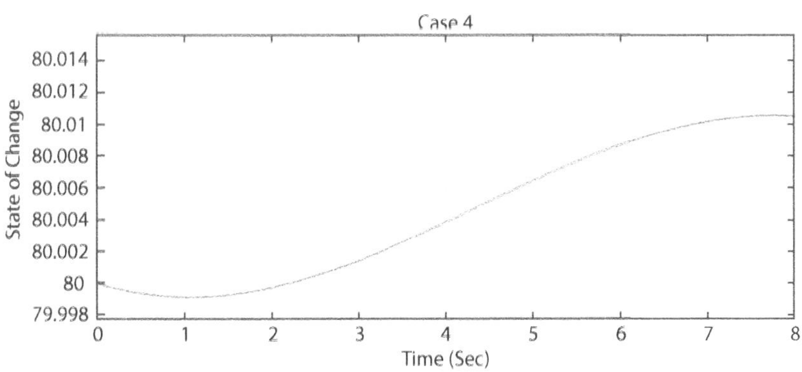


**Figure 1.23** BES wind SoC.

The incorporation of the wind system into a hybrid renewable energy configuration constitutes a viable means of fulfilling the energy needs of the EV charging station, owing to the BES station's consistent and dependable power supply. Given the dynamic nature of the wind power output, the system requires continual monitoring and optimization to sustain optimal and reliable performance.

### 1.5.5 Case 5: BES FC Setup

For the Case 5 setup, the output power characteristics and SoC are shown in Figures 1.24, 1.25.

The power requirements of the BES system and the output power of the fuel cell, which is rated at 82 W and has been set aside for station usage, appear to be somewhat correlated. As a result, it is shown that the SoC rises from its initial value, indicating that it absorbs more power than it is using.

Several factors may be involved in this scenario, including the fuel cell efficiency and the power consumption profile of the BES setup. If the fuel

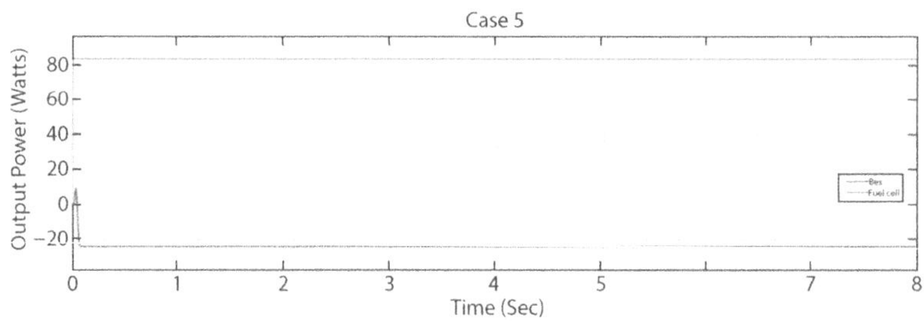


**Figure 1.24** BES FC power.

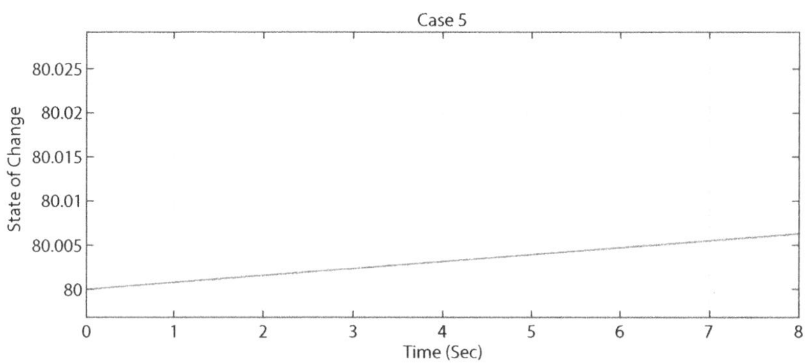


**Figure 1.25** BES FC SoC.

cell does not operate at peak efficiency, it may not be capable of generating the full 82 W of power, thereby explaining the observed partial support of the BES capacity. Similarly, the BES setup may not consume the maximum power available from the fuel cell, possibly owing to the reduced demand or built-in power-saving features.

This observed trend of increasing SoC for the BES is encouraging, as it suggests that the system can fulfill its power requirements with some surplus capacity. Nonetheless, vigilance in monitoring the system performance is paramount to guarantee that the power output from the fuel cell is sufficient to fulfill the power demands of the BES setup.

### 1.5.6 Case 6: BES Wind FC Setup

For the Case 6 setup, the output power characteristics and SoC are shown in Figures 1.26, 1.27.

This setup outlines a hybrid system comprising a wind turbine, fuel cell, and electric vehicle (EV) charging station. The system was designed to utilize the fuel cell's reserved power output of 12 W to power the BES station. The integrated power generated from the wind and fuel cell setup was harnessed to energize the BES station, thereby ensuring a reliable energy supply for the EV charging station.

During the initial 0 s to 0.5 s, the SoC of the BES station decreases, after which it starts to increase from 0.5 s to 8 s. Notably, the wind power during the first second was 8 m/s,followed by a linear increase from 1 s to 7 s before decreasing to 13 m/s from 7 s to 8 s. This trend demonstrates that the generated output from the wind and fuel cell setup is sufficient to

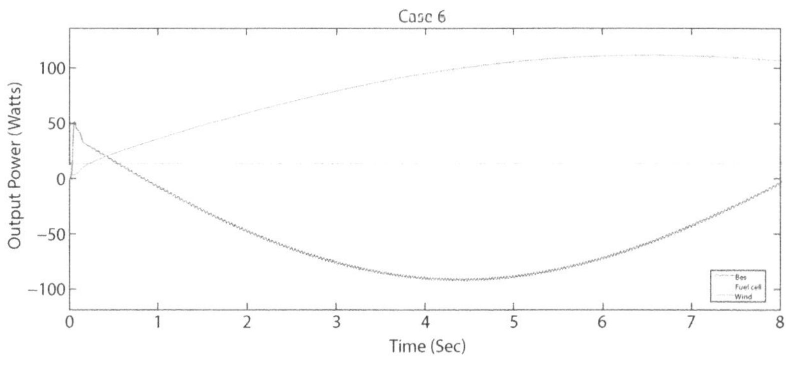


**Figure 1.26** BES wind FC power.

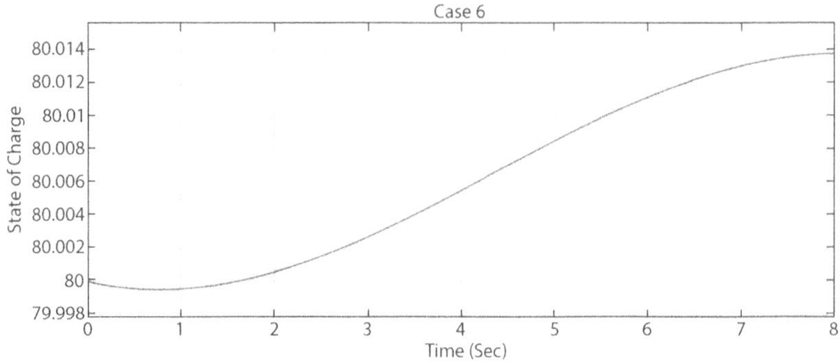


**Figure 1.27** BES wind FC SoC.

maintain the BES station's requirements to deliver power to EVs, even after the initial 0.5 s of operation.

The utilization of a hybrid renewable energy system featuring wind and fuel cell power generation technologies presents an innovative solution to address the energy demands of modern society, while promoting sustainable and eco-friendly energy practices. The reliability and stability of such systems, as illustrated by the efficient operation of the BES station, highlight viable hybrid technologies for meeting the energy demands of the future.

### 1.5.7 Case 7: PV BES Wind FC Setup

For the Case 7 setup, the output power characteristics and SoC are shown in Figures 1.28, 1.29.

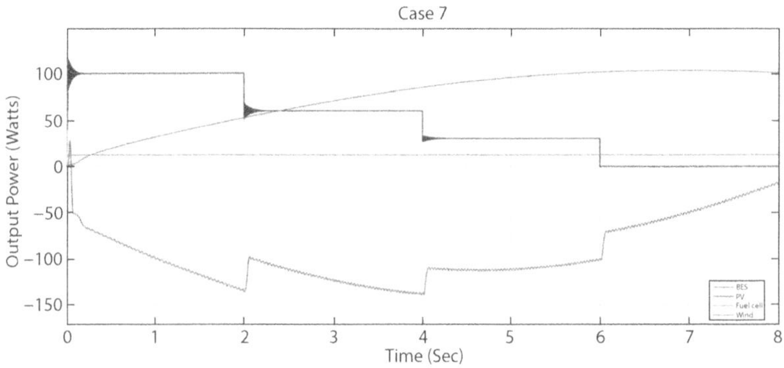


**Figure 1.28** PV BES wind FC power.

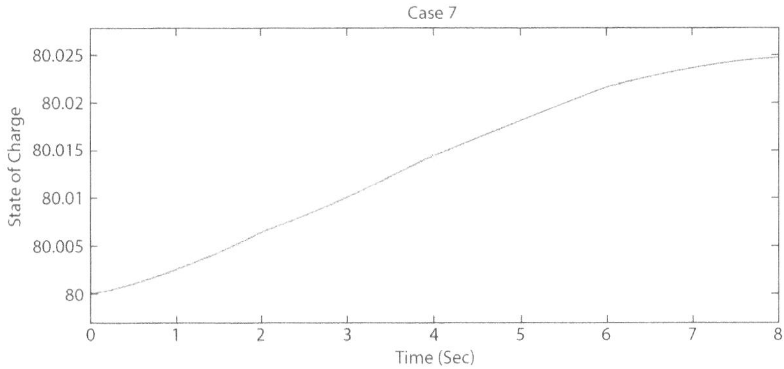


**Figure 1.29** PV BES wind FC SoC.

This scenario examines an integrated power-generation setup that includes photovoltaic (PV), wind, fuel cells, and electric vehicle (EV) systems. Notably, the reserved power from the fuel cell with a power output of 12 W was utilized for the BES station. As a result of the integration of these power sources, the generated power is channeled into energizing the station BES, and the SoC of the station BES setup starts increasing from its initial state. The observed outcomes of this integrated setup show that the generated output is fully capable of meeting the requirement of a station BES to deliver power to EVs compared to Case 2. This suggests that the use of various power sources improves the system's overall effectiveness and produces better outcomes.

## 1.6 Conclusion and Future Outlook

This study analysed the combinations of various renewable energy sources to power the EVCS. The energy needed for an autonomous EVCS has been met by integrating renewable energy sources, such as solar, wind, and hydrogen-powered fuel cells, to create a hybrid renewable energy configuration. A battery energy system provides a dependable and stable supply to the system. A BES plays an important role in balancing energy input and output and ensures that EV energy needs are met even when solar and wind energy outputs fluctuate. The reserve power output of the fuel cell provides a novel approach to enhance the system's overall capacity for producing and storing energy while minimizing the consequences of transient energy swings. Seven different configurations were analyzed.

Of the seven potential cases, it was found that the optimal combination for the station BES setup was Cases 2 and 7. In this pairing, Case 7 comprised a fuel cell that generated reserved power, rendering it superior to Case 2. It is important to remember that when choosing the ideal design, both the fuel cell efficiency and the BES system's power consumption must be considered.

As a result, it is essential to continue a watchful monitoring routine to ensure that the fuel cell's power output is sufficient to meet the setup's power requirements. In conclusion, Case 7, with its reserved power from the fuel cell, presents an optimal solution for the station BES setup, particularly when combined with Case 2. Therefore, to counteract climate change, hybrid renewable energy systems must be combined to meet the demand.

Future studies may focus on creating complex energy management algorithms that optimize the use of the hybrid renewable energy system and investigating the robustness and reliability of the hybrid system under various circumstances, including extreme weather or equipment failure.

## References


1. Lahiri-Dutt, K., The Diverse Worlds of Coal in India: Energising the Nation, Energising Livelihoods. *Energy Policy*, 99, 203–213, 2016.
2. Al-Thani, H., Koç, M., Fountoukis, C., Isaifan, R.J., Evaluation of particulate matter emissions from non-passenger diesel vehicles in Qatar. *J. Air Waste Manage. Assoc.*, 70, 2, 228–242, 2020.
3. Sun, X., Li, Z., Wang, X., Li, C., Technology Development of Electric Vehicles: A Review. *Energies*, 13, 1, 2020.
4. Lima, T., Franco, J., Lezama, F., Soares, J., Vale, Z., Joint Optimal Allocation of Electric Vehicle Charging Stations and Renewable Energy Sources Including CO2 Emissions. *Energy Inf.*, 4, suppl, 2, 2021.
5. https://e-amrit.niti.gov.in/benefits-of-electric-vehicles.
6. Minh, P., Quang, S., Pham, M., Technical Economic Analysis of Photovoltaic-Powered Electric Vehicle Charging Stations under Different Solar Irradiation Conditions in Vietnam. *Sustainability*, 13, 6, 2021.
7. Rafi M, A.H. and Bauman, J., A Comprehensive Review of DC Fast Charging Stations with Energy Storage: Architectures, Power Converters, and Analysis. *IEEE Trans. Transp. Electrif.*, 7, 2, 345–368, 2021.
8. Nicholas, M. and Hall, D., Lessons Learned on Early Fast Electric Vehicle Charging Systems, International Council on Clean Transportation, 2018.
9. Weitemeyer, S., Kleinhans, D., Vogt, T., Agert, C., Integration of renewable energy sources in future power systems: the role of storage. *Renew. Energy*, 75, 14–20, 2015.

10. Kabir, E., Kumar, P., Kumar, S., Adelodun, A., Kim, K., Solar energy: Potential and future prospects. *Renew. Sustain. Energy Rev.*, 82, 894–900, 2018.
11. Sampaio, P.G.V. and González, M.O.A., Photovoltaic solar energy: conceptual framework. *Renew. Sustain. Energy Rev.*, 74, 590–601, 2017.
12. Kumar, V., Teja, V.R., Singh, Mishra, S., PV Based Off-Grid Charging Station for Electric Vehicle. *IFAC-PapersOnLine*, 52, 4, 276–281, 2019.
13. Bhatti, A.R., Salam, Z., Aziz, M.J.B.A., Yee, K.P., Ashique, R.H., Electric vehicles charging using photovoltaic: Status and technological review. *Renew. Sustain. Energy Rev.*, 54, 34–47, 2016.
14. McCormick, P.G. and Suehrcke, H., The effect of intermittent solar radiation on the performance of PV system. *Sol. Energy*, 171, 667–674, 2018.
15. Lee, Y. and Hur, J., A simultaneous approach implementing wind-powered electric vehicle charging stations for charging demand dispersion. *Renew. Energy*, 144, 172–179, 2019.
16. Mehrjerdi, H. and Hemmati, R., Stochastic model for electric vehicle charging station integrated with wind energy. *Sustain. Energy Technol. Assess.*, 37, 100577, 2020.
17. Noman, F., Alhatani, A.A., Agelidis, V., Tiong, K.S., Alkawski, G., Ekanayake, J., Wind energy powered electric vehicle charging stations: Resource availability data analysis. *Appl. Sci.*, 10, 5654, 2020.
18. Lokar, J. and Virtic, P., The potential for integration of hydrogen for complete energy self-efficiency in residential buildings with photovoltaic and battery storage systems. *Int. J. Hydrogen Energy*, 45, 60, 34566–34578, 2020.
19. Ogbonnaya, C., Abeykoon, C., Nasser, A., Turan, A., Ume, C.S., Prospects of integrated photovoltaic-fuel cell systems in a hydrogen economy – A comprehensive review. *Energies*, 14, 20, 2021.
20. Dhongade, N., Dhopare, R., Malode, A., Dandwate, H., Hybrid solar wind-powered charging station for electric vehicles. *Int. Res. J. Modern. Eng. Technol. Sci.*, 04, 5, 565–573, 2022.
21. Jyothi, P., Saketh, P., Vignesh, C., Krithikadevi, V.S., Renewable energy powered DC charging system for electric vehicle. *J. Phys. Conf. Ser.*, 1706, 2020.
22. Atawi, I.E., Hendawi, E., Zaid, S.A., Analysis and design of a standalone electric vehicle charging station supplied by photovoltaic energy. *Processes*, 9, 7, 1246, 2021.
23. Hernández-Callejoa, L., Gallardo-Saavedraa, S., Alonso-Gómez, V., A review of photovoltaic systems: Design, operation and maintenance. *Sol. Energy*, 188, 426–440, 2019.
24. Fathabadi, H., Novel wind powered electric vehicle charging station with vehicle-to grid (V2G) connection capability. *Energy Convers. Manage.*, 136, 229–239, 2017.
25. https://sepuplhs.org/high/hydrogen/hydrogen.html.
26. Bounechba, H., Bouzid, A., Snani, H., Lashab, A., Real time simulation of MPPT algorithms for PV energy system. *Int. J. Electr. Power Energy Syst.*, 83, 67–78, 2016.

27. Hassoune, A., Khafallah, M., Mesbahi, M., Breuil, D., Electrical Design of photovoltaic grid system for electric vehicles charging station. *14th International Multi-Conference on Signals, Systems, and Devices (SSD)*, IEEE, 2017.

# 2

# Innovating EV Charging Infrastructure: A Hybrid Energy Storage System Approach for Solar Powered-Based DC Microgrid

**Sandeep S. D., Satyajit Mohanty* and Shashi Bhushan**

*School of Electrical Engineering, Vellore Institute of Technology, Vellore, Tamil Nadu, India*

***Abstract***

The rise of electric vehicles (EVs) demands innovative solutions for charging infrastructure, particularly for harnessing renewable energy sources such as solar power. This study presents a promising concept: a hybrid energy storage system (HESS) for a photovoltaic (PV)-powered EV charging station (EVCS), aiming to address the challenge of power fluctuations. It includes a hybrid energy storage system (HESS) that comprises a battery and supercapacitor (SC). In the case of variations in the PV power, a quick response is required from the storage system. In addition, power fluctuations occur during the extraction of power from the storage system. A rapid change in supply cannot be compensated for using a single battery. To address these issues, a HESS with both a battery and an SC is suggested for the EV charging point powered by solar energy. The HES also helps adjust the power variations. The results were obtained using both a conventional PI regulator and ANN regulator.

***Keywords***: Artificial neural network, battery storage, energy management, electric vehicle charging, hybrid energy storage, supercapacitor

## 2.1 Introduction

Over the past few years, the output of energy has been outpaced by the requirement for electrical power, largely owing to the introduction of new

**Corresponding author*: satyajit.mohanty@vit.ac.in

A. Chitra, W. Razia Sultana and V. Indragandhi (eds.) Smart Charging Infrastructures, (29–40)

loads such as EVCS [1]. A shift towards a renewable energy foundation is necessary because of the limited quantity of non-renewable resources and their negative impact on the environment. Non-conventional energy sources such as hydro, wind, and solar energy are easily accessible and environmentally friendly. Solar energy [2], in particular, shows great potential, but is constrained by factors such as location, time of day, and season. An electric vehicle charging station can be continuously powered using a high-capacity PV array system. However, most alternative energy sources are inconsistent, leading to fluctuations in the power output at the charging station. Two methods can be used to deal with power fluctuations: utilizing the grid or implementing an HESS system [3]. As suggested by several sources, the grids may contribute to pollution [4]. A means to regulate the fluctuations in the power output is recommended in this study through the implementation of the HESS. Dynamic variations on the PV side are effectively managed by HESS, which incorporates power-balancing mechanisms that consider both steady-state and transient conditions [5, 6]. The steady-state changing conditions are compensated for by battery storage, while transient conditions are compensated for by the storage system of the SC [7, 8]. In [9], power regulation strategies (PRS) were provided in many studies to control the power distribution among solar panels, batteries, and alternative storage devices such as fuel cells and flywheels.

In this study, a unique energy-regulation system was introduced to handle the supply of electrical power between SC, storage batteries, and PV power. The fundamental structure of the electric vehicle charging point is shown in Figure 2.1. This study presents the development of a DC charging station enabled by combining solar photovoltaic with an SC and a battery. Effective management of the power supply is achieved among the solar energy, battery, SC, and load of the EV charging point.

## 2.2 System Architecture

Photovoltaic panels and HESS constitute the architecture. HESS consists of a combination of SC and battery energy storage. A single DC bus-based electric vehicle charging point connects all components, as depicted in Figure 2.1.

### 2.2.1 Modeling of PV System

The analogous circuit design of the PV array is displayed in Figure 2.2 within a PV system, which often includes an array of PV modules.

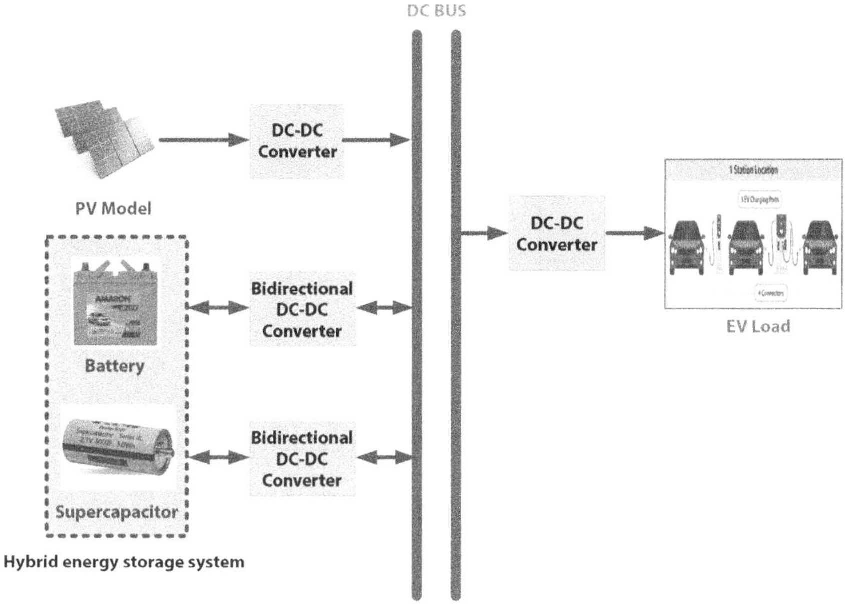


**Figure 2.1** Control logic of the PV system.

Equation (2.1) expresses the current generated by the solar power. The irradiance measured in W/m$^2$ is denoted by γ, the temperature in SI units is indicated by Ta, the short circuit current coefficient is α, and the rated values are represented by $I_{sref}$, $T_{ref}$, and $\gamma_{ref}$. The source current *Is* is expressed in amperes, the current through the resistance $R_p$ is $I_p$ in amperes, the diode current is $I_d$ in amperes, the PV array voltage is $V_{PV}$ in volts, and the voltage across the diode is $V_d$ in volts.

$$I_{pv} = \left(\frac{\gamma}{\gamma_{ref}}\right) I_{sref} + \alpha I_{sc}(T_\alpha - T_{ref}) - I_o\left[exp\left(\frac{V_d}{V_t}\right) - 1\right] - \frac{V_{pv} + R_s I_{pv}}{R_p} \tag{2.1}$$

Variations in maximum power point tracking (MPPT) and generated power are caused by irradiance in a PV array. The incremental conductance (INC) method was employed to track the MPPT. By adjusting the dimensions of the increments, MPPT was traced in a PV system. The step size adaptation coefficient allows for dynamic adjustment of the step size based on the conditions of the PV array, this method simplifies the design

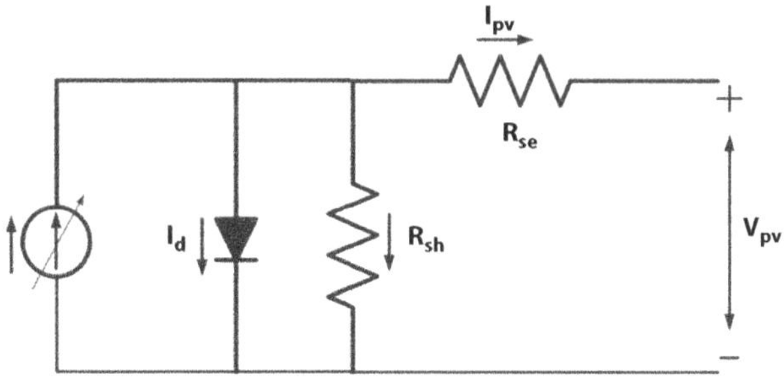


**Figure 2.2** Control logic of the PV system.

of the PV system and eliminates the requirement for a user-specified constant value at the junction of this MPPT methodology [10].

## 2.2.2 Battery Storage System

Batteries containing electrochemical cells with one or more components are the primary components of electrical power sources. Figure 2.3 shows a comparable design. Battery storage systems reduce the impact of fluctuations in the solar power generation over time.

The battery's state of charge (SOC) is calculated using the current integrating technique expressed by Equation (2.2). *I* stands for current, *Q(to)* for the battery's starting charge at time *to*, and discharge/charge efficiency.

$$V_{bat} = U_{oc} - Ux \tag{2.2}$$

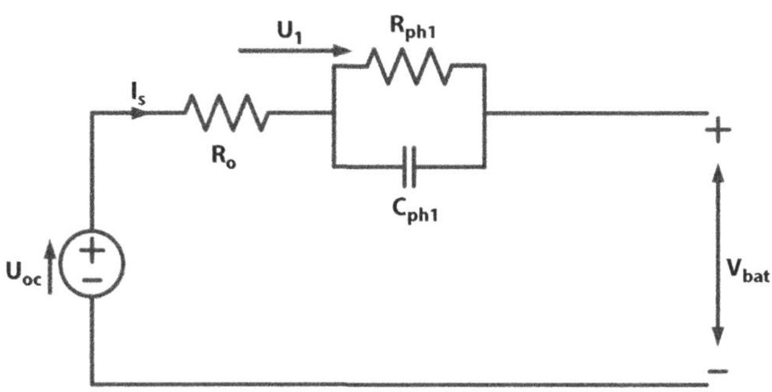


**Figure 2.3** Control logic of the PV system.

### 2.2.3 Supercapacitor

The proposed system aims to use an SC to resolve the rapid power fluctuations experienced by the solar PV system. As a temporary power source and energy buffer, SC enhances the visibility of charging stations for electric vehicles. Equation (2.3) was used to determine the SC SOC, which was determined by the total energy $Q_c$ as a percentage of the rated energy $Qq$.

$$SOC = \frac{Q_c}{Q_0} = \frac{CV_c^2}{\frac{CV_{max^2}}{2}} \tag{2.3}$$

The overall energy storage capacity of the SC bank is denoted by C. The voltage is represented by $V_c$, where $Vmax$ indicates the maximum voltage of the SC bank when it is fully charged.

## 2.3 Power Management System

The control block diagrams for the recommended ANN-based controller and the traditional PI controller are shown in Figures 2.4, 2.5. In this configuration, a two-sided converter regulates HESS charging and discharging, whereas PV systems are connected to electric vehicle loads *via* boost converters. The charging and discharging of the SC and SB systems were controlled by a two-sided converter. Variations in solar irradiation can lead to changes in the sun's power output. Therefore, by coordinating the variations in power flow, a hybrid energy storage system can effectively meet the EV load demands in this study. While the storage battery system handles

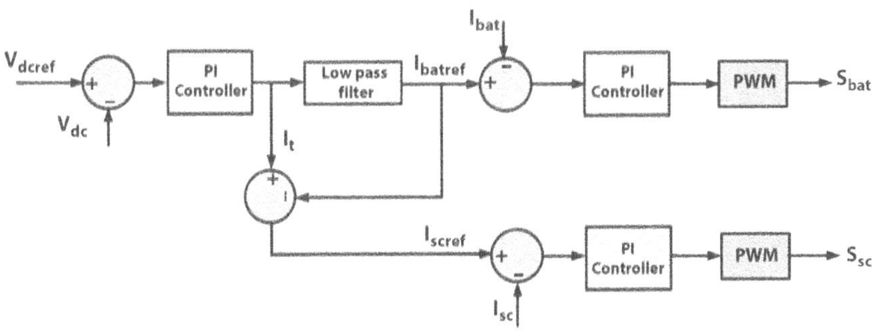


**Figure 2.4** Control strategy of the conventional PI controller.

Table 2.1 Specification of PV, battery, and supercapacitor.

| Variables | Pmax | Voc | Isc | Vmpp | I mpp | Standard voltage | Nominal capacity | Capacitor rating | Charge voltage |
|---|---|---|---|---|---|---|---|---|---|
| **Specification** | 250 W | 37.3 V | 8.66 A | 30.7 V | 8.15 A | 240 V | 48 Ah | 100 F | 300 V |

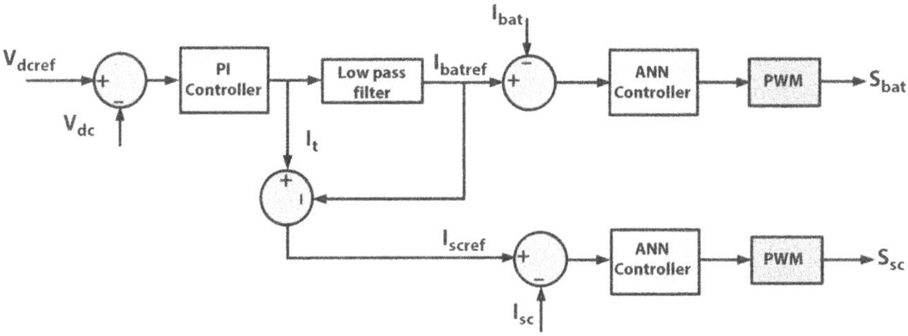


**Figure 2.5** Control strategy of the ANN controller.

progressive power shifts, the SC storage system addresses dynamics that change quickly. The system parameters and specifications are detailed in Table 2.1.

Equations 2.4, 2.5, and 2.6 serve as the foundation for the operation of the energy management system.

$$Pev = Ppv + Pstorage \tag{2.4}$$

$$Pstorage = Pbat + Psc \tag{2.5}$$

$$Pstorage = Ppv - Pev \tag{2.6}$$

In this case, $P - pv$, $Pbat$, and $Psc$ are the total powers supplied by the solar panel, storage battery, and supercapacitor, respectively. A positive

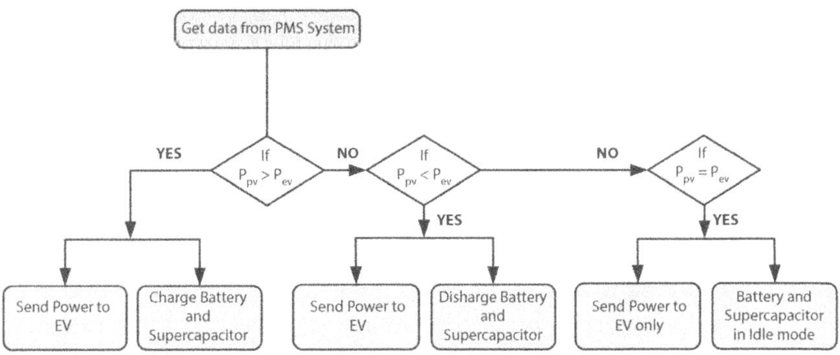


**Figure 2.6** Energy management system flowchart.

symbol indicates that the SC and storage battery are in draining mode when the charging mode is turned on for both. The electric vehicle load was powered by a PV array in this situation. An MPPT controller is utilized to optimize power generation. However, the power output decreases as the solar system's irradiance fluctuates. A delay is implemented for the storage battery owing to its time responsiveness, and a voltage controller is used to regulate the HESS to meet the EV demand. The current flowing from the storage battery is referred to as *I bat* current. The storage battery handles slow-changing dynamics, whereas the SC manages fast-changing ones. The current flowing through the SC is known as *Isc* current. A PMS flowchart is shown in Figure 2.6. Solar PV systems are used to generate electricity specifically for charging electric vehicles (EVs), batteries, and SCs when the solar output surpasses the load requirement. Solar photovoltaic and hybrid storage supply energy to the electric car for charging when the solar PV power is insufficient to meet the load. When the HSS delivers power, the SC and storage battery are both in the draining mode. Assuming there is a perfect match between the load demand and solar panel output, the EV charging station will solely receive power from the solar PV system. Both the SC and storage batteries were in an inactive state.

## 2.4 Results and Discussion

The planned EV charging point utilizes a PV system and HESS to meet EV demand. The impact of irradiance on the PV power variation is shown in Figure 2.7. Figures 2.8 & 2.9 represents batteries voltage, current and power and Battery SoC-time graph respectively. Also Figures 2.10 & 2.11 represents SC's voltage, current and power and SC SoC-time graph respectively. Every 1 s, the starting power of a solar PV panel is 2,000 W, which then decreases to 1,500 W after 1 s, and so on. The minimum power of the solar PV system was observed between t = 4 s and t = 5 s at 150 W. The proposed system in Figure 2.12, consists of a steady direct-current electric vehicle that requires a constant supply of 1,000 W of direct current power from the solar photovoltaic over a period of 2 s. This demand is consistent and does not fluctuate during this period, as shown in Figure 2.7. Power is extracted from the solar panels and HESS between t = 2 s and t = 5 s, as shown in Figures 2.8, 2.10.

An SC with battery is used to maintain the charging station demand and solar power. The solar power decreased continuously after 3 s, with the load demand being less than the accessible power. To achieve load demand, both the SC and battery are utilized. Instant SC support is shown at t = 3 s

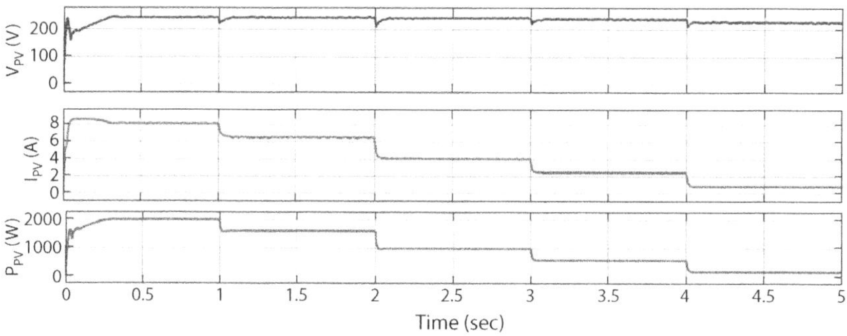


**Figure 2.7** Voltage, current, and power of the PV panel.

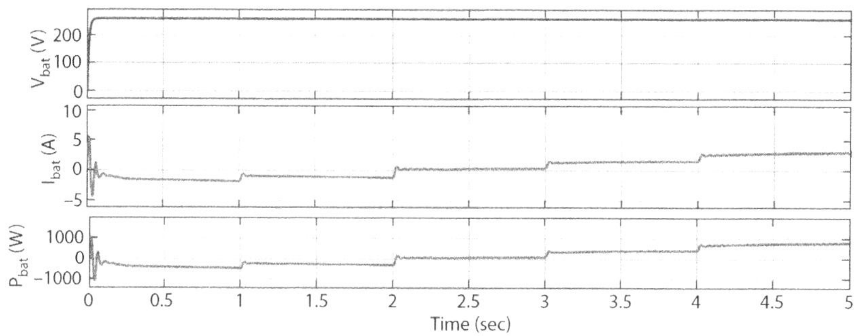


**Figure 2.8** Voltage, current, and power of the battery.

and t = 4 s in Figures 2.10, 2.11. The battery experienced a delay because of its constant time. Figures 2.8, 2.9 illustrate how batteries compensate for fluctuations in solar power over prolonged periods of time. Figures 2.12, 2.13 demonstrate that the proposed ANN controller surpasses traditional PI controllers by maintaining a steady DC bus voltage and meeting the charging load demands seamlessly.

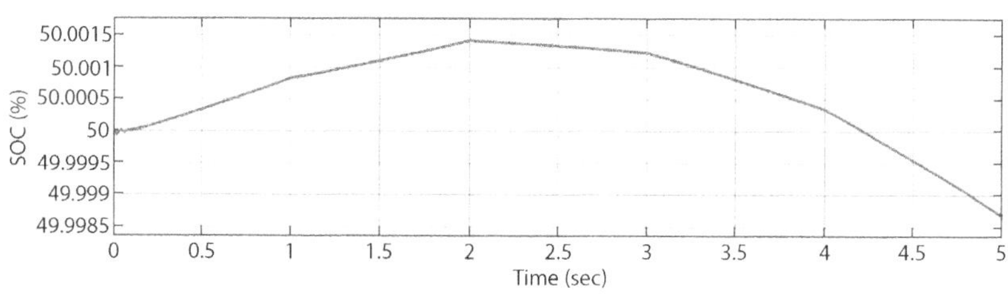


**Figure 2.9** Battery SOC v/s time.

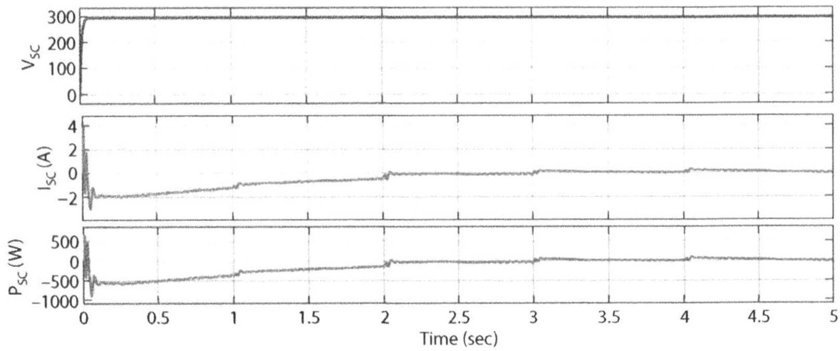


**Figure 2.10** Voltage, current, and power of the supercapacitor.

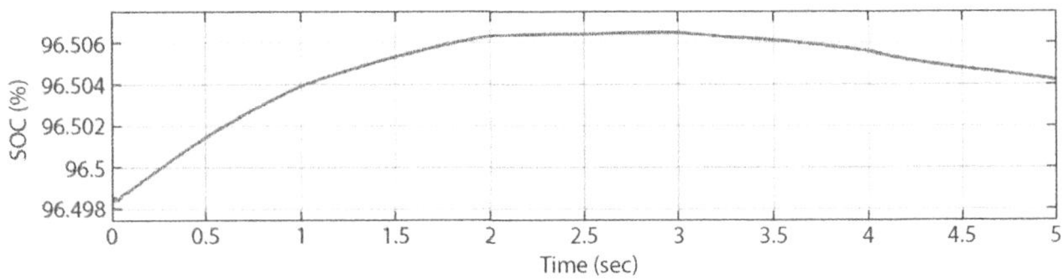


**Figure 2.11** Supercapacitor SOC v/s time.

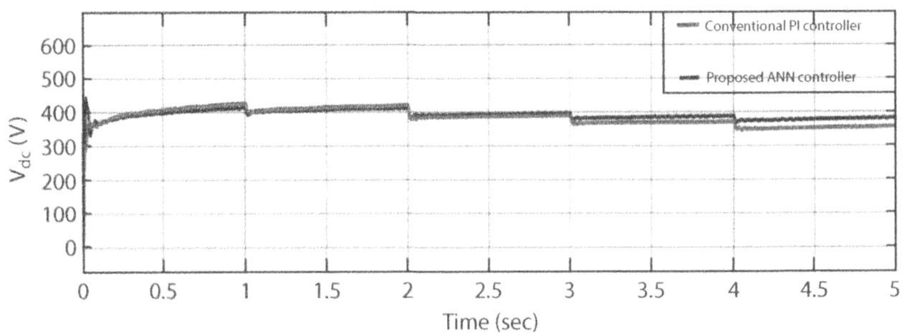


**Figure 2.12** Comparison of DC voltage with ANN controller v/s PI controller.

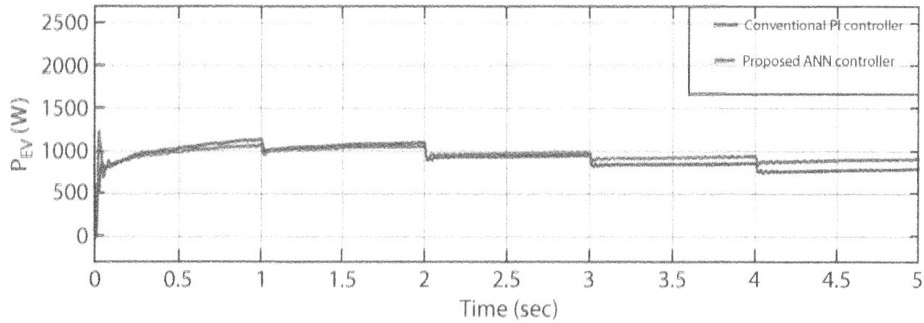


**Figure 2.13** Comparison of EV load with ANN controller and conventional PI controller.

## 2.5 Conclusion

A solar photovoltaic and HESS-based EV charging point is suggested in this study. Short-term power fluctuations are compensated for by SCs, whereas long-term power variances are aided by the storage batteries. Thus, the EV load criteria were met. The regulation of the DC bus voltage and load power was effectively controlled using the recommended ANN controller. The ANN controller provides better outcomes than the ordinary PI controller. The proposed system is supported by the simulation findings.

## References

1. Mahmood, H., Michaelson, D., Jiang, J., A power management strategy for PV/battery hybrid systems in islanded microgrids. *IEEE J. Emerging Sel. Top. Power Electron.*, 2, 4, 870–882, 2014.
2. Badawy, M.O. and Sozer, Y., Power flow management of a grid tied PV-battery system for electric vehicles charging. *IEEE Trans. Ind. Appl.*, 53, 2, 1347–1357, 2016.
3. Deshmukh, R.R., Ballal, M.S., Suryawanshi, H.M., Mishra, M.K., An adaptive approach for effective power management in DC microgrid based on virtual generation in distributed energy sources. *IEEE Trans. Ind. Inf.*, 16, 1, 362–372, 2019.
4. Kewat, S., Singh, B., Hussain, I., Power management in PV-battery-hydro based standalone microgrid. *IET Renew. Power Gener.*, 12, 4, 391–398, 2018.
5. Hong, J., Yin, J., Liu, Y., Peng, J., Jiang, H., Energy management and control strategy of photovoltaic/battery hybrid distributed power generation systems with an integrated three-port power converter. *IEEE Access*, 7, 82838–82847, 2019.

6. Abouobaida, H., de Oliveira-Assis, L., Soares-Ramos, E.P., Mahmoudi, H., Guerrero, J.M., Jamil, M., Energy management and control strategy of DC microgrid based hybrid storage system. *Simul. Modell. Pract. Theory*, 124, 102726, 2023.
7. Yi, Z., Dong, W., Etemadi, A.H., A unified control and power management scheme for PV-battery-based hybrid microgrids for both grid-connected and islanded modes. *IEEE Trans. Smart Grid*, 9, 6, 5975–5985, 2017.
8. Singh, A.P. and Kumar, Y., Advanced Power Management System for Renewable energy-based fusion Microgrid, IEEE, pp. 1–4, 2022.
9. Naik, K.R., Rajpathak, B., Mitra, A., Kolhe, M., Adaptive energy management strategy for optimal power flow control of hybrid DC microgrid, IEEE, pp. 1–6, 2020.
10. Behera, P.K., Mishra, B., Pattnaik, M., Geometrical Interpretation of Incremental Conductance MPPT Algorithm for a Stand-alone Photovoltaic System, IEEE, pp. 1–6, 2021.

3

# Design of Intermediate Charging Facilitated Port Configuration of Charging Station with Consideration of Reliability and Cost

**K. Vaishali and D. Rama Prabha***

*School of Electrical Engineering, Vellore Institute of Technology, Vellore, Tamil Nadu, India*

***Abstract***

As electric vehicles (EVs) become more prevalent in transportation, manufacturing businesses are pivotal for developing charging infrastructure. Ensuring the reliability of charging ports is a challenging aspect for the moderate charging circumstances of EVs, despite the charging station industries adhering to the criteria of the distribution system while building charging stations. Additionally, the inclusion of the vehicle-to-grid (V2G) feature is a significant advantage, as it allows for the discharge of EVs during periods of high demand. This leads to increased customer satisfaction due to the economic savings achieved by reducing the charging rates. This study examines the evaluation method of reliability probability in terms of the failure rate of the charging ports in the charging station of the power distribution system. It also explored the use of the binomial distribution probability approach. The quantitative analyses conducted in this study relied on the criteria outlined in the MILHDBK-217F and MILHDBK-338B.

***Keywords***: Electric vehicles, charging infrastructure, V2G, failure rate evaluation, reliability probability, power system reliability

**Corresponding author*: dramaprabha@vit.ac.in

A. Chitra, W. Razia Sultana and V. Indragandhi (eds.) Smart Charging Infrastructures, (41–56)

## 3.1 Introduction

The worldwide demand for and installation of charging stations has surged significantly because the increasing usefulness of EVs for road transportation. The researchers complied with charging station standards while implementing the guidelines required for industrial implementation. The installation of charging stations is influenced by numerous factors, including the surrounding consumer base, station sites, and economic crises faced by investors. The parking lot charging port capacity is determined by the overall size of the land and the distribution station's power supply facilities [1].

The global economy has grown because of a consistent increase in EV manufacturing. However, it is important to acknowledge that the development of EVs has led to increased power consumption and environmental issues. The unplanned integration of EVs results in a power grid imbalance. The economics of the system will also be impacted by several other factors, including the consistency of power supply parameters, cost of system maintenance, frequency of failures, ability to recover or replace spare parts, and quality preservation. The unstable and unpredictable behavior of a power distribution system is caused by several significant variables [2].

In [3], the location of the charging stations depended on the setup parameters of the chosen system, such as the availability of slow and quick charging capabilities. Even with charging stations that adhere to power system regulations, load changes can result in energy loss, voltage deviation, and damage to the system's supporting electrical and electronic components. Efficient fulfilment of charging needs at various locations designated for EV recharge is vital for mitigating the degradation aspects of power system networks.

The charging demand influences how various locations, including residences, transportation hubs, and supermarkets, are weighed. To optimize the supply of EVs while minimizing installation costs, energy loss, voltage deviation in the power system network, and land cost have been thoroughly addressed, with an emphasis on addressing these concerns [4]. The charging station establishment process is divided into various zones, each of which serves as a distribution point. A variety of auxiliary variables must be involved in a system to produce or transfer output energy while efficiently using its resources. Supporting components could be essential for completing a specific task, depending on how the system functions.

In [5], EVs frequently plug in and out of parking lots, which increases the risk of port failure at charging stations. The system's overall reliability could be compromised, and maintenance expenses could arise from a maximum port failure that causes the system to shut down entirely. Appropriate equipment purchases and routine system maintenance are required for better reliability. This study aims to predict the system's failure rate and reliability to minimize maintenance expenses, as it is anticipated that maintaining the system will result in a financial loss. The increasing prevalence of electronic devices necessitates the replacement of charging station components. The reliability of electronic components is significantly affected by the manufacturing quality of the product. These problems have resulted in a significant increase in charging-station maintenance costs. Using the above-mentioned characteristics, an estimate of the 50 kW–300 kW featured a charging terminal's reliability probability in terms of failure rate and costs has been made [6, 7].

## 3.2 Methodology for Estimating the Reliability Probability of Charging Ports

The reliability of the charging system was assessed using a Markov analysis, specifically focusing on the system's failure rate. Furthermore, the Monte Carlo simulation incorporated the system simulation's failure rate. The intricate analysis and conclusions required in these techniques make the software and its implementation extremely expensive and challenging. A cost-effective and simple-to-implement approach for determining failure rates is presented.

A range of equipment faults has the potential to impact both the regular operation of the power system and the customer's ability to receive electricity. Power system reliability is the capacity of a power system to consistently provide electrical energy and electricity to users in accordance with recognized quality standards and necessary quantities.

Numerous approaches have been explored to increase the network resilience of utilities. The reliability study uses the loss of load variations and anticipated energy decline indices [8]. These indicators include the load profile of the peak, voltage, and energy-loss characteristics of the distribution system.

The creation of electricity and its subsequent supply to customers depend on transmission and distribution networks. Any careless mistakes made throughout this process can result in significant financial losses and social unrest. However, the issue at hand is the reliability of the system. Stochastic behavior and uncertainty can be incorporated into quantitative dependability using probabilistic quantification of reliability. The system's reliability is crucial for effective planning and operation as well as for maintaining the right level of supply reliability at a fair price. Figure 3.1 shows an example of the charging process and its impact at EV charging stations.

The elements pertaining to the process observations of the charging system for EV applications are shown in Figure 3.1. Reliability assessment is essential for the operation, design and planning of power systems. To assess the reliability of the system, the selected unit(s) were employed to satisfy the actual or anticipated loads. The process of applying reliability indices to assess the effectiveness of a specific generator configuration can satisfy the load requirements. Because the indices are sensitive to fundamental factors, such as unit size and availability, they are particularly helpful in assessing the general reliability of various generation configurations. The reliability assessment of the electricity system is sufficient to meet the peak load or highest demand [9, 10].

The charging station establishment spectrum is determined by the allocated area of the parking plots. The occupation potential of parking lots is insufficient to facilitate recharge services for customers. Installing a charging station requires paying the full cost and financial commitment necessary for the location's maximum charging-port capacity. To determine the budget allocation for procuring the appropriate ports, a reliability test of the selected port design should be conducted prior to charging station installation [11]. Considering the aforementioned assertion, the reliability quantization approach was presented and assessed, as shown in Figure 3.1.

Examining the ambiguous plug-in scenario is the first step toward establishing the design of the port configuration. The design considers both identical and non-identical port designs to facilitate EV charging services, as shown in Figure 3.1. Charging station load variation causes a higher failure rate in EVs under intermediate operating conditions. If there is a malfunction in the charging panel, the charging ability of the vehicle may be affected by the available power ratings. Service interruptions can occur if the rate of port failure is high. One solution to ensure continuous charging is to replace the failing port.

The replacement of a failing port is determined by the material's quality compared to the capital investment criterion for charging port maintenance. The cost estimate was used to allocate the maintenance budget to replace the failed product with quality products and upgrade charging facilities. The cost estimate was used to allocate the maintenance budget for replacing the failed product with quality products and upgrading the charging facilities. The product's usefulness period was evaluated to ensure its quality in compliance with the MILHDBK-217F (military handbook)

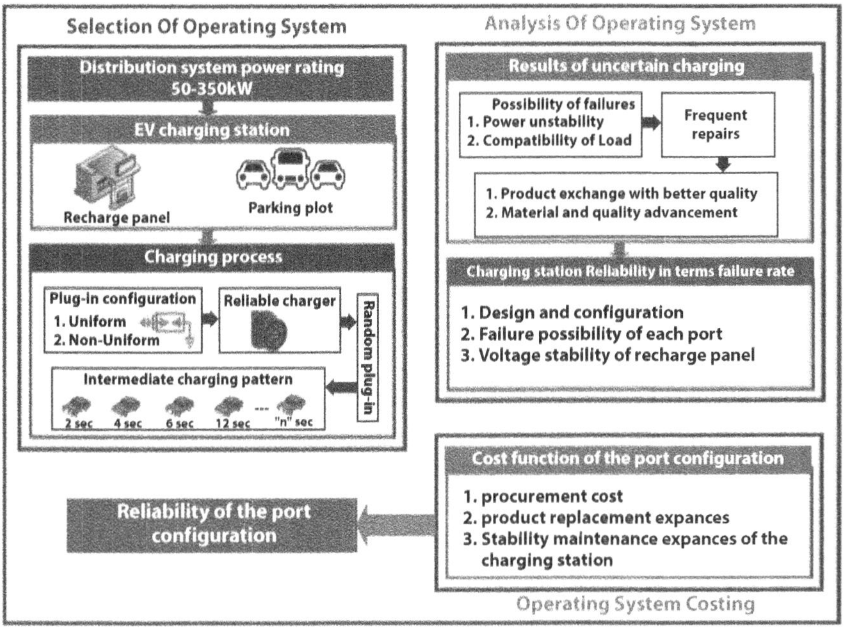


**Figure 3.1** The sequential approach for reliability estimation.

criteria [12]. The proposed methodology assesses reliability by calculating the failure rate of each port configuration. The station range and features depend on the port composition and combinations used. Identical port layouts are commonly used but require more occupation potential areas.

Providing an equivalent space for the parking plot occupation of EVs is a complicated aspect. Identical ports, on the other hand, have lower failure diagnostic and maintenance costs than non-identical ports because of the lower to higher power capability ratings. While identical ports are better for a long life, little maintenance, and constant performance, non-identical port designs are compatible with narrow occupation potentials. For both identical and non-identical port layouts, the aforementioned claims have been utilized to enhance installation, failure, reliability, and flexible cost [13]. A 12-port charging station was designed after considering various factors related to the charging station configuration, such as identical and non-identical port configurations. The next section provides a detailed description of the port positioning pattern of the proposed 12-port configuration.

## 3.3 Introduced Pattern Identical and Non-Identical Configuration

This study proposes a charging station structure with a compound of identical and non-identical port configurable patterns of 12 ports. The suggested charging ports prioritize reliability, lower maintenance costs, and ease of plugging in and unplugging cars while parked. It states that An appropriate 12-port charging station structure has been introduced, and it is divided into 6-port identical and non-identical designs. Figure 3.2 depicts identical and non-identical port-configured charging stations with 12 ports.

Figure 3.2 displays the proposed charging station that has 12 ports and offers various port layouts based on a maximum port count of 6. An identical configuration with six ports has been suggested, as demonstrated in Figure 3.2, which consists of a consistent arrangement of three ports in each batch. Figure 3.2 displays a non-identical arrangement of six ports with irregular layouts from different batches. The recommended configuration is shown in Figure 3.2, which includes both identical and non-identical port layouts. This configuration represents the port population. An analysis of the reliability probability and cost function was conducted to improve our understanding of both identical and non-identical system performance. The proposed 12 port pattern and operates at a power rating of 50 kW–300 kW to ensure that power requirements are maintained.

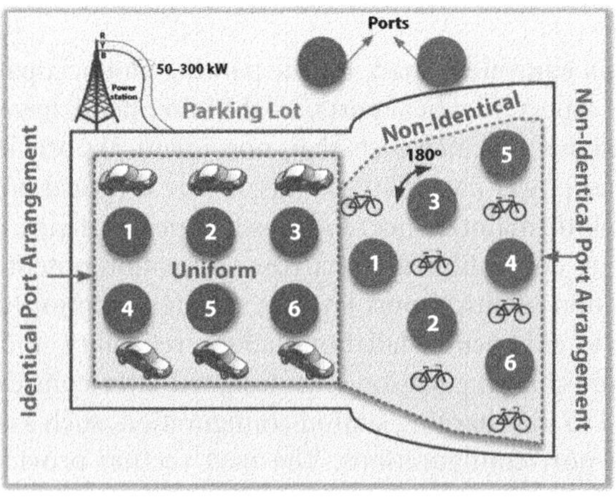


**Figure 3.2** Proposed 12-ported identical and non-identical charging station.

The method for assessing the layout that combines both identical and non-identical charging port configurations of the proposed 12-port charging station is detailed through Equations (3.1)–(3.8). To attain the intended functional characteristics of a reliable charging panel, the installation area distribution system selection process, system configuration, and suitable probability strategy are largely impacted by the reliable recharge panel. The binomial distribution is the preferred method for determining the ability of a station with 12 ports occupation potential. The assessment was conducted following the criteria set for processes of both identical and non-identical systems.

A dual-batched system of charging outlets was installed to facilitate consideration of parking lots. The system has six ports, which are not identical. The reliability of the product was determined using a repeatability method. The identical system has six separate ports, two of which are vulnerable. Repeatability occurs every time a random arrangement configuration is selected. According to [14], the MILHBK-338B standards were utilized to assess the system's interface failure rate. Equations (3.1)–(3.8) were used to assess the suggested port configuration estimation to start the reliability study.

Estimated failure rate ($\lambda_E$)

$$\lambda_E = \frac{\lambda_{physical}}{operationg\ time\ of\ ports \times yearly\ period} \tag{3.1}$$

$\lambda_{physical} = \lambda_b * \pi_T * \pi_R * \pi_S * \pi_A * \pi_Q * \pi_E / 10-^6$ h

$\pi_T$, Thermal coefficient;

$\pi_R$, Flow of current;

$\pi_S$, Withstand voltage;

$\pi_A$, Type of application;

$\pi_Q$, Material factor;

$\pi_E$, Operating environment.

The lifespan of electrical components is significantly affected by the temperature, which depends on the specifications of the component. The thermal coefficient is indicated below.

$$\pi_T = \exp\left(-3082\left(\frac{1}{T_j + T_r} - \frac{1}{298}\right)\right) \tag{3.2}$$

where $T_j$ represents the environmental temperature and $T_r$ is the environmental temperature.

When selecting components, it is crucial to consider the application's settings and environment. The application of a product determines its environmental constant. The charge application (Ns) is discussed below.

$$\text{Environment factor } (\pi_E) = N_S = \text{ constant value.}$$

The type of material JAN, JANTX, or JANTXV used in the product's construction affects both its longevity and quality. Material grade has a direct impact on the component failure rate, making it an important indicator of product quality. The symbol represents $\pi_Q$.

$$\text{Quality grade } (\pi_Q) = \text{material} = \text{constant} \tag{3.3}$$

The voltage applied to power devices determines the operational failure possibilities of the product. The blocking voltage and peak current have the potential to maximize the failure rates. When working with electrical circuits, it is essential to consider two critical elements: the voltage stress factor and current rating factor. These elements are key to ensuring the circuit's performance and safety.

$$\text{Current rating } (\pi_R) = (I_{rms})^{0.40} \tag{3.4}$$

Where

$$I_{rms} = \text{port current}$$

$$\text{Voltage stress } (\pi_S) = (V_s)^{1.9} \tag{3.5}$$

Failure rate of the system (λ)

$$\frac{\textit{Total failures}}{\textit{Total operating time}} \tag{3.6}$$

Reliability probability in terms of success P(s)

$$P(s) = \sum_{i=s}^{r} \frac{r!}{S!(r-S)!} * P^S * q^{r-S} \tag{3.7}$$

where r represents the plug population, P is the individual port probability, q = (1 – P), q is the probability of individual channel, X is the cumulative success of channel, and $U_\lambda$ is the uncertainty factor.

$$U_\lambda = \frac{1}{4r}\left(Z_{0.95} + \sqrt{4r + 3^2}\right) \tag{3.8}$$

The 12-port pattern probability reliability was evaluated based on the reliability assessment process. The compound-batched charging ports, which have a maximum capacity of 12 ports, have an estimated system reliability probability in terms of the failure rate, as illustrated in Figures 3.3, 3.4, 3.5.

# 3.4 Results and Discussions

## 3.4.1 Identical Port Configuration

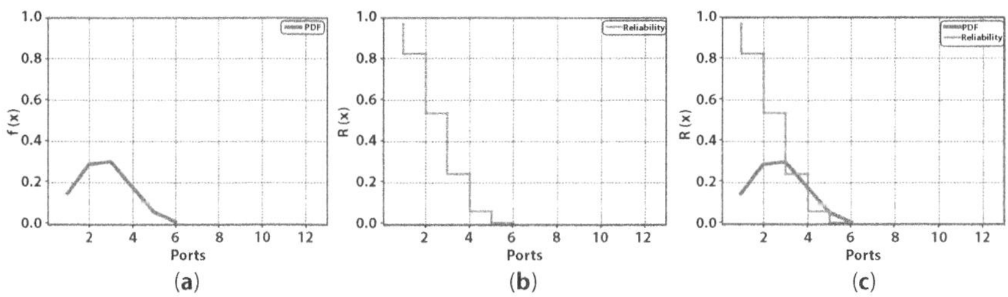


**Figure 3.3** (a) Failure probability of the 12 ported identical port configuration, (b) reliability of the proposed configuration, and (c) cumulative comparison of reliability.

## Non-Identical 3-Repeatability

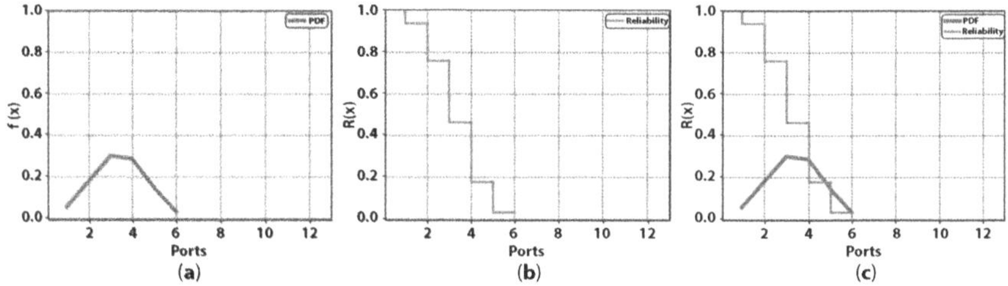


**Figure 3.4** (a) Failure probability of the 12-ported 3-batch charging oriented parking lot for EV, (b) reliability of the proposed configuration, and (c) cumulative comparison of reliability.

## 2-Repeatability

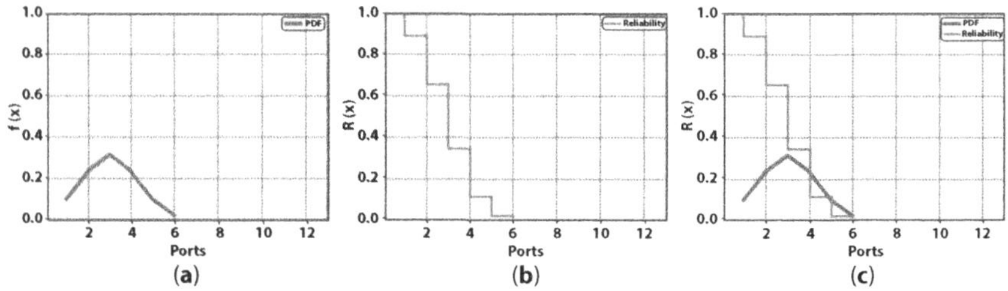


**Figure 3.5** (a) Failure probability of the 12 ported 2-batch charging oriented parking lot for EV, (b) reliability of the 12-ported 3-batch charging oriented parking lot for EV, and (c) cumulative comparison of reliability.

The reliability and likelihood of charging port failures in the parking lot are depicted in Figures 3.3, 3.4. As shown in Figure 3.3, random charging for the parking lot with 12 ports resulted in a maximum failure rate involving charging ports 3 to 4. The expected failure probabilities in a batch of charging ports are divided into two ports, as shown in Figure 3.3(a). Figures 3.3(a,b) show that the port failure rate determines the reliability of the system service during the charging process. It is evident from Figure 3.4(a) that the random charging for the 12-ported parking lot resulted in a maximum failure rate involving charging ports of 3. Table 3.1 lists the reliability charging panel basis of charging port failure chances organized by batch sequence. On the other hand, Table 3.2 shows the actual failure rate of the 12-port pattern.

From Table 3.1, it can be concluded that the proposed port pattern is capable of supplying power with an expected allowable success rate of 8.0

Table 3.1 Individual batch failure rate of the 12-port pattern.

| Batches | Port count | Healthy ports of pattern | Success of pattern |
|---|---|---|---|
| Identical port configuration | | | |
| B-1 | 3 | 0.02 | 8.0 |
| B-2 | 3 | 0.02 | 8.0 |
| Non-identical configuration | | | |
| B-11 | 1 | 0.0067 | 0.0067 |
| B-22 | 2 | 0.0116 | 0.02293 |
| B-33 | 3 | 0.02 | 8.0 |

Table 3.2 Reliability probability of the 50 kW–300 kW distribution system.

<table>
<tr><th>Charging ports (n)</th><th>Individual batch port count (ni)</th><th>Probability of failure rate</th><th>System failure rate (q)</th><th>Success probability of system p(s)</th></tr>
<tr><td rowspan="3">12</td><td>6 (identical)</td><td>2%</td><td>2%</td><td>0.44</td></tr>
<tr><td rowspan="2">6 (non-identical)</td><td rowspan="2">2%</td><td>3%</td><td>0.56</td></tr>
<tr><td>2%</td><td>0.5</td></tr>
</table>

per $10^6$ h for identical ported configurations. A non-identical port configuration was designed with three batched configurations with various port quantities because the configuration had maximum and minimum success rates of 0.0067 and 8.0 per $10^6$ h. For better observation of the proposed 12-port pattern, the reliability was evaluated and is tabulated in Table 3.2.

Table 3.2 shows that, with a repeating combination of three ports, the suggested 12-port charging station may provide the maximum three-port potential for identical port patterns of individual batches. It is possible to obtain a combination of three ports that are not identical. This non-identical port compound can be linked to six ports of higher potential in any of the batches and to at least one port with minimal potential for the EV charging station. Because there is an identical number of healthy port possibilities in every batch, Table 3.2 indicates that the identical 6-ported classification has the same success rate of $0.44/10^6$ h. Nonetheless, a non-identical configuration with six ports has been organized using distinct port structures, causing the success rate of every batch to differ based on the number of ports. Based on each batch port pattern, it can operate successfully up to 0.56 times per $10^6$ h for repetitive combinations of three ports, as tabulated in Table 3.2. Table 3.2 makes it is evident for that, in the 6-non-identical ported charging station, the identical 6-port pattern is the better configuration category. Despite the allowed success rate provided by the inconsistent system, it is essential to perform regular upkeep to ensure steady performance, which leads to increased maintenance expenses. The product's reliability and quality determine the cost to maintain. However, the cost of investment increases when reliable materials are purchased for installation. As a result, an estimate of the product maintenance costs for the suggested 12-port charging station layout was made. The necessary criteria to determine the 12-ported charging station are covered in the following section, according to the authors in [15, 16].

Purchasing or replacing reliable products regularly can be challenging and costly. Investors should focus on the costs associated with installing and maintaining the charging stations. Because there are more ports, failure rates could necessitate routine repairs. Even installing a charging station and purchasing reliable goods are preferable for routine maintenance. A single charging station port failure impacts 20% of the revenue generated by clients every 2 h. To preserve technician safety, the charging station must be closed to replace the charging port. Customers will be inconvenienced and investors will suffer financial losses as a result of the charging station shutdown for 1 h. To ensure that the setup of the EVs charging station does not capture investor attention. Researchers have provided optimal maintenance cost-based charging station designs to draw investors to the development of eco-oriented vehicles worldwide [17, 18].

The availability of the product and its selling price in relation to the city or municipality determine the maintenance costs of ports in charging stations. The cost is divided into fixed, variable, and mixed costs based on the aforementioned statement. Given the cost variance by location, it can be inferred from the authors [19, 20] that variable cost is the most crucial element for rural station areas. Even in cases where location costs are fixed, the amount of product will still have an impact on the final cost because of variations in the dealer's fixed costs. Product quantity affects fixed costs, which could result in financial losses. Thus, the distribution of charging stations is crucial. For the charging system configuration under consideration, which is engaged in the assessment of the failure rate of charging ports, the cost of maintenance has been calculated. The implementation of the maintenance cost evaluation procedure is predicated on the assessment of charging port reliability and failure rates for intermediate EV charging circumstances. Equations (3.9) and (3.10) were used to determine the system maintenance cost for the charging lot based on the operational capabilities and reliability considerations. Because of the cost function assessment process's involvement with the charging system's power parameters, this evaluation method can also be used for various charging station layouts.

Each port individual voltage

$$V_{port}^{ind} = \frac{Total\ voltage}{\max\ voltage} \tag{3.9}$$

Installation cost of the system

$$C.F = N_{port} + \alpha\ V_{port}^{ind} \tag{3.10}$$

where $N_{port}$ is the population of charging ports and $\alpha$ represents thecurrent rating of the port.

The costs of the 12-port pattern of the parking lot have been tabulated in Table 3.3.

**Table 3.3** Costs of proposed 12-ported configuration.

| Port patterns | Batches | Ports/batch | Failure voltage maintenance cost (F.VMC) | Stable voltage maintenance cost (S.VMC) |
|---|---|---|---|---|
| 6-port identical system | | | | |
| 2 | b-1 | 3 | 25 | 26 |
| | b-2 | 3 | 25 | 26 |
| 6-port non-identical system | | | | |
| 3 & 2 | b-1 | 1 | 24.33 | 24.67 |
| | b-2 | 2 | 24.85 | 25.16 |
| | b-3 | 3 | 25 | 26 |

Utilizing a per-unit value, the maintenance expenses of the proposed 12-port pattern were calculated. Based on the information provided in Table 3.3, the maintenance costs for the 6-ported identical design are comparable to those for 25 p.u. quantities that have a port arrangement consisting of a repeated combination of two ports. The 6-port identical pattern can maintain consistency in functionality for an additional cost of 25 p.u. in maintenance and at a unit cost of 26. The maintenance cost of the 6-port non-identical pattern varies depending on the ports used in the building of the charging station, as indicated in Table 3.3. Based on the assessment of the expenditures associated with the 6-ported non-identical configuration, it is possible to infer that the cost per unit to maintain the charging services could range between 24.33 and 25. In relation to maintenance, the 6-ported identical configuration exhibited greater economic efficiency than the non-identical configuration. This study demonstrates that a 12-ported charging station, whether identical or non-identical, can effectively provide charging services for EVs applications. The highest maintenance cost allowed is 24.33 p.u.

## 3.5 Conclusion

The present study used a reliability probability evaluation methodology to assess the failure rate of EVs charging panels with both identical and non-identical port layouts. With a 50–300 kW distribution system, a 12-port charging station design has been presented for market adoption. 6-port identical and non-identical charging-port combinations make up the configuration of the suggested 12-ported charging station. The logic of repeated combinations was used to assess the port configuration's reliability. However, because of the uneven port arrangements in each batch, non-identical ported configurations are more likely to fail.

The proposed work presents a mathematical approach for evaluating port reliability in each configuration based on port layout. This approach was implemented using the standards of MILHBK-217F. Based on the failure rate evaluations of the 12-port pattern, it is reasonable to conclude that the 6-port identical configuration can provide charging services with a failure rate of 2% and predicted failure probability of $0.44/10^6$ h. The configured of 6-ported non- identical can provide that the operation of the charging process is possible with the expected failure rate of 0.56 and $0.5/10^6$ h with the combinations of repeatability 3 and 2.

The replacement of failed ports in the 12-port pattern is combined with the cost of maintenance at the failure rate of a particular individual port.

According to the failure rate of ports, the estimated cost of product replacement is calculated in relation to maintenance expenses. The charging stations featuring a 12-port design offer maintenance services for 24.33 per unit for failure rates and 25 per unit for success rates, especially considering the upper-level port arrangement with two repeated configurations. The study found that facilities can maintain 24.85 p.u regarding a failure rate and a success rate of 26 p.u. It was determined that using an identical port design resulted in more efficient charging capabilities than systems with varied designs. A detailed study suggests that the introduction of 12-port configurations, both identical and non-identical, could provide EV users with more reliable charging solutions, lower maintenance costs, and reduced failure rates. From the proposed port configuration reliability and maintenance cost, it can also be suggested for V2G operation.

## References

1. Galiveeti, H.R., Goswami, A.K., Choudhury, N.B.D., Impact of plug-in electric vehicles and distributed generation on reliability of distribution systems. *Eng. Sci. Technol. Int. J.*, 21, 1, 50–59, Jan. 2018.
2. Pal, A., Bhattacharya, A., Chakraborty, A.K., Allocation of electric vehicle charging station considering uncertainties. *Sustainable Energy Grids Networks*, 25, 100422, Dec. 2020.
3. Archana, A.N. and Rajeev, T., Reliability index based approach for allocating EV charging station in a distribution system, in: *IEEE International Conference on Power Electronics, Smart Grid and Renewable Energy (PESGRE2020)*, Jan. 2020, pp. 1–6.
4. Moghaddam, Z., Ahmad, I., Habibi, D., Masoum, M.A.S., A Coordinated Dynamic Pricing Model for Electric Vehicle Charging Stations. *IEEE Trans. Transp. Electrif.*, 5, 1, 226–238, March. 2019.
5. Guner, S. and Ozdemir, A., Reliability improvement of distribution system considering EV parking lots. *Electr. Power Syst. Res.*, 185, 106–353, Mar. 2020.
6. Vaishali, K. and Rama Prabha, D., Reliability and economic analysis of an electric vehicle charging station in the distribution system. *AIP Conf. Proc.*, 2966, 1, pp. 020025-1-020025-6, AIP Publishing, Mar. 2024.
7. Haji-Aghajani, E., Hasanzadeh, S., Heydarian-Forushani, E., A novel framework for planning of EV parking lots in distribution networks with high PV penetration. *Electr. Power Syst. Res.*, 217, 109156, Jan. 2023.
8. Gupta, M. and Bhargava, A., Optimal selection and analysis of microgrid energy system using Markov process. *Sustain. Energy Technol. Assess., 62*, 103623, Feb. 2024.

9. Sripriya, R., Kumar, C., Xavier, F.J., Kumar, J.S., Kotsampopoulos, P., Fayek, H.H., Reliability Improvement of a Hybrid Electric Vehicle Integrated Distribution System. *Energies*, 16, 10, 3984, May. 2023.
10. Khamis, A., Aiman, M.H., Faizal, W.M., Khor, C.Y., Charging strategy in electric vehicle chargers by utilizing demand side management scheme. *Electr. Power Syst. Res.*, 220, 109240, Feb. 2023.
11. Krishnachaitanya, D. and A., C., Quantitative Analysis of Asymmetric Multilevel Inverters With Reduced Device Count From Reliability and Cost Function Perspective—A Review. *IEEE Trans. Power Electron.*, 36, 10, 11068–11086, Oct. 2021.
12. *Reliability Prediction of Electronic Equipment (MIL-HDBK-217F),* U.S. Department of Defense, Washington, D.C., USA, 1986.
13. Vaishali, K. and Prabha, D.R., The Reliability and Economic Evaluation Approach for Various Configurations of EV Charging Stations. *IEEE Access*, 12, 26267–26280, Feb. 2024.
14. *Military Handbook Electronic Reliability Design Handbook, MIL-HDBK-338B*, U.S. Department of Defense, Washington, DC, USA, 1998.
15. Karthikeyan, D., Vijayakumar, K., Kumar, D.S., Krishnachaitanya, D., Mathematical analysis of cost function and reliability condition for new proposed multilevel inverter topology. *Indones. J. Electr. Eng. Comput. Sci.*, *20*, 2, 654–661, Nov. 2020.
16. Krishnachaitanya, D. and Annamalai, C., Real time implementation of a new seven level multilevel inverter with design considerations for feasible and reliable operation. *Int. J. Circuit Theory Appl.*, *51*, 10, 4839–4863, Oct. 2023.
17. Firouzjah, K.G., Profit-based electric vehicle charging scheduling: Comparison with different strategies and impact assessment on distribution networks. *Int. J. Electr. Power Energy Syst.*, 138, 107977, Jan. 2022.
18. Mohammadi-Landi, M., Rastegar, M., Mohammadi, M., Afrasiabi, S., Stochastic Optimal Sizing of Plug-in Electric Vehicle Parking Lots in Reconfigurable Power Distribution Systems. *IEEE Trans. Intell. Transp. Syst.*, 23, 10, 17003–17014, Oct. 2022.
19. Krishnachaitanya, D., Chitra, A., Biswas, S.S., Reliability Approach for the Power Semiconductor Devices in EV Applications, in: *Artificial Intelligent Techniques for Electric and Hybrid Electric Vehicles*, pp. 115–124, Jul. 2020.
20. Jin, Y., Acquah, M.A., Seo, M., Han, S., Optimal siting and sizing of EV charging station using stochastic power flow analysis for voltage stability. *IEEE Trans. Transp. Electrif.*, 10, 1, 777–794, May 2024.

# 4

# AI-Based Smart Charging Infrastructures: Revolutionizing Electric Vehicle Integration

**V. Bagyaveereswaran, S.L. Arun, M. Manimozhi and B. Jaganatha Pandian***

*School of Electrical Engineering, Vellore Institute of Technology, Vellore, Tamil Nadu, India*

***Abstract***

The integration of electric vehicles (EVs) into transportation infrastructure is a critical step towards achieving sustainability and reducing greenhouse gas emissions. However, the widespread adoption of EVs poses significant challenges, particularly in terms of the charging infrastructure. Traditional charging methods are often inefficient, resulting in long wait times and grid congestion. In response, AI-based smart-charging infrastructure has emerged as a promising solution to address these challenges and optimize the charging process for EVs.

One of the key advantages of AI-based smart charging infrastructures is their ability to optimize charging schedules based on various factors such as grid capacity, energy demand, and user preferences. Through real-time data analysis and predictive modeling, these systems can forecast demand and dynamically adjust the charging mechanism to minimize costs and maximize efficiency. Furthermore, AI-based smart charging infrastructure plays a crucial role in balancing supply and demand on the grid, particularly as the penetration of renewable energy sources continues to increase. By coordinating charging schedules with renewable energy generation patterns, these systems can help maximize the utilization of clean energy resources and reduce reliance on fossil fuels. This study provides a comprehensive overview of AI-based smart-charging infrastructures and their implications for the future of electric vehicle integration.

***Keywords***: Electric vehicles (EVs), AI-based smart charging, charging infrastructure, grid integration, predictive analytics, vehicle-to-grid (V2G), cybersecurity and interoperability

**Corresponding author*: jaganathapandian@vit.ac.in

A. Chitra, W. Razia Sultana and V. Indragandhi (eds.) Smart Charging Infrastructures, (57–90)

## 4.1 Introduction

Electric vehicles (EVs) represent a shift in perspective for both the automotive and electric power sectors, with the potential to accelerate their decarbonization by integrating them. Although the automobile industry now has an extremely low proportion of power generation from renewables, it is undergoing a significant transformation, particularly in passenger daily road transportation, where EVs are emerging. Owing to recent advancements in the power sector, the renewable energy resource-based generation cost is significantly reduced; hence, many countries have adopted power as an appealing low-cost fuel for the transportation sector. However, a substantial increase in EV penetration introduces additional opportunities in the electricity sector. Furthermore, connecting many EVs to the grid may result in a large energy storage capacity. They can function either as flexible demands or virtual energy storage units and provide additional operational support to grid operators. With the help of smart charging features, EVs can alter their charging/discharging patterns. The change in the demand pattern of end users may significantly reduce the grid operational costs by supporting the grid operation in several ways, such as reducing the peak-to-average ratio, avoiding the operation of peak power plants, and effective utilization of generation from conventional and non-conventional energy resources. In general, smart charging refers to the optimal control of the EV charging/discharging pattern, considering both the desires of vehicle owners and the dynamics of grid operations. This allows EV integration while satisfying the transportation demands.

Electric vehicles (EVs) have emerged as promising solutions for reducing carbon emissions and mitigating the impacts of climate change. As the world shifts towards sustainable transportation, demand for EVs is steadily increasing. However, this surge in EV adoption presents new challenges, particularly in the realm of charging infrastructures. Smart charging, empowered by artificial intelligence (AI), is revolutionizing the charging of EVs, offering solutions to optimize energy usage, enhance grid stability, and streamline the charging process. Smart charging refers to the intelligent management of electric vehicle charging processes, leveraging advanced technologies, such as AI, the Internet of Things (IoT), and data analytics. Unlike conventional charging methods, which often lead to peak demand spikes and strain on the grid, smart charging solutions aim to distribute charging loads efficiently, by considering factors such as grid capacity, energy demand, and user preferences.

AI-based smart charging systems for electric vehicles typically consist of several key components, such as data collection sensors, communication infrastructure, AI algorithms, charging infrastructure, user interface, grid integration, security measures, energy management software and predictive analytics. Data collection sensors utilize various sensors to gather data, such as electricity demand, grid load, weather conditions, and vehicle charging statuses. Smart charging systems rely on communication networks to facilitate data exchanges between different components. This includes communication between charging stations, vehicles, grid operators, and other smart devices. The core component of AI-based smart-charging systems is intelligent algorithms that analyze the collected data and make decisions accordingly. These algorithms may use machine learning techniques, such as neural networks, reinforcement learning, or optimization algorithms, to optimize charging schedules, predict energy demand, and manage grid congestion.

Additionally, smart charging infrastructure can facilitate bidirectional energy flows between EVs and the grid, enabling vehicle-to-grid (V2G) integration and providing opportunities for improved energy storage and grid stabilization. AI-based smart charging infrastructures not only possess advanced technical abilities, but also prompt significant concerns regarding data privacy, cybersecurity, and interoperability. Given their heavy reliance on data collection, robust security measures are vital to safeguard sensitive information and maintain the integrity of charging transactions. In addition, standardizing communication protocols and interoperability standards is crucial for seamless integration across diverse charging networks and platforms.

Beginning with an exploration of the current landscape of the EV charging infrastructure, this chapter examines the need for more intelligent and adaptive solutions. It then delves into the core principles of AI and machine learning algorithms that strengthen smart charging systems, including predictive modeling, optimization algorithms, and data-driven decision-making processes.

## 4.2 Fundamentals of Smart Charging

The smart-charging feature provides significant control over EV charging patterns, which includes several pricing strategies and technical alternatives for charging. Presently, service providers mostly adopt time-of-use pricing strategies in which EV users may reduce the electricity bill by scheduling their charging schedule during off/mid peak intervals.

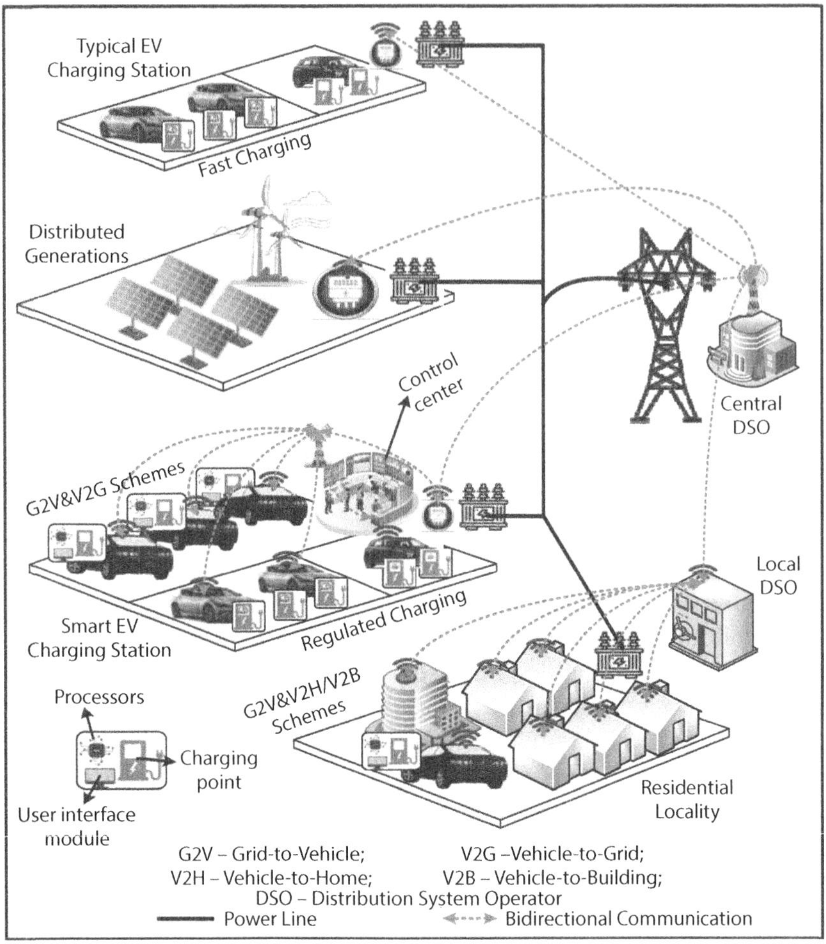


**Figure 4.1** Architectural difference between the typical and smart charging infrastructure.

Furthermore, upgraded smart EV charging techniques, such as direct control approaches, are required for long-term benefits with high EV penetration. These techniques can be as simple as turning ON/OFF the EV charging, or as complex as unidirectional grid-to-vehicle control (G2V), which will have feature controls of the charging rate, and bidirectional vehicle-to-grid (V2G), which is a difficult mechanism that enables EVs to offer grid services by discharging batteries. Furthermore, the bidirectional operation of EVs, such as vehicle-to-home (V2H) and vehicle-to-building (V2B), allows EVs to be utilized as a backup power source for homes during grid power interruptions or to increase the amount of energy that is generated locally. The architectural difference between a typical EV charging station and a smart EV charging station in a smart distribution system is shown in Figure 4.1.

### 4.2.1 Benefits of Smart-Charging Infrastructure

Uncontrolled EV charging has the potential to raise system peaks because charging patterns may coincide with load peaks that are already in place. This might lead to overloading and requirements for transmission and distribution system modifications. Furthermore, increased demand would need to upgrade the generating capacity. However, because e-mobility is a power-dense, movable, and controlled load, the adoption of smart charging for electric mobility is anticipated to create a positive feedback loop with the integration of renewables. Most self-owned cars, including EVs, spend more than 90% of their lives in parking spaces. This and their ability to store energy may make EVs a desirable flexible option for supporting grid operations. In addition to reducing the demand peaks brought on by EVs (mostly at the distribution level), smart charging can also modify the load curve to incorporate renewable energy resources more effectively.

Services rendered to the power grid: EVs with smart charging infrastructure may improve grid stability by enhancing the local utilization of RER generation and preventing the need to invest in peak power plants. Depending on the smart charging strategy, EVs that are parked most of the time and stand idle might offer the power system a variety of services, including G2V, V2G, and V2H/B.

Because EVs are kept idle for longer durations than they need to be charged fully, EV users should be encouraged to schedule charging during mid-peak intervals, such as late morning/afternoon, with high penetration of solar generation and off-peak intervals, such as nighttime, which could be adjusted with nighttime wind generation. This entails flattening the load curve by shaving the peaks and filling valleys. This would regulate the investment in peak power plants.

Smart charging enhances the grid balance in real time by altering the EV charging patterns to achieve steady frequency and voltage. Transmission system operators have made significant progress in developing flexibility at the system level, whereas distribution system operators mostly lack the flexibility of dispersed energy resources to operate their grids.

The smart charging mechanism improves the savings of EV users by assisting them in purchasing the electricity from the utility during off-peak intervals at low prices and supporting their demand during peak intervals in which the price of electricity is high. Additionally, utilizing in-house RER generation effectively might greatly reduce reliance on the grid.

### 4.2.2 Deployment Factors for Smart Charging

To enhance system observability, controllability, and integrity, smart-charging mechanisms widely use several sensors, embedded processors, and digital communication systems. Hence, an efficient and sustainable smart charging infrastructure requires advanced computational intelligence, bi-directional secured communication protocols, EVs connection points with smart meters, and user interface modules.

**Charging infrastructure**: Presently, there are few viable business models for private parties, and the development of charging infrastructure necessitates large financial outlays. The government may encourage the establishment of charging stations at public or residential access points. An initial focus on aggressive EV objectives may be utilized to assist in the development of the infrastructure for charging EVs, followed by a focus on funding projects for actualization. A basic and continuous problem is also necessary to comprehend the optimal methods for charging, aggregating, and managing EV demand on the grid. The best way to satisfy consumers' desires and comfort depends on key decisions made during the construction of the charging infrastructure, including the placement of the smart charging stations, the technology to be used, and the way to integrate fast chargers with slow smart chargers. Smart charging stations can detect, interpret, and react to signals from other parties or energy system operators to determine the optimal timing for charging or discharging in accordance with the overall supply and demand for energy. Local governments that want to set up household charging stations on the street can construct a similar scheme.

**Responsibilities of stakeholders**: Another significant and distinctive feature of smart charging is its location at the intersection of the energy market and e-mobility. In contrast to typical charging strategies, which involve the market of e-mobility (EV customers, charging point workers, and mobile service vendors) acting independently of the energy market, smart charging integrates them to work together to accommodate the requirements of e-mobility in the power system with due consideration of the power system flexibility needs.

**Regulation for V2G integration**: The economic benefit to EV users will be merely based on the pricing strategy followed by smart-charging vendors. Similarly, the V2G feature shall be succeeded by accounting for stack revenue from many sources of income and allowing for flexibility at the local and system levels. This cannot occur in the absence of functional energy markets. Even in a developing e-mobility industry, there are not always competitive retail and wholesale marketplaces. While wholesale electricity markets are present in most countries, competitive retail and balancing markets usually do not exist. However, these services are still centrally governed and managed by the TSO. To encourage the assessment of EV grid services, even in cases where such markets already exist, their design will need to be advanced and rules will need to be changed. These changes may include the following:

- Modifying market limits and access requirements for various wholesale segments. The minimum ability and availability criteria for important grid services are still intended for large-scale power systems, even in markets where aggregation access is permitted.
- Preventing duplicate charging of storage for the grid, which penalizes both second-life batteries and V2G.
- Update laws that forbid the resale of power from the grid without a provider while considering EVs.

**Aggregators**: Although EV batteries have a limited storage capacity, they can deliver the quick reaction required for some auxiliary services. As a result, an EV cannot supply these services for the length of time required by the power system. However, when EVs are combined, they may work in concert to create a virtual power plant that can respond quickly and sustain operations as long as required. It is easier to deploy EVs as flexible energy sources when aggregator corporate models are in place. To make EV power provisioning feasible at the wholesale level, a minimum capacity of 1 MW to 2 MW must be exchanged. This calls for the gathering of approximately 500 EVs and associated charging stations.

**ICT tools**: Bidirectional communication protocols must be created to optimize the system and make it easier for all parties involved to share information. The process of charging EVs through bidirectional secure communication between multiple entities optimizes grid management, the utilization of RER generation, and all customer requirements in terms of system costs, constraints, dependability, safety, and security.

**Artificial Intelligence (AI) and big data for smart charging**: Smart charging with a V2G scheme optimally manages the EV demands either from the response of the EV user for the price signal or from a preprogrammed automatic response with respect to the market scenarios or a combination of both responses. Hence, the user requirements for EV availability are essential when scheduling charging. Scheduling includes shifting the EV demand to low price intervals or adjusting the power based on certain limitations such as user requirements, connection capacity, and RER generation. Technological developments in AI and big data have the potential to enhance and maximize the services offered by smart-charging systems. The integration of ICT improvements, such as data management and analytics, can improve smart charging features and optimize grid service provision by analyzing data from drivers, charging trends, charging-point operators, and charging stations. Furthermore, data analytics and digital technologies will make it feasible to determine the best locations for charging stations and maximize the compatibility between mobility demand and power supply dynamics. Additional services may be added to the grid without compromising the demands of customers if direct control techniques facilitated by the EV and charging station are in place. For instance, EV users can specify the reserve capacity of the battery or departure time of the EV. The charging station determines the status of the battery and computes the energy required to attain the target state in the most efficient manner to enhance the environmental and economic aspects of the power system.

## 4.3 Role of AI in Smart Charging

The integration of AI has revolutionized the world of charging infrastructure, particularly for electric vehicles. AI offers exciting possibilities for optimizing efficiency, improving the user experience, and supporting the transition to a more sustainable future by unlocking the power of data analysis and machine learning.

As electric vehicles continue to gain traction worldwide, the need for robust charging infrastructure has become increasingly important. With the advent of AI and ML, charging infrastructure has undergone significant transformations, enabling predictive charging, real-time data analytics, optimization techniques, and demand response management. In this chapter, we delve into the intricate workings of AI-driven solutions in charging infrastructure, highlighting their roles in enhancing efficiency, reliability, and sustainability.

### 4.3.1 Understanding Artificial Intelligence in Charging Infrastructures

Artificial Intelligence (AI) has emerged as a foundation for transforming the charging infrastructures for electric vehicles (Figure 4.2). By leveraging AI technologies, charging stations can adapt to dynamic conditions,

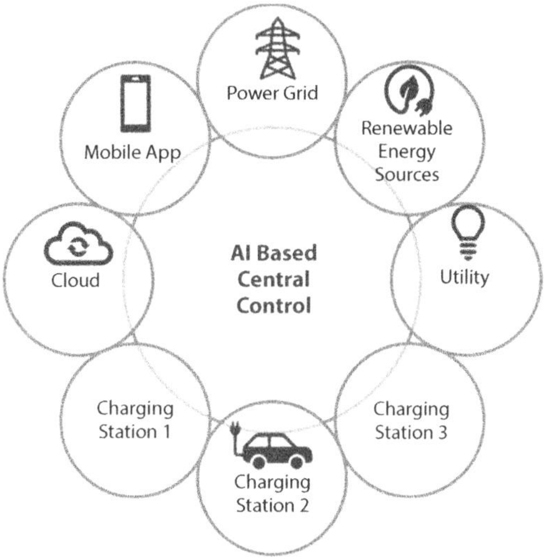


**Figure 4.2** AI-based charging infrastructures.

ensure optimal energy distribution, and enhance the user experience. The integration of AI facilitates predictive maintenance, fault detection, load balancing, and the seamless operation of charging stations. AI-driven algorithms empower charging infrastructure operators to analyze various data to uncover insights and improve overall system performance. AI-integrated charging stations can predict demand patterns, adjust charging rates, and allocate resources efficiently using powerful machine learning models. This proactive approach not only minimizes operational costs but also reduces the environmental impact by optimizing energy consumption.

Artificial Intelligence (AI) plays a crucial role in optimizing the charging infrastructure for electric vehicles (EVs) in several ways:

**Demand Prediction**: AI algorithms can analyze historical data on charging patterns, weather conditions, events, and other relevant factors to predict the future demand for charging stations. This helps operators allocate resources efficiently and avoid unnecessary congestion.

**Dynamic Pricing**: AI can optimize pricing strategies based on real-time factors, such as electricity demand, energy costs, and traffic conditions. Dynamic pricing encourages users to charge during off-peak hours so that load balancing on the grid is ensured and the cost is reduced for both operators and consumers.

**Load Balancing**: AI algorithms can dynamically distribute charging loads across different stations to prevent grid congestion. By analyzing real-time data on charging patterns and grid capacity, AI can optimize the utilization of the charging infrastructure and prevent holdups.

**Predictive Maintenance**: AI can analyze data from charging stations to predict the need for maintenance, minimize downtime, and ensure reliable operation. By detecting potential risks early, operators can proactively schedule maintenance, reduce costs, and improve the overall reliability of the charging infrastructure.

**Grid Integration**: AI can facilitate integration between charging infrastructure and the electrical grid by optimizing energy flow, managing peak demand, and supporting renewable energy utilization. AI algorithms can coordinate charging schedules to align with maximizing the utilization of clean energy sources.

**Route Planning**: AI-powered navigation systems can recommend optimal routes for EV drivers by considering factors such as traffic conditions, charging station availability, and energy consumption. This ensures that drivers can find charging stations conveniently along their routes, minimizing range anxiety, and optimizing travel time.

**User Experience Enhancement**: AI-powered interfaces and mobile apps can provide personalized recommendations and assistance to EV drivers. Users can obtain facilities such as suggestions on nearby charging stations, optimization of charging schedules, and real-time updates on availability and pricing.

Overall, AI enables smarter, more efficient, and more user-friendly charging infrastructure for electric vehicles, helping accelerate the transition to sustainable transportation while optimizing the use of energy resources.

### 4.3.2 Machine Learning Algorithms for Predictive Charging

Predictive charging involves leveraging historical data, real-time information, and various predictive algorithms to forecast charging demand and optimize charging schedules. By analyzing factors such as user behavior, weather conditions, traffic patterns, and grid load, predictive charging systems can intelligently manage charging sessions to minimize costs, reduce grid stress, and enhance the user experience.

Some important charging station related parameters, which can be monitored and predicted using machine learning based on historical data, data collected from sensors, user interactions, and external factors, are listed in Table 4.1, along with their benefits.

Machine learning algorithms play a pivotal role in predictive charging, enabling charging stations to anticipate user requirements and optimize

**Table 4.1** Charging station parameters to predict and the benefit.

| Parameter to predict | Benefit |
|---|---|
| Charging demand | Prepare for future demand based on the time of day, day of the week or any specific event |
| Energy consumption | Optimize energy usage and distribution |
| Charging station availability | Manage demand and avoid congestion |
| Battery state of charge (SOC) | Optimize charging schedules and ensure efficient use of resources |
| Charging speed | Handle vehicle's battery capacity, charging technology, and environmental conditions |
| Fault prediction | Avoid potential faults or malfunctions in charging station components |
| Weather conditions | Adjust charging schedules or recommend optimal times for charging |
| Grid demand and pricing | Optimize charging schedules and minimize costs for both users and operators |
| Peak load | Avoid overloading the grid or incurring peak demand charges |
| User behavior | Improve user experience, and tailor marketing strategies |
| Predictive maintenance | Prevent downtime and ensure reliability |
| Energy storage capacity | Balance supply and demand and improve overall efficiency |
| Load balancing | Optimize resource utilization and reduce congestion across multiple charging stations |
| Vehicle arrival and departure | Minimize wait times and optimize charging schedules |
| Predictive analytics on grid operations | Improve grid stability, reliability, and efficiency |

charging schedules accordingly. By analyzing historical charging patterns, ML models can forecast future demand and facilitate proactive resource allocation and load management. Predictive charging, enabled by machine learning (ML) algorithms, has emerged as a promising approach for optimizing charging operations, enhancing the user experience, and facilitating grid integration. In this section, we explore various machine learning algorithms used for predictive charging and their applications.

**Regression**: Regression models can be built using algorithms such as linear, polynomial, and support vector regression. These models can be employed to model the relationship between input and target variables. This can be used for the prediction of future charging demand based on historical data and external factors, such as weather, time of day, and events.

**Decision Trees**: A tree-like structure of decisions built in this algorithm based on input features, enabling the identification of charging patterns and preferences. This can be used to predict the optimal charging schedules based on factors such as vehicle type, charging station availability, and battery capacity. Decision trees are particularly effective for capturing nonlinear relationships and interactions between different variables, making them suitable for complex charging scenarios.

**Random Forest**: Random Forest is an ensemble learning technique that constructs multiple decision trees and combines their predictions to improve accuracy and robustness. This can be used to predict the availability of charging stations and optimize charging schedules in real time. Random forest can effectively handle noisy or incomplete data from charging stations by training the model using a diverse subset of data.

**Gradient Boosting Machines (GBM)**: GBM builds an ensemble of weak learners (typically decision trees) sequentially, where each learner corrects the errors of its predecessor. This algorithm can be used to predict the battery state of charge (SoC) to improve the charging speed based on the vehicle characteristics and environmental conditions.

**Support Vector Machines (SVM)**: SVMs are excellent tools for classifying and recognizing patterns. Support vector machines algorithm determines the optimal hyperplane that best separates different classes in the feature space, allowing for the classification of charging station conditions. This will be useful for predicting charging station faults based on the sensor data and historical maintenance records.

**Artificial Neural Networks (ANNs)**: ANNs mimic the structure and function of the human brain, consisting of interconnected layers of neurons that learn from input data through iterative training. An ANN can be used to predict nonlinear and complex charging patterns and optimize charging schedules based on a wide range of input features from charging stations.

**K-Nearest Neighbors (KNNs)**: KNN is a classification algorithm that assigns a new data point to the majority class of its k-nearest neighbors. This allows the prediction of the availability of a charging station and recommendation of nearby stations based on historical usage patterns.

**Long Short-Term Memory (LSTM)**: LSTM is a type of recurrent neural network (RNN) designed to capture long-term dependencies in time series data. LSTM is suitable for predicting charging patterns over time and battery state of charge (SoC), and thus optimizing charging schedules for e-vehicles over extended periods.

**Gaussian Processes**: This used to model the distribution over functions, allowing probabilistic predictions and uncertainty quantification in predictive charging scenarios. The uncertainty predictions of the charging demand help optimize the charging schedules under uncertain conditions.

**Time-Series Analysis**: Time-series forecasting techniques, including autoregressive integrated moving average (ARIMA), seasonal autoregressive integrated moving average (SARIMA), exponential smoothing methods, and recurrent neural networks (RNNs), can be utilized to predict upcoming charging patterns based on historical charging data. Time series forecasting algorithms capture temporal dependencies and seasonal patterns to accurately forecast the charging demands.

#### *4.3.2.1 Benefits of ML-Powered Predictive Charging*

- **Reduced Grid Strain:** Optimized charging schedules minimize the peak hour demand and prevent grid overload.
- **Improved Resource Management:** Charging stations can prioritize vehicles based on urgent needs, leading to their efficient utilization.
- **Enhanced User Experience:** Predictive insights allow users to optimize charging times and reduce waiting periods.
- One such application is predictive maintenance, in which ML algorithms analyze sensor data to detect anomalies and predict potential equipment failures. Operators can schedule timely maintenance by identifying potential risks before they escalate, preventing costly downtimes, and ensuring an optimal system performance.
- Additionally, ML-based predictive algorithms enhance the user experience by recommending optimal charging times and locations based on individual preferences, traffic

conditions, and energy tariffs. By personalizing the charging experience, EV owners can maximize convenience while minimizing charging costs, thereby fostering the widespread adoption of electric vehicles.

### 4.3.3 Real-Time Data Analytics and Optimization Techniques

Real-time data analytics form the backbone of AI-driven charging infrastructure, enabling operators to monitor system performance, analyze trends, and make informed decisions on the fly. Through advanced data processing techniques, charging stations can react dynamically to fluctuating demand and optimize energy distribution in real time. Figure 4.3 shows a list of potential optimization tools that can be used to achieve optimization targets under different pricing schemes.

Furthermore, real-time optimization algorithms adjust the charging rates based on factors such as grid congestion, energy prices, and renewable energy availability. By harnessing AI technologies, charging infrastructure operators can maximize the utilization of renewable energy sources, reduce reliance on fossil fuels, and mitigate their environmental impacts.

Moreover, real-time analytics enables predictive pricing strategies, in which charging stations dynamically adjust tariffs based on demand and supply conditions. By incentivizing off-peak charging and discouraging peak demand, operators can alleviate the strain on the grid, minimize energy costs, and promote sustainable charging practices.

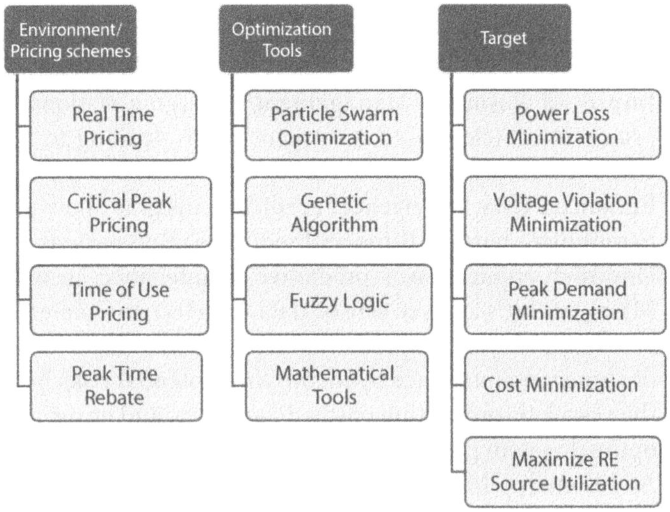


**Figure 4.3** Utilizing scheduling for optimization.

#### 4.3.3.1 Real-Time Data Analytics

Real-time data analytics involves the collection, processing, and analysis of generated data, enabling charging station operators to make informed decisions instantaneously. Through the deployment of various sensors and monitoring devices, charging stations can gather data on parameters, such as energy consumption, charging patterns, grid demand, and station utilization.

One of the primary benefits of real-time data analytics is its ability to provide insights into charging station performance and user behavior. By analyzing these data, operators can identify trends, detect anomalies, and optimize the charging processes to improve efficiency and reliability. For example, they can predict peak demand periods and adjust charging rates accordingly to prevent grid overload and minimize waiting times for users.

Moreover, real-time data analytics enables proactive maintenance by early detection of equipment malfunctions or performance degradation. By monitoring key metrics, such as voltage levels, current flow, and temperature, operators can identify potential issues before escalating into costly downtime or safety hazards.

#### 4.3.3.2 Optimization Techniques

In addition to data analytics, charging station operators employ optimization techniques to maximize the utilization of their infrastructure and minimize operational costs. These techniques leverage advanced algorithms and computational models to optimize various aspects of charging station operations, including energy management, resource allocation, and scheduling.

One common optimization approach is forecasting demand, which uses historical data and machine-learning algorithms to accurately predict future charging demand. By forecasting demand at different timescales (e.g., hourly, daily, and weekly), operators can optimize station capacity planning and scheduling to meet user needs while avoiding underutilization or congestion.

Another optimization technique is dynamic pricing, in which charging rates are adjusted in real time based on factors such as grid demand, energy costs, and user preferences. By incentivizing users to charge during off-peak hours or at less congested stations, dynamic pricing helps balance the demand across the network and reduces the overall cost of electricity procurement for operators.

Furthermore, optimization techniques can facilitate smart grid integration by enabling bidirectional communication between charging stations and the grid. Through demand response programs and vehicle-to-grid (V2G) technologies, operators can manage EV charging in response to grid conditions such as fluctuations in renewable energy generation or peak demand events.

### 4.3.4 AI-Based Demand Response Management

Demand response management lies at the heart of AI-driven charging infrastructure, enabling operators to balance supply and demand in real time while ensuring grid stability and reliability. By leveraging AI-based algorithms, charging stations can participate in demand response programs by adjusting the charging rates based on grid conditions and electricity market dynamics.

One key application of AI-based demand response management is peak shaving, where charging stations reduce energy consumption during periods of high demand, alleviating strain on the grid and preventing potential blackouts. Through intelligent load management techniques, AI algorithms

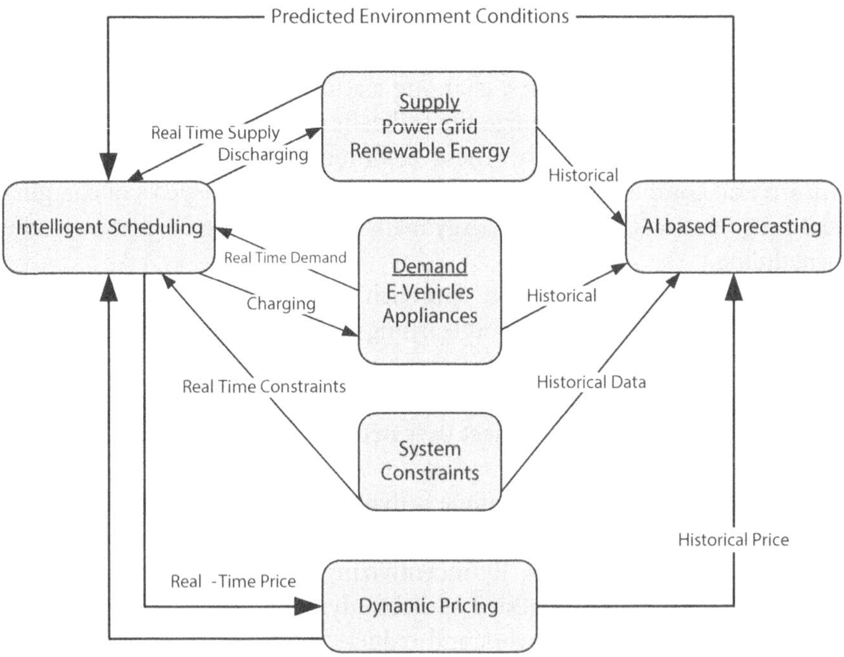


**Figure 4.4** Illustration of an AI-based charging station demand response management.

prioritize critical charging tasks while optimizing overall energy usage, ensuring uninterrupted service for EV owners. A simple illustration of the AI-based charging station demand response management system is shown in Figure 4.4.

#### *4.3.4.1 Understanding Demand Response Management*

Demand response management (DRM) involves adjusting electricity consumption patterns in response to supply conditions, grid constraints, or price signals. Traditionally, DRM has been applied in industrial and commercial settings; however, with the rise of EVs, it has gained relevance in the realm of transportation electrification. The goal is to optimize the utilization of the charging infrastructure while ensuring grid reliability and minimizing costs.

Artificial Intelligence (AI) plays a pivotal role in enhancing the efficiency and effectiveness of DRM for charging stations. By leveraging advanced algorithms and machine learning techniques, AI enables the real-time monitoring, prediction, and optimization of charging processes. Here is how AI enhances DRM for charging stations:

Predictive Analytics: AI algorithms analyze historical data, weather patterns, traffic conditions, and user behavior to predict charging demand. This proactive approach allows charging stations to anticipate peak periods and adjust operations accordingly, thereby optimizing resource allocation and grid integration.

Dynamic Charging Scheduling: AI dynamically adjusts charging schedules based on the grid load, electricity prices, and renewable energy availability. By prioritizing charging during off-peak hours or when renewable energy generation is high, AI maximizes the utilization of clean energy sources and minimizes the stress on the grid.

User Behavior Modeling: AI models learn from user preferences, driving patterns, and charging habits to personalize charging recommendations. This not only enhances the user experience, but also facilitates load balancing across charging stations, preventing congestion and grid overloads.

Grid Integration and Coordination: AI-based DRM systems facilitate seamless integration with the grid infrastructure, enabling bidirectional communication and coordination between charging stations and utility providers. This allows for load shedding or load shifting during grid emergencies or peak demand periods, thereby ensuring grid stability and resilience.

#### *4.3.4.2 Benefits of AI-Based DRM for Charging Stations*

The AI-based DRM for charging stations has multiple advantages for stakeholders:

Grid stability: AI optimizes charging patterns to reduce grid congestion and volatility, leading to increased stability and reliability.

Cost savings: AI-enabled predictive analytics help schedule charging during off-peak hours or when the usage of renewable energy sources is high, leading to a reduction in electricity costs.

User-friendliness: Recommendations for charging levels and dynamic scheduling ensure a high level of user-friendliness and satisfaction, which helps accelerate the adoption of EVs.

Environmental benefits: AI-based DRM helps in the optimal utilization of renewable energy sources and the reduction of greenhouse gas emissions through the efficient usage of resources due to optimal charge scheduling. AI-powered DRM-based DRM further promotes vehicle-to-grid integration by giving electric vehicles the opportunity to become energy storage devices. By intelligently managing EV batteries' charging and discharging cycles, charging stations can stabilize the grid, support renewable energy integration, and unlock new revenue streams for EV owners.

In summary, Artificial Intelligence and machine learning are at the forefront of changing the worldview on electric vehicle charging systems. Enhanced predictive charging, real-time data analytics and forecasting, optimization methods, and demand response support have been democratized. These solutions allow operators to improve efficiency, reliability, and sustainability, thereby opening the doors for the planet's evolution into a clean, intelligent mobility standard.

## 4.4 Components of AI-Based Smart Charging Systems

The charging infrastructure includes physical charging stations where electric vehicles are connected. These stations may vary in complexity and capabilities from basic Level 1 chargers to more advanced Level 2 or DC fast chargers. A user-friendly interface is essential for users to interact with a smart-charging system. This interface could be a mobile app, a web portal, or integrated directly into the vehicle's infotainment system, allowing users to monitor the charging status, schedule charging sessions, and adjust their preferences. Smart charging systems often need to interact with the electrical grid to optimize charging schedules based on grid conditions such as electricity prices, grid capacity, and renewable energy availability. Grid integration components enable communication among the smart charging system, utility providers, and grid operators.

The sensitive nature of the data involved potential impact of cyberattacks on the electrical grid, and robust security measures are crucial for AI-based smart charging systems. This includes encryption protocols, authentication mechanisms, and intrusion detection systems to safeguard the integrity of data and infrastructure. Some smart charging systems incorporate energy management software to optimize energy usage within a given ecosystem. This software can help balance the energy supply and demand, integrate renewable energy sources, and prioritize charging based on user preferences and grid constraints. In addition, AI algorithms may employ predictive analytics to forecast future electricity demand, grid conditions, and user behavior. These predictions can help optimize charging strategies to minimize costs, reduce grid congestion, and maximize the utilization of renewable energy resources.

### 4.4.1 Sensors and IoT Devices for Data Collection

Several sensors and Internet of Things (IoT) devices are used in smart charging systems for electric vehicles to gather data for management and decision making. Smart charging systems for electric vehicles (EVs) rely heavily on data collected from sensors and IoT devices. These systems take advantage of IoT networks to streamline the deployment of charging infrastructure, improve the user experience *via* smooth operation, and enable effective energy consumption monitoring. As accurate energy consumption assessment is made possible by the integration of sensors into EV charging procedures, and real-time data transmission between vehicles, infrastructure, and service providers is made possible by IoT technology. Blockchain technology is also used in shared EV charging areas to manage monetary transactions and authentication procedures. The integration of sensors, IoT gadgets, and blockchain technology guarantees efficient data gathering, administration, and optimization in EV smart charging systems, supporting environmentally friendly and productive electric mobility. The list of frequently used sensors and IoT devices is as follows:

**Electricity Meters**: These meters measure the electricity consumption at charging stations and provide data on energy usage, helping in billing, load management, and grid balancing.

**Current Sensors**: Current sensors monitor the flow of electric current through charging cables and can detect abnormalities, such as overloading or short circuits, ensuring safety during charging operations.

**Voltage Sensors**: Voltage sensors measure the electrical potential difference between two points and provide data on voltage levels at charging stations, helping to monitor the charging infrastructure's health and performance.

**Temperature Sensors**: Temperature sensors monitor the temperature of charging cables, connectors, and other components to prevent overheating, which can lead to safety hazards or damage to equipment.

**Humidity Sensors**: Humidity sensors measure the moisture content in the environment surrounding charging stations, helping to prevent corrosion and electrical faults due to moisture ingress.

**RFID Readers**: Radio-Frequency Identification (RFID) readers are used for vehicle identification and authentication, allowing seamless access control and billing based on user accounts or vehicle profiles.

**GPS Trackers**: GPS trackers enable the location tracking of electric vehicles, facilitating fleet management, route optimization, and geofencing for automated charging initiation or restriction in designated areas.

**Accelerometers and Gyroscopes**: These motion sensors detect vehicle movement and orientation, providing data on vehicle status (e.g., parked, driving) and enabling smart charging scheduling based on predicted arrival times or departure patterns.

**Power Quality Analyzers**: Power quality analyzers monitor the quality of the electrical power supply and detect issues such as voltage fluctuations, harmonic distortions, or power factor variations that can affect the charging efficiency and equipment performance.

**Communication Gateways**: Communication gateways serve as interfaces between charging stations, sensors, and the central control system, enabling data exchange and the remote monitoring/control of charging operations.

**Smart Electric Meters**: These meters provide advanced metering capabilities, such as real-time monitoring of energy consumption, demand response capabilities, and two-way communication with utility providers for dynamic pricing and grid integration.

**Environmental Sensors**: Environmental sensors measure parameters, such as air quality, ambient temperature, and solar radiation, providing data for optimizing charging schedules based on environmental conditions and promoting sustainable charging practices.

By integrating these sensors with IoT devices, smart charging systems can benefit from real-time monitoring, predictive analytics, and adaptive-control strategies. This promotes user convenience, grid stability, and effective energy management when charging the electric vehicles. Some control functions using controllers with the IoT are shown in Figure 4.5.

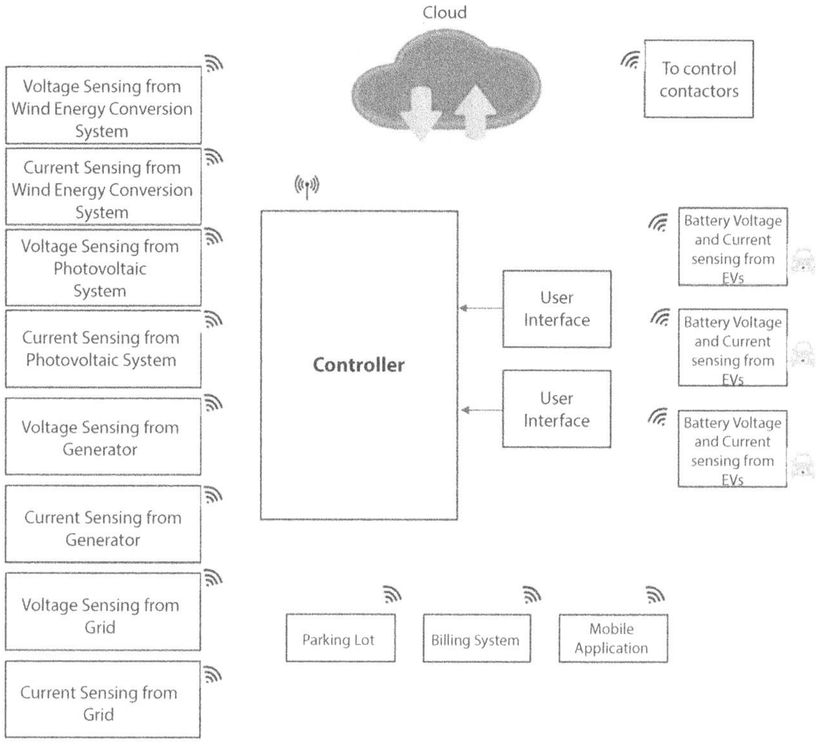


**Figure 4.5** Control functions using controller with IoT.

### 4.4.2 Cloud Computing and Edge Computing Platforms

Both cloud computing and edge computing platforms are essential for facilitating effective data processing, instantaneous decision-making, and smooth interaction with the electric grid in electric vehicle (EV) smart charging systems. These platforms offer safe and lightweight charging-scheduling frameworks for Moving EVs (MEVs) and Parking EVs (PEVs) in 6G heterogeneous vehicular networks (HetVNETs), help with customized charging schedules through Software-Defined Networking (SDN), and coordinate Power Electronic Converters (PECs). Furthermore, a cloud-based framework for electric vehicle (EV) charging is presented by integrating cloud computing with the Internet of Vehicles (IoV). This framework handles high-demand difficulties at charging stations during peak hours, improving the system performance and quality of service for EV consumers. In the rapidly changing world of smart grids and sustainable energy solutions, these platforms maximize EV charging efficiency, grid stability, and overall system management using advanced control algorithms, SDN support, and collaborative computing resource allocation. These platforms were used as follows:

#### *4.4.2.1 Cloud Computing Platforms*

**Data Storage and Management**: Cloud computing platforms provide scalable and reliable storage solutions for the vast amount of data generated by EV charging stations, sensors, and IoT devices. They offer data management capabilities, including data aggregation, indexing, and archival, ensuring easy access to and retrieval of historical charging data for analysis and reporting.

**Data Analytics and Insights**: Cloud-based analytics tools leverage the computational power of the cloud infrastructure to perform advanced data analytics, including predictive modeling, anomaly detection, and demand forecasting. These analytics help optimize charging schedules, identify usage patterns, and provide insights for grid management and energy planning.

**Remote Monitoring and Control**: Cloud computing enables remote monitoring and control of the EV charging infrastructure, allowing operators to monitor charging station status, track energy consumption, and remotely configure charging parameters. This facilitates proactive maintenance, troubleshooting, and optimization of charging operations from a centralized management console.

**Integration with Grid Services**: Cloud-based platforms facilitate integration with utility providers and grid operators, enabling demand response programs, dynamic pricing schemes, and grid-balancing services. They support communication protocols such as the Open Charge Point Protocol (OCPP) for interoperability with third-party systems and adherence to industry standards.

**Scalability and Flexibility**: Cloud computing offers scalability to accommodate varying workloads and scale resources up or down based on demand. This flexibility allows EV charging networks to adapt to changing requirements, accommodate growing fleets of electric vehicles, and support future innovations in smart grid technologies.

#### *4.4.2.2 Edge Computing Platforms*

**Real-Time Data Processing**: Edge computing platforms process data locally at or near the source of generation, reducing latency and enabling real-time decision-making for time-sensitive applications such as vehicle-to-grid (V2G) communication and load balancing.

**Edge Analytics and Machine Learning**: Edge computing enables on-device analytics and machine learning inference, allowing EV charging stations to perform local analytics and make intelligent charging decisions autonomously, without relying solely on cloud-based services. This improves responsiveness and reduces the dependence on continuous connectivity to the cloud.
**Fault Tolerance and Resilience**: Edge computing enhances system reliability by reducing reliance on central cloud infrastructure. Local processing capabilities enable EV charging stations to continue operating autonomously, even in the event of network disruptions or cloud service outages, thereby ensuring uninterrupted charging services for users.
**Privacy and Data Security**: Edge computing platforms help address privacy concerns by processing sensitive data locally and minimizing the transmission of raw data over networks. This approach enhances data security and privacy compliance by reducing the exposure to potential cyber threats and unauthorized access to sensitive information.
**Distributed Intelligence**: Edge computing fosters distributed intelligence across the EV charging network, allowing for collaborative decision making and peer-to-peer communication between charging stations. This decentralized approach promotes scalability, fault tolerance, and adaptability to local conditions, thereby enhancing the resilience and efficiency of the overall system.

In summary, edge computing and cloud computing platforms work best for EV smart-charging systems. They combined the real-time processing and resilience of edge computing with the scalability and analytics capabilities of the cloud to provide intelligent, dependable, and effective charging services for electric vehicles.

### 4.4.3 Communication Protocols and Network Infrastructure

Different communication protocols and network infrastructure are employed in electric vehicle (EV) smart charging systems to provide smooth data sharing, interoperability, and coordination between various ecosystem components. Communication protocols and network infrastructure play vital roles in EV charging systems. Smart grids in EV charging systems rely heavily on modern communication networks and digital-control techniques. Software-Defined Networking (SDN) is proposed for effective charge scheduling and personalized charging services, in which a centralized controller receives charging requests from Vehicular Edge Computing (VEC) servers. The integration of distributed generation and renewable energy in smart grids necessitates smart monitoring and control of interconnected systems, where EV technologies can contribute significantly. Moreover, the future of the EV charging infrastructure involves innovative concepts such as dynamic and quasi-dynamic wireless charging, emphasizing the importance of smart control and communication techniques for efficient EV charging. This comprehensive approach ensures reliable and sustainable EV charging systems in the evolving smart city landscape. The following are some of the most important network architectures and communication protocols often used:

**Open Charge Point Protocol (OCPP)**: The OCPP is a widely adopted open communication protocol for managing charging stations and EVs. It enables interoperability among charging station hardware, network operators, and energy management systems, allowing for remote monitoring, control, and firmware updates.

**ISO 15118 (Vehicle-to-Grid Communication)**: ISO 15118 is the standard for bidirectional communication between electric vehicles and charging infrastructure. It facilitates vehicle-to-grid (V2G) communication, allowing EVs to exchange information with charging stations and the grid, thus enabling functionalities such as smart charging, vehicle authentication, and grid service participation.

**Modbus TCP/IP**: Modbus is a widely used communication protocol in industrial automation systems, including EV charging infrastructure. Modbus TCP/IP enables communication between charging stations, energy management systems, and control devices, providing real-time data exchange and control capabilities.

**Message Queuing Telemetry Transport (MQTT)**: MQTT is a lightweight messaging protocol suitable for IoT applications, including EV smart charging systems. It facilitates efficient and reliable communication among IoT devices, cloud services, and backend systems, supporting publish-subscribe messaging patterns for data streaming and event-driven architectures.

**Representational State Transfer APIs (RESTful APIs)**: RESTful APIs provide a standardized way for web-based applications to interact with EV charging infrastructure and backend systems. They enable integration with third-party software applications, mobile apps, and web portals, allowing users to monitor the charging status, initiate charging sessions, and access billing information *via* HTTP-based APIs.

**Wi-Fi**: Wi-Fi connectivity is commonly used for local communication between EV charging stations, IoT devices, and access points within premises or public charging networks. It provides high-speed wireless connectivity for data exchange, configuration, and management of the charging infrastructure.

**Cellular Networks (3G/4G/5G)**: Cellular networks play a vital role in enabling remote monitoring, control, and management of the EV charging infrastructure deployed in diverse locations. They provide ubiquitous connectivity, allowing charging stations to communicate with backend systems, cloud services, and utility providers in cellular data networks.

**Ethernet**: Ethernet connectivity is used for wired communication between charging stations, controllers, and network switches within a local area network (LAN) or industrial Ethernet infrastructure. It offers high-speed data transfer and reliable connectivity for the real-time monitoring and control of charging operations.

**Long Range Wide Area Network (LoRaWAN)**: LoRaWAN is a low-power, wide-area networking protocol suitable for IoT applications in remote or outdoor environments. It enables long-range communication among EV charging stations, sensors, and gateways, providing connectivity for monitoring and control over large geographic areas.

**Bluetooth Low Energy (BLE)**: BLE is used for short-range wireless communication among EVs, mobile devices, and charging stations. It facilitates proximity-based interactions, authentication, and data exchange between EVs and the charging infrastructure, supporting features such as mobile app integration and user authentication.

These network infrastructures and communication protocols allow for smooth connectivity and interoperability in EV smart charging systems, providing a variety of features such as energy management, vehicle-grid integration, and real-time monitoring and control.

### 4.4.4 Control Algorithms for Dynamic Charging Control

Dynamic charging control in electric vehicle (EV) smart charging systems is crucial for their efficient operation. Various control algorithms have been proposed to address this problem, including machine learning-based charge management systems, adaptive super-twisting sliding mode controllers, adaptive error convergence techniques, gain adaptive sliding mode control with modified phase-shift algorithms, and approximate dynamic programming. These algorithms focus on improving charging dynamics, achieving unity power factor correction, tight voltage regulation, adaptation to varying parameters, tracking load profile variations, and optimizing charging processes efficiently. By utilizing techniques such as deep neural networks, genetic algorithms, and fitted value iterations, these control algorithms aim to enhance the reliability, sustainability, and cost-effectiveness of EV charging systems within smart cities. EV smart charging systems with dynamic charging control algorithms attempt to maximize charging times by considering several variables, including user preferences, grid demand, electricity pricing, and the availability of renewable energy sources. Several popular control algorithms for dynamic charge control are as follows:

**Load Balancing Algorithms**: These algorithms distribute charging loads among available charging stations to avoid overloading specific circuits or transformers. Load balancing helps optimize resource utilization and prevents grid congestion, ensuring the efficient operation of the charging infrastructure.

**Peak Demand Management**: Algorithms for peak demand management aim to reduce electricity consumption during peak demand periods, when energy prices are typically higher. These algorithms schedule charging sessions to minimize the grid impact during peak hours, thereby reducing the electricity costs for EV owners and alleviating strain on the grid.

**Time-of-Use (ToU) Pricing Optimization**: ToU pricing optimization algorithms schedule charging sessions to coincide with off-peak hours when the electricity prices are lower. By charging during periods of low demand, EV owners can take advantage of cheaper electricity rates while balancing the grid and promoting renewable energy integration.

**Renewable Energy Integration**: Algorithms for renewable energy integration prioritize charging during times of high renewable energy generation, such as when the solar or wind power output is abundant. By aligning charging schedules with renewable energy availability, these algorithms promote the use of clean energy and reduce the reliance on fossil fuels.

**Grid Services Participation**: Some algorithms enable EVs to participate in grid services, such as frequency regulation, demand response, and ancillary services. These algorithms adjust charging rates or schedules in response to signals from grid operators, helping to stabilize the grid and supporting its reliability and resilience.

**User Preference Optimization**: User preference optimization algorithms consider individual user preferences, constraints, and priorities when scheduling charging sessions. They may consider factors such as desired departure times, travel distance, and battery state of charge, ensuring that EV owners' needs are met while optimizing the overall charging efficiency.

**Predictive Charging Algorithms**: Predictive charging algorithms use historical data, weather forecasts, traffic patterns, and other relevant information to predict the future energy demand and grid conditions. By anticipating future charging requirements, these algorithms can proactively adjust charging schedules to optimize energy utilization and minimize costs.

**Machine-Learning-Based Optimization**: Machine-learning algorithms analyze large datasets to identify patterns, trends, and optimal charging strategies. They can learn from past charging behavior and adapt charging schedules dynamically based on real-time data, thereby improving accuracy and efficiency over time.

**Distributed Control Strategies**: Distributed control strategies decentralize decision making and coordination among charging stations, allowing them to communicate and collaborate autonomously. These strategies enable peer-to-peer communication, load sharing, and self-organization, thereby enhancing the scalability, reliability, and resilience of the charging network.

**Adaptive Control Algorithms**: Adaptive control algorithms continuously monitor the system dynamics and adjust the charging parameters in response to changing conditions. They can dynamically optimize the charging rates, voltages, and power flows to adapt to variations in grid conditions, user behavior, and environmental factors.

These control algorithms provide dynamic and intelligent regulation of charging processes, promoting efficient energy consumption, grid stability, and customer satisfaction in smart-charging EV systems. They can be applied in energy management systems, cloud-based platforms, and EV charging infrastructures.

## 4.5 Challenges and Future Directions

Challenges in smart charging infrastructures include the effective management of electric vehicle (EV) charging demands, integration with the smart grid for efficient charging schedules, and resolving security and privacy risks offered by AI approaches. Future options include using artificial intelligence (AI) to automate charging infrastructure, placing self-charging technologies in place, and giving electric vehicles (EVs) the ability to drive themselves. AI may also be used to improve automation, save manual labor, and reducing operating costs in the installation and maintenance of smart infrastructures. Smart charging infrastructure can adapt to the problems provided by growing EV use, renewable energy integration, and power loads. Applying AI to optimize charging procedures to reduce bottlenecks and improve grid efficiency. Upgrading energy trading paradigms with FL and blockchain, EV data security, charging point location optimization, and AI-based charging time planning. Future directions for AI-powered smart-charging infrastructure will improve reliability and reduce costs by automating deployment and operation.

### 4.5.1 Security and Privacy Concerns in AI-Driven Infrastructures

Smart charging infrastructure has many advantages, including serious security and privacy issues.

**Data privacy**: Users' locations, charging habits, and even car usage trends are collected by smart charging systems. To protect user privacy, these data must be treated with extreme caution to avoid misuse.

**Authentication and Access Control**: It is critical to ensure that only those with permission can access and operate charging stations. Unauthorized access or misuse of charging facilities may result from weak authentication procedures or flaws in the access control systems.

**Data Integrity**: It is critical to preserve the accuracy of the data that smart charging systems produce and handle. Any manipulation of these data may result in misleading energy use figures, incorrect invoicing, or even potential safety risks.

**Third-Party Risks**: Smart charging systems frequently enter into relationships with other service providers to provide features like payment processing and data analytics. If appropriate controls are not in place, these relationships can pose significant threats to privacy and security.

Innovative techniques are used to solve security and privacy problems in AI-driven smart-charging infrastructure, specifically in EV charging networks. The suggested mechanisms include Federated Learning frameworks with adaptive differential privacy, privacy preservation techniques based on blockchain technology, Federated Learning (FL) utilizing, and Practical Deep Reinforcement Learning-based Rechargeable Battery assist Privacy Preserving Method (PRoP) to maximize trade-offs between privacy protection and electricity costs. Furthermore, optimal charging control for electric vehicles, anonymity, and fairness in power transactions are guaranteed by a blockchain-based smart EV charging station energy management system.

### 4.5.2 Scalability and Interoperability Issues

Scalability and interoperability play a major role in the design and erection of charging infrastructure.

**Scalability**: As the number of electric cars (EVs) increases, smart charging infrastructures must be able to handle more vehicles without affecting reliability or performance. If infrastructure is unable to keep up with the increasing demand for charging services, scalability problems may occur, causing traffic jams, delays, and user discomfort.

**Interoperability**: Interoperability refers to the capacity of various platforms, devices, and systems to function as units. Interoperability is crucial for facilitating coordination and communication among different elements of smart charging infrastructure, such as energy management systems, grid operators, cars, and charging stations.

**Charging Station Compatibility**: Owners of electric vehicles should have no trouble utilizing any kind of charging station, regardless of the brand or supplier. The ability of charging stations from various suppliers to interact with one another and with other components of the system is ensured by interoperability standards such as the Open Charge Point Protocol (OCPP).

**Grid Integration**: To maximize energy consumption, prevent grid overloads, and facilitate the integration of renewable energy sources, smart charging infrastructures must efficiently communicate with the electrical grid. To facilitate grid-friendly charging techniques, such as demand response and dynamic load balancing, communication between the grid management systems and charging infrastructure is necessary.

**Future-Proofing**: Future technological developments, modifications to laws or industry standards, and scalability and interoperability issues should all be considered. Infrastructures for smart charging must be versatile and flexible to meet changing needs and new technologies as they arise.

Scalability is demonstrated by an Adaptive Charging Network (ACN), which uses an Adaptive Scheduling Algorithm based on convex optimization to address real-world issues, including uneven infrastructure and less-than-ideal battery behavior. To handle peak demand, the Internet of Vehicles (IoV) framework suggests cloud-based EV charging options, highlighting the significance of dependable communication infrastructure for scalability. In addition, it has been determined that AI technologies are essential for automating the installation and maintenance of smart grids and other smart infrastructure to save costs and improve reliability. The application of cooperative multi-agent reinforcement learning for smart charging strategies, assuring scalability and profitability, has been highlighted in research on shared autonomous electric vehicles.

Collaboration between many stakeholders, including government agencies, academic institutions, industry companies, and standards groups, is necessary to address difficulties related to scalability and interoperability. Overcoming these obstacles and realizing the full potential of AI-driven smart charging infrastructures may be accomplished by creating and upholding open standards, investing in modular and adaptable designs and encouraging innovation through trial projects and experimentation.

### 4.5.3 Regulatory and Policy Implications

Smart charging infrastructures powered by AI have great potential for improving grid management, optimizing energy use, and encouraging sustainable behaviors. To guarantee efficient and fair deployment, they also present several legislative and policy issues that must be resolved. The following are some significant policy and regulatory ramifications:

**Data Security and Privacy**: Large volumes of data, including the energy usage and charging habits of users, are gathered and analyzed by smart-charging infrastructure. To prevent unauthorized access to or exploitation of users' sensitive information, regulations must provide strong data privacy and security protection.

**Consumer Protection and Accessibility**: Regulations should prioritize consumer protection by ensuring pricing, standards, and accessibility to diverse socioeconomic backgrounds.

**Interoperability Standards**: Policymakers should create interoperability standards for AI-based smart-charging infrastructures to promote universal adoption and compatibility among various charging networks and EV types. This makes it simpler for different systems and platforms to integrate and communicate with one another.

**Tariffs and Pricing Structures**: For smart-charging services, policymakers should create fair and transparent tariff structures and pricing models. To promote effective use and investment in renewable energy sources, this may include dynamic pricing algorithms that consider current energy costs, periods of peak demand, and grid congestion are required.

**Ethical and Social Implications**: Potential employment displacement, algorithmic biases, and environmental justice issues are just a few of the ethical and social issues that policymakers should consider when developing AI-based smart charging infrastructures. Fairness, accountability, and openness should be incorporated into regulatory frameworks to reduce risks and encourage responsible innovation.

### 4.5.4 Emerging Technologies and Trends in Smart Charging

The following new developments influence how smart EV charging infrastructure will be developed in the future:

**Vehicle-to-Grid (V2G) Integration**: EVs and the electrical grid may exchange energy in both directions owing to the V2G technology. When the demand is at its highest, electric vehicle (EV) batteries can act as distributed energy storage devices, store excess energy from renewable sources, and return them to the grid. Maximizing the value of EVs as grid assets, lowering energy costs, and improving grid stability are all possible with the V2G integration.

**Wireless Charging**: By eliminating the need for physical wires and connectors, wireless charging technology enables electric vehicles to be charged by parking their vehicles over a charging pad. This technology can be implemented in a variety of venues, including residences, offices, and public parking lots, and it provides ease for electric vehicle drivers. As wireless charging technology advances, the smart-charging infrastructure may be equipped with wireless charging as a standard.

**Advanced Metering Infrastructure (AMI)**: AMI systems allow energy consumption at each individual meter to be managed and monitored in real time. Utilities may obtain insights into electric vehicle charging patterns, enhance grid operations, and provide dynamic pricing plans to encourage off-peak charging by combining AMI with a smart charging infrastructure.

**Blockchain Technology**: Blockchain offers a safe, decentralized environment for transaction recording and verification. Blockchain can enable peer-to-peer energy trading between EV owners and grid operators, speed up payment processing for charging services, and offer transparent and tamper-proof recording of charging transactions in the context of a smart-charging infrastructure.

**Integration with Smart Grids**: EV charging stations, grid operators, renewable energy sources, and other distributed energy resources can communicate and coordinate seamlessly because of the growing integration of smart-charging infrastructure into larger smart-grid ecosystems. This integration supports the shift to a decarbonized energy system, while improving the flexibility, dependability, and efficiency of the grid.

## Bibliography

1. Arikumar, K.S., Prathiba, S.B., Moorthy, R.S., Srivastava, G., Gadekallu, T.R., Software Defined Networking Assisted Electric Vehicle Charging: Towards Smart Charge Scheduling and Management. *IEEE Trans. Netw. Sci. Eng.*, 11, 1, 163–173, 2023.
2. Chen, N., Wang, M., Zhang, N., Shen, X., Energy and information management of electric vehicular network: A survey. *IEEE Commun. Surv. Tutor.*, 22, 2, 967–997, 2020.

3. Chung, Y.W., Khaki, B., Li, T., Chu, C., Gadh, R., Ensemble machine learning-based algorithm for electric vehicle user behavior prediction. *Appl. Energy*, 254, 113732, 2019.
4. Ejaz, W., Naeem, M., Sharma, S.K., Khattak, A.M., Ramzan, M.R., Ali, A., Anpalagan, A., IoV-based deployment and scheduling of charging infrastructure in intelligent transportation systems. *IEEE Sens. J.*, 21, 14, 15504–15514, 2020.
5. Emodi, N.V., Akuru, U.B., Dioha, M.O., Adoba, P., Kuhudzai, R.J., Bamisile, O., The role of Internet of Things on electric vehicle charging infrastructure and consumer experience. *Energies*, 16, 10, 4248, 2023.
6. Florea, B.C. and Taralunga, D.D., Blockchain IoT for smart electric vehicles battery management. *Sustainability*, 12, 10, 3984, 2020.
7. Gebbran, D., Barragán-Moreno, A., Gómez, P.I., Subroto, R.K., Mardani, M.M., López, M., Dragičević, T., Cloud and edge computing for smart management of power electronic converter fleets: A key connective fabric to enable the green transition. *IEEE Ind. Electron. Mag.*, 17, 2, 6–19, 2022.
8. Hafeez, A., Alammari, R., Iqbal, A., Utilization of EV charging station in demand side management using deep learning method. *IEEE Access*, 11, 8747–8760, 2023.
9. Hasan, M.K., Habib, A.A., Islam, S., Balfaqih, M., Alfawaz, K.M., Singh, D., Smart grid communication networks for electric vehicles empowering distributed energy generation: Constraints, challenges, and recommendations. *Energies*, 16, 3, 1140, 2023.
10. Islam, S., Badsha, S., Sengupta, S., Khalil, I., Atiquzzaman, M., An intelligent privacy preservation scheme for ev charging infrastructure. *IEEE Trans. Ind. Inf.*, 19, 2, 1238–1247, 2022.
11. Kazemtarghi, A., Mallik, A., Chen, Y., Dynamic pricing strategy for electric vehicle charging stations to distribute the congestion and maximize the revenue. *Int. J. Electr. Power Energy Syst.*, 158, 109946, 2024.
12. Lee, Z.J., Lee, G., Lee, T., Jin, C., Lee, R., Low, Z., Low, S.H., Adaptive charging networks: A framework for smart electric vehicle charging. *IEEE Trans. Smart Grid*, 12, 5, 4339–4350, 2021.
13. Li, D., Yang, Q., Zhang, F., Wang, Y., Qian, Y., An, D., Research on privacy issues in smart metering system: An improved tcn-based nilm attack method and practical drl-based rechargeable battery assisted privacy preserving method. *IEEE Trans. Autom. Sci. Eng.*, 21, 3, 2882–2899, 2023.
14. Lin, Y.J., Chen, Y.C., Zheng, J.Y., Shao, D.W., Chu, D., Yang, H.T., Blockchain-based intelligent charging station management system platform. *IEEE Access*, 10, 101936–101956, 2022.
15. Martins, J.P., Ferreira, J.C., Monteiro, V., Afonso, J.A., Afonso, J.L., IoT and blockchain paradigms for EV charging system. *Energies*, 12, 15, 2987, 2019.
16. Mosayebi, M., Gheisarnejad, M., Farsizadeh, H., Andresen, B., Khooban, M.H., Smart extreme fast portable charger for electric vehicles-based artificial intelligence. *IEEE Trans. Circuits Syst. II Express Briefs*, 70, 2, 586–590, 2022.

17. Masood, U., Azeem, M.K., Ahmad, I., ul Jabbar, A., Robust adaptive nonlinear control of plugin hybrid electric vehicles for vehicle to grid and grid to vehicle power flow with hybrid energy storage system. *ISA Trans.*, 139, 406–424, 2023.
18. Mazhar, T., Asif, R.N., Malik, M.A., Nadeem, M.A., Haq, I., Iqbal, M., Ashraf, S., Electric vehicle charging system in the smart grid using different machine learning methods. *Sustainability*, 15, 3, 2603, 2023.
19. Mishra, D., Singh, B., Panigrahi, B.K., Bi-directional EV Charging with robust power controlled adaptive phase-shift algorithm. *IEEE Trans. Veh. Technol.*, 72, 12, 15491–15501, 2023.
20. Mishra, D., Singh, B., Panigrahi, B.K., Implementation of a robust PMAE algorithm to limit large gain variation in a fuel-cell integrated EV charging architecture. *IEEE Trans. Energy Convers.*, 38, 4, 2671–2683, 2023.
21. Paudel, D. and Das, T.K., A deep reinforcement learning approach for power management of battery-assisted fast-charging EV hubs participating in day-ahead and real-time electricity markets. *Energy*, 283, 129097, 2023.
22. Razmjouei, P., Kavousi-Fard, A., Dabbaghjamanesh, M., Jin, T., Su, W., DAG-based smart contract for dynamic 6G wireless EVs charging system. *IEEE Trans. Green Commun. Netw.*, 6, 3, 1459–1467, 2022.
23. Rimal, B.P., Kong, C., Poudel, B., Wang, Y., Shahi, P., Smart electric vehicle charging in the era of internet of vehicles, emerging trends, and open issues. *Energies*, 15, 5, 1908, 2022.
24. Rivera, S., Goetz, S.M., Kouro, S., Lehn, P.W., Pathmanathan, M., Bauer, P., Mastromauro, R.A., Charging infrastructure and grid integration for electromobility. *Proc. IEEE*, 111, 4, 371–396, 2022.
25. Ruan, G., Qiu, D., Sivaranjani, S., Awad, A.S., Strbac, G., Data-driven energy management of virtual power plants: A review. *Adv. Appl. Energy*, 14, 100170, 2024.
26. Shahriar, S., Al-Ali, A.R., Osman, A.H., Dhou, S., Nijim, M., Machine learning approaches for EV charging behavior: A review. *IEEE Access*, 8, 168980–168993, 2020.
27. Shao, S., Sartipizadeh, H., Gupta, A., Scheduling EV charging having demand with different reliability constraints. *IEEE Trans. Intell. Transp. Syst.*, 24, 10, 11018–11029, 2023.
28. Teimoori, Z. and Yassine, A., A review on intelligent energy management systems for future electric vehicle transportation. *Sustainability*, 14, 21, 14100, 2022.
29. Xiong, Y., Wang, B., Chu, C.C., Gadh, R., Vehicle grid integration for demand response with mixture user model and decentralized optimization. *Appl. Energy*, 231, 481–493, 2018.
30. Yu, H. and Chin, K.W., Learning Algorithms for Data Collection in RF-Charging IIoT Networks. *IEEE Trans. Ind. Inf.*, 19, 1, 88–97, 2022.

5

# EV Smart Charging Using RES—Challenges

**Sowmya Ramachandradurai*, Joylin Mary J. and D.F. Jingle Jabha**

*Department of EEE, SRM TRP Engineering College, Trichy, India*

***Abstract***
These emissions are more significant owing to the use of fossil fuels for transportation. By considering population growth and environmental concerns, an efficient model of an electric vehicle (EV) smart charging system is proposed in this chapter with the integration of renewable energy sources (RES) in distribution networks. The existing EV charger related to the power demand profile was modified to enhance the efficiency of the charger. Two different cases were studied to understand the impacts of RES penetration and the smart-charging capacity of EVs. The optimization of EVs without the injection of RES evolved in case one. In case two, the RES was injected into the EVs. The IEEE 33 bus system was used for the implementation of the proposed method.

***Keywords*:** Electric vehicles (EVs), renewable energy sources (RES), distributed generation (DG), particle swarm optimization (PSO) technique, passive detection (PD)

## Acronyms

| | |
|---|---|
| EVs | electric vehicles; |
| DG | distributed generation; |
| RES | renewable energy sources; |
| PSO | particle swarm optimization; |
| PD | passive detection; |
| PV | photovoltaic; |
| BDF | beta distribution function; |
| EVCS | electric vehicle charging stations; |
| MOPSO | multi objective optimization algorithm; |

**Corresponding author*: sowmya2621994@gmail.com

A. Chitra, W. Razia Sultana and V. Indragandhi (eds.) Smart Charging Infrastructures, (91–104)

TOPSIS technique for order of preference by similarity to ideal solution detection (PD)

## 5.1 Introduction

DG units, categorized as distributed generation, have garnered significant attention owing to several factors, including the high investment in establishing new generating units, rising demand for electricity, and depletion of fossil fuels. The implementation of DGs plays a crucial role in reducing the need for extensive grid reinforcement which minimizes power loss. However, DGs integrated with EVs into a radial configuration bring about changes in current flow and voltage magnitude, which can impact the functioning of protection relays, as highlighted in recent studies (Selim *et al.*, 2021; Mohamed *et al.*, 2021; Ji *et al.*, 2021).

During a fault, the utility grid disconnects automatically and sends line workers to repairs. However, RES and EVs may continue to supply power, creating a passive island within the power system. This islanding poses risks to the line workers. Therefore, it is vital for these homes to autonomously detect islanding and disconnect from the grid to ensure the safety of line workers (Irshad and Rafique, 2020).

One of the key challenges associated with DG integration is the occurrence of unintentional islanding, which can cause damage to customer appliances (Shahid *et al.*, 2021; Lopez *et al.*, 2021). Detecting unintentional islanding is crucial for maintaining the system stability. This detection can be achieved using both remote and local methods. Remote methods rely on communication signals to identify islanding events, whereas local methods can detect islanding without such signals (Abokhalil *et al.*, 2018; Ra-machandradurai *et al.*, 2023). Efficiently addressing these issues is essential for ensuring the seamless integration and safe operation of DG units within the power grid.

This chapter proposes the allocation of DGs and EVs using the particle swarm optimization (PSO) technique, and the passive detection (PD) method is performed to ensure the islanding event in the 33-bus system with EV-based RES.

## 5.2 System Description

The installation of DGs for 33 bus systems was based on insights gathered from the existing literature. The analysis delved into the modeling equations utilized in various studies to understand the specific methodologies employed in modeling and installing DGs within these buses (Koundinya *et al.*, 2019; Ramachandradurai and Naravanan, 2021).

### 5.2.1 Description of Photovoltaic (PV) Source

Solar energy is captured *via* the photovoltaic (PV) phenomenon; sunlight is a sustainable energy source that is converted into electric current by solar panels. The initial cost is relatively high but decreases gradually with improved efficiency. Power generation is influenced by factors such as module rating, atmospheric temperature, and solar insolation, as defined in the literature (Ramachandradurai and K, 2020; Vijay and Sowmya, 2017; Bukhari *et al.*, 2021).

$s$ in (kW/m$^2$), $\Gamma$, and $K_F(x)$ are the solar radiation, gamma function, and BDF-beta distribution function of solar power, respectively. $\mu$ is 0.055 from Equation (5.2), and σ is 0.999 from Equation (5.3).

$$KF(x) = s^{\times(\sigma-1)}\frac{(\mu+\sigma)\Gamma}{(\sigma)\Gamma(\mu)\Gamma}(1-s)^{(\mu-1)\times} \qquad 0 \leq s \leq 1 \tag{5.1}$$

$$\mu = \frac{(v(1+v))}{\zeta^2} \times (1-v) - 1 \tag{5.2}$$

$$\sigma = \frac{v\mu}{1-v} \tag{5.3}$$

### 5.2.2 Description of Wind Energy

The electricity output from a wind turbine is not constant and fluctuates owing to the turbine's changing speed. This variability in the turbine speed directly influences the power generation pattern, leading to intermittent energy production. Wind speed modeling commonly uses the Weibull probability distribution function (PDF) to analyze these fluctuations. The correlation between wind speed and power output is usually represented by a mathematical function tailored to each turbine's design and features. This dynamic characteristic of electricity generation is a fundamental aspect of wind energy systems (Soroudi *et al.*, 2012).

### 5.2.3 Description of EV

Electric vehicles are considered compact storage units. Furthermore, the converters are integrated into electric vehicle charging stations and exhibit notable flexibility in adjusting both real and apparent power. Integrating electric vehicles (EVs) can be used to enhance reactive power management in a distribution grid. By establishing bidirectional charging links with the distribution network, EVs can significantly contribute to the regulation of reactive power (Balasundar *et al.*, 2021).

$$Car_{(in/out)}P = \frac{V_C \times V_S \times Sin(\delta)}{L_C \times \omega} \tag{5.4}$$

Equation (5.4) represents the modeling of EV with active power.

$$\sqrt{(P_{car})^2 - (S_{car})^2} = Q_{(car)max}P \tag{5.5}$$

$$-\sqrt{(P_{car})^2 - (S_{car})^2} = Q_{(car)min}P \tag{5.6}$$

Equations (5.4)–(5.6) represent the modeling of EV with active and reactive powers. $Car_{(in/out)}P$ is the input/output car power, and $V_c$ *and* $V_s$ are the charging voltage and voltage in the grid, respectively. $\delta$ is the phase-angle difference. $\omega$ is the angular frequency and $L_c$ is the line inductance. $S_{car}$, $Q_{(car)max}P$, and $Q_{(car)min}P$ are the car capacity, final, and initial bound reactive powers, respectively (Wang *et al.*, 2019).

Figure 5.1 represents the block diagram of renewable based EV system.

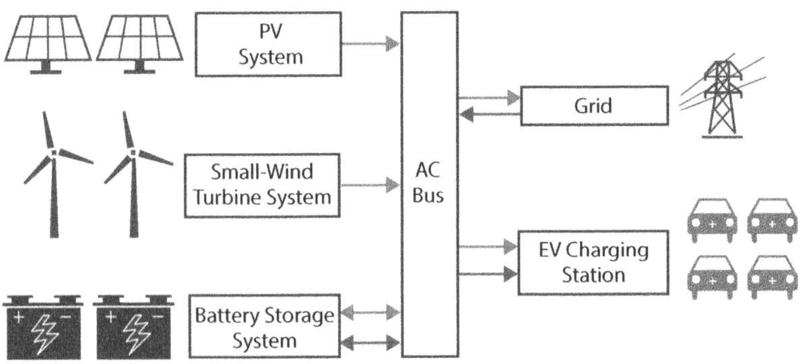


**Figure 5.1** Block diagram representation of PV, Wind, and EV.

### 5.2.4 Objective Function

In this study, three objectives were targeted for optimization. Line loss minimization is related to the economy of the power grid because the minimization of voltage deviation and maximization of the stability margin is crucial for enhancing grid operation and security. In addition, these objectives have led to conflicts. To achieve a Pareto optimal solution with good convergence and diversity, a Multi-Objective Evolutionary Algorithm (MOEA) was employed to manage the above objectives simultaneously. Under specific conditions, a Pareto optimal set was selected. To reconcile the contradiction between objectives, maximizing the stability margin is transformed into solving the reciprocal of the minimum singular value of the minimum converging power-flow Jacobian matrix. This conversion is essential for simultaneously minimizing all the three objectives. The mathematical equations for the three objective functions are outlined in Equation (5.7).

$$\begin{cases} X_1 = \sum_{i,j\in N_L} g_{ij}(-2V_iV_jCos\theta_ij + V_j^2 + V_i^2) = min(f_1) \\ \sum_{j\in N_i} (V_j^* - V_j)^2 = min(f_2) \\ \dfrac{1}{\delta_m in} = min(f_3) \end{cases} \tag{5.7}$$

$N_L$ is the branch, $N_t$ is the node, $Vj^*$ is the rated voltage, $\delta_m in$ is the minimum singular value, $Vi$ and $Vj$ are the voltage magnitudes, $g_{ij}$ is the admittance voltage, and $f_2$, $f_1$, and $f_3$ are power losses (Wang *et al.*, 2019; Ma *et al.*, 2018).

### 5.2.5 Constraint Conditions

The following constraints are followed for the modeling.

#### 5.2.5.1 *Equality Constraint*

$$\begin{cases} -P_{Di} + P_{Gi} = N_0 \in 0, i \\ -Q_{Di} + Q_{Gi} = N_{PQ} \in 0, i \end{cases} \tag{5.8}$$

In Equation (5.8), $-P_{Di} + P_{Gi}$ and $-Q_{Di} + Q_{Gi}$ represent the sum of generation node and *i*th nodes of active power and reactive power (Iba, 1994).

#### *5.2.5.2 Generator Constraint*

$$\begin{cases} Q_{minG} \leq Q_G \leq Q_{maxG} \\ V_{minG} \leq V_G \leq V_{maxG} \end{cases} \tag{5.9}$$

Equation (5.9) represents the generator constraints, in which $Q_{minG} \leq Q_G \leq Q_{maxG}$ and $V_{minG} \leq V_G \leq V_{maxG}$ are the limits of the active and apparent power (Zhang *et al.*, 2022).

### 5.2.6 Framework of Optimization Algorithm

To enhance the scheduling and capacity setup of Electric Vehicle Charging Stations (EVCS) powered by wind energy, this study introduces a novel hybrid optimization strategy that combines multi-objective particle swarm optimization (MOPSO) with the Technique for Order Preference by Similarity to Ideal Solution (TOPSIS). MOPSO is leveraged for the dual-objective optimization problem and generates a spectrum of Pareto-optimal results. Subsequently, TOPSIS was deployed to identify the most suitable solution.

Step 1: Identify Objectives and Set Constraints
The first step is to clearly articulate the optimization objectives and set boundaries. For an EVCS system, these objectives typically revolve around the following:

- Reducing costs: This includes both capital and operational expenditure.
- Enhancing efficiency: This could focus on maximizing wind energy utilization or minimizing the time required to charge vehicles.

Potential constraints may include the following:

- Maximum wind-turbines output.
- Storage capacity of batteries.
- Compliance with grid-connection standards.

Step 2: Implement MOPSO (Multi Objective Optimization Algorithm)
MOPSO is employed to address multiple objectives by generating a range of efficient solutions that demonstrate the necessary trade-offs among objectives, ensuring that no single solution is superior across all criteria. The process involves a population of candidate solutions evolving towards an optimal state through iterations.

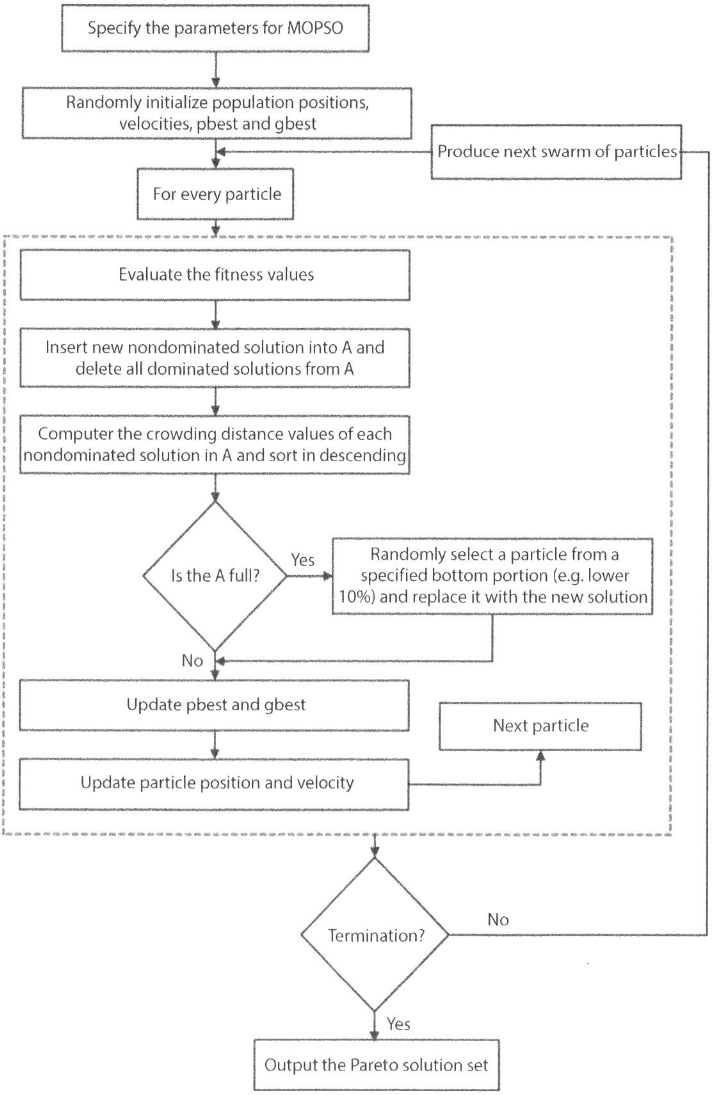


**Figure 5.2** Flow chart for the optimization algorithm.

- Initialization: The initial swarm is populated with randomly distributed particles within the defined space.
- Evaluation: Assess the position of each particle relative to the objectives.
- Update: Revise the velocities and positions based on the best results for individual particles and the entire swarm.

- Pareto Front Refinement: Continually refine the set of top nondominated solutions.

Step 3: Employ TOPSIS for End Selection
After establishing a Pareto front using MOPSO, TOPSIS helps select the ultimate solution by evaluating the proximity of each solution and its distance from the least desirable result.

- Formulate the Decision Matrix: Include all Pareto-efficient solutions and catalog their values across various objectives.
- Normalization: The matrix is adjusted using Euclidean norms to normalize the values.
- Ideal and Nadir Points: Identify the most and least favorable values for each objective.
- Distance Calculation: Assess the distance of each solution from both ideal points.
- Optimal Solution Selection: Choose the solution closest to the ideal point.

Step 4: Deploy and Monitor
Implement the selected solution in the EVCS system, adjusting capacity, and scheduling as guided by the TOPSIS analysis. Continuous monitoring and adaptive adjustments are crucial to cater to changes in wind conditions, energy demands, and technological progress. Figure 5.2 represents the optimal allocation of the TOPSIS and MOPSO algorithms.

## 5.3 Results and Discussion

The design of 33-bus system is illustrated in Figure 5.3. In this chapter, the value of the Doubly Fed Induction Generator (DFIG) is 300 kW and that of the photovoltaic (PV) is 21 kW. Additionally, the value of the electric vehicle (EV) charging and battery swapping stations is 80 kW. The wind turbine's active power output, influenced by wind speed, was segmented into three stages, with wind speeds denoted as $v_{in}^{w}$ set at 3 m/s, $v_{out}^{w}$ set at 25 m/s, and $v_{base}^{w}$ set at 12 m/s. The initial solar irradiation for the PV system was 600 W/m$^2$, with a temperature coefficient of 0.2 and a fixed temperature of 2°C.

Various energy sources were influenced by distinct environmental factors, as outlined in Table 5.1, which details the initial parameter disparities.

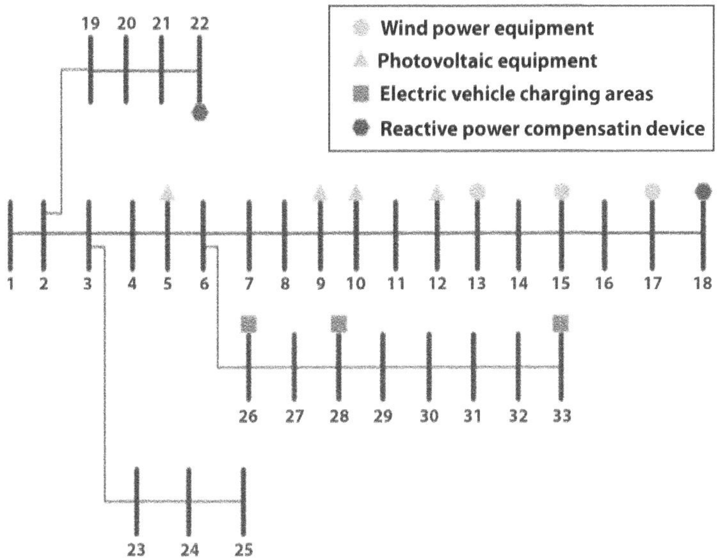


**Figure 5.3** IEEE-33 bus system with renewables.

Figure 5.4 represents the optimal changes in renewable energy with active power, reactive power, and overall performance of the system.

## 5.4 Conclusion

In conclusion, this study presents a comprehensive framework showing the adaptability of the TOPSIS method in managing distribution networks incorporating new energy sources and electric vehicles (EVs). The framework encompasses the following key aspects:

First, a distribution network model was developed to incorporate the dynamics of energy sources and EVs, particularly focusing on reactive power regulation across diverse network configurations.

Second, the TOPSIS method was applied to the model, with a detailed elucidation of its operational procedures and suitability for various network scenarios. A comparative analysis highlights the efficacy of Multi-Objective Particle Swarm Optimization (MOPSO) over other algorithms, demonstrating stable adaptation and superior performance across different indices, especially in smaller systems.

Third, an adaptive strategy is integrated into the TOPSIS method to enhance the precision of the optimization process by dynamically adjusting objective priorities according to real-time requirements.

**Table 5.1** Allocation of renewable and EV in 33 bus system.

| Number | Reactive power capacity | Solar irradiation | Speed (wind) | Active power |
|---|---|---|---|---|
| PV | | | | |
| 1 | – | 600 | 12 | [–17.23,17.23] |
| 2 | | 700 | 14 | [–15.65,15.65] |
| 3 | | 800 | 16 | [–13.60,13.60] |
| 4 | | 900 | 18 | [–10.82,10.82] |
| Wind | | | | |
| 1 | 9 | – | 200 | [–136.60,151.11] |
| 2 | 11 | | 266.67 | [–92.131,121.48] |
| 3 | 13 | | 300.00 | [–69.90,106.67] |
| EV and battery | | | | |
| 1 | – | – | –42.80 | [–67.59,67.59] |
| 2 | | | –49.02 | [–63.22,63.22] |
| 3 | | | –31.93 | [–73.35,73.35] |

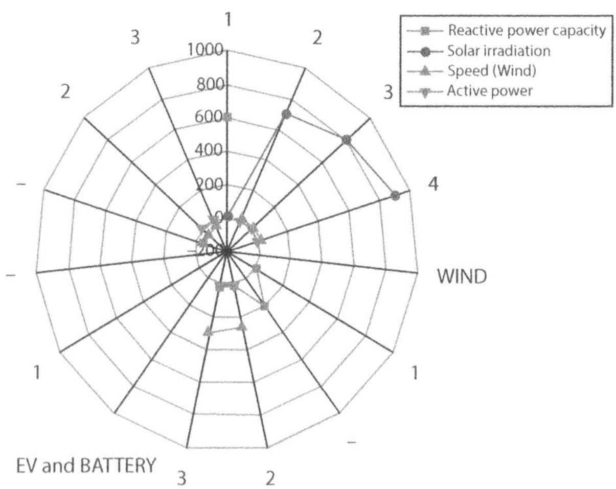


**Figure 5.4** Flow chart for the optimization algorithm.

Finally, this study examines the resilience of the proposed model to environmental factors, such as changes in wind speed, solar irradiation, and modifications in reactive power compensation devices. Using MOPSO as a benchmark, the analysis illustrated the model's robustness in adapting to dynamic environmental conditions.

In essence, this framework not only contributes to advancing the understanding of TOPSIS applications in distribution network optimization, but also underscores its potential for addressing complex challenges associated with the integration of new energy sources and EVs. By enhancing adaptability and resilience, these findings have significant implications for practical implementation of distribution network management strategies in the context of evolving energy landscapes.

## References

Abokhalil, A.G., Awan, A.B., Al-Qawasmi, A.-R., Comparative study of passive and active islanding detection methods for pv grid-connected systems. *Sustainability*, 10, 6, 2018, ISSN 2071-1050. doi: 10.3390/su10061798. URL https://www.mdpi.com/2071-1050/10/6/1798.

Balasundar, C., Sundarabalan, C.K., Sharma, J., Srinath, N.S., Guerrero, J.M., Design of power quality enhanced sustainable bidirectional electric vehicle charging station in distribution grid. *Sustainable Cities Soc.*, 74, 103242, 2021, ISSN 2210-6707. doi: https://doi.org/10.1016/ j.scs.2021.103242. URL https://www.sciencedirect.com/science/article/pii/ S2210670721005199.

Bukhari, S.B.A., Mehmood, K.K., Wadood, A., Park, H., Intelligent islanding detection of microgrids using long short-term memory networks. *Energies*, 14, 18, 2021, ISSN 1996-1073. doi: 10.3390/en14185762. URL https://www.mdpi.com/1996-1073/14/18/5762.

Iba, K., Reactive power optimization by genetic algorithm. *IEEE Trans. Power Syst.*, 9, 2, 685 692, 1994, doi: 10.1109/59.317674.

Irshad, U.B. and Rafique, S., Stochastic modelling of electric vehicle's charging behaviour in parking lots, in: *2020 IEEE Transportation Electrification Conference & Expo (ITEC)*, pp. 748–752, 2020, doi: 10.1109/ITEC48692.2020.9161566.

Ji, X., Zhang, X., Zhang, Y., Yin, Z., Yang, M., Han, X., Three-phase symmetric distribution network fast dynamic reconfiguration based on timing-constrained hierarchical clustering algorithm. *Symmetry*, 13, 8, 2021, ISSN 2073-8994. doi: 10.3390/sym13081479. URL https://www.mdpi.com/2073-8994/13/8/1479.

Lopez, J.R., Ibarra, L., Ponce, P., Molina, A., A decentralized passive islanding detection method based on the variations of estimated droop characteristics.

*Energies*, 14, 22, 2021, ISSN 1996-1073. doi: 10.3390/en14227759. URL https://www.mdpi.com/1996-1073/14/22/ 7759.

Ma, Y., Liu, C., Zhou, X., Gaol, Z., Reactive power compensation method for distribution network from electric vehicles, in: *2018 37th Chinese Control Conference (CCC)*, pp. 8826–8830, 2018, doi: 10.23919/ChiCC.2018.8482930.

Mohamed, A.A., Kamel, S., Selim, A., Khurshaid, T., Rhee, S.-B., Developing a hybrid approach based on analytical and metaheuristic optimization algorithms for the optimization of renewable dg allocation considering various types of loads. *Sustainability*, 13, 8, 2021, ISSN 2071-1050. doi: 10.3390/su13084447. URL https://www.mdpi.com/2071-1050/ 13/8/4447.

Nihith Koundinya, S.P.V.S., Vignesh, S., Sowmya, R., Girish Ganesan, R., Narayanan, K., Framework for computationally efficient outage detection, in: *2019 IEEE Innovative Smart Grid Technologies - Asia (ISGT Asia)*, pp. 3980–3985, 2019, doi: 10.1109/ISGT-Asia.2019.8881703.

Ramachandradurai, S. and K., N., A novel islanding detection method with reduced non-detection zones for different distributed generation units, in: *2020 International Conference on Smart Grids and Energy Systems (SGES)*, pp. 309–313, 2020, doi: 10.1109/SGES51519.2020.00061.

Ramachandradurai, S. and Naravanan, K., An improved (f&v) based passive islanding detection strategy with reliability evaluation, in: *2021 IEEE PES Innovative Smart Grid Technologies Conference - Latin America (ISGT Latin America)*, pp. 1–5, 2021, doi: 10.1109/ISGTLatinAmerica52371.2021.9543002.

Ramachandradurai, S., Krishnan, N., Sharma, G., Bokoro, P.N., Islanding detection with reduced non-detection zones and restoration by reconfiguration. *Energies*, 16, 7, 2023, ISSN 1996-1073. doi: 10.3390/en16073035. URL https://www.mdpi.com/1996-1073/16/7/3035.

Selim, A., Kamel, S., Mohamed, A.A., Elattar, E.E., Optimal allocation of multiple types of distributed generations in radial distribution systems using a hybrid technique. *Sustainability*, 13, 12, 2021, ISSN 2071-1050. doi: 10.3390/su13126644. URL https://www.mdpi.com/2071-1050/ 13/12/6644.

Shahid, M.U., Alquthami, T., Siddique, A., Munir, H.M., Abbas, S., Abbas, Z., Res based islanded dc microgrid with enhanced electrical network islanding detection. *Energies*, 14, 24, 2021, ISSN 1996-1073. doi: 10.3390/en14248432. URL https://www. mdpi.com/1996-1073/14/24/8432.

Soroudi, A., Aien, M., Ehsan, M., A probabilistic modeling of photo voltaic modules and wind power generation impact on distribution networks. *IEEE Syst. J.*, 6, 254–259, 06 2012, doi: 10.1109/JSYST.2011.2162994.

Vijay, R. and Sowmya, R., Optimal sitting of pv-wind-energy storage system integrated micro grid using artificial bee colony optimization technique. *Int. J. Innov. Res. Comput. Commun. Eng.*, 80, 2017.

Wang, Y., Wang, T., Zhou, K., Cao, K., Cai, D., Liu, H., Zhou, C., Reactive power optimization of wind farm considering reactive power regulation capacity of wind generators, in: *2019 IEEE Innovative Smart Grid Technologies - Asia (ISGT Asia)*, pp. 4031–4035, 2019, doi: 10.1109/ISGT-Asia.2019.8881439.

Zhang, X., Li, C., Xu, B., Pan, Z., Yu, T., Dropout deep neural network assisted transfer learning for bi-objective pareto agc dispatch. *IEEE Trans. Power Syst.*, 1–1, 01 2022, doi: 10.1109/TPWRS.2022.3179372.

6

# Green Energy-Based Active Grid Optimization Using Deep Learning for EV Charging Infrastructure

**D. Shruthi[1], R. Raja Singh[2]*, S. L. Arun[3] and R. Rengaraj[4]**

*[1]Department of Electronics and Communication Engineering, PSN College of Engineering and Technology, Tirunelveli, India*
*[2]Automotive Research Centre, Vellore Institute of Technology, Vellore, India*
*[3]Department of Electrical and Electronics Engineering, School of Electrical Engineering, Vellore Institute of Technology, Vellore, India*
*[4]Department of Electrical and Electronics Engineering, Sri Sivasubramaniya Nadar College of Engineering, Chennai, India*

***Abstract***
Sustainable transportation has been revolutionized by integrating active grid technology with artificial intelligence. An active grid enables the integration of renewable energy sources, including solar, wind, and hydroelectric energy into an EV charging network. The network can effectively prioritize charging activities by dynamically adapting to fluctuations in renewable energy availability and grid demand. Deep-learning-based active grid optimization has abundant potential for electric vehicle (EV) charging infrastructure by maximizing the utilization of green energy resources and minimizing carbon emissions. Deep learning algorithms are trained using extensive datasets that include the energy output, grid demand, weather patterns, and past charging behavior. It renders accurate predictions in real time by forecasting energy generation and consumption patterns with precision. Furthermore, bidirectional power flow technologies in active grid systems enable EV batteries to serve as grid storage resources, enhancing grid flexibility and resilience through vehicle-to-grid (V2G) functionalities. Grid-interactive charging algorithms optimize charging schedules based on real-time data, ensuring environmentally friendly charging operations while minimizing grid impact. In this chapter, two DC microgrids with renewable energy sources

**Corresponding author*: rrajasingh@gmail.com

A. Chitra, W. Razia Sultana and V. Indragandhi (eds.) Smart Charging Infrastructures, (105–136)

(solar and wind) and an EV battery-charging system are designed. A logic-based control algorithm was developed for the dynamic optimization of the active grid for EV charging. A deep-learning-based dynamic model was adapted to predict renewable energy generation, grid demand, and charging patterns to optimize the active grid. Overall, a significant step towards a sustainable transportation ecosystem, where green EV charging infrastructure actively contributes to reducing carbon emissions and promoting renewable energy adoption.

***Keywords***: Active grid, DC microgrid, deep learning, electric vehicle, EV battery-charging system, green energy, renewable energy, sustainable transportation

## 6.1 Introduction

In recent years, the rising energy demand has become a major source of concern for current power systems. Microgrids, which consist of an energy-renewable networked group and dispersed demands, are known as an intriguing approach to lowering both the environmental and operational costs of normal fossil fuel-based energy generation [1]. Microgrids are low-voltage distribution systems that combine modular dispersed energy sources with storage devices and programmed loads such as solar, wind, and fuel cells. This increases grid reliability and ensures the delivery of long-term, high-quality electricity. Microgrids, such as the power systems of physical islands, can be linked to major power networks or run independently. However, in today's world, centralized generation and distribution are being replaced by more dynamic, distributed microgrids and two-way power flow. This necessitates real-time synchronization, monitoring, and maintenance. Consequently, the digital grid is an excellent initial step toward grid modernization. However, owing to the ever-changing terrain, the grid should be capable of gathering and delivering data for future studies. An active grid continually analyzes data at the network's edge, and intelligent devices inside the grid connect and collaborate directly [2]. For next-generation smart grids, active grid management offers real-time monitoring and control of the infrastructure to attain situational awareness. The active grid is based on a multipurpose Internet of Things (IoT) network architecture that is unified, scalable, and multipurpose for smart utilities and citizens [3]. Using several adaptive communication technologies, such as radio frequency, power line carriers, Wi-Fi, and cellular, an active grid creates a guaranteed connection and network resilience. Distributed intelligence, machine-to-machine interactions, and multi-application network architectures are all parts of IoT [4]. Data analytics, cloud computing, and the new wave of battery-operated edge devices and sensors are among the topics covered. By utilizing this feature, utilities can have access to information that allows them to evaluate usage trends. Consequently, issues and solutions may be discovered more immediately, and resources can be allocated more efficiently from the start [5]. With the growing edge computing architecture, storage, control, and data analytics have been brought closer to the point of sensing. Additionally, this enables programs with incorporated artificial intelligence to react within milliseconds or less. This enables us to shift the computational power from centralized cloud servers to edge nodes, as well as analyze time-sensitive data at edge devices to reduce latency and network traffic [6].

Owing to the increased energy needs of industrial and residential areas in the framework of sustainable development goals, the discipline of solar irradiance and wind speed forecasts has evolved over the last decade [7]. The development of many renewable energy systems depends on their ability to make accurate fine-grained projections. For example, the configuration and orientation of solar panels in a photovoltaic (PV) plant or a wind power plant can have a significant influence on the total quantity of energy generated throughout the facility's lifetime. As the number of solar PV and wind plants increases and they are incorporated into the electric grid, it is necessary to forecast the quantity of energy generated to minimize overloads and anticipate energy shortages. Furthermore, reliable projections are required to management of electric vehicles to accumulate energy. Deep learning (DL) is a subset of machine learning in which artificial neural networks (ANNs) are more sophisticated and better approximate complicated functions than typical machine learning techniques. These networks are distinguished by several layers, each of which represents a specific function specified by its weights and biases. The network's final function is inferred by combining all the functions, which are then fitted to the available data and forecast solar irradiance, wind speed, and load demand [8]. This chapter discusses the detailed mathematical modeling of resources in the active grid system, integration of the active grid system, cloud computing, and control strategies followed for reliable operation. Furthermore, the implementation of a deep learning algorithm for microgrid resources is elaborated.

## 6.2 Active Grid and Edge Computing

DC microgrids have various advantages in integrating renewable sources and making them a part of an active grid. This is mainly due to the interoperability of local DC power networks with existing AC electrical infrastructure.

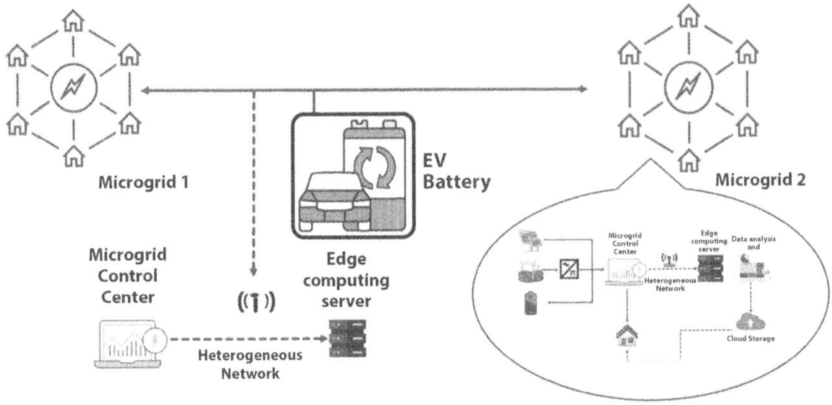


**Figure 6.1** Active grid and edge computing modeling.

DC storage devices such as batteries in electric vehicles (EV), capacitors, and fuel cells also satisfy the needs of local DC electricity in terms of power storage [9]. In essence, the microgrid, which is a self-sufficient power network of energy generation and storage sources, is a smaller counterpart to the larger power grid. The microgrid does not require a connection to the main grid when there is no external link. PV and wind power systems that are DC-based are more dependable than those that are AC-based [10]. While inverters account for less than 20% of the cost of a PV system, any system failure might cause the system to shut down, resulting in a complete loss of energy output. Wind energy can be more dependable in the DC form because the mechanical transmission system, which is necessary for wind turbines that create AC, is substantially simplified. Energy losses can be reduced by up to 30% or more when locally generated DC power from renewable energy sources, such as solar panels and windmills, is combined with minimal conversion (DC to AC or AC to DC) and transmission [11]. The cost of producing local electricity from solar PV and wind systems is decreasing daily, in contrast to the 20th-century technology, and the cost can be further reduced by using DC power instead of AC [12]. Figure 6.1 represents two integrated microgrid systems running in parallel with an EV charging station that compensates for any power deficiency in the system. The entire process was controlled using edge computing as the communication protocol.

Edge computing (EC) is required to receive real-time data from a model for analysis. Massive amounts of data must be transported to cloud datacenters for real-time operation to take place. If all tasks are offloaded to the cloud, the network is significantly burdened. This can be solved using edge computing, which is thought to reduce offloading costs while still ensuring performance. Because cloud computing resources are housed in far-flung datacenters, communication latency and network bandwidth have become major issues. Consequently, edge computing is a superior option because computing resources are positioned closer to the user [13]. The device, edge, and cloud layers are the three layers of edge computing. The device layer is the initial layer and serves as a communication link between the microgrid and datacenter. Bluetooth, Wi-Fi, ZigBee, 4G/5G, and other wireless standards are frequently used. The framework's primary layer is Edge. It is located at the network's edge and comprises a significant number of edge nodes. The data created in the device layer are filtered and preprocessed in this layer before being transmitted to the cloud [14]. The Microgrid system's edge nodes deliver real-time data to the edge server, which performs the necessary computations and sends the results to the cloud's central datacenter. EC devices ensure safe access to diverse objects in the device layer, and they keep themselves and the cloud computing layer working together *via* application program interfaces (APIs). EC can minimize the latency for end devices and deliver real-time responses for end-user applications by deploying edge servers near the users and providing storage and computing resources at the edge. The framework's third component is cloud computing. It is still a vital aspect of the hierarchical structure and serves as a storage and processing platform according to the EC. It is composed of storage devices and a variety of high-performance servers capable of storing and processing enormous amounts of data as well as providing a variety of application services. This oversees the long-term data storage and dataset calculations. This layer collects summary data from each edge node and performs global analysis of the information received. In addition, to improve the quality of latency-sensitive services, the cloud computing layer passes policies to the edge layer [15].

## 6.3 Modeling of Standalone Hybrid System

### 6.3.1 Solar PV Cell Model

An analogous arrangement of PV cells is shown in Figure 6.2. $I_{ph}$ represents the photocurrent in the cell. The solar cell's series and shunt resistances are represented by the symbols $R_s$ and $R_{sh}$, respectively. $R_s$ is typically substantially lower, whereas $R_{sh}$ is significantly higher. PV modules are higher-order components that are composed of PV cells. These modules are connected in series or parallel to create PV arrays that are used to produce energy in solar power plants, as shown in Figure 6.3 [16].

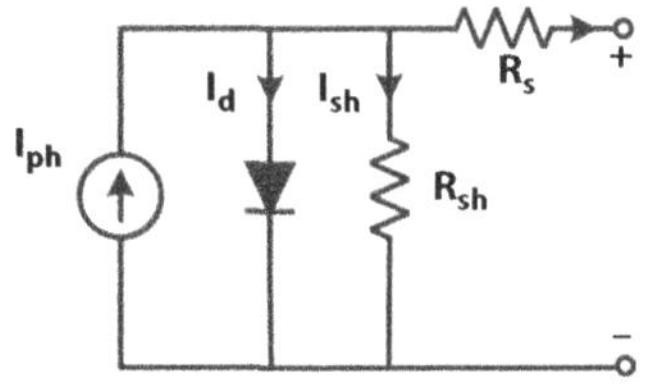


**Figure 6.2** Equivalent circuit of PV cell.

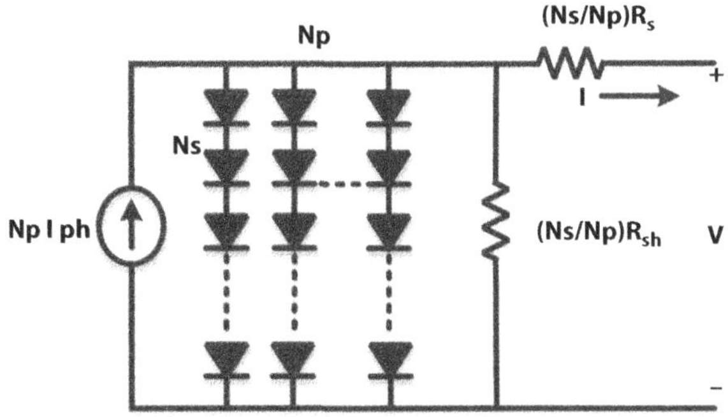


**Figure 6.3** Solar array circuit model.

The module photocurrent could be calculated as,

$$I_{ph} = \left[ I_{sc} + P_j(T - 298) \right] * \frac{I_{sr}}{1{,}000} \tag{6.1}$$

where $P_j$ is the equivalent $I_{sc}$ at 25°C, $I_{sr}$ is the solar irradiation (W/m$^2$), $I_{ph}$ is the current flowing through photovoltaic cells, and $I_{sc}$ is the short-circuit current passing through the shunt resistance. The PV module's reverse saturation current ($I_{rs-pv}$) can be computed as follows:

$$I_{rs-pv} = \frac{I_{sc}}{\left[ \exp\left( \frac{q\,V_{oc}}{N_s knT} \right) - 1 \right]} \tag{6.2}$$

where n is the diode ideality factor, k is Boltzmann's constant, q is the electron charge, $V_{oc}$ is the open circuit voltage, and $N_s$ is the series connected cell.

*Module saturation current* $I_o$

It is not the same as a photovoltaic cell's temperature, which is determined by,

$$I_o = I_{rs-pv}\left[\frac{T_k}{T_r}\right]^3 \exp\left[\frac{q * E_g}{nk}\left(\frac{1}{T_k} - \frac{1}{T_r}\right)\right] \tag{6.3}$$

where, $T_k$ denotes the temperature of the PV panel, nominal temperature $T_r$ and semiconductor band gap energy $E_g$ are given. The current output of the solar PV module can be written as,

$$I = \left[\left(I_{ph}N_p\right) - I_d - I_{sh}\right] \tag{6.4}$$

where $I_{sh}$ represents the shunt current and $I_d$ the diode current. The diode current may be calculated using the aforementioned formulae as,

$$I_d = N_p * I_o * \left[\exp\left(\frac{\frac{V}{N_s} + I * \frac{R_s}{R_p}}{n * V_t}\right) - 1\right] \tag{6.5}$$

where $V_t$ is the thermal voltage of the diode. Here are the values for the shunt current and thermal voltage:

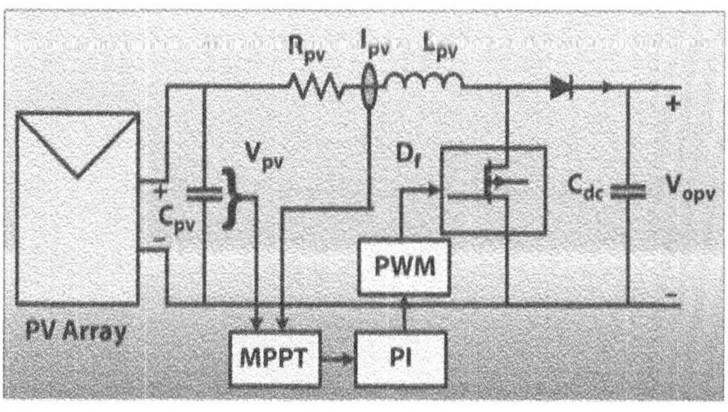


**Figure 6.4** PV array with MPPT algorithm.

$$V_t = \frac{kT}{q} \tag{6.6}$$

$$I_{sh} = \frac{V * \frac{N_p}{N_s} + I * R_s}{R_{sh}} \tag{6.7}$$

where Np represents number of PV modules linked in parallel. The MPPT algorithm, which is illustrated in Figure 6.4, is used to extract the maximum power from the PV panels and transmit the maximum power from the PV modules to the loads *via* DC-to-DC converters. An MPPT perturb and observation strategy was developed to operate a stationary PV module at the MPPT [17].

### 6.3.2 Wind Turbine Model

The following equation represents the wind power generated by the turbine blades:

$$P_\omega = \frac{1}{2}\rho\pi r^2 V_\omega^3 \tag{6.8}$$

where Vω denotes the wind velocity m/s, r is the blade radius m, and ρ is a constant value based on the air density. The Bentz constraint Cp (λ,β) determines the power supplied by the wind generator.

$$P_t = \frac{1}{2}\rho\pi r^2 V_\omega^3 C_p(\lambda, \beta) \tag{6.9}$$

where β is the pitch angle and λ is the tip speed ratio.

$$\lambda = \frac{(\omega_m * R)}{V_\omega} \tag{6.10}$$

where $C_p$ is the power coefficient and $\omega_m$ is the generator's speed (rad/sec). Many models of power coefficients have been developed, most notably those that include $C_p$ by,

$$C_p(\lambda,\beta)=0.517\left(\frac{116}{\lambda_i}-0.4\beta-5\right)e^{\left(\frac{-21}{\lambda_i}\right)}+0.006795\lambda_i \quad (6.11)$$

$$\lambda_i=\frac{1}{\frac{1}{\lambda+0.008\beta}-\frac{0.03}{\beta^3+1}} \quad (6.12)$$

The relationship between the generated output power (W) and the wind velocity $V_\omega$ (m/s) is shown in Figure 6.5. The cut-in and cut-off speeds for the wind energy conversion system were 3.1 m/s and 25 m/s, respectively [18]. The wind turbine should always operate at maximum efficiency to harvest the maximum amount of power from the wind. A permanent magnet synchronous generator's rotor speed may be calculated as,

$$\omega_{opt}=\frac{\lambda_{opt}*V_\omega}{R} \quad (6.13)$$

The ideal tip speed ratio is denoted by $\lambda_{opt}$. We derive the turbine torque equation as follows:

$$T_t=\frac{P_t}{\omega_m} \quad (6.14)$$

Hence, the torque equation can be written as,

$$T_t=\frac{0.5\,\rho\,\pi\,r^2V_\omega^3C_p(\lambda,\beta)}{\omega_m} \quad (6.15)$$

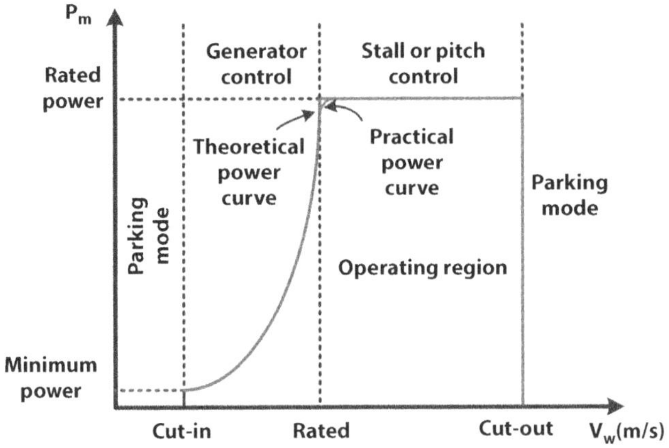


**Figure 6.5** Output power and wind speed relationship curve.

### 6.3.3 EV Battery Model

A microgrid is a system composed of transportation, industrial, commercial, and residential loads, energy storage, power conversion, and at least one distributed energy source (renewable or non-renewable). The transportation loads included EV charging stations with V2G and G2V features. Its most distinguishing feature is its capacity to function as both connected and unplugged from the main electrical grid. The total of all daily charge/discharge transfers is the EV battery's State of Charge (SoC) [19]. The battery condition at each given hour t is determined by the system's energy output or consumption between t – 1 and t, as well as the prior level of charge. The battery bank capacity accessible at hour t during the EV charging process can be explained as follows:

$$E_{EV}(t) = E_{EV}(t-1) + [E_{SUR} - DC(t)]\eta_{CHG} \tag{6.16}$$

$$SoC(t) = \left[1 - \frac{E_{Req}(t)}{E_{EV}(t)}\right] * 100 \tag{6.17}$$

Nonetheless, the battery's charged capacity is limited by the following:

$$SoC_{min} \le SoC(t) \le SoC_{max} \tag{6.18}$$

The maximum depth of discharge (DoD) determines the lowest SoC, and the maximum value of SoC is 100%.

$$SoC_{min} = 1 - DoD \tag{6.19}$$

Energy storage devices are necessary in most microgrids to improve power quality and preserve power and energy balance. Although there are many different kinds of storage technologies on the market today, none of them can match the requirements of an energy storage system used in a microgrid, which requires a high energy density to provide the microgrid with autonomy and a high power density to handle sudden fluctuations in power.

## 6.4 Deep Learning and Its Implementation

Demand-response management is essential for the autonomous functioning of smart active grids. The demand response control strategy is economically and technically beneficial to both consumers and grid operators. A flowchart of the steps required to create an optimization model is shown in Figure 6.6. After careful consideration of all environmental restrictions, a neural network model was built using the dataset received from the power grid. The data gathered from consumer-side smart sensors are used to constantly train the optimization model [20]. To optimize the grid through the demand response, two different factors must be predicted, namely time-series demand and power availability from each power source.

The demand response was predicted using the deep learning method. One type of machine learning based on the anatomy of the human brain is called deep learning. Similar to human analysis, deep learning computers draw conclusions by analyzing data according to a predefined logical framework [21]. Neural networks, a multilayered structure of algorithms, are used in deep learning to achieve this. Different algorithms, such as Artificial Neural Networks (ANN), Support Vector Machine (SVM), K-Nearest Neighbor (KNN), and multilayer perceptron (MLP) algorithms have been used for demand forecasting [22]. All these algorithms had positive and negative values, and there was no middle ground to make it balanced and perfect without affecting other parameters. ANN and SVM have high model complexity, and the computational speed is very low in SVM algorithms and better in the ANN model [23]. In both cases, the accuracy was high in both models. In KNN algorithms, the amount of data

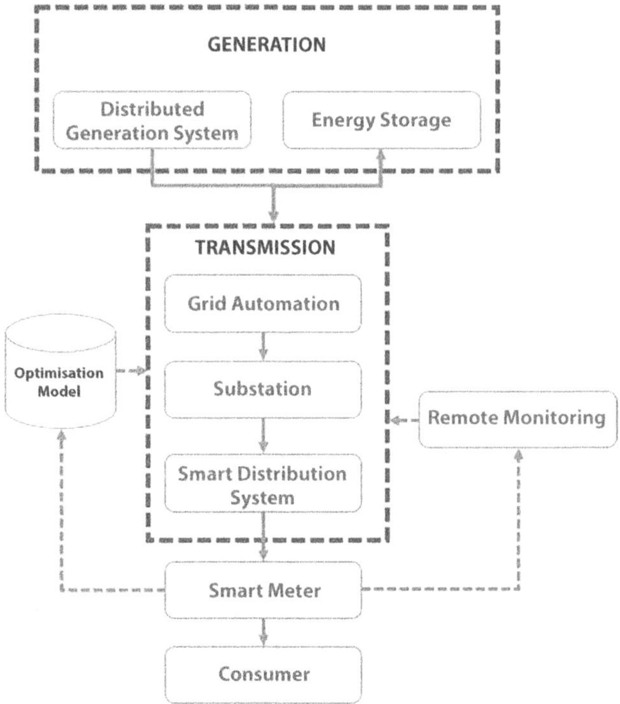


**Figure 6.6** Flow chart of a smart grid system involving a demand response system.

slows down the prediction stage, and the accuracy of the data depends completely on the quality of the data, unlike in other algorithms. It also requires high computational power compared to other algorithms to prepare the same operation. MLP models have many parameters for applying differential changes in values to obtain accurate results. All nodes across various layers are connected, and the assumptions in different nodes can cause insignificant results. It can cause redundancy and inefficiency in large datasets, such as energy forecasting predictions [24]. In this chapter, the Long Short-Term Memory (LSTM) algorithm is used. LSTMs modify data by multiplying and adding them. Cell states are a method by which information moves in the LSTMs. This is how LSTMs selectively remember or forget things. Three distinct dependencies on the data in each cell state are known [25].

The deep learning model is composed of three gates: the input gate, forget gate, and output gate. Sigmoid activation (output of 0 or 1) functions are used as gates for the LSTM. The following equations form the basis of LSTM for use in deep learning.

$$i_t = \sigma(\omega_t[h_{t-1}, x_t] + b_i) \tag{6.20}$$

$$f_t = \sigma(\omega_t[h_{t-1}, x_t] + b_f) \tag{6.21}$$

$$o_t = \sigma(\omega_t[h_{t-1}, x_t] + b_o) \tag{6.22}$$

The first equation represents the input gate, and provides the amount of new data to be saved in the cell state. The second equation indicates data that must be removed from the cell state. The output gate, which is utilized to activate the final output of the LSTM block at timestamp "t," is represented by the final equation. The following equations represent the cell state, candidate cell state, and ultimate output:

$$c_t = \tanh(\omega_c[h_{t-1}, x_t] + b_c) \tag{6.23}$$

$$c_t = f_t * c_{t-1} + i_t * c_t \tag{6.24}$$

$$h_t = o_t * \tanh(c^t) \tag{6.25}$$

In the above equations, the cell state understands what must be forgotten from the prior state (i.e., $f_t * c_{t-1}$) and what needs to be considered from the current timestamp (i.e., $i_t * c_t$). The activation function forecasts the proportion of the LSTM unit output at a certain timestamp (t). To obtain the anticipated output $y_t$ from the present block, it can send this $h_t$ from the current LSTM block through the Softmax layer.

### 6.4.1 Energy Demand Pattern

Time-series data are subjected to numerous levels of optimization, visualization, and analysis for several reasons, which will be discussed in this section. After parsing into date and time using Pandas, the data were transformed into a time-series format. Consequently, the data may be resampled and utilized to investigate various aspects over a period. Several visualizations are offered for deep learning analysis to select the resampling interval, size, and co-relevant factors [26]. As shown in Figure 6.7, the panels resampled the data over the course of the day. The total, mean, and standard deviation of the resampled parameters were among the statistical features investigated. The plots demonstrate that the plot pattern remains comparable even when using different statistical measures owing to scale discrepancies. This makes it possible to rescale and resample any statistical measure. This seems to be true only when the mean and sum were used as statistical parameters. The rescaled figures seemed to vary when standard deviation was used. Any resampling that varies one parameter with another shows that it can be used to forecast the correlation and can be ignored if it gives a negative correlation, as the patterns remain consistent throughout resampling.

Two parameters, voltage, and active power are resampled of the month in the plots Figures 6.8(a,b). It can be shown that despite the variance in active power, the voltage appears to be constant, making it unsuitable for deep learning. The scales of active power and submetering appear to be equivalent in the plots in Figure 6.9. Because reactive power has a lower scale than intensity and intensity have a larger scale, the scales need to be changed to execute deep learning.

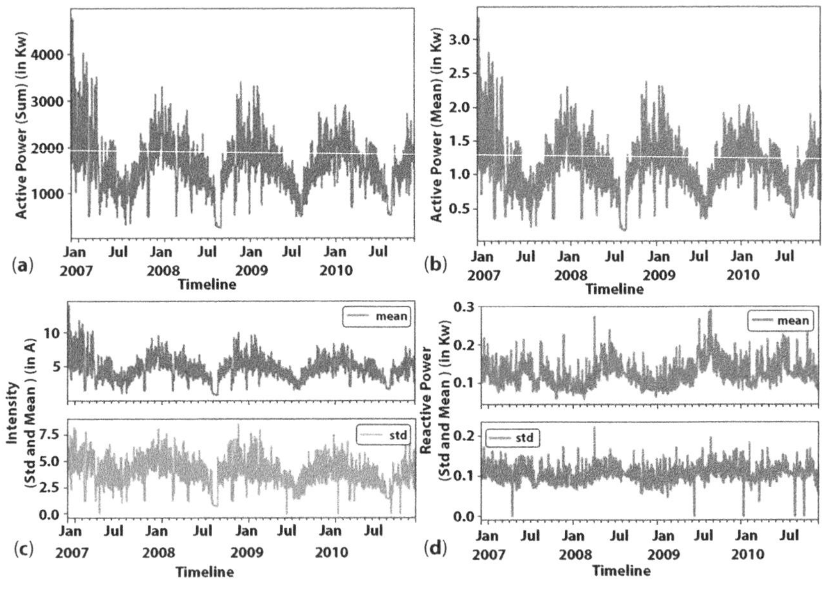


Figure 6.7 Visualization trends of input and output parameters; (a) total active power, (b) average active power, (c) intensity, (d) reactive power on two different parameters.

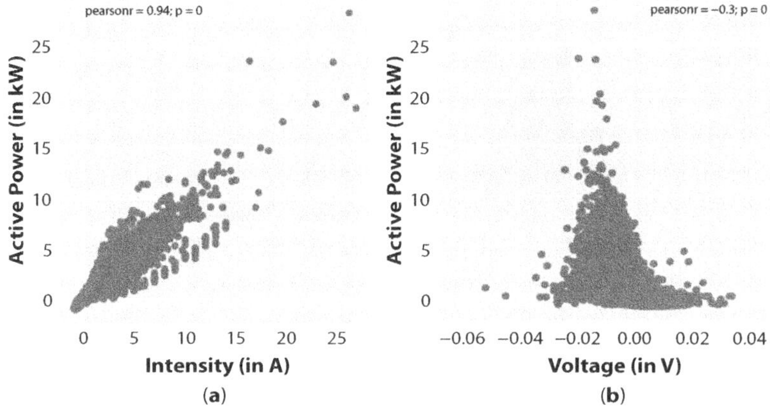


**Figure 6.8** Resampled month data of voltage and active power. (a) Active power, (b) voltage.

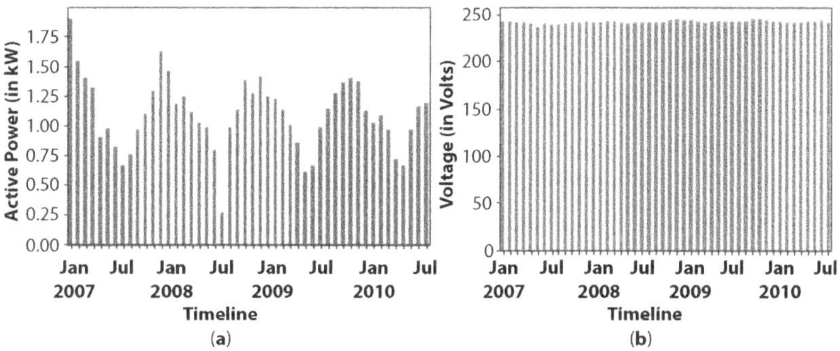


**Figure 6.9** Scales of global power and submetering power. (a) Histogram plot for scales, (b) linear plots of parameters.

Two types of correlations were considered during feature selection. Pearson's correlation is shown in Figures 6.10(a,b). Except for the voltage, which agrees with the assumption drawn based on the visualization of the values, each factor indicated a positive connection. As a result, we exclude the voltage from the feature selection and rely on the remaining criteria. In Figure 6.11, the Spearman correlation heatmap is generated for all seven features available in comparison to one another. This demonstrates the correlation once more, demonstrating only voltage as a negatively linked element and removing it from the deep-learning data structure. It can also be observed that when the resampling period is increased, the correlation increases. However, as resampling increased, the amount of data available

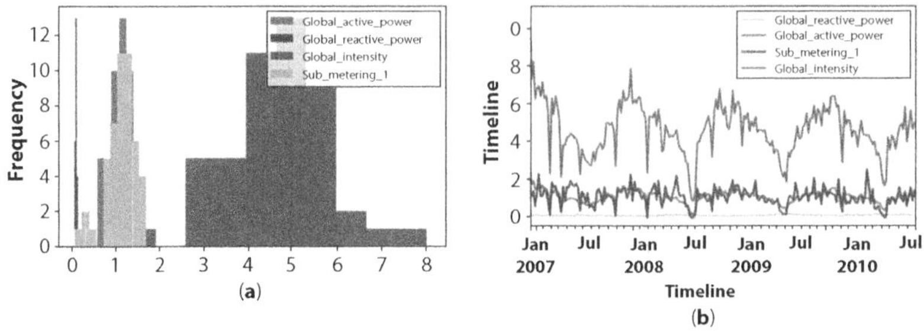


**Figure 6.10** Pearsons Correlation of electrical parameters. (a) Active power, (b) reactive power.

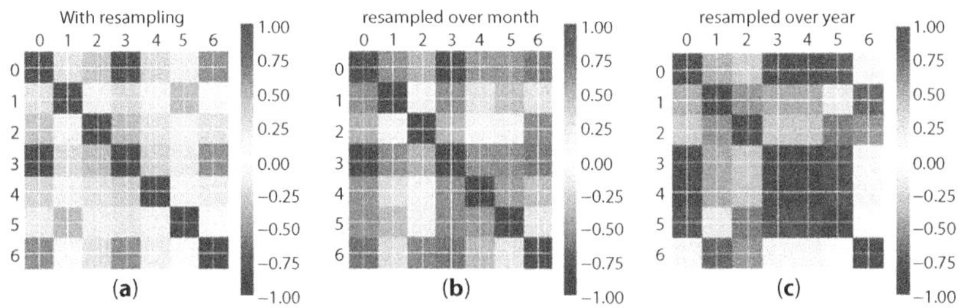


**Figure 6.11** Spearman correlation heatmap. (a) Without resampling, (b) resampled over month, (c) resampled over year.

for deep learning decreased. Consequently, every minute of data was resampled for an hour for deep learning.

## 6.4.2 Wind Speed

A standard must be established for wind turbine energy. This aids in defining the basic features of wind turbines. The data for this study were obtained from a 12-month energy bill. During the 12-month period, approximately 1,600 kWh of power was consumed. A total of 1.6 MWh was used. Based on this, the basic capacity of the wind turbine that needs to be developed can be calculated. A wind turbine's annual energy output is determined by its capacity (and other turbine design features), number of days it operates, number of hours it operates, and capacity factor. The capacity factor is calculated by dividing the actual yearly energy output by the potential maximum outputif the machine ran at its rated (maximum) power for the whole 8,766-hour year. The LSTM looks for an array of n inputs and a single output, such as n consecutive readings followed by the

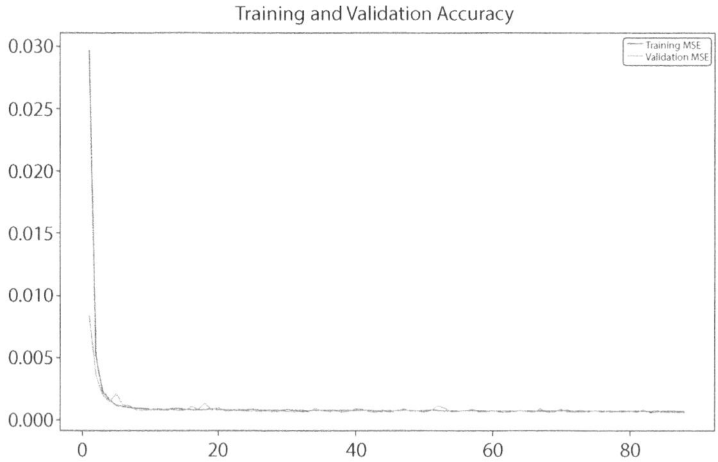


**Figure 6.12** Training and validation accuracy curve.

next reading. Therefore, we forecast a single output based on n inputs [27]. Figure 6.12 shows the training and validation accuracy after running for 100 epochs using the Adam decent optimizer, and it can be seen that the LSTM Neural Network learned well.

### 6.4.3 Solar Irradiation

To simulate solar irradiance accurately, other meteorological characteristics of the dataset should be used. After importing the information, the first step was to transform the time and date parameters into a more usable format and add other columns that could be used for visualization, modeling, and analysis [28]. The hourly and monthly means of numerous variables were then visualized using bar plots in Figure 6.13 to help with a better understanding of the data. It is evident from the graphs above that the temperature and sun irradiance have a strong relationship. Pressure/humidity and solar irradiance have fewer apparent relationships; however, humidity appears to have a negative relationship with sun irradiance, temperature, and pressure. Solar irradiation and temperature peaked at approximately around 12:00, as expected. The monthly means of temperature and sun irradiance seem to decrease as winter approaches, with the exception of a very slight increase in solar irradiance from September to October. A Pearson correlation heatmap was created to assist in visualizing the correlations between variables. The graphics in the section above clarify that there is no linear relationship between solar irradiation and the time of day.

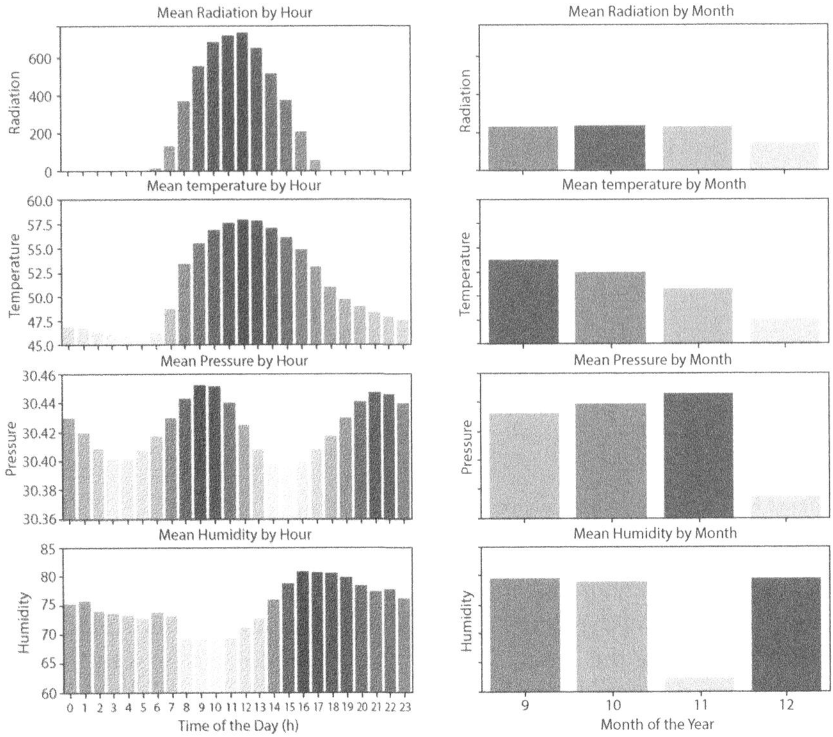


**Figure 6.13** Bar plots for visualization.

As a result, despite their significant link, the "Time of Day" columns were left out of the heatmap. "UNIX Time," "Month of Year," and "Week of Year" were also removed since a combination of "Time of Day" and "Day of Year" is likely to be more effective in training and prediction. The correlation heatmap in Figure 6.14 backs up the suggestions made in the previous sections. It also shows that, in comparison to temperature, the day of the year has far less impact on solar irradiance. Except for solar irradiation, all reported meteorological factors were included as independent variables. To indicate date and time, the variables "Day of Year" and "Time of Day(s)" were chosen. This would ensure that no complications arose if projections for the following year were made. The independent variable was solar irradiance. The dataset was then split between the training and test sets with split percentages of 80% and 20%, respectively.

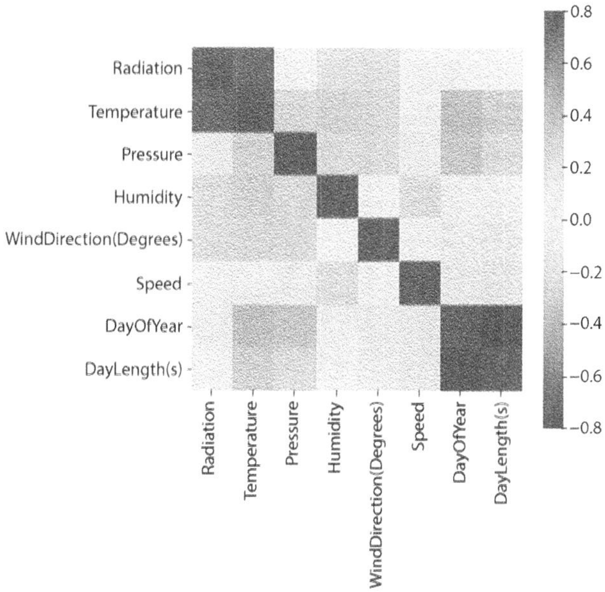


**Figure 6.14** Correlation heatmap.

## 6.5 Micro-Grid and Control Mechanism

To develop an active grid network system that is optimized using deep learning through edge computing. A Simulink model must be developed by integrating two microgrids, each of two renewable resources (solar and wind), a battery, and a load. The next objective is to design a logic-based control algorithm to atomize the charge/discharge conditions of a battery based on the demand. Edge computing is then integrated by assigning nodes to dynamically collect data, decentralizing the computation, and increasing the grid efficiency. Deep learning algorithms, such as LSTM, can be used to create an optimized model and provide an automated prediction model based on demand response. Figure 6.15 depicts the overall model, which consists of various steps and levels. The control center acts as a medium for the interface that connects the microgrid for further data analysis. Wi-Fi is used as the node to communicate the data extrapolated from the Simulink model to create datasets which is used for deep learning.

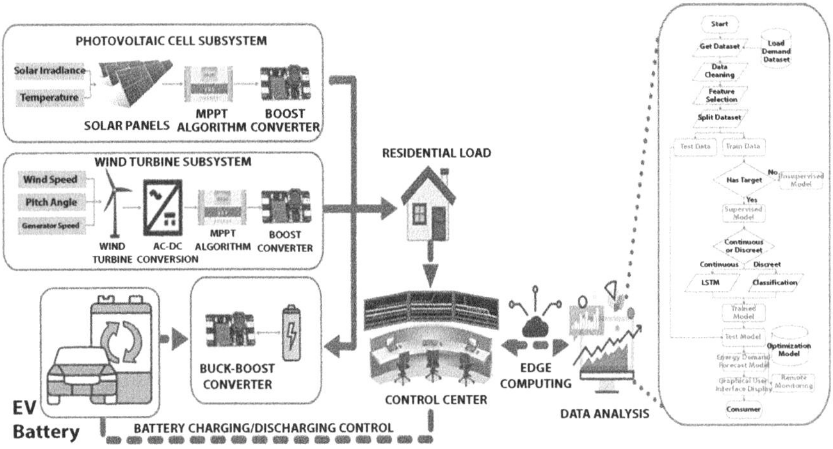


**Figure 6.15** Functioning of active grid using deep learning and edge computing.

## 6.5.1 Microgrid Functioning in Different Modes

A crucial aspect of microgrid management is maintaining a balance between the supply and demand of power. In the grid-interconnected mode, the microgrid achieved balance by exchanging electricity with an interconnected grid. In contrast, the microgrid should achieve balance in the islanded mode by lowering the generation or load shedding.

Management, control, protection, power quality, pilot plants, and field testing have all been researched for islanded microgrid operations. Microgrid energy management and power control have also been investigated. An emulated laboratory microgrid system was used to create and evaluate protection methods for microgrids during power sags. Microgrid prototype plants have been built, and field testing for frequency and voltage control algorithms, as well as utility connecting devices, have been conducted. The microgrid operates normally in grid-connect mode; however, it should disconnect and enter islanded operation mode in the event of an issue with the upstream grid. In grid-connect mode, the main grid maintains the microgrid's frequency and voltage within a specific range. However, in an islanded operation with a small number of microsources, controlling the microgrid's local frequency and voltage is more difficult. The power balance between supply and demand during islanding is currently unbalanced. The project aims to manage and optimize the power between two grids when operating in the islanding mode under critical load conditions. A DC microgrid, which consists of two renewable resources (solar and wind) and battery storage units from EV charging stations, is shown in the diagram. The sources were attached to a variable DC load, and an optimized control technique was designed to distribute power.

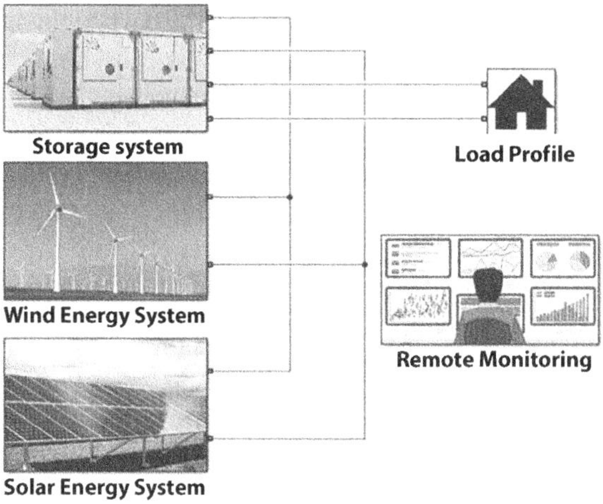


**Figure 6.16** Microgrid islanding mode functioning of microgrid.

#### 6.5.1.1 *Islanded Mode*

The microgrid's frequency and voltage may fluctuate, and the system may face a blackout unless an appropriate power-balance matching method is implemented. It is challenging to guarantee the strong dynamic performance of a microgrid made entirely of renewable energy sources and traditional combined heat and power units such as diesel generators, gas engines, and microturbines, during islanded operation because of the intrinsic characteristics of these generation systems. Because their power outputs are dependent on the availability of the primary source, such as wind or sunlight, RES is intermittent and cannot ensure the power supply required by the loads. The EV charging station-based energy storage system is implemented on a common DC link to supplement the energy sources' slower power supply. The microgrid may run steadily during the islanded mode even if the load is altered abruptly by including an energy storage system in a distributed generation system with a somewhat slow response primary energy source. Figure 6.16 depicts the simulation model of a microgrid operating in islanding mode.

#### 6.5.1.2 *Multiple Microgrid Control with Centralized Energy Storage System*

With a centralized energy storage system, the microgrids function automatically with the help of a central battery. The central battery provides stability and is vital to the system as it helps compensate for the power deficiencies in any microgrid system. The central battery functions when the voltage levels of any microgrids do not meet the load requirements. Most importantly, a central battery system was used to handle blackouts and voltage fluctuations. The system functions in such a way that the load automatically connects to the central battery, isolating the load from the renewable sources. In another situation, where there is no required charge available with the microgrid battery, the system automatically disconnects from it and functions with the central battery. In this manner, the power requirements and voltage levels are constantly maintained for the load, and a consistent power supply is maintained.

### 6.5.2 Energy Storage System Simulation

The operation of a solar system varies constantly owing to variations in the load and weather. Dynamic tracking techniques are essential to guarantee that the solar array produces an optimum amount of power. The maximum power point tracking (MPPT) of a solar array is required for efficient PV system construction and operation. MPPT is a lifespan booster that increases the power provided by the PV system to the load. Solar panels, a DC-DC converter, an MPPT controller, and grid-connection equipment comprise a grid-connected PV system. All photovoltaic systems connect to the grid *via* converters, which are utilized to balance the system. The designed solar-powered energy system and wind-powered energy system are shown in Figures 6.17 and 6.18. Table 6.1 depicts the parameters of the PV array. It can be observed that the renewable sources are intermittent, and we designed a PID controller for each energy system. A solar cell's

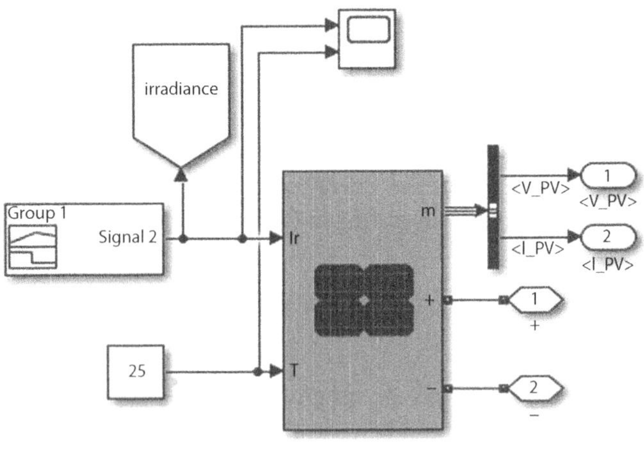


**Figure 6.17** Solar energy system.

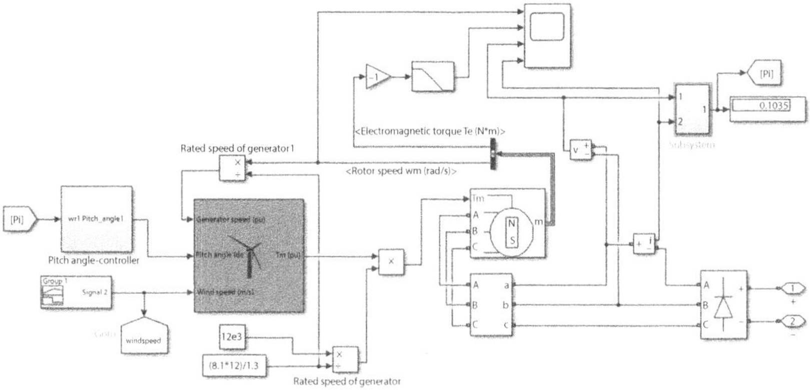


**Figure 6.18** Wind turbine model.

**Table 6.1** Solar PV array specification.

| | |
|---|---|
| Maximum power output value | 213.15 W |
| Open circuit output voltage Voc | 36.3 V |
| Short-circuit output current Isc | 7.84 A |
| Voltage at maximum power point Vmp | 29 V |
| Current at maximum power point Imp (A) | 7.35 A |
| Temperature coefficient of Voc (%/°C) | −0.36099°C |
| Temperature coefficient of Isc (%/°C) | 0.102°C |

efficiency is extremely low. Approaches to correctly match the source and load must be considered to improve the efficiency. One such method is MPPT, which controls the gating pulse for the boost converter.

### 6.5.3 Wind Energy Storage System Simulation

The permanent-magnet synchronous generator (PMSG) of a wind turbine generates three-phase alternating electricity from the kinetic energy generated by blades rotating with the wind. The voltage and frequency are both determined by the wind speed. The wind speed provided as an input is continually changing. These settings were programmed to vary at predetermined times. The produced energy must be transformed into AC power at steady frequency and voltage. Consequently, the PMSG output voltage must be adjusted. MPPT is utilized in addition to the rectifier circuit to achieve a high energy conversion efficiency. The MPPT algorithm was used to compute the torque reference based on the wind speed variable. The rectified wind speed was used to provide the torque reference, whereas the DC voltage served as the current reference. A hysteresis controller was utilized to generate the switch signal for the MPPT. The rectified wind speed was used to provide the torque reference, whereas the DC voltage served as the current reference. The switch signal for MPPT was generated using a hysteresis controller. Figure 6.19 shows inputs from deep learning converted and input as a continuous time-series signal using a signal builder. Figure 6.20 depicts how the boost converter stepped up the input voltage magnitude to a required output voltage magnitude without the use of a transformer. Table 6.2 depicts the parameters of the wind turbine used in the simulation.

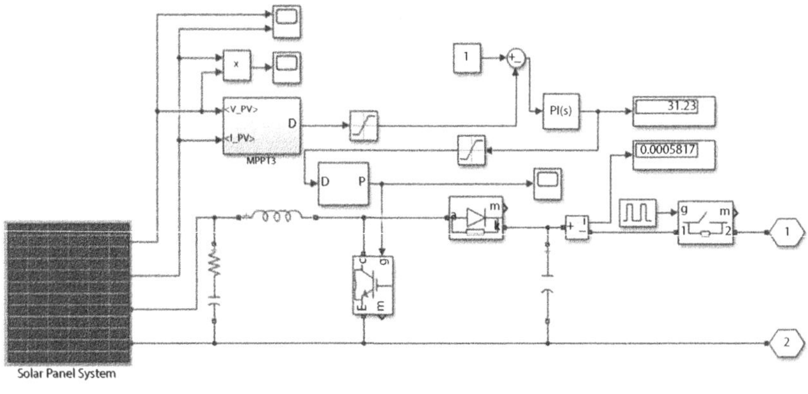


**Figure 6.19** Solar energy system.

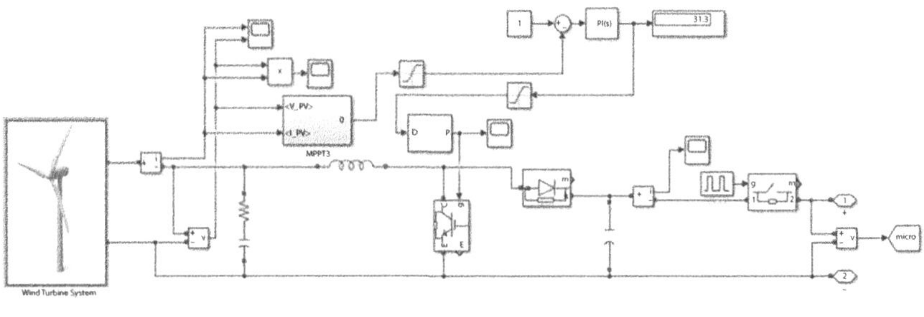


**Figure 6.20** Wind energy system.

**Table 6.2** Wind turbine parameters.

| | |
|---|---|
| Mechanical output power (W) | 12,300 W |
| Base power of the electrical generator (VA) | 13,666 VA |
| Base wind speed (m/s) | 12 m/s |
| Maximum power at base wind speed | 0.85 |
| Base wind turbine rotational speed | 1.2 |
| Pitch angle | 0° |

### 6.5.4 EV Battery Control Mechanism

The microgrid model consists of a hybrid power system and derives power from both solar and wind sources. This system uses a PV array and wind turbine to function as a hybrid system. Owing to the constant variations in both wind speed and solar irradiation, there is a need to implement the maximum power point tracking (MPPT) algorithm. The model used a constant-voltage-type MPPT algorithm. This algorithm functions based on comparisons of the voltage generated from a renewable source to a constant voltage. This constant voltage was maintained as a reference; thus, an error signal was generated and the duty cycles were controlled. The controller ensures that a constant output voltage is provided despite variations in the input voltage to the MOSFET. The microgrid is designed such that the battery storage system acts as a backup for the power supply to the load, as well as a buffer for the voltage to be maintained at the load. With an inconsistent power supply, an issue in renewable resources, the battery system ensures stability in the model, pushing away the need to integrate the model with the utility grid. With the MPPT algorithm, whichensures a stable supply from renewable sources, the control mechanism for the activation of the storage system uses looping structures to switch on the charging and discharging of the battery [29]. The switch ensures that a minimum threshold voltage is provided by renewable sources and stable power is supplied by the battery when the voltage requirement is not met.

A precise battery cell model required to control the DC bus voltage in the islanding mode is shown in Figure 6.21. During operation, an estimate of the battery terminal voltage and state of charge is required. The lead acid battery model is represented by a high-fidelity electrical model. We also designed a control based on the switch case to determine the charge and discharge conditions of the battery. Table 6.3 depicts the parameters of the battery used in the simulation.

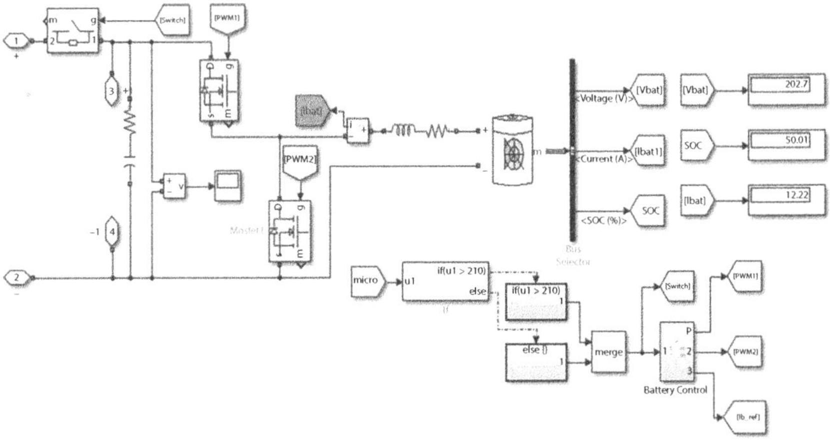


**Figure 6.21** EV battery design.

**Table 6.3** EV battery parameters.

| | |
|---|---|
| Maximum capacity of battery | 50 Ah |
| Cut-off voltage value | 153.75 V |
| Fully charged voltage value | 220 V |
| Nominal discharge current value | 9.6 A |
| Internal resistance value | 0.042708 Ω |
| Exponential zone [voltage (V), capacity (Ah)] | 14.8933 Ah |

## 6.6 Results and Discussion

### 6.6.1 Deep Learning

***Load***: One neuron was utilized in the output layer to forecast the activity, and an LSTM with 100 neurons in the first visible layer and a dropout of 20 was used in the model. The efficient Adam version of stochastic gradient descent and Mean Absolute Error (MAE) loss function were applied to the input shape, which is a one-time step with six features. The model was fitted for 20 training epochs with a batch size of 70. The curves in Figure 6.22 show a comparison between the actual and predicted values after the analysis of the house.

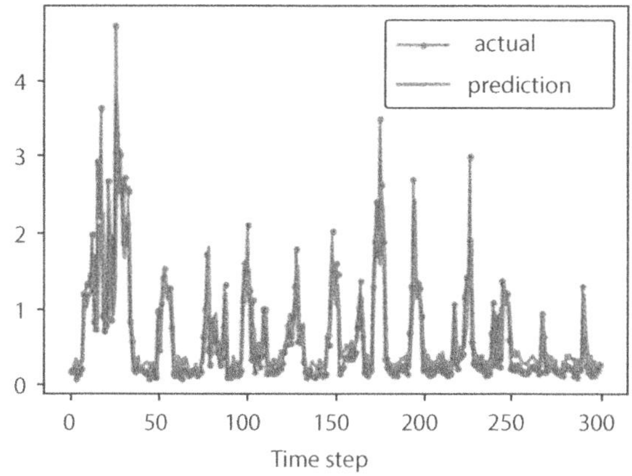


**Figure 6.22** Load actual vs prediction curve.

***Wind Speed***: Time-series data were used, which consisted of hourly wind speed and wind direction data. The input form consists of a single step that includes two features: the efficient Adam version of the stochastic gradient and Mean Absolute Error (MAE) loss function (Figure 6.23). To perform LSTM analysis, we divided the data into 200 epochs with a batch size of 280. The curves in Figure 6.23 show a comparison between the actual and predicted values after deep learning analysis of the wind turbine data.

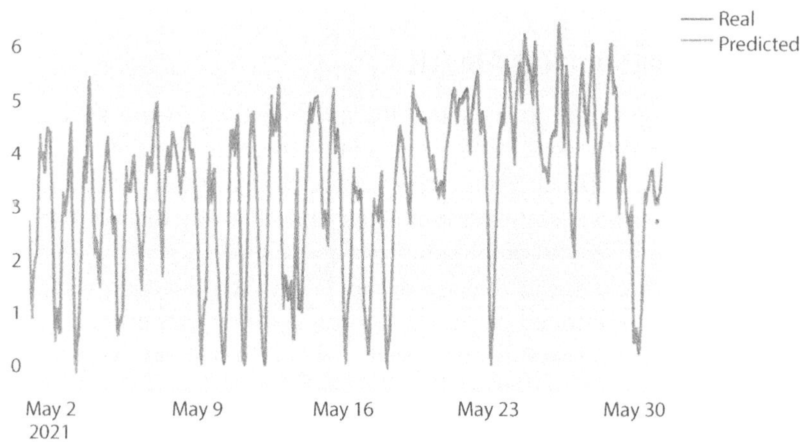


**Figure 6.23** Load actual vs prediction curve.

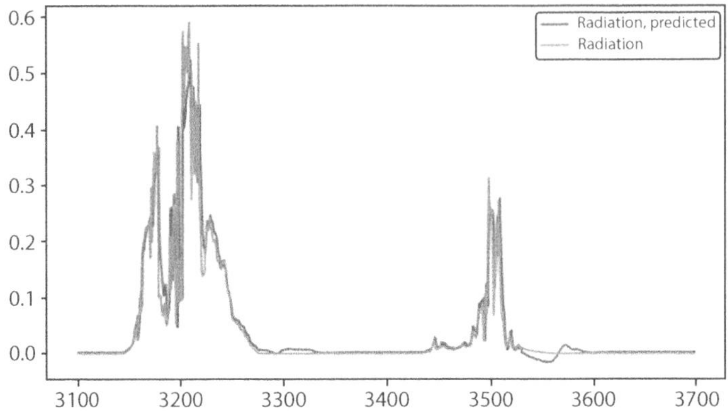


**Figure 6.24** Solar irradiance actual vs prediction curve.

***Solar Irradiance***: Time-series data consisting of 5 min of data on temperature, irradiance, humidity pressure, and other parameters were used. The input form consists of a single step with two features: the efficient Adam version of the stochastic gradient descent and Mean Absolute Error (MAE) loss function. To perform the LSTM analysis, we divided the data into 30 epochs with a batch size of 772. The curves in Figure 6.24 show a comparison between the actual and predicted values after the deep learning analysis of the solar PV array data. As can be observed, the prediction was accurate for all three deep learning models.

### 6.6.2 Matlab/Simulink Model

Figure 6.25 shows the input data of the irradiance and wind speed. The figure also depicts the load voltage, current, and power. The SoC of the EV charging station is also depicted, showing the charging and discharging of the battery. The power supply is simulated in such a way that for each 0.5 s simulation, a different combination of energy sources is active. Sudden spikes indicate a change in the power supply between the energy sources. The simulation functioned in an islanded mode of operation for a period of 2 s. In the next 2-second time period the central battery system came into play and considered simulated blackouts. The input parameters for the solar and wind energy systems were constants. This microgrid model is used to depict the functioning of the microgrid and its compatibility when it is connected to various systems.

The curve in Figure 6.26 depicts the functioning of the charging station and its charging/discharging scenarios. There is a sharp discharge

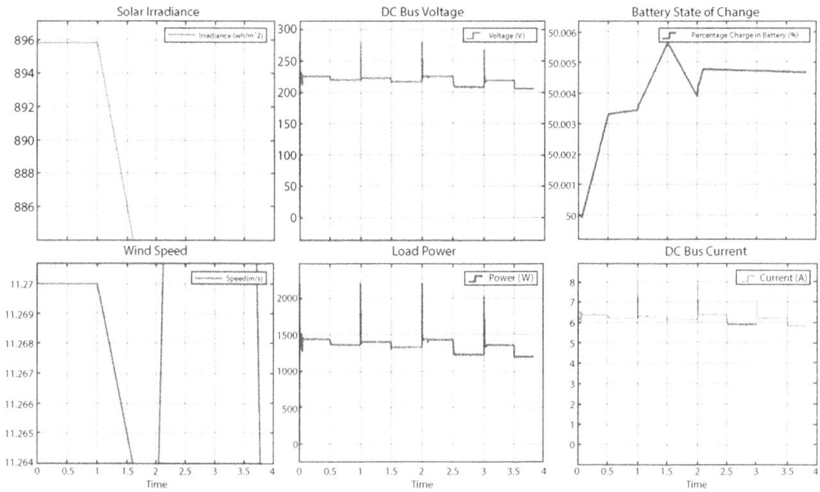


**Figure 6.25** Input and output data for microgrid.

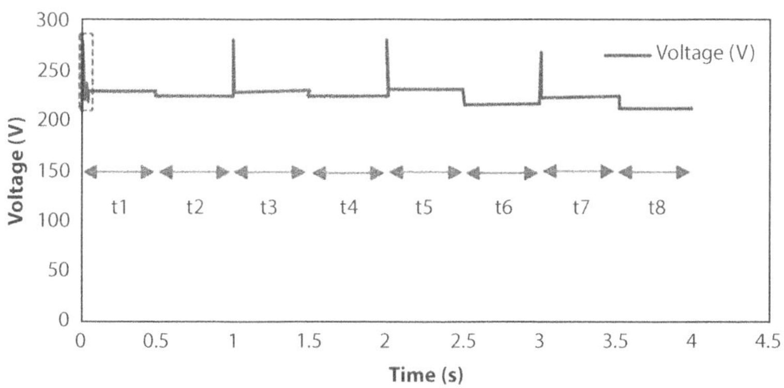


**Figure 6.26** DC bus voltage for microgrid.

depicting the power compensation for the microgrids as the renewable sources are yet to reach the voltage levels. The following periods depict the battery as nonfunctional, charging, and discharging. Figure 6.26 depicts the load voltage and is used to depict how the change in the power supply source affects the microgrid system. The control mechanism of the system was developed such that the voltage at the load was close to the nominal voltage of 220 V.

*t1*—Power is supplied by both solar and wind.
*t2*—Power is supplied by solar.
*t3*—Power is supplied by wind.
*t4*—There is no power supplied.
*t5*—Power is supplied by both solar and wind.
*t6*—Power is supplied by solar.
*t7*—Power is supplied by wind.
*t8*—There is no power supplied.
*(t1 to t3)*—EV battery charging.
*t4*—EV battery discharging
*(t5 to t7)*—Central battery charging
*t8*—Central battery discharging

As the individual microgrid system takes time to reach the required voltage level, the power is compensated by the central battery and is automatically switched to the power output by the microgrid when the voltage level is reached. This situation can be observed whenever the microgrids are unable to meet the voltage level.

## 6.7 Conclusion

The objective of this chapter is to create an active grid system that considers a DC microgrid with an EV charging station and integrates deep learning techniques. For the DC microgrid, renewable energy sources, such as solar and wind, were modeled along with the storage system. The first stage of the islanded-mode operation of the microgrid was performed. Various parameters had to be included in the control algorithms to obtain the ideal model. This was then integrated with an EV charging system and connected to a second microgrid to analyze its function during the simulated blackouts. Deep learning has been integrated into the model to make it autonomous and reliable, as it helps predict the demand as well as the availability of resources at particular times to be prepared for additional demand or shortage. The prediction model can be further improved by adding additional layers to the neural network structure or by increasing the computational power and processing loads of the data. There can be more work put in the active grid structure with a focus on making it more appropriate and feasible for real-time applications.

## References

1. Howell, S., Rezgui, Y., Hippolyte, J.-L., Jayan, B., Li, H., Towards the next generation of smart grids: Semantic and holonic multi-agent management of distributed energy resources. *Renew. Sustain. Energy Rev.*, 77, 193–214, 2017.
2. Alotaibi, I., Abido, M.A., Khalid, M., Savkin, A.V., A comprehensive review of recent advances in smart grids: A sustainable future with renewable energy resources. *Energies*, 13, 23, 6269, 2020.
3. Feng, C., Wang, Y., Chen, Q., Ding, Y., Strbac, G., Kang, C., Smart grid encounters edge computing: Opportunities and applications. *Adv. Appl. Energy*, 1, 100006, 2021.
4. Ai, Y., Peng, M., Zhang, K., Edge computing technologies for Internet of Things: a primer. *Digital Commun. Netw.*, 4, 2, 77–86, 2018.
5. Zhang, Y., Huang, T., Bompard, E.F., Big data analytics in smart grids: a review. *Energy Inf.*, 1, 1, 1–24, 2018.
6. Chen, S., Wen, H., Wu, J., Lei, W., Hou, W., Liu, W., Xu, A., Jiang, Y., Internet of things based smart grids supported by intelligent edge computing. *IEEE Access*, 7, 74089–74102, 2019.
7. Adenle, A.A., Assessment of solar energy technologies in Africa opportunities and challenges in meeting the 2030 agenda and sustainable development goals. *Energy Policy*, 137, 1111805, 2020.
8. Abdolrasol, M.GM., Hussain, S.M., Ustun, T.S., Sarker, M.R., Hannan, M.A., Mohamed, R., Ali, J.A., Mekhilef, S., Milad, A., Artificial Neural Networks Based Optimization Techniques: A Review. *Electronics*, 10, 21, 2689, 2021.
9. Kumar, D., Zare, F., Ghosh, A., DC microgrid technology: system architectures, AC grid interfaces, grounding schemes, power quality, communication networks, applications, and standardizations aspects. *IEEE Access*, 5, 12230–12256, 2017.
10. Keller, J. and Kroposki, B., Understanding fault characteristics of inverter based distributed energy resources, No. NREL/TP-550-46698, National Renewable Energy Lab.(NREL), Golden, CO (United States), 2010.
11. Jahdi, S., Lai, L.L., Nankoo, D., Grid integration of wind-solar hybrid renewables using AC/DC converters as DG power sources, in: *2011 World Congress on Sustainable Technologies (WCST)*, IEEE, pp. 171–177, 2011.
12. Singh, R., Alapatt, G.F., Bedi, G., Why and how photovoltaics will provide cheapest electricity in the 21st century. *Facta Univ. Ser. Electron. Energ.*, 27, 2, 275–298, 2014.
13. Anuradha, M., EDGE Computing Application in SMART GRID-A Review, in: *2021 Second International Conference on Electronics and Sustainable Communication Systems (ICESC)*, IEEE, pp. 1–6, 2021.
14. Zhang, Y., Di, B., Wang, P., Lin, J., Song, L., HetMEC: Heterogeneous multilayer mobile edge computing in the 6 G era. *IEEE Trans. Veh. Technol.*, 69, 4, 4388–4400, 2020.

15. Li, H., Ota, K., Dong, M., Learning IoT in edge: Deep learning for the Internet of Things with edge computing. *IEEE Netw.*, 32, 1, 96–101, 2018.
16. Islam, N., Modeling of photovoltaic module under varying solar irradiance, 2014.
17. Ou, T.-C. and Hong, C.-M., Dynamic operation and control of microgrid hybrid power systems. *Energy*, 66, 314–323, 2014.
18. Gite, S.S. and Pawar, S.H., Modeling of wind energy system with MPPT control for DC microgrid, in: *2017 second international conference on electrical, computer and communication technologies (ICECCT)*, IEEE, pp. 1–6, 2017.
19. Ghanbari, N., Mobarrez, M., Bhattacharya, S., A review and modeling of different droop control-based methods for battery state of the charge balancing in dc microgrids, in: *IECON 2018-44th Annual Conference of the IEEE Industrial Electronics Society*, IEEE, pp. 1625–1632, 2018.
20. Lpez, K.L., Gagn, C., Gardner, M.-A., Demand-side management using deep learning for smart charging of electric vehicles. *IEEE Trans. Smart Grid*, 10, 3, 2683–2691, 2018.
21. Liu, W., Wang, Z., Liu, X., Zeng, N., Liu, Y., Alsaadi, F.E., A survey of deep neural network architectures and their applications. *Neurocomputing*, 234, 11–26, 2017.
22. Kaensar, C., A comparative study on handwriting digit recognition classifier using neural network, support vector machine and k-nearest neighbor, in: *The 9th International Conference on Computing and Information Technology (IC2IT2013)*, pp. 155–163, Springer, Berlin, Heidelberg, 2013.
23. Ahmad, A.S., Hassan, M.Y., Abdullah, M.P., Rahman, H.A., Hussin, F., Abdullah, H., Saidur, R., A review on applications of ANN and SVM for building electrical energy consumption forecasting. *Renew. Sustain. Energy Rev.*, 33, 102–109, 2014.
24. Rohith, B., *et al.*, GUI Energy Demand Forecast using LSTM Deep Learning Model in Python Platform, in: *2021 Innovations in Power and Advanced Computing Technologies (i-PACT)*, IEEE, pp. 1–6, 2021.
25. Sundermeyer, M., Schlter, R., Ney, H., LSTM neural networks for language modeling, in: *Thirteenth annual conference of the international speech communication association*, 2012.
26. McKinney, W., *Python for data analysis: Data wrangling with Pandas, NumPy, and IPython*, O'Reilly Media, Inc., 2012.
27. Yao, W., Huang, P., Jia, Z., Multidimensional LSTM networks to predict wind speed, in: *2018 37th Chinese Control Conference (CCC)*, IEEE, pp. 7493–7497, 2018.
28. Qing, X. and Niu, Y., Hourly day-ahead solar irradiance prediction using weather forecasts by LSTM. *Energy*, 148, 461–468, 2018.
29. Bao, K., Li, S., Zheng, H., Battery charge and discharge control for energy management in EV and utility integration. *2012 IEEE power and energy society general meeting*, IEEE, 2012.

7

# Bearing Fault Diagnosis in Permanent Magnet Synchronous Motor Using Deep Neural Network

**Geetha G., Shanthini C., Geethanjali P.* and Yokkeshwaran K.**

*School of Electrical Engineering, Vellore Institute of Technology, Vellore, India*

***Abstract***

The diagnosis of bearing faults poses an essential problem in the monitoring of rotating machinery and has gained increasing attention. Rolling bearings are prone to various problems under demanding operating conditions that can lead to complete machine failure. This is reflected in the machine performance. If these faults are left unattended, they result in high levels of friction, which further causes immense heat in the machinery, higher than the machine could probably handle, eventually leading to equipment failure. This highlights the necessity of monitoring the machinery's condition to anticipate any potential issues arising from bearings. This study proposed and validated the use of deep learning techniques to diagnose and detect bearing faults in permanent magnet synchronous motors. In this study, a Visual Geometry Group (VGG) neural network was employed to diagnose the inner race fault and outer race fault against healthy data with the help of images obtained through wavelet analysis and kurtogram. The current and vibration signals from the permanent magnet synchronous motor have been taken for analysis. The Paderborn University bearing dataset is used to validate the training model's accuracy.

***Keywords*:** Fault diagnosis, deep learning, wavelet transform, kurtogram, current signal, vibration

**Corresponding author*: pgeethanjali@vit.ac.in

A. Chitra, W. Razia Sultana and V. Indragandhi (eds.) Smart Charging Infrastructures, (137–156)

## 7.1 Introduction

Permanent magnet synchronous motors (PMSMs) have been the preferred choice in recent years. This is because of the advantages they provide over conventional motors. PMSM motors exhibit highly efficient performance in almost all operations. They are also effective for operations involving a wide range of speeds and loads (Singh *et al.*, 2023; Gerada and Mu, 2020). With PMSM, a wide range of advanced control techniques can be employed to exercise precise control over the required speed and torque. These advanced control techniques mainly include direct torque control (DTC), field-oriented control (FOC) (Shriwastava *et al.*, 2019), fuzzy direct torque control (FDTC), and model predictive direct torque control (MPDTC) (Kakouche *et al.*, 2023). The long life and better heat transfer characteristics of the PMSM over the DC motors and induction motor provide the PMSM with a low maintenance feature (Mishra *et al.*, 2014). They have a compact design that allows the use of these motors, in which the available space is a parameter to be considered. The high-power density and regenerative breaking feature of the PMSM are exploited in electric vehicle propulsion systems (Huang *et al.*, 2023). With upcoming technology, PMSMs are important electrical components that drive systems on a large scale. With a PMSM being an electrical component, faults associated with the motor are unavoidable. Moreover, these cannot be neglected.

PMSM motors have three types of major faults: electrical, mechanical, and magnetic faults. Electrical faults refer to faults that occur due to the windings of the motor, or the short circuit and open circuit of the stator windings. Stator faults, one of the most prominent electrical faults, account for approximately 38% of all the faults experienced by a PMSM (Moosavi *et al.*, 2017). Magnetic faults in PMSM generally refer to the demagnetization faults that have a severe impact on the operation of the motor. They may affect the stator current of the motor, increasing the chance of machine failure (Faiz and Nejadi-Koti, 2015). Mechanical faults include bending of the shaft, eccentricity of the air gap, and bearing faults.

Bearing faults are responsible for almost 50–60% of the motor faults (Zhongming and Bin, 2000). Fatigue-related breakdowns may occur even under circumstances with balanced loads and correct alignment. This eventually results in problems, such as bearing flaking or spalling, in which parts of the bearing break free. Aside from the conventional internal strains generated by variables like vibration, intrinsic eccentricity, and bearing currents from solid-state drives, exterior problems such as improper mounting can also cause bearing deterioration leading to bearing faults that might damage the equipment to an irreversible extent (Rosero *et al.*, 2006). Fragments of the metal detach when the fatigue crack begins beneath the metal surface and progresses towards the surface, leaving behind a tiny depression or flaking. This results in a bearing failure, potentially causing problems with the cage, inner race, outer race, and ball components (Chen *et al.*, 2019). The diagnosis of bearing faults becomes imperative, as failure to do so might result in system failure along with damage to equipment.

Advanced bearing fault diagnosis methods can be classified into model-based, signal-based, artificial-intelligence-based, and hardware-based methods. Model-based procedures require the use of a specific system model that can be obtained using mathematical equations, physical components, or data-driven methods. Model-based fault diagnosis involves two steps: residual generation and evaluation. A signal is typically synthesized by computing the system's input and output. This signal is then passed to the evaluation phase, where potential faults are checked. In this case, the signal is used directly. Signal-based methods for diagnosing faults, as opposed to analyzing a system's input and output data, focus on signal measurement for problem identification and extraction. This measurement analysis may be of various types like spectrum and phase in the frequency domain and deviations and magnitudes in the time domain (Gao *et al.*, 2015).

The extent of diagnosis depends on the extent of feature extraction from the signal taken for analysis. Artificial intelligence (AI) methods for diagnosing faults depend on the use of artificial intelligence models. These data were fed either as input or output data or signals. Therefore, these methods rely on the previously stated methods for the input. The input is processed through an artificial network that can be any form of AI-based model as a neural network (Sharma *et al.*, 2019), fuzzy logic control, random forest, linear discriminant analysis, support vector machine, k-nearest neighbor, decision tree, and so on (Bhuiyan *et al.*, 2020). In PMSM machines, determining the location, nature, and extent of a fault depends on the utilization of hardware. One of the most widely used hardware-based methods is online order analysis for bearings (Lu *et al.*, 2018).

Various signals from the motor can be used in bearing fault diagnosis. These include the signal of the vibration of the motor, current, temperature, flux, speed, and noise from the motor. Vibration signals have been widely used in studies as the features of the vibration signal portray the effect of faults, making the diagnostic process more accurate. Vibration signals have been pre-processed and used for diagnosis (Chen *et al.*, 2017). An accuracy of 99.62% was achieved at the highest level using the stacked auto-encoders. White noise was been added by Kang *et al.* (2023) to the vibration signal data to improve the features of the fault characteristics, and was processed through a progressive lattice method-based optimized ResNet, resulting in an accuracy of 94.75%. The use of current signals for the diagnosis of faults has recently increased. With current signals (Jokic *et al.*, 2018), various signal processing techniques have been used to extract the features associated with faults.

Signal processing techniques are of high importance when current and vibration signals are fed through a neural network for diagnosis. With preprocessing, the faulty features of the original signal are expected to be prominent, allowing the accuracy of the diagnosis to be better. For this, various techniques are employed such as the Fast Fourier transforms (FFT) (Wang et al., 2024), Short-Time Fourier Transforms (STFT) (Boudinar *et al.*, 2019), Power Spectral Density (PSD), Wavelet Transforms (WT) (Malhotra *et al.*, 2021), and Hilbert Transforms (HT) (Rai and Upadhyay, 2016).

Motor current signals have been used in fault diagnosis using various methods, with neural networks being the most dominant. This is due to the difficulty in extracting features from the current signals, and hence, the requirement of an advanced technique of feature identification and extraction. The wavelet function that has been scaled and translated is convolved with the input signal to perform wavelet transform. The wavelet function is a brief oscillating waveform that is frequently temporal and frequency-localized. This transform can capture various frequency components of the signal at different resolutions by adjusting the scale and position of the wavelet function.

Discrete wavelet transform (DWT) was employed for the analysis of digital data or discrete-time signals. It includes down-sampling and filtering the signal repeatedly to produce a multiresolution representation. With a high-resolution representation at lower frequencies and coarse resolution at higher frequencies, the DWT succeeds in tiling the signal time and frequency. The father wavelet (low-pass filter) and mother wavelet (high-pass filter) are two sets of functions used by the DWT. Two sets of coefficients, referred to as approximation coefficients representing the low-frequency components and detail coefficients representing the high-frequency components, were produced by convolving the input signal with these filters. To acquire more decomposition levels, the procedure is performed recursively on the approximation coefficients.

Yeolekar *et al.* (2017) studied the processing of the current signal using a discrete wavelet transform (DWT) to identify the features of outer-race faults. The difficulty in feature extraction brings forth the need for additional techniques like information fusion (Hoang and Kang, 2019), long-short-term memory with a signal processed through wavelet packet decomposition (Habbouche *et al.*, 2021), multiresolution analysis, and FFT feature-based feature selection along with support vector machine (Sabir *et al.*, 2019). A maximum accuracy of 98.3% for fault diagnosis using the current signal was given by Agustin *et al.* (2023), where a combination of multilayer perceptron and information fusion was exploited.

This study uses the current and vibration signals of a PMSM motor dataset from the Paderborn University bearing dataset for bearing fault diagnosis. The work is performed on a three-class classification: healthy, inner race fault, and outer race fault. Previous studies have been conducted extensively in the field with vibration signals. This study aims to employ discrete wavelet transform and kurtogram images for the diagnosis of bearing faults to increase the accuracy of discrimination between faults using a deep neural network.

## 7.2 Methodology

The proposed system is based on the VGG-19 neural network for diagnosing faults in a 3-class. The given data have two major faults: the inner race fault (KI04) and the outer race fault (KA04). These are diagnosed against

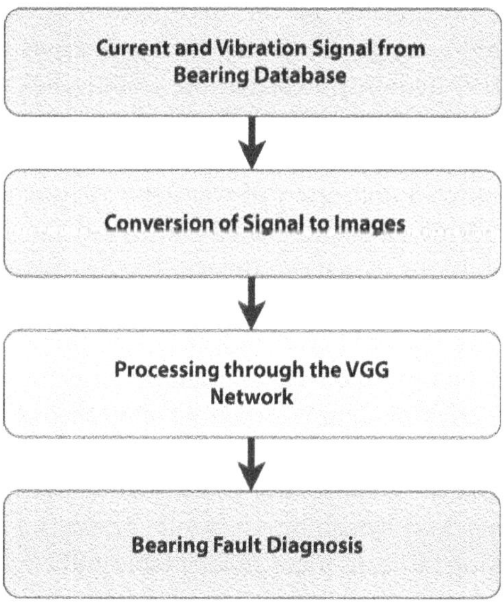


**Figure 7.1** Block diagram of the proposed system.

the healthy data (K001) considered from the Paderborn University bearing database (Zhou *et al.*, 2023). VGG-19 works well with images; hence, the signal acquired from the dataset was pre-processed into images to meet the criteria. Two different methods were used in this study to validate the extent of feature extraction from the signals: the discrete wavelet transform and kurtogram. The signals that were taken for analysis were the current and vibration signals. A simplified block diagram of this method is shown in Figure 7.1.

### 7.2.1 Discrete Wavelet Transform

The discrete wavelet transform (DWT) is a technique used to convert the given data into equivalent images to retain the characteristics of the original signal (Toma and Kim, 2020). The plot of the coefficients of decomposition through the levels was used for further analyses. They are of the prism spectrum of colors, allowing better distinction in the images. When a signal is processed using discrete wavelets, it is simultaneously subjected to high-pass and low-pass filters. With a high-pass filter, the detailed components are obtained, and with a low-pass filter, the approximate components are obtained. Thus, the obtained approximate components are taken for level 2 of decomposition, and the cycle continues until a specified level is reached. With DWT, there is downsampling of samples by 2 at each successive level (Skodras, 2007).

To obtain the coefficients of the decomposition at each level, the Daubechies 5 (db5) wavelet, a subset of the Daubechies family, was used. Meftah *et al.* (2019) demonstrated that the Daubechies wavelet family is best suited for analyzing bearing fault defects.

The Daubechies wavelet, also referred to as a db wavelet, is a versatile and extensively utilized collection of wavelets. They derived their name from Ingrid Daubechies, a distinguished mathematician renowned for her significant contributions to wavelet theory. The distinguishing features of the Daubechies wavelets include their compact support, orthogonality, and vanishing moments. These characteristics enable them to strike a favorable balance between time and frequency localization, rendering them well suited for a wide array of signal processing applications. The Daubechies wavelet family encompasses various members, such as db1, db2, db3, and up to db45. Overall, the Daubechies wavelet family, with its compact support, orthogonality, and vanishing moments, presents a valuable tool set for signal processing tasks. It offers an adaptable and effective solution for activities such as denoising, compression, and feature extraction, enabling comprehensive analysis and manipulation of signals in both time and

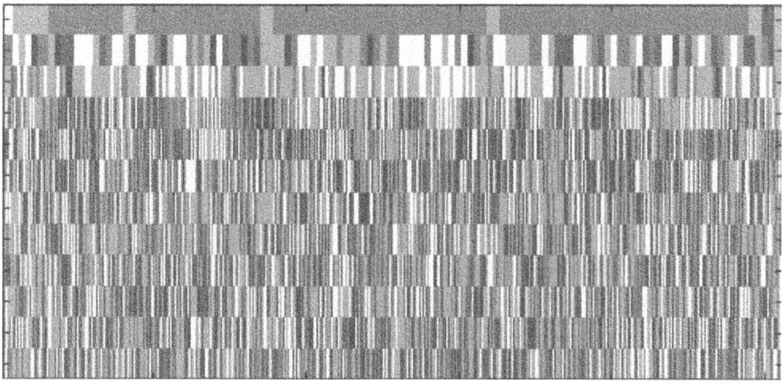

(a) Healthy

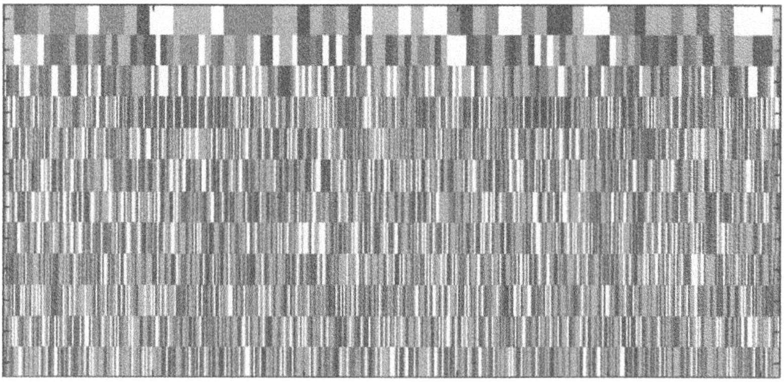

(b) Inner Race Fault

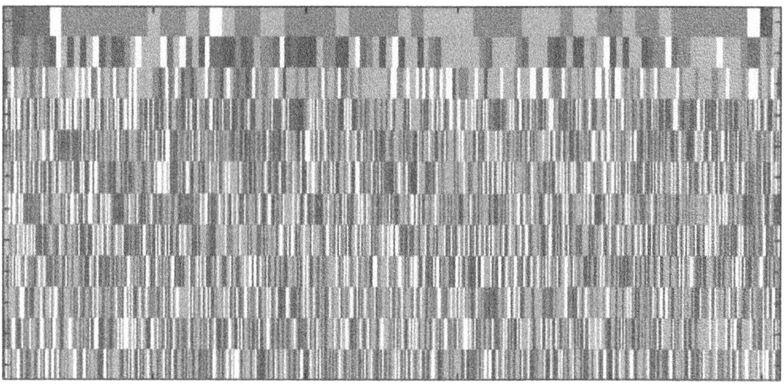

(c) Outer Race Fault

**Figure 7.2** Coefficient plots for different bearing conditions with current signal.

frequency domains. The equation for a Daubechies (db) wavelet, irrespective of order, can be expressed using Equation (7.1).

$$\psi(t) = \sum[h[n] * \phi(2t - n)] \tag{7.1}$$

Where,

$\psi(t)$ is the Daubechies wavelet function at time t.

h[n] represents the filter coefficients associated with the wavelet.

$\phi(t)$ is the scaling function (low-pass filter) associated with the wavelet.

The sum is taken over the filter coefficients h[n] multiplied by the scaling function $\phi$, evaluated at 2t – n. The specific values of filter coefficients h[n] depend on the chosen wavelet order. Different orders of Daubechies wavelets have different numbers of vanishing moments and filter coefficients with different lengths.

The numerical value indicates a higher degree of smoothness and increased number of vanishing moments. The number indicate the length of the filter associated with the respective wavelet. The decomposition level was set to 12 to obtain the maximum variation in the frequency scale. Coefficients at different levels were plotted against the samples to obtain the required plot for further analysis. The plots of coefficients for the current signal when it is healthy, has an inner race fault, and has an outer race fault are shown in Figures 7.2a–c. A clear distinction among the three specified conditions can be seen at the highest level of decomposition, i.e., the 12th level. The sparsity of the red color is highly distinct. With inner-race faults, red is very sparse, while with outer-race, it is moderately sparse. With healthy data, the coefficients of the 12th level are characterized highly by red, allowing a better probability of discrimination between the different conditions.

### 7.2.2 Kurtogram

The kurtogram is a spectral analysis tool intended to identify and characterize nonstationary signals. It operates at a fourth-order level of analysis. This is based on the claim that each type of temporary event is connected to an appropriate combination that maximizes kurtosis. The major function of a kurtogram is to identify and determine the location of faults in mechanical systems by evaluating an input signal's kurtosis across various time-frequency ranges. The elevated regions of the kurtogram refer to the location of the faults or transient features allowing the diagnosis of faults in the given signal. Because the kurtogram specifically highlights the

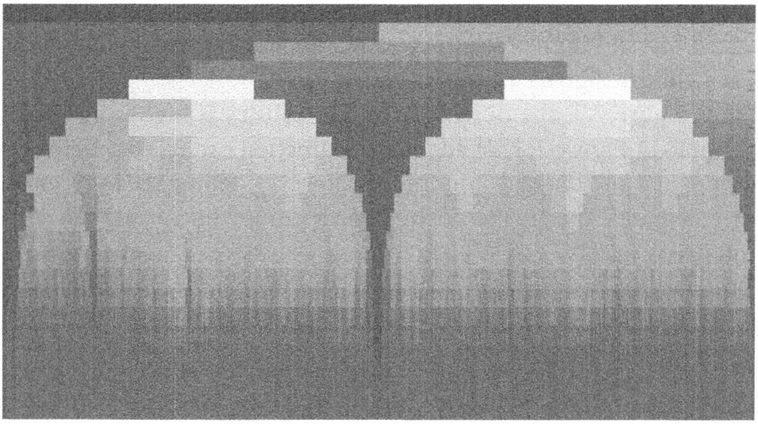

(**a**) Healthy condition

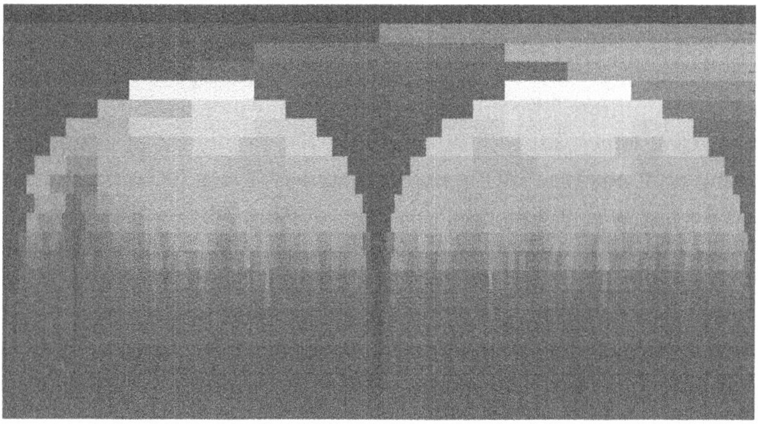

(**b**) Outer Race Fault

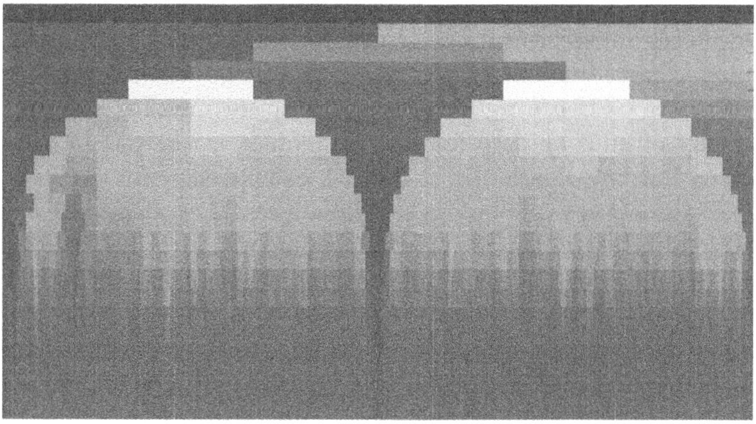

(**c**) Inner Race Fault

**Figure 7.3** Kurtogram plots for different conditions of the current signal.

transient features of a signal, feature extraction from the kurtogram plot is expected to yield higher accuracy rates. The kurtograms for the different types of current signals are shown in Figure 7.3.

From Figure 7.3, the difference in the features is higher in the vibration signal. In Figure 7.3, an adequate distinction can be seen between the healthy signal and the fault conditions. However, among the inner race and outer race faults, the characteristic differences are noticeable yet not very distinctive.

However, the features were highly noticeable in each class when a vibration signal was used. This is expected to provide better accuracy than the other conditions presented above.

### 7.2.3 Deep Neural Network-VGG

There is a growing trend towards the use of deep learning (DL)-based methodologies to enhance performance in various operating settings and noisy surroundings. The number of studies has increased dramatically in recent years, which suggests a significant rise in interest in utilizing deep learning methods for bearing defect diagnosis. Deep learning attains significant capability and adaptability by acquiring knowledge to depict the world as a layered structure of ideas, where each idea is defined in connection to simpler ideas and more general representations are derived from less general ones. Classical machine-learning algorithms have the potential to rival or surpass deep-learning networks on smaller datasets. As the volume of data increases, deep learning (DL) can significantly outperform the performance of most traditional machine learning (ML) methods.

The process of training deep neural network models aims to enhance their speed, convergence, and generalization. Training deep networks requires a large amount of processing power; however, using a high-performance GPU can significantly speed up this training process. The advantage of utilizing deep learning techniques, in contrast to standard machine learning algorithms, is that DL exhibits superior performance that surpasses previous solutions in various areas. The data are transmitted directly to the network, which then autonomously learns the characteristics of the unprocessed data by adjusting the weights in the network.

Convolutional Neural Networks (CNNs) (Qin and Shi, 2022) are key components of deep learning and are designed to extract intricate characteristics from image data. CNNs have been extensively applied and are the prevailing method in the domain of defect diagnosis. In recent research, an evaluation was conducted to assess the performance of advanced pre-trained networks, such as AlexNet, VGG-16, VGG-19, GoogLeNet, and

ResNet-50, to evaluate the status of bearings using images acquired from signals.

In this study, the VGG-19 neural network is a convolutional neural network design used in pattern recognition, image classification, and computer vision. VGG-19 is composed of 19 layers, which encompasses 16 convolutional layers and three fully connected layers, which are also called dense layers. The convolutional layers were deeply stacked. Max pooling layers are present in between the blocks of convolutional layers to reduce the spatial dimensions that help in the prevention of overfitting of data.VGG-19 also includes rectified linear unit (ReLU) activation functions. These are functions that introduce nonlinearity in the model properties. The architecture of the VGG-19 model used in this study is listed in Table 7.1.

In Table 7.1, there are 16 convolutional layers, as mentioned above. Each layer's output shape is specified in the format (None, x, y, z), where 'None' refers to the fact that this model can be trained for any batch size, such as 28, 32, 64, and 128. x and y refer to the height and width, respectively, whereas z refers to the number of feature maps produced by the layer.

**Table 7.1** VGG-19 architecture.

| Layer | Output Shape |
|---|---|
| Input layer | (None,250,250,3) |
| Block-1:Convolution layers (2) | (None,250,250,64) |
| Block-1: Max pooling layer | (None,125,125,64) |
| Block-2: Convolution layers (2) | (None, 125, 125, 128) |
| Block-2: Max pooling layer | (None, 62, 62, 128) |
| Block-3: Convolution layers (4) | (None, 62, 62, 256) |
| Block-3: Max pooling layer | (None, 31, 31, 256) |
| Block-4: Convolution layers (4) | (None, 31, 31, 512) |
| Block-4: Max pooling layer | (None, 15, 15, 512) |
| Block-5: Convolution layers (4) | (None, 15, 15, 512) |
| Block-4: Max pooling layer | (None, 7, 7, 512) |
| Flatten layer | (None, 25088) |
| Dense layer | (None,3) |

With the dense layer, a softmax activation function was used to estimate the probability of the processed image as a member of one of the three classes.

The bearing dataset was obtained from the Paderborn University bearing dataset. The images obtained from the preprocessing techniques were not sufficient to train the model. Hence, image augmentation was implemented and the number of images was extended to 3,000 for each class of training data and 500 for each class of validation data. Thus, 9,000 images were used to train the model, and 1,500 images were used to validate the model.

## 7.3 Results and Discussion

Two major cases were analyzed in this study. The first is using DWT to diagnose the fault for different signals, and the second is where the kurtogram is used to preprocess for fault diagnosis. Each of these models was trained separately using the VGG-19 model.

### 7.3.1 Case 1: Using DWT

When DWT was used for the current signal, an accuracy of 94.63% was obtained, whereas vibration data provided a better accuracy of 97.102%. The confusion matrix that represents the accuracy obtained for the current signal is shown in Figure 7.4, and the confusion matrix for the vibration signal using the DWT is shown in Figure 7.5.

For the current signal, a batch size of 28 was used with a learning rate of 0.1. This was run for 35 epochs to obtain an accuracy of 94%. However, with the vibration signal, a batch size of 28 was used with a learning rate of 0.1 as well. However, the number of epochs required to attain a 97.102% accuracy was only 35. The fault features were extracted better with the vibration signals.

### 7.3.2 Case 2: Using Kurtogram

With the exploitation of the kurtogram, the features of the faults were highly noticeable in the coefficient matrix using the DWT. The model diagnoses the faults in the current signal with an accuracy of 96.943%, for which the confusion matrix is shown in Figure 7.6. With the vibration signal, the features were prominent in the kurtogram plot. This allows for a better accuracy of diagnosis, providing an accuracy of 99.728%, proving its dominance over the other cases and the type of signal. A confusion matrix for the same is shown in Figure 7.7.

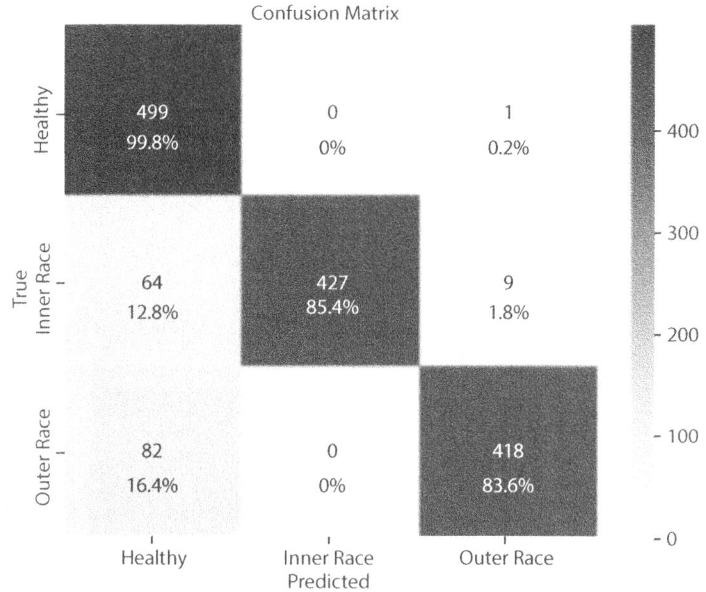


**Figure 7.4** Confusion matrix of the current signal using DWT.

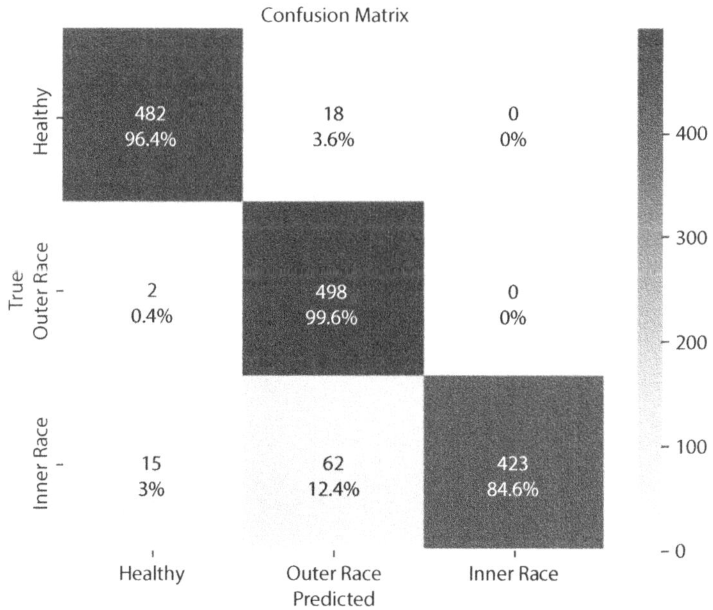


**Figure 7.5** Confusion matrix of the vibration signal using DWT.

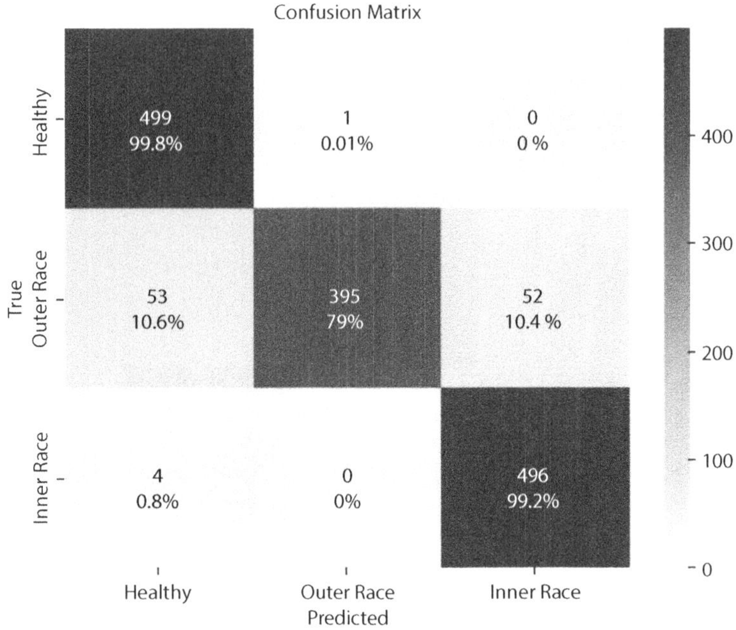


**Figure 7.6** Confusion matrix of the current signal using kurtogram.

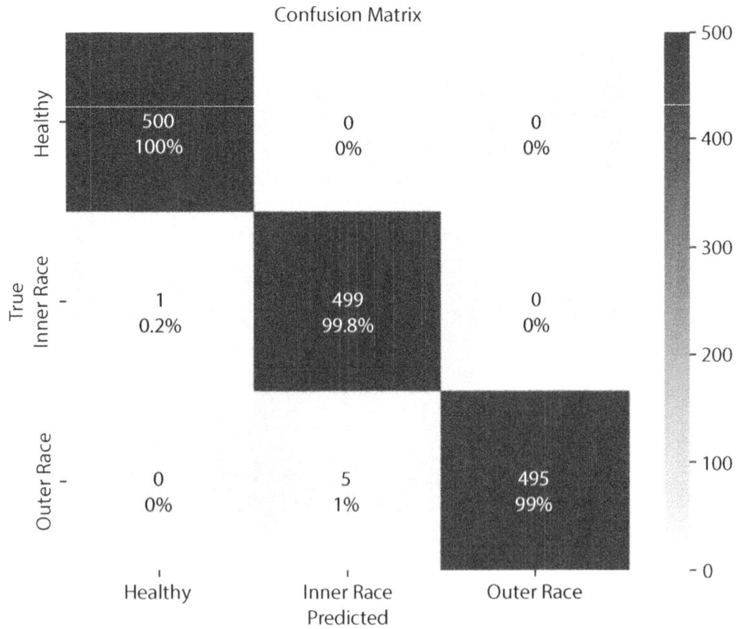


**Figure 7.7** Confusion matrix of the vibration signal using kurtogram.

While using the kurtogram for analysis, the batch size for both the current and vibration was set to 32, and the learning rates were set equal to 0.1 as well. However, the kurtogram of the current signal took 20 epochs to attain an accuracy of 96.943%, whereas the kurtogram of the vibration signal only took 10 epochs to achieve an accuracy of 99.728%. The rate of convergence was faster for a vibration signal. It can be observed that the vibration signal

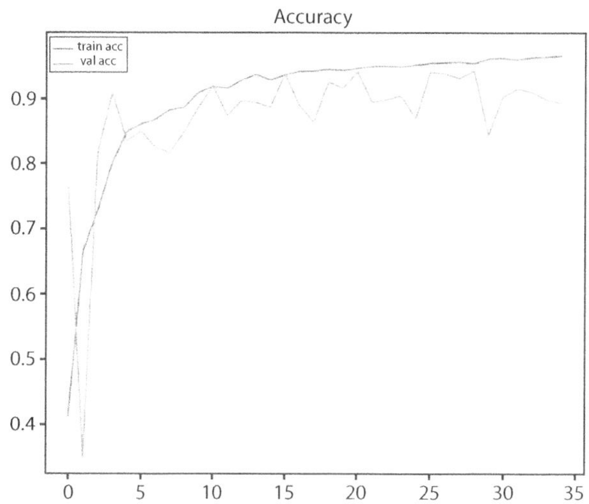


**Figure 7.8** Accuracy plot of the vibration signal using DWT.

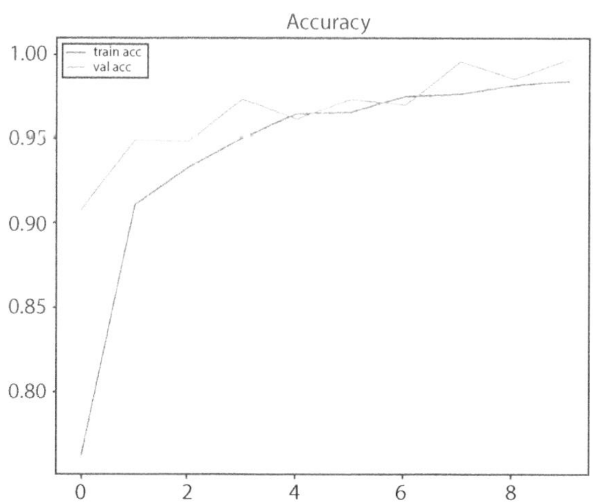


**Figure 7.9** Accuracy plot of the vibration signal using kurtogram.

**Table 7.2** A summary of the results.

| | DWT | | Kurtogram | |
|---|---|---|---|---|
| **Parameter** | **Current** | **Vibrations** | **Current** | **Vibrations** |
| **Epochs** | 35 | 35 | 20 | **10** |
| **Batch size** | 32 | 28 | 32 | **32** |
| **Learning rate** | 0.1 | 0.1 | 0.1 | **0.1** |
| **Accuracy** | **94.633%** | **97.102%** | **96.943%** | **99.728%** |

helps in the diagnosis of the fault to a greater extent than the current signal. In addition, the results were better with kurtogram plots.

The better training and validation accuracy of bearing fault diagnosis, providing an accuracy greater than 99.7% using kurtogram and 97.1% using DWT, proves its dominance over the current signal. The accuracy plots for the same are presented in Figures 7.8, 7.9.

A summary of the accuracies and major parameters that have been constantly tuned is provided in Table 7.2. From Table 7.2, it can be said that the model predicts the faults best when the signal used in the vibration signal and the processing technique is a kurtogram.

## 7.4 Conclusion

This study proposes a bearing fault diagnosis method using a VGG-19 neural network. The need to diagnose bearing faults is important to ensure the safety of the equipment. This study was validated against the Paderborn dataset. Wavelet transform and kurtogram were used for signal processing, and the results were the best with the kurtogram images. The signals used are the current and vibration, among which vibration provides better accuracy when compared to the current signal. An accuracy of 99.728% was obtained at the highest value using kurtogram images of the vibration signal.

## References

Agustin, X.M., Samson, E.J., Ostia, C., Application of SVM Classification Technique in Single-phase AC Motor Bearing Fault Diagnosis using Motor Current Analysis with MRA-FFT as Feature Extractor and CFFS as Feature

Selection Method, in: *2023 IEEE 14th Control and System Graduate Research Colloquium (ICSGRC)*, 2023, August, IEEE, pp. 208–213.

Bhuiyan, E.A., Akhand, M.M.A., Das, S.K., Ali, M.F., Tasneem, Z., Islam, M.R., Moyeen, S.I., A survey on fault diagnosis and fault tolerant methodologies for permanent magnet synchronous machines. *Int. J. Autom. Comput.*, *17*, 763–787, 2020.

Boudinar, A.H., Aimer, A.F., Khodja, M.E.A., Benouzza, N., Induction motor's bearing fault diagnosis using an improved short time fourier transform, in: *Advanced Control Engineering Methods in Electrical Engineering Systems*, pp. 411–426, Springer International Publishing, 2019.

Chen, Y., Liang, S., Li, W., Liang, H., Wang, C., Faults and diagnosis methods of permanent magnet synchronous motors: A review. *Appl. Sci.*, *9*, 10, 2116, 2019.

Chen, Z., Deng, S., Chen, X., Li, C., Sanchez, R.V., Qin, H., Deep neural networks-based rolling bearing fault diagnosis. *Microelectron. Reliab.*, *75*, 327–333, 2017.

Djaballah, S., Meftah, K., Khelil, K., Tedjini, M., Sedira, L., Detection and diagnosis of fault bearing using wavelet packet transform and neural network. *Frat. Integrità Strut.*, *13*, 49, 291–301, 2019.

Faiz, J. and Nejadi-Koti, H., Demagnetization fault indexes in permanent magnet synchronous motors—An overview. *IEEE Trans. Magn.*, *52*, 4, 1–11, 2015.

Gao, Z., Cecati, C., Ding, S.X., A survey of fault diagnosis and fault-tolerant techniques—Part I: Fault diagnosis with model-based and signal-based approaches. *IEEE Trans. Ind. Electron.*, *62*, 6, 3757–3767, 2015.

Habbouche, H., Benkedjouh, T., Zerhouni, N., Intelligent prognostics of bearings based on bidirectional long short-term memory and wavelet packet decomposition. *Int. J. Adv. Manuf. Technol.*, 114, 1, 145–157, 2021.

Hoang, D.T. and Kang, H.J., A motor current signal-based bearing fault diagnosis using deep learning and information fusion. *IEEE Trans. Instrum. Meas.*, *69*, 6, 3325–3333, 2019.

Huang, Q., Huang, Q., Guo, H., Cao, J., Design and research of permanent magnet synchronous motor controller for electric vehicle. *Energy Sci. Eng.*, *11*, 1, 112–126, 2023.

Jokic, S., Cincar, N., Novakovic, B., The analysis of vibration measurement and current signature in motor drive faults detection, in: *2018 17th International Symposium INFOTEH-JAHORINA (INFOTEH)*, 2018, March, IEEE, pp. 1–6.

Kakouche, K., Oubelaid, A., Mezani, S., Rekioua, D., Rekioua, T., Different control techniques of permanent magnet synchronous motor with fuzzy logic for electric vehicles: analysis, modelling, and comparison. *Energies*, *16*, 7, 3116, 2023.

Kang, O., Xu, H., Wang, C., Research on Fault Diagnosis of Rolling Bearings Based on Progressive Grid Optimization ResNet, in: *2023 IEEE International Conference on Image Processing and Computer Applications (ICIPCA)*, 2023, August, IEEE, pp. 1678–1683.

Lu, S., He, Q., Zhao, J., Bearing fault diagnosis of a permanent magnet synchronous motor *via* a fast and online order analysis method in an embedded system. *Mech. Syst. Signal Process.*, *113*, 36–49, 2018.

Luo, X., Wang, H., Han, T., Zhang, Y., FFT-Trans: Enhancing Robustness in Mechanical Fault Diagnosis with Fourier Transform-Based Transformer under Noisy Conditions. *IEEE Trans. Instrum. Meas.*, 26, 73, 1–2, 2024 Mar.

Ma, C., Gao, Y., Degano, M., Wang, Y., Fang, J., Gerada, C., Mu, Y., Eccentric position diagnosis of static eccentricity fault of external rotor permanent magnet synchronous motor as an in-wheel motor. *IET Electr. Power Appl.*, *14*, 11, 2263–2272, 2020.

Malhotra, A., Minhas, A.S., Singh, S., Zuo, M.J., Kumar, R., Kankar, P.K., Bearing fault diagnosis based on flexible analytical wavelet transform and fuzzy entropy approach. *Mater. Today Proc.*, *43*, 629–635, 2021.

Mishra, A., Agarwal, P., Srivastava, S.P., A comprehensive analysis and implementation of vector control of permanent magnet synchronous motor. *Int. J. Power Energy Convers.*, *5*, 1, 1–23, 2014.

Moosavi, S.S., Esmaili, Q., Djerdir, A., Amirat, Y.A., Inter-turn fault detection in stator winding of PMSM using wavelet transform, in: *2017 IEEE Vehicle Power and Propulsion Conference (VPPC)*, 2017, December, IEEE, pp. 1–5.

Nishat Toma, R. and Kim, J.M., Bearing fault classification of induction motors using discrete wavelet transform and ensemble machine learning algorithms. *Appl. Sci.*, *10*, 15, 5251, 2020.

Qin, Y. and Shi, X., Fault diagnosis method for rolling bearings based on two-channel CNN under unbalanced datasets. *Appl. Sci.*, *12*, 17, 8474, 2022.

Rai, A. and Upadhyay, S.H., A review on signal processing techniques utilized in the fault diagnosis of rolling element bearings. *Tribol. Int.*, *96*, 289–306, 2016.

Rosero, J.A., Cusido, J., Garcia, A., Ortega, J.A., Romeral, L., Broken bearings and eccentricity fault detection for a permanent magnet synchronous motor, in: *IECON 2006-32nd Annual Conference on IEEE Industrial Electronics*, 2006, November, IEEE, pp. 964–969.

Sabir, R., Rosato, D., Hartmann, S., Guehmann, C., LSTM based bearing fault diagnosis of electrical machines using motor current signal, in: *2019 18th IEEE International Conference on Machine Learning and Applications (ICMLA)*, 2019, December, IEEE, pp. 613–618.

Sharma, A., Jigyasu, R., Mathew, L., Chatterji, S., Bearing fault diagnosis using frequency domain features and artificial neural networks, in: *Information and Communication Technology for Intelligent Systems: Proceedings of ICTIS 2018, Volume 2*, pp. 539–547, Springer Singapore, 2019.

Shriwastava, R.G., Bhise, D.R., Nagrale, P., Comparative analysis of FOC based three level DCMLI driven PMSM drive, in: *2019 International Conference on Innovative Trends and Advances in Engineering and Technology (ICITAET)*, 2019, December, IEEE, pp. 26–31.

Singh, S., Singh, S.N., Tiwari, A.N., PMSM drives and its application: An overview. *Recent Adv. Electr. Electron. Eng. (Formerly Recent Pat. Electr. Electron. Eng.)*, *16*, 1, 4–16, 2023.

Skodras, A.N., Discrete wavelet transform: an introduction. Hellenic Open University, Patras, Greece, Rep. HOU-CS-TR-2003-02-EN, 2003.

Yeolekar, S., Mulay, G.N., Helonde, J.B., Outer race bearing fault identification of induction motor based on stator current signature by wavelet transform, in: *2017 2nd IEEE International Conference on Recent Trends in Electronics, Information & Communication Technology (RTEICT)*, 2017, May, IEEE, pp. 2011–2015.

Zhou, H., Cheng, P., Shao, S., Zhao, Y., Yang, X., Intelligent bearing fault diagnosis method based on a domain aligned clustering network. *Meas. Sci. Technol.*, *34*, 4, 044001, 2023.

Zhongming, Y.E. and Bin, W.U., A review on induction motor online fault diagnosis, in: *Proceedings IPEMC 2000, Third International Power Electronics and Motion Control Conference (IEEE Cat. No. 00EX435)*, 2000, August, vol. 3, IEEE, pp. 1353–1358.

# 8

# Enhancing Efficiency in Bidirectional CLLC Resonant Converters: A Hybrid Control Approach

**Aryan Chaturvedi, M. Rajalakshmi and Razia Sultana W.***

*School of Electrical Engineering, Vellore Institute of Technology, Vellore, India*

## *Abstract*

The bidirectional CLLC resonant converter is a sophisticated power electronics system created to enable efficient energy transfer between two voltage sources and is commonly utilized in scenarios demanding bidirectional power flow, such as vehicle chargers. This paper presents a comprehensive examination of the bidirectional CLLC resonant converter, focusing on its setup, operational principles, and an innovative hybrid control technique that integrates frequency control and phase-shift approaches. The bidirectional CLLC resonant converter is designed with full-bridge configurations on both the primary and secondary sides, ensuring balance and enabling a smooth energy transfer in both directions. The key components of the system include the switching elements, body diodes, output capacitors, high-frequency transformers, resonant inductances, and capacitors. The ratio of turns in the transformer and excitation inductance is pivotal in determining the converter's performance. This study explores the operational principles of frequency control by employing an underlying examination to comprehend the operational properties of the converter. It discusses the influence of critical parameters, such as the inductance coefficient (k) and the quality factor (Q), on the voltage gain, providing an in-depth analysis of their impact under different conditions. A significant portion of this study is dedicated to an innovative hybrid control strategy that merges phase-shift control and frequency control methods. This strategy overcomes the limitations of using either control method independently by broadening the range of the voltage gain and developing the overall performance and stability of the converter. The hybrid control strategy, which comprises the steady current and voltage charging phases, is particularly advantageous during the vehicle charging process.

**Corresponding author*: wraziasultana@vit.ac.in

A. Chitra, W. Razia Sultana and V. Indragandhi (eds.) Smart Charging Infrastructures, (157–174)

***Keywords*:** Resonant converter, smart charging, bi-directional EV charging, hybrid control

## 8.1 Introduction

New energy challenges are posed by the scarcity of fossil resources and environmental considerations. In total, traditional transportation consumes half of the global oil production, resulting in huge emissions [1]. These challenges, when considered collectively, have an impact on the automotive industry and are critical for the research and development of electric vehicle (EV) technologies as a solution to these issues [2]. Electrical energy storage is currently one of the most popular study topics. Electrical energy storage technology has progressed to a point where it now has a suitable mass density of energy and power to meet automobile needs. The most significant disadvantage of these storage systems is their high manufacturing cost [3]. Researchers are currently working to develop good storage solutions and improve their charging methods and reliability to minimize the vehicle's overall cost.

In this field, numerous technological storage systems have been created and integrated into electric power train systems, resulting in improved performance [4]. Flawless management of the main electrical engine or perfect control of the battery recharge system aids in reducing the loss of the vehicle's power system [5]. To improve the system's efficiency, researchers have investigated various control methods. In addition, various investigations on the battery's internal structure have been conducted to improve the overall productivity [6]. Other options have been offered to improve the energy efficiency of EV transportation systems. This incorporates a solid track record of autonomy in contemporary electric vehicle models [7].

The CL3C resonant converter could be a future portable bidirectional EV charger without any distrust [8]. The CL3C converter satisfies all the major criteria for developing an EV charger with high power handling capacity with ZVS and ZCS operation to minimize switching losses [9]. The established V2X technology in smart city infrastructure development for road safety, traffic efficiency, energy savings, and mass surveillance can be extended to energy transfer using bidirectional high-frequency wireless charging with a CL3C resonant converter [10].

## 8.2 Bidirectional CLLC Resonant Converter

In Figure 8.1, a bidirectional CLLC resonant converter arrangement is shown. The primary side features switching elements $S_1$–$S_4$ forming a full bridge, while $S_5$–$S_8$ establish a full bridge on the secondary side. Corresponding to $S_1$–$S_8$, $D_1$–$D_8$ represent the body diodes, and $C_{coss1}$–$C_{coss8}$ represent the output capacitors for $S_1$–$S_8$. The transformer turns ratio is n:1; $L_m$ denotes the transformer's excitation inductance, $L_{r1}$, $L_{r2}$, $C_{r1}$, and $C_{r2}$ pertain to the resonating inductance and capacitance on the primary and secondary sides, respectively; and the high-frequency transformer enables electrical isolation, each representing a specific function. $U_{AB}$ denotes the primary voltage, $U_{CD}$ indicates the secondary voltage, and $C_{in}$ and $C_o$ represent the capacitors for filtering. In the converter's forward operation, power is circulated from the $U_{AB}$ to the $U_{CD}$. Given that the converter retains the same operational state in both the forward and reverse modes, the examination concentrates exclusively on the positive working period.

The structures on the left and right sides comprise full-bridge configurations, demonstrating symmetry. Energy transfer in both the forward and reverse modes allows for bidirectional flow, with the converter operating as an LLC resonant converter in both directions. During forward operation, switches $S_1$–$S_4$ receive the necessary actuating signal for inverter functionality, whereas $S_5$–$S_8$ facilitate rectification.

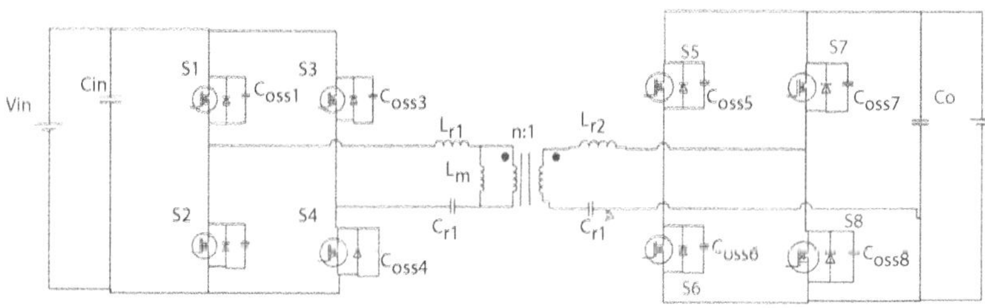


**Figure 8.1** Circuit diagram of CLLC converter.

## 8.3 Working by Controlling Conversion of Frequency

This type of analysis method was utilized to examine the operational behavior of the converter, with the resultant circuit depicted in Figure 8.2. Specifically, $V_{AB\_FHA(t)}$ denotes the square-wave intrinsic component of the DC bus voltage input following the full-bridge inverter. The values of $C_{r2}$ and $L_{r2'}$ represent the capacitance and inductance transformed from $C_{r2}$ and $L_{r2}$, respectively, to the primary side of the transformer. $R_{eq}$ signifies the equivalent load that has been transformed to the primary side and is expressed as follows:

$$Req = \frac{8n^2}{\pi^2}\frac{Vout}{Iout} = \frac{8n^2}{\pi^2}\frac{Vout^2}{Pout}$$

where n is the the transformer ratio and Iout, Vout, and Pout denote the output current, voltage, and power, respectively.

When the output voltage limits the voltage across the terminals of Lm, the resonant frequency that results in the main resonant frequency is:

$$f_{r1} = \frac{1}{2\pi\sqrt{L_{r1}C_{r1}}}$$

When $L_y$ is not constrained by the resultant output, the corresponding resonant frequency becomes the secondary resonant frequency:

$$f_{r2} = \frac{1}{2\pi\sqrt{(L_{r1}+L_m)C_{r1}}}$$

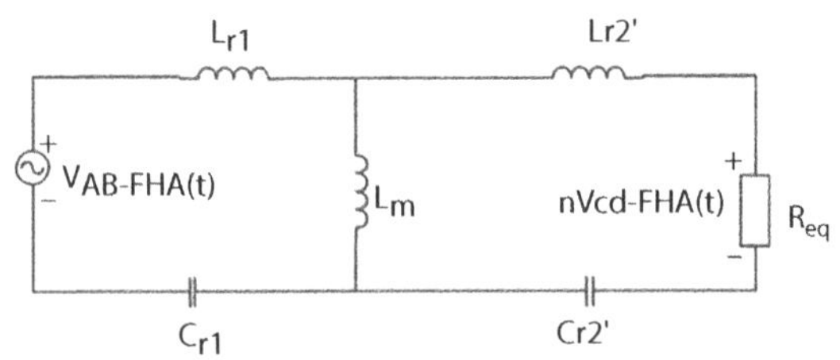


**Figure 8.2** Equivalent circuit of CLLC converter.

The impedance can be defined as:

$$\begin{Bmatrix} Z1 = j\omega_s L_{r1} + 1/(j\omega_s C_{r1}) \\ Z2 = j\omega_s L_{r2}' + 1/(j\omega_s C_{r2}'), \\ Z_m = j\omega_s L_m \end{Bmatrix}$$

The converter's transfer function can be expressed as, where Z1 represents the series resonant impedance on the primary side, Z2 represents the equivalent series resonant impedance on the secondary side, Zm is the excitation inductance impedance, and ωs is the switching angular frequency, where ωs is equal to 2πfs, as depicted in Figure 8.2.

$$H_{(j\omega s)} = \frac{nV_{CD\_FHA(t)}}{V_{AB\_FHA(t)}} = \frac{Z_m //(Z_2 + R_{eq})}{Z_1 + Z_m //(Z_2 + R_{eq})} \cdot \frac{R_{eq}}{Z_2 + R_{eq}'}$$

By substituting the equations for the impedance and transfer function of the converter,

$$M_{(fn)} = \frac{1}{\sqrt{\left(1 + \frac{1}{k} - \frac{1}{kf^2_n}\right)^2 + \left[Qf_n\left(2 + \frac{1}{k}\right) - \frac{Q}{fn}\left(2 + \frac{2}{k}\right) + \frac{Q}{kf^3_n}\right]^2}}$$

the inductance coefficient, denoted as k, is defined as the ratio of $L_m$ to $L_{r1}$. The quality factor, represented by Q, is determined by the reciprocal of L1, $C_{r1}$, and Req. $f_n$ corresponds to the normalized frequency, where $f_n$ is calculated as the ratio of $f_s$ to $f_{r1}$ and f indicates the actual switching frequency. The equation for the voltage gain (M) reveals that the voltage gain (M) of the CLLC resonating converter is influenced by the parameters Q, k, and f. Among these parameters, k and Q significantly contributed to determining the voltage gain, as discussed in the subsequent analysis.

## 8.4 How the Inductance Factor (k) Affects Voltage Gain (M)

Figure 8.3 depicts the relationship between the normalized frequency and the voltage gain with varying coefficients of inductance k and given quality factor (Q) = 0.3. At $f_n = 1$, the resonating frequency aligns with the switching frequency, resulting in operation at the point of resonance, where the voltage gain remains constant at 1 despite the effect of k. In the sub-resonant region, a low value of k indicates the maximum or high voltage gain and a narrow range of frequency modulation, facilitating wide gain adjustment. Conversely, increasing k causes a gradual decrease in the peak converter voltage gain, normalized frequency at maximum gain, and broadening of the range of frequency modulation. In the over-resonant region, the curve becomes smoother for voltage gain, which restricts the effectiveness of adjusting the gain through the switching frequency. To maintain gain stability around the resonance point, a larger k value is recommended. However, exceeding a certain k value results in the converter's peak voltage gain falling below the required maximum, which is accompanied by an excessively low minimum switching frequency.

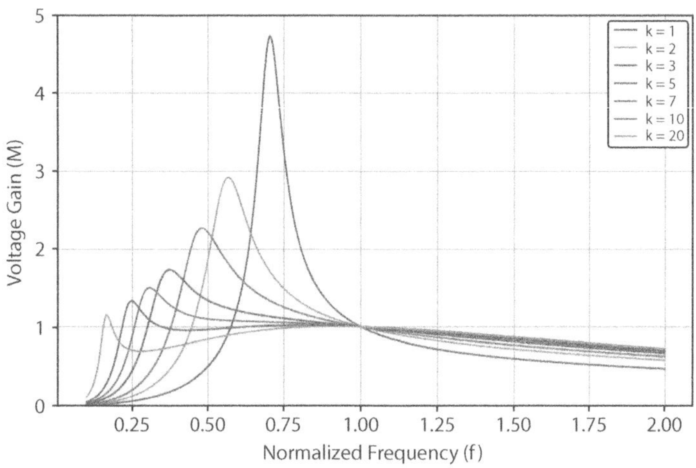


**Figure 8.3** Gain characteristic curve for different k values.

## 8.5 How the Quality Factor (Q) Influences Voltage Gain (M)

Figure 8.4 illustrates such plots that depict normalized frequency versus voltage gain for varying quality factors with a value of k = 5. At fn = 1, the resonating frequency aligns with the switching frequency, operating it at the resonance point where the voltage gain remains constant at 1 despite changes in Q. Under light load conditions, characterized by small Q values, reducing the switching frequency in the under-resonant region significantly boosts the converter's gain. However, increasing the switching frequency in the over-resonant region only slightly reduces the converter's gain, exhibiting a low-frequency adjustment effect. High frequency is essential for voltage regulation but leads to increased switching loss. Hence, selecting an appropriate Q value is crucial for ensuring that the converter encounters the minimum requirement for voltage gain under light-load conditions without exceeding a very high maximum switching frequency. As Q increases, the resultant load becomes more substantial. In the over-resonant region, the switching frequency changes the converter gain. However, under an excessive load, the peak gain value in the under-resonant region diminishes. Lowering the switching frequency to broaden the frequency modulation is necessary to achieve maximum voltage gain. The curve for the voltage gain displays two peak points, which

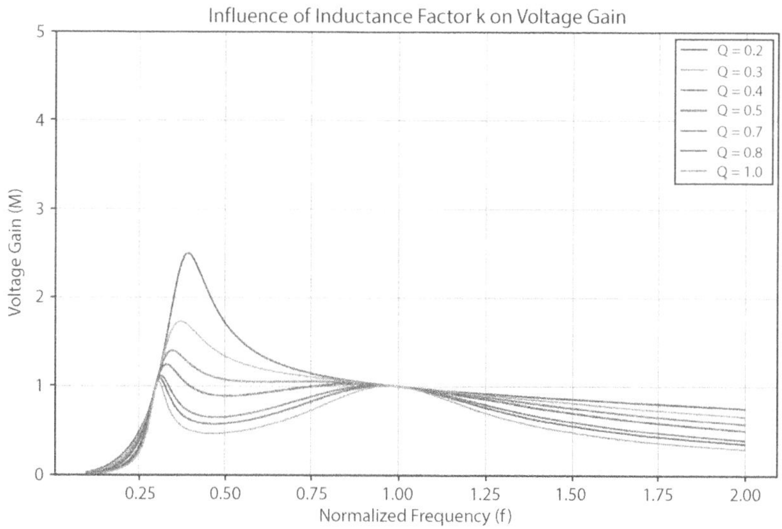


**Figure 8.4** Gain characteristics of CLLC converter for different Q values.

show the challenges in ensuring converter stability and designing the control system. Therefore, a balanced approach is crucial for selecting the Q value.

After the completion of the first half-cycle in the converter, the primary-side switching tube continues to have an inductor current $i_{Lr}$ flowing across the circuit. This current is responsible for discharging and recharging parasitic capacitance ($C_{oss}$). It is presumed that the current in the switching tube, denoted by $i_{Lr}$, remains constant during $t_d$ (dead time), and $C_{oss}$ for the switching tube remains constant. In case zero-voltage switching (ZVS) conditions are required, the current i must exceed the minimum necessary for charging and discharging the output capacitance (Coss) during the dead interval.

$$i_{Lr}t_d \geq CossU_{Coss'}$$

## 8.6 Understanding Frequency-Conversion Control

When the converter uses the phase-shift control technique, a new voltage waveform appears in the input resonant cavity (Uxp). This waveform was different from the original square wave with a 50% duty cycle. The new waveform is a square wave with a duty cycle of not more than 50% and at the zero-voltage level. Based on this circuit model and the analysis in Figure 8.2, we can calculate the most important component (AC component) of this new, phase-shifted square wave.

$$U'\,AB1(t) = \frac{2[1+\cos(D\pi)]U_1}{\pi}\sin(\omega t = \varphi),$$

where D represents the phase shift, D = ¢ /7, 0 < D < 1, and ¢ represents the phase shift angle. From the above equation and the transfer function of the converter, we derived a voltage equation under phase-shift control:

$$M_{PS} = \frac{1+\cos(D\pi)}{2}$$

Phase-shift control significantly affects voltage behavior. The gain, which can be thought of as a multiplier for the voltage, becomes roughly like a cosine function when plotted against a parameter called "D." This function oscillates between zero and one, affecting the overall voltage level.

There is a specific period, 0.5(1 – D)Ts, during which the voltage across the Lm2 component (a two-terminal element) is denoted as U2. To achieve a smooth switching process (soft switching) during dead time (td), a crucial condition must be met. This condition essentially states that the voltage across a capacitor (Coss) must be greater than a certain threshold ($U_{Coss}$) during this dead time.

$$M_{\min} = \frac{8L_{m2}C_{oss}}{(1-D)T_s t_d'}$$

## 8.7 Combining Frequency Conversion and Phase Shifting with a Hybrid Control Strategy

The voltage gain relationship curve with the normalized frequency fn and phase-shift ratio D can be derived by combining equations. The curve is shown in Figure 8.5. Frequency conversion and phase-shift control were applied to the bidirectional CLLC resonant converter. With the quality factor set at 0.3, controlling the converter solely with frequency conversion results in a narrow voltage gain range, requiring significant adjustments in the switching frequency. However, using phase-shift control limits the maximum voltage gain to 1, which is achievable in step-down mode, with the minimum voltage gain significantly lower than that under frequency-conversion control. To address this, a novel approach of hybrid control involving both phase shift and frequency conversion is proposed in this study to expand the range of the voltage gain. At this resonance point, both the control methods exhibited identical working conditions. By defining this as a point of transition, a smooth shift in voltage amplification is accomplished: frequency-conversion regulation is applied when M is greater than 1, whereas phase-shift regulation is implemented when M is less than 1.

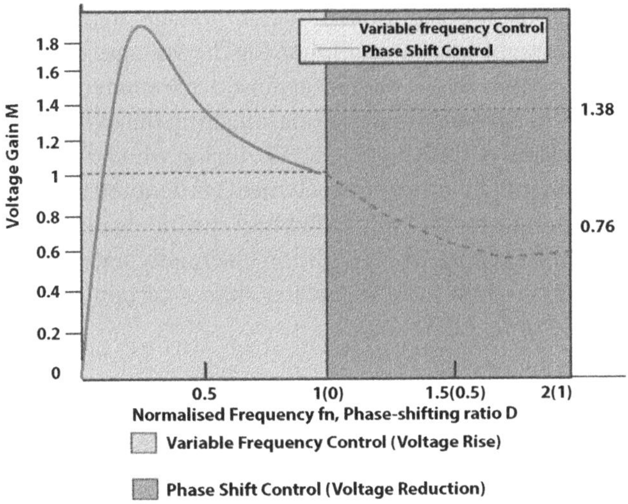


**Figure 8.5** Hybrid control of CLLC converter.

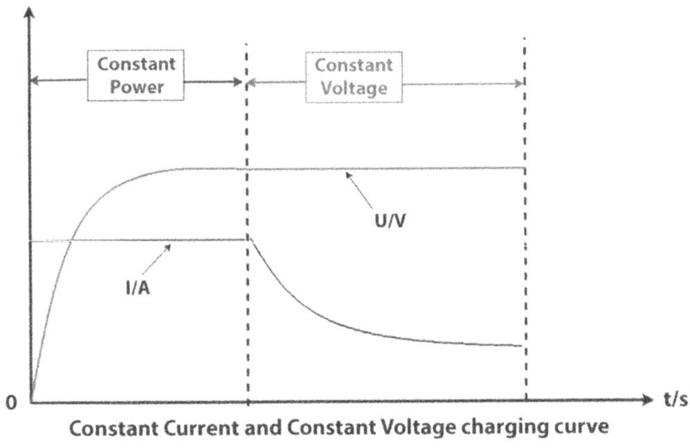


**Figure 8.6** CC-CV control of CLLC converter.

The bidirectional CLLC resonant converter developed in this study was utilized at the backend of an electric vehicle charger. The charging procedure typically involves two phases: initial constant-current charging followed by constant-voltage charging, as illustrated in Figure 8.6. In the constant-current charging phase, a set current was employed for charging, starting with the voltage of the battery below the specified level. The voltage loop remained saturated and was regulated solely by the current loop. As the charging advances, the voltage increases gradually until it reaches the specified level, indicating a shift to the constant-voltage charging phase. Throughout the phase, the voltage loop transitions out of saturation, resulting in a gradual reduction in the output value until it is under the regulation of the voltage loop, thereby setting up a scenario of constant-voltage charging scenario. Simultaneously, as the present loop becomes saturated, there is a gradual decrease in the charging current until it matches the battery's self-discharge current, thus concluding the charging procedure.

Figure 8.7 shows a block diagram illustrating the utilization of the hybrid control mode involving phase shift and frequency conversion. Throughout the procedure, the resistance load was employed by the load, with the voltage output and current serving as the criteria for assessment. To enable an automated transition between constant voltage and current loops, both current and voltage loops operate concurrently in the forward direction. By contrasting the sampled battery voltage with the reference value Uref, the system selects the stable current control mode if the voltage of the battery is below $U_{ref}$, and the stable voltage control mode if the voltage of battery is equal or exceed $U_{ref}$. In the reverse mode, a dual closed-loop control strategy for voltage and current was employed to transfer electrical energy from the battery to the primary side *via* the resonant cavity, ensuring a consistent output voltage of 400 V.

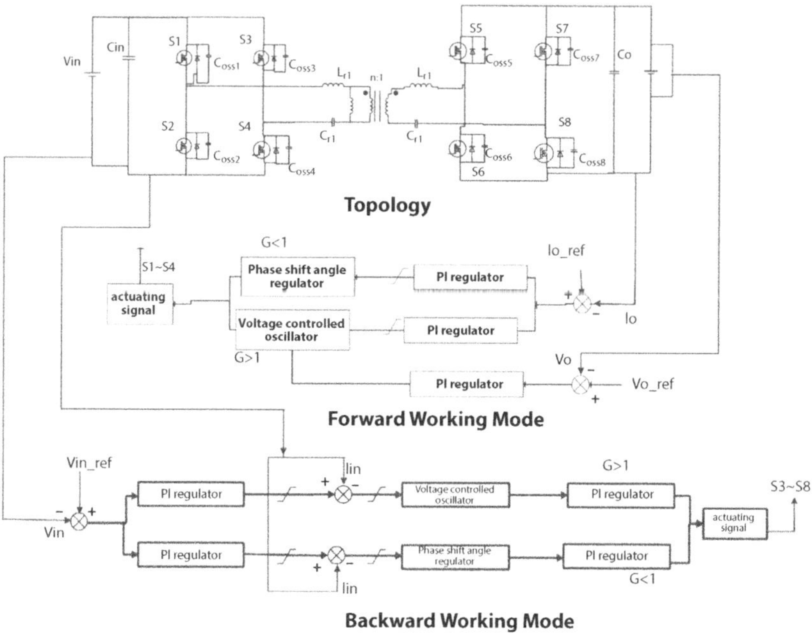


**Figure 8.7** Block diagram of hybrid controlled CLLC converter.

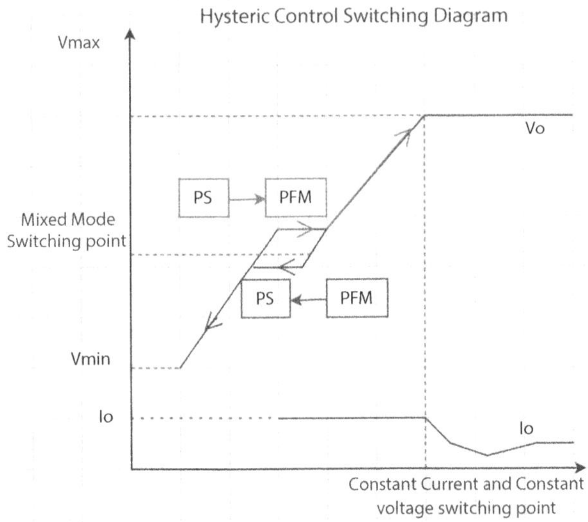


**Figure 8.8** Switching diagram with hysteresis control.

Figure 8.8 depicts the switching diagram with hysteresis control for the bidirectional CLLC resonant converter. This study utilized both the frequency and phase-shift control methods. To prevent unsteady oscillations, mode switching should be controlled *via* hysteresis rather than a single threshold transition. The system transitions from phase-shift control to frequency control upon reaching the maximum set point for voltage and from frequency control to phase-shift control when the voltage falls below the minimum set point. When setting the mode-switching threshold, we ensured that the maximum value for phase-shift control was higher than the minimum value for frequency control. The introduction of a buffer region enhances the reliability of the transition between these control modes.

## 8.8 Simulation Results and Discussion

The simulation of CLLC DC-DC converter is carried out for the following design specifications stated in Table 8.1.

**Table 8.1** Design parameters specifications.

| **Parameters** | **Specifications** |
|---|---|
| Power rating | 10 kW |
| Input DC voltage | 380–600 V |
| Resonant frequency | 100 kHz |
| Primary inductor | 22.6 μH |
| Primary capacitor | 112 nF |
| Magnetizing inductance | 180.8 μ H |
| Secondary inductor | 20.6 μH |
| Secondary capacitor | 90.7 nF |
| Battery capacity | 30.2 kWh |
| Battery voltage | 320 |

To analyze the converter's performance, a simulation was run for the aforementioned requirements in both the forward and reverse directions, that is, for charging and discharging batteries at different switching frequencies. The circuit is intended for a 10-kW power rating at a 400 V input voltage, as shown in Figure 8.9. Converter performance at different frequencies, i.e., below, at, and above the magnetizing inductance current, secondary-side resonant current and voltage, and primary-side resonant current and voltage at a resonant frequency of 110 kHz. Figure 8.10 displays the 90 kHz frequency primary-side resonant current and voltage, secondary side resonant current and voltage, and magnetizing inductance current. At the resonant frequency (100 kHz), Figure 8.11 displays the primary-side resonant current and voltage, secondary-side resonant current and voltage, and magnetizing inductance current. In Figure 8.12, the magnetizing inductance current, secondary-side resonant current and voltage, and primary-side resonant current and voltage at 110 kHz. Figure 8.13 displays the waveforms after the converter's reverse operation was examined. The output voltage and current waveforms, which are pure DC appropriate for battery charging, are shown in Figure 8.14.

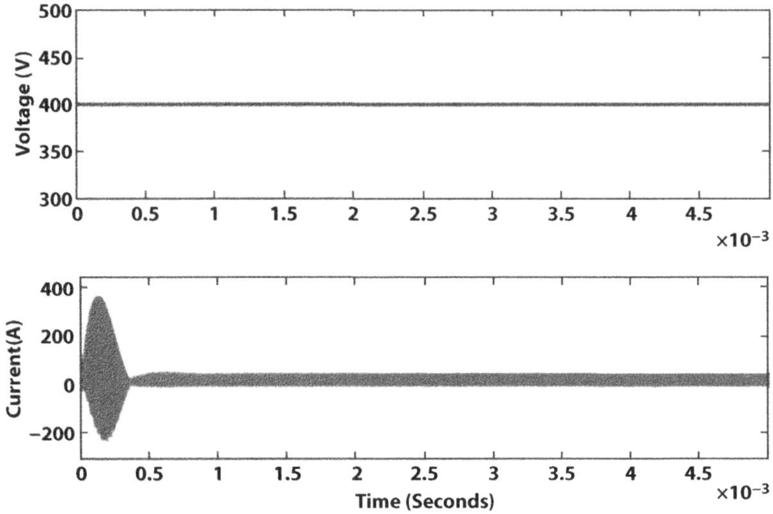


**Figure 8.9** Input voltage and current.

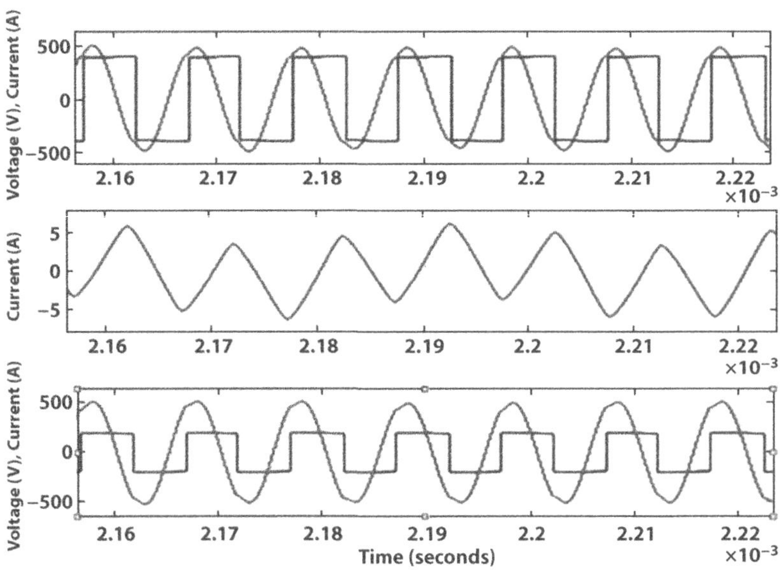


**Figure 8.10** Resonant tank current and voltage below resonant frequency.

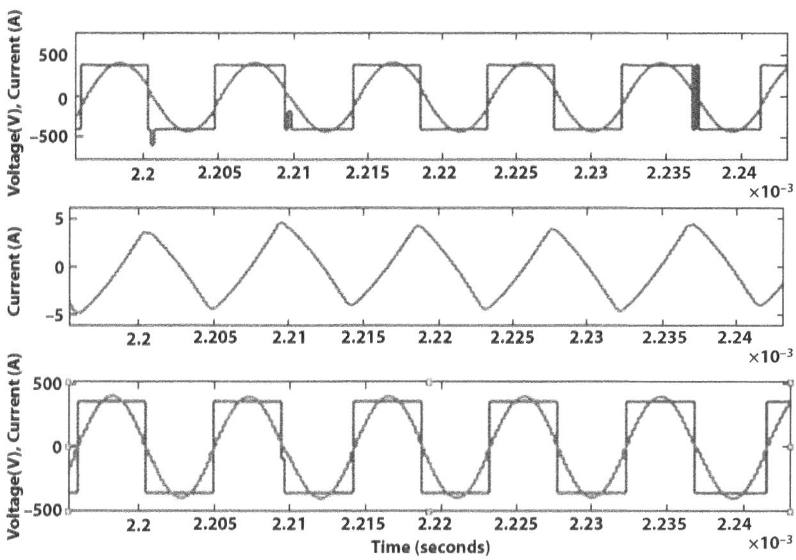


Figure 8.11 Resonant tank current and voltage at resonant frequency.

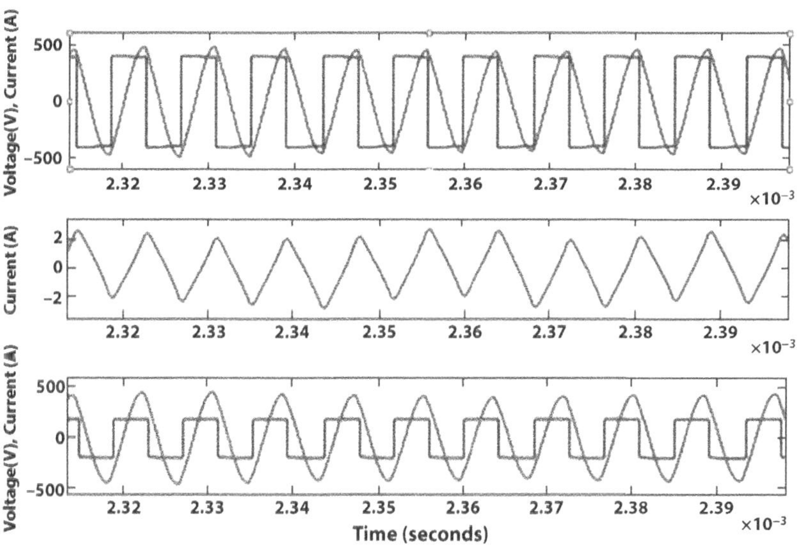


Figure 8.12 Resonant tank current and voltage above resonant frequency.

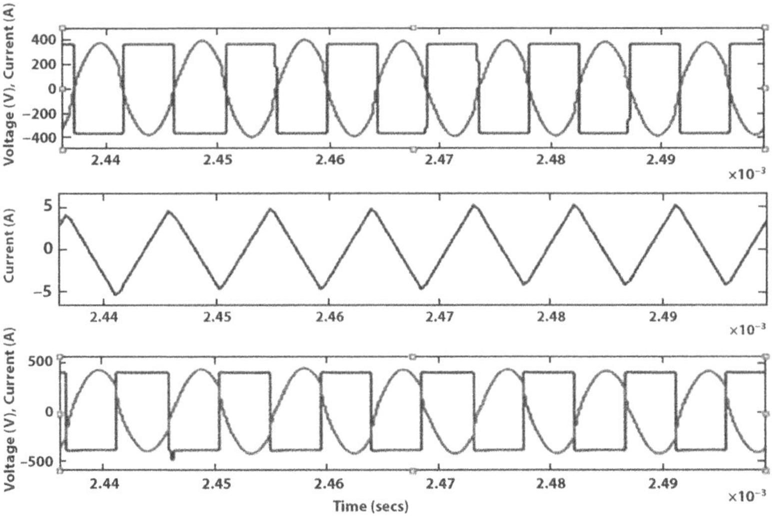


Figure 8.13 Resonant tank current and voltage in reverse direction.

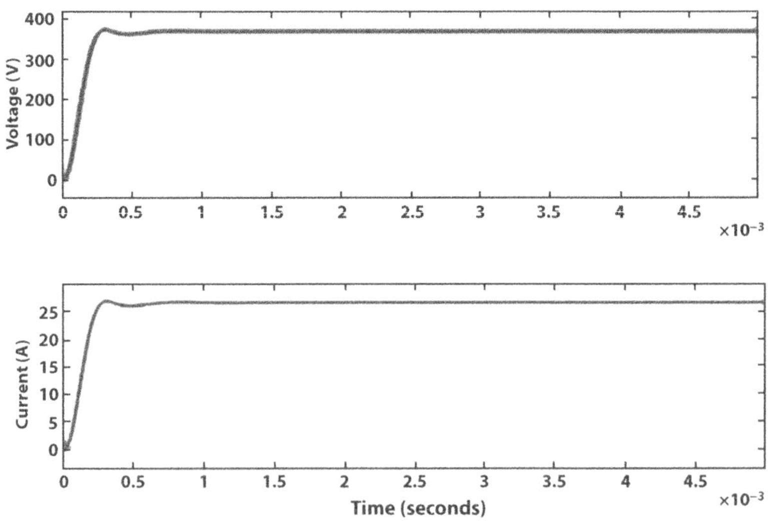


Figure 8.14 Output voltage and current.

## 8.9 Conclusion

In the current investigation, a new and innovative hybrid control approach that integrates frequency conversion and phase-shift techniques was devised for a bidirectional CLLLC resonant converter utilized in vehicle chargers. This unique strategy effectively broadens the voltage gain range and overcomes the constraints associated with the individual use of each control technique. When the voltage gain exceeds one (M >1), frequency-conversion control is implemented, while phase-shift control is utilized for voltage gains below one (M <1), ensuring a smooth and seamless transition of voltage gain at the resonance point, thereby optimizing the overall performance of the converter. The study conclusively shows that the proposed bidirectional CLLLC resonant converter functions efficiently throughout the charging process, which involves phases of constant current and voltage. This converter guarantees steady energy transfer and precise regulation of voltage and current, which are essential for the successful operation of vehicle chargers. The integration of this dual-mode control strategy not only extends the voltage gain range of the converter, but also guarantees reliable operation under diverse load conditions, thereby enhancing the overall efficiency and stability of the system. The outcomes of the research underscore the importance of carefully selecting suitable quality factors and inductance coefficients to fine-tune the converter's voltage gain, thereby ensuring consistent and efficient operational performance.

## References


1. Chen, H., Sun, K., Lu, L., Wang, S., Ouyang, M., A constantcurrent control method with improved dynamic performance for CLLC converters. *IEEE Trans. Power Electron.*, 37, 2, 1509 1523, 2021.
2. Wang, Y., Zhao, W., Liu, B., Li, W., Optimal design of resonant network for resonant converter. *IEEE Trans. Ind. Appl.*, 58, 6, 7469–7478, 2024.
3. Jin, N.Z., Feng, Y., Chen, Z.Y., Wu, X.G., Bidirectional CLLLC Resonant Converter Based on Frequency-Conversion and Phase-Shift Hybrid Control. *Electronics*, 12, 7, 1605, 2023.
4. Yang, N., Zeng, J., Hu, R., Liu, J., Analysis and design of an isolated high step-up converter without voltage-drop. *IEEE Trans. Power Electron.*, 37, 6, 6939–6950, 2021.
5. Min, J. and Ordonez, M., Bidirectional resonant CLLC charger for wide battery voltage range: Asymmetric parameters methodology. *IEEE Trans. Power Electron.*, 36, 6, 6662–6673, 2020.

6. Bai, C. and Kim, M., Bidirectional resonant converter with minimized switching loss over wide operating voltage range. *IEEE J. Emerg. Sel. Top. Power Electron.*, 10, 3, 2975–2988, 2021.
7. Park, H.P., Kim, M., Jung, J.H., Bidirectional current-fed CLLC resonant converter employing asymmetric PWM. *IEEE Trans. Energy Convers.*, 36, 4, 3167–3177, 2024.
8. Seminar, P.S.D., Designing an LLC Resonant Half-Bridge Power Converter, Hong Huang, Texas Instruments, Slup263, 2021.
9. Zou, S., Mallik, A., Lu, J., Khaligh, A., Sliding mode control scheme for a CLLC resonant converter. *IEEE Trans. Power Electron.*, 34, 12, 12274–12284, 2019.
10. Zhu, T., Zhuo, F., Zhao, F., Wang, F., Yi, H., Zhao, T., Optimization of extended phase-shift control for full-bridge CLLC resonant converter with improved light-load efficiency. *IEEE Trans. Power Electron.*, 35, 10, 11129–11142, 2023.

# 9

# IoT-Based Smart Charging Systems

**Tanmay Sharma, Pramatha S. Vasishtha and Razia Sultana W.***

*School of Electrical and Electronics, Vellore Institute of Technology, Vellore, Tamil Nadu, India*

***Abstract***

This study explores the profound impact of IoT integration in electric vehicles (EVs), ushering in an era of smart, connected, and sustainable transportation. It delves into various aspects, including user experience enhancement through remote monitoring and telematics, for real-time data gathering on vehicle performance and location. IoT facilitates efficient charging infrastructure connectivity, enabling smart stations to optimize energy usage and contributing to grid stability through vehicle-to-grid (V2G) technology. Moreover, IoT enhances autonomous driving capabilities, advanced driver assistance systems (ADAS), fleet operations, and consumer comfort by offering tailored in-car experiences and value-added services. Overall, the study advances the understanding of how IoT revolutionizes transportation, fosters innovation, and provides insights into its implications for the future of EVs.

***Keywords***: ADAS (advanced driver assistance system), Dijkstra's algorithm, Bellman Ford algorithm, A* search algorithm, Floyd Warshall algorithm, bidirectional search algorithm, RRT (rapidly exploring random tree) algorithm, PRM (probabilistic road map algorithm)

## Abbreviation

| | |
|---|---|
| EV | electric vehicle |
| IoT | Internet of Things |
| ADAS | advanced driver-assistance systems |

**Corresponding author*: wraziasultana@vit.ac.in

A. Chitra, W. Razia Sultana and V. Indragandhi (eds.) Smart Charging Infrastructures, (175–194)

## 9.1 Introduction

An era of smart, connected, and sustainable transportation has been ushered in by the automotive industry's revolution through the integration of Internet of Things (IoT) technologies in electric cars (EVs) [1]. The implications of various IoT technologies in electric vehicles (EVs) are examined in this study, with a focus on how these technologies affect vehicle performance, energy efficiency, user experience, and sustainability of the ecosystem as a whole.

This study explores the complex network of sensors, communication systems, and data analytics that enables EVs to communicate in real time with their surroundings, other users, and the charging infrastructure *via* the IoT lens. It examines how smart grid integration, energy efficiency, vehicle diagnostics, maintenance, and user convenience are all improved by telematics and remote monitoring.

This study also examines how IoT enables autonomous driving capabilities and advanced driver assistance systems (ADAS) in EVs, enhancing road safety and efficiency. This study delves into the application of IoT in fleet, logistics, and energy management, highlighting the ways in which real-time data and analytics can propel operational efficiency and sustainability in commercial electric vehicle fleets.

Additionally, this study examines the consequences of IoT-powered services and customized in-car experiences, showing how EVs are evolving into whole mobility solutions catered to specific requirements and tastes rather than just being cars.

Through a thorough analysis of the implications of IoT technology in electric vehicles, this study seeks to offer important insights into how the IoT can revolutionize transportation in the future. It aims to foster more innovation in this exciting and rapidly developing subject while adding to the body of information already available on IoT applications in EVs [1].

## 9.2 Remote Monitoring and Telematics

In electric vehicles (EVs) [5], telematics and remote monitoring are essential for improving the vehicle performance, safety, and user experience. By utilizing the Internet of Things (IoT), these technologies enable users, cars, and external systems to communicate and collect data in real-time.

The monitoring and transmission of vehicle-related data through the integration of informatics and telecommunications are known as telematics.

Sensors, GPS receivers, and onboard diagnostic systems are common components of telematics systems for electric vehicles (EVs) that gather and send data on location, driving style, and vehicle performance.

Users and manufacturers can access and manage vehicle functions and data remotely using remote monitoring. This includes functions such as vehicle tracking, over-the-air software updates, and remote diagnostics. Proactive vehicle health management is made possible *via* remote monitoring, which also improves maintenance efficiency. The IoT, which offers a framework for linking cars to the Internet and other devices, is essential for enabling telematics and remote monitoring in electric vehicles. The IoT facilitates smooth data transfer between EVs, smart grids, and charging stations, enabling predictive maintenance, effective energy management, and improved user experience.

Advantages of Remote Monitoring and Telematics for EVs:

Effective Maintenance: By enabling preventive maintenance and decreasing downtime, telematics data can be utilized to track the health of vehicles in real time. Enhanced Driving Experience: Through remote monitoring, users can monitor energy usage, vehicle performance, and driving habits, which helps them improve the efficiency of their driving. Enhanced Safety: Real-time notifications from telematics systems about malfunctions or accidents in vehicles allow for prompt assistance and response. Energy Management: By offering insights into energy usage trends and suggesting effective driving routes, IoT-enabled telematics systems can optimize the energy consumption. User Convenience: Remote monitoring options to improve user comfort and convenience include car tracking and remote climate control.

## 9.3 Infrastructure Connectivity for Charging

Smart charging solutions for electric vehicles (EVs) are made possible by integrating Internet of Things (IoT) [5] technologies with infrastructure connectivity. Through the use of these technologies, EVs, charging stations, the electricity grid, and other equipment can communicate with each other, improving the efficiency and convenience of charging.

Smart charging stations that can interact with EVs to control charging schedules depending on variables like electricity pricing, grid demand, and user preferences are made possible by the Internet of Things. Dynamic charging rates are made possible by this connectivity, which maximizes the energy efficiency and lowers the expenses for EV owners.

Moreover, vehicle-to-grid (V2G) technology is made possible by IoT, enabling EVs to take energy from the grid and provide extra energy back when needed [5]. In addition to enhancing grid stability, this reciprocal flow of electricity can provide EV owners access to new cash streams.

In general, IoT technologies are essential for improving the EV charging infrastructure connectivity, which results in a more intelligent, effective, and sustainable charging process.

## 9.4 Autonomous Driving and Advanced Driver Assistance Systems (ADAS)

IoT technologies have improved [6] advanced driver assistance systems (ADAS) and autonomous driving in electric cars (EVs), especially when it comes to charging.

EVs can connect with grid systems, other cars, and charging infrastructure owing to IoT. Because cars may communicate information, such as location, speed, and traffic conditions, to make decisions about where to drive in real time, this connectivity is essential for autonomous driving. IoT also helps the ADAS by supplying the data required for functions such as collision avoidance systems, adaptive cruise control, and lane-keeping assistance. These systems use cameras and sensors to gather information regarding the environment around a car. Real-time analysis and processing of these data is possible owing to the Internet of Things technologies.

IoT is crucial to the operation of ADAS and autonomous driving in EVs because it offers the connectivity and data processing power required for these systems to function effectively and securely.

## 9.5 Logistics and Fleet Management

Internet of Things (IoT) technologies have a significant impact on [5] fleet management and logistics for electric vehicles (EVs), particularly when it comes to charging.

With the help of the IoT, fleet managers can track and monitor electric vehicle fleets in real time, plan maintenance, and minimize downtime. To maintain cars in top condition, this connectivity also makes remote diagnostics and predictive maintenance possible.

The IoT also provides smart charging options for EV fleets. To control charging schedules based on variables such as energy pricing and grid demand, charging stations can interact with one another as well as with cars. This reduces operating expenses and downtime by ensuring that the cars are charged effectively and economically. IoT technologies are essential for enhancing EV fleet management and logistics because they offer real-time data and connections that facilitate productive, economical, and environmentally friendly operations.

## 9.6 Sustainability and Energy Management

Integration of Renewable Energy Sources: IoT makes it possible for EVs to interact with renewable energy sources, such as solar panels. Through the use of IoT, EVs may plan their charging to occur during times when renewable energy production is at its highest, optimizing the usage of clean energy and lowering dependency on fossil fuels.

Smart Grid Interaction: To improve charging patterns, EVs with IoT capabilities can interact with the smart grid. For instance, when the electricity demand is low during off-peak hours, EVs can charge, which might ease the burden on the grid and possibly cut consumer energy bills. Demand Response: IoT-enabled electric vehicles (EVs) have the option of participating in demand response programs, in which they modify their charging speeds in response to grid operator signals. This increases the stability and efficiency of the grid by balancing the supply and demand. IoT sensors in electric vehicles (EVs) can be used for energy monitoring and optimization. They can also be used to gather information regarding driving and charging habits. Using these data, energy expenses can be decreased overall, battery life can be increased, and energy consumption can be optimized.

Vehicle-to-Grid (V2G) Technology: Made possible by the Internet of Things, V2G technology enables EVs to take energy from and return excess energy to the grid. In addition to providing EV owners with a source of income, this two-way flow of electricity can help stabilize the grid and reduce the need for additional energy storage.

Lifecycle Assessment: From production to disposal, the environmental impact of EVs can be monitored *via* the Internet of Things. Policymakers and manufacturers can use this information to make informed decisions that will lower the overall environmental footprint of EVs.

## 9.7 Services and User Experience

Personalized Charging Experience: With the help of IoT, EVs can interact with charging stations to modify the charging parameters according to user preferences and energy costs. EV users can charge their cars at the most affordable and convenient time because of our customized charging experience.

Remote Monitoring and Control: Using online interfaces or mobile apps, EV owners can use the Internet of Things to remotely monitor and control the charging state of their vehicles. This function allows customers control their charging needs anywhere, giving them convenience and peace of mind.

Cost savings and energy efficiency: IoT-enabled EVs may optimize their charging schedules in response to grid demand and energy prices, which helps users save money on charging costs. Furthermore, energy waste can be decreased, and a more sustainable energy system can be promoted *via* smart charging systems. Integration with Smart household Systems: EVs can be seamlessly integrated with household appliances, energy management systems, and vehicles owing to the Internet of Things. Overall, the user experience can be improved, and energy usage can be further optimized with this integration.

Value-Added Services: Predictive maintenance, remote diagnostics, and location-based services are just a few of the value-added services that the Internet of Things makes possible. These services can boost safety, improve vehicle performance, and make EV use more convenient. Data-Driven insights: IoT sensors in electric vehicles can gather and examine data on driving habits, charging habits, and overall vehicle performance. Insights from this data can help manufacturers, service providers, and owners of electric vehicles (EVs) enhance their offerings.

## 9.8 Algorithms for Shortest Path Finding

### 9.8.1 Dijkstra's Algorithm

Dijkstra's algorithm [2] is used to determine the shortest paths between nodes in a weighted graph, which can model a road network. This algorithm computes the shortest path from a starting node to all other nodes in the graph. If the nodes represent cities and the edge weights denote the driving distances between these cities (disregarding traffic signals, tolls, and other obstacles), Dijkstra's algorithm effectively determines the shortest route

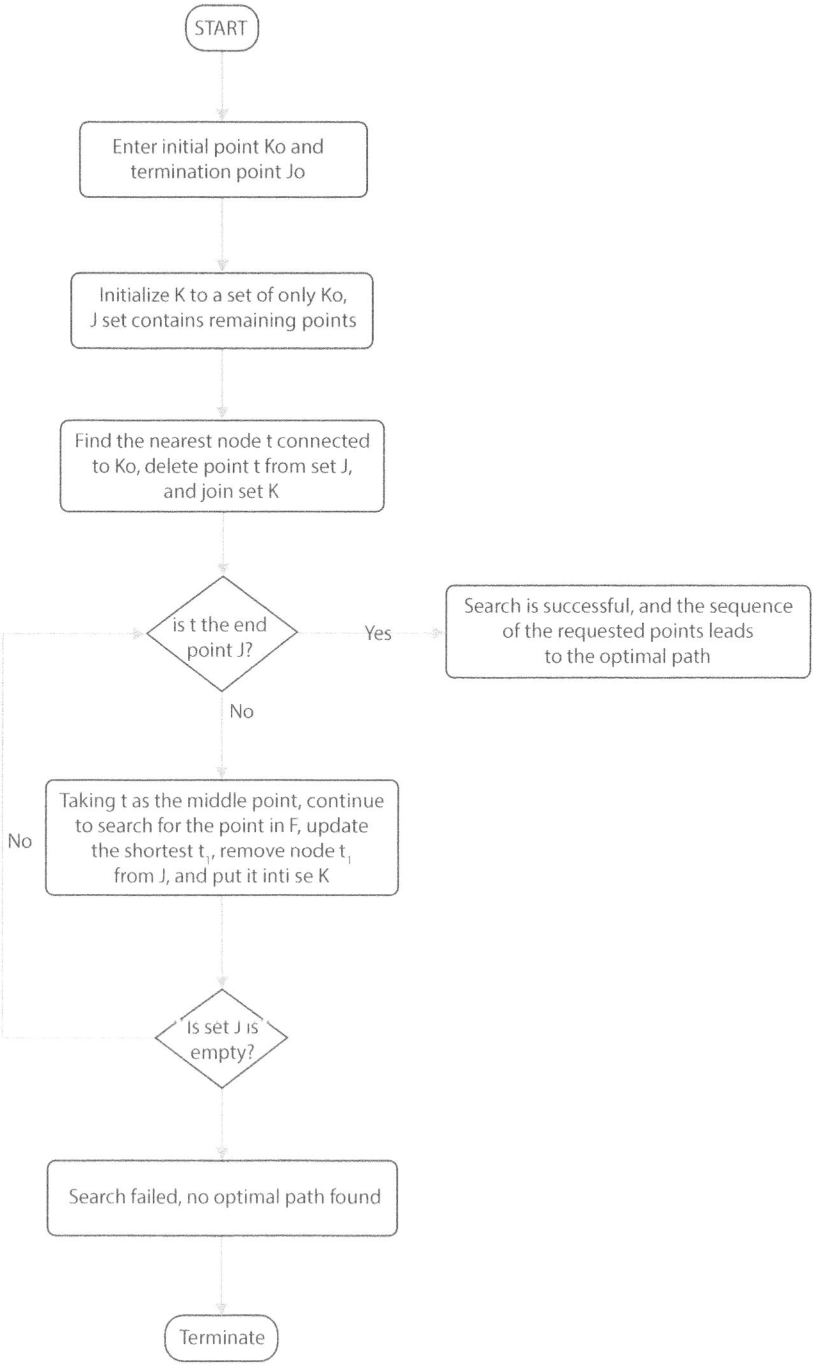


**Figure 9.1** Flowchart for Dijkstra's algorithm.

between any pair of cities. The algorithm utilizes real numbers or positive integers for its labels and relies on a data structure to manage and retrieve partial solutions based on their distance from the starting point. The original version of Dijkstra's algorithm operates with a specific time complexity and does not employ a min-priority queue. The detailed flow of operations is illustrated in Figure 9.1, which provides a step-by-step representation of how the algorithm progresses through the graph. $\vartheta(|v|2)$ (where $|v|$ denotes the number of nodes). The running time complexity of Dijkstra's algorithm can be enhanced by employing a Fibonacci heap as a min-priority queue. This optimization reduces the complexity of $\vartheta(E + V\ log\ V)$. This is asymptotically the fastest single-source shortest-path algorithm available for any directed graph with non-negative weights. Dijkstra's algorithm, or its variations, is often referred to as a "uniform cost search" in various domains, including artificial intelligence. It serves as an example of the more general concept of best-first search.

### 9.8.2 Bellman–Ford Algorithm

The Bellman–Ford algorithm [3] is used in weighted directed graphs to find the shortest paths from a single source vertex to all the other vertices. Unlike Dijkstra's algorithm, Bellman–Ford can handle graphs with negative edge weights, making it more flexible for certain applications where negative weights are present. Negative edge weights are common in various graph problems, which is one of the reasons for the algorithm's effectiveness. If there is a "negative cycle" reachable from the source, the path cost can be continually reduced by repeatedly traversing this cycle, preventing the identification of the shortest path. In such cases, the Bellman–Ford algorithm can detect and report the presence of negative cycles.

### 9.8.3 A* Search Algorithm

The A* algorithm is a widely used graph traversal and pathfinding technique in various fields of computer science owing to its efficiency, optimality, and completeness. It works on weighted graphs to find the shortest path from a source node to a target node by considering the given weights. However, a significant practical limitation of A* is the $O(b^d)$. A major drawback of the A* algorithm [2] is its high space complexity because it stores all generated nodes in memory. This can lead to performance issues, especially in large-scale applications such as real-world travel routing systems, where memory-efficient algorithms or preprocessing techniques often outperform A*. However, A* remains the preferred choice in several scenarios. This can be viewed as an enhancement of Dijkstra's algorithm, improving performance by guiding its search using heuristics. Unlike Dijkstra's algorithm, which finds the shortest-path tree from a source to all possible targets, A* focuses solely on finding the shortest path from a specific source to a specified goal.

### 9.8.4 Floyd–Warshall Algorithm

The visual characteristics of the open space, determined by the local planner, affect the convergence rate of the algorithm. The Probabilistic Roadmap

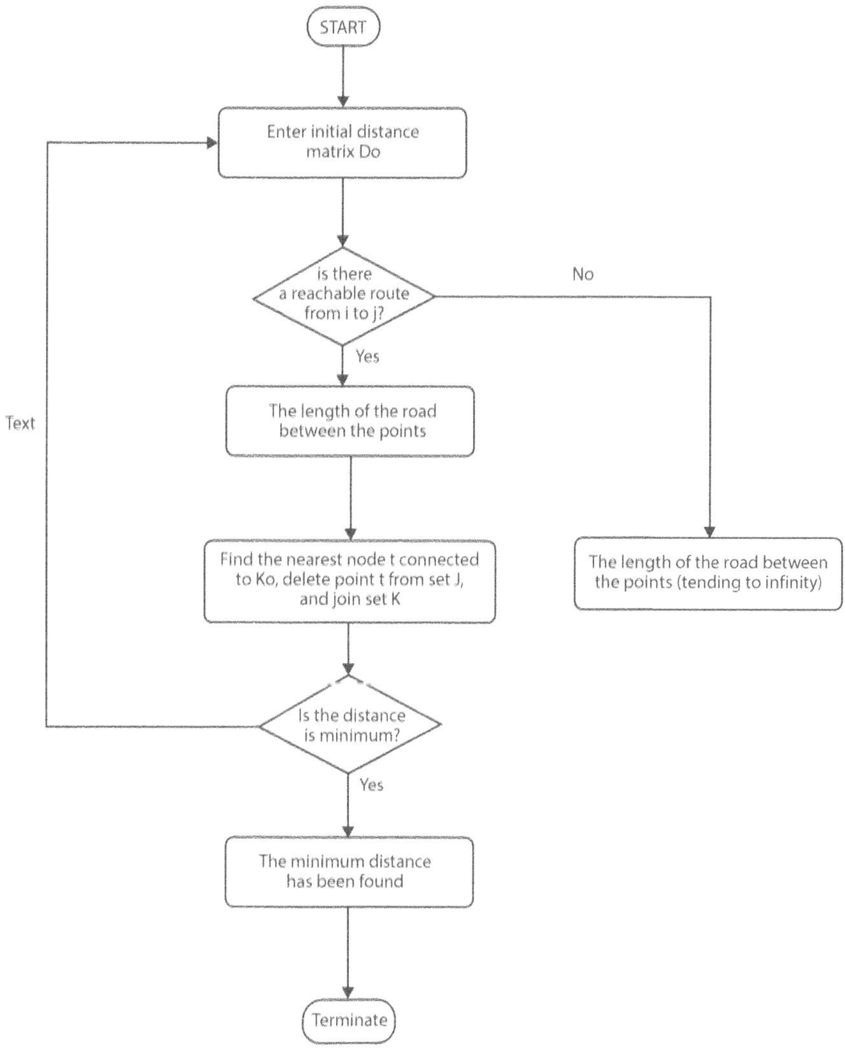


**Figure 9.2** Flowchart for Floyd–Warshall algorithm.

(pPRM) algorithm is known to be probabilistically complete, meaning that the likelihood of failing to find a path, if one exists, approaches zero as the number of sampled points increases indefinitely, given some relatively simple conditions on the free space's structure. The performance of the Floyd–Warshall algorithm, which is used to determine the shortest paths in a directed weighted graph with positive or negative edge weights (but no negative cycles), is also influenced by these observable features of the open space set by the local planner. The algorithm, also known as Floyd's algorithm, the Roy–Warshall algorithm, the Roy–Floyd algorithm, or the WFI algorithm, calculates the shortest path lengths (summed weights) between all pairs of vertices in a single execution. Although it does not directly provide the paths, it can be reconstructed with minor modifications to the method. Variations in this algorithm are also used to determine the transitive closure of a relation in the Schulze voting system or to find the widest paths between all pairs of vertices in a weighted graph. The detailed flow of operations is illustrated in Figure 9.2, which provides a step-by-step representation of how the algorithm progresses through the graph.

### 9.8.5 Bidirectional Search Algorithm

Bidirectional search is a graph-search technique used to find the shortest path between a starting vertex and a goal vertex in a directed graph. This method performs two simultaneous searches, one forward from the starting point and one backward from the goal, meeting somewhere in the middle. This approach is often preferred because it is significantly faster than a single-direction search. In a basic model of search problem complexity, each search tree has a branching factor of $b$ and depth of $d$ from the start to the goal. By dividing the search into two parts, the overall complexity is significantly reduced, making the process more efficient. O $(b^{d/2})$ (in Big O notation), and the sum of these two search times is much less than $O(b^d)$. This bidirectional search strategy effectively reduces the complexity compared to a single search from the start to the goal. Similar to the A* algorithm, bidirectional search [3] can also be guided by heuristics, in which heuristics estimate the distance from the start, whereas in the forward search, they estimate the remaining distance to the goal. This heuristic guidance makes the search process even more efficient by focusing the search direction towards the intersection point of the two searches. The detailed flow of operations is illustrated in Figure 9.3, which provides a step-by-step representation of how the algorithm progresses through the graph.

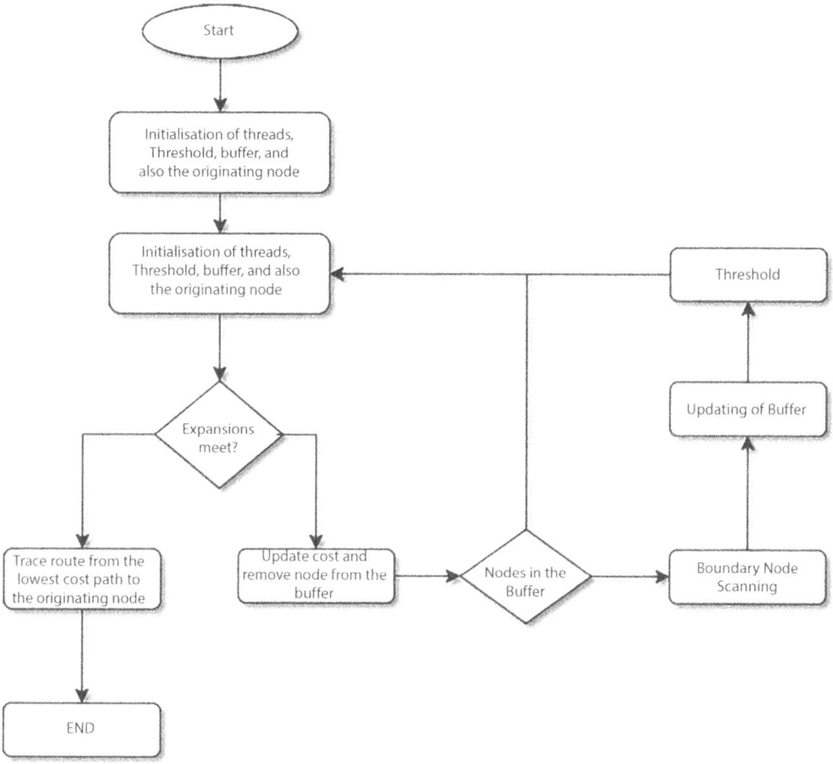


**Figure 9.3** Flowchart for bi-directional search algorithm.

### 9.8.6 Rapidly Exploring Random Tree Algorithm

The Rapidly Exploring Random Tree (RRT) algorithm [4] is an efficient method for searching high-dimensional, nonconvex spaces by incrementally building a space-filling tree using randomly sampled points from the search area. Owing to its progressive construction from random samples, RRT inherently tends to expand into unexplored, large regions of the problem space, making it highly suitable for handling barriers and constraints, such as nonholonomic and kinodynamic limitations, which are common in autonomous robotic motion planning.

RRTs are often used to generate open-loop trajectories for nonlinear systems with state constraints. Conceptually, RRTs [4] can be viewed as a Monte Carlo method that biases the search toward the largest Voronoi regions of the graph, similar to stochastic fractals. They are also employed to compute approximate control laws for complex high-dimensional nonlinear systems with restrictions on states and actions.

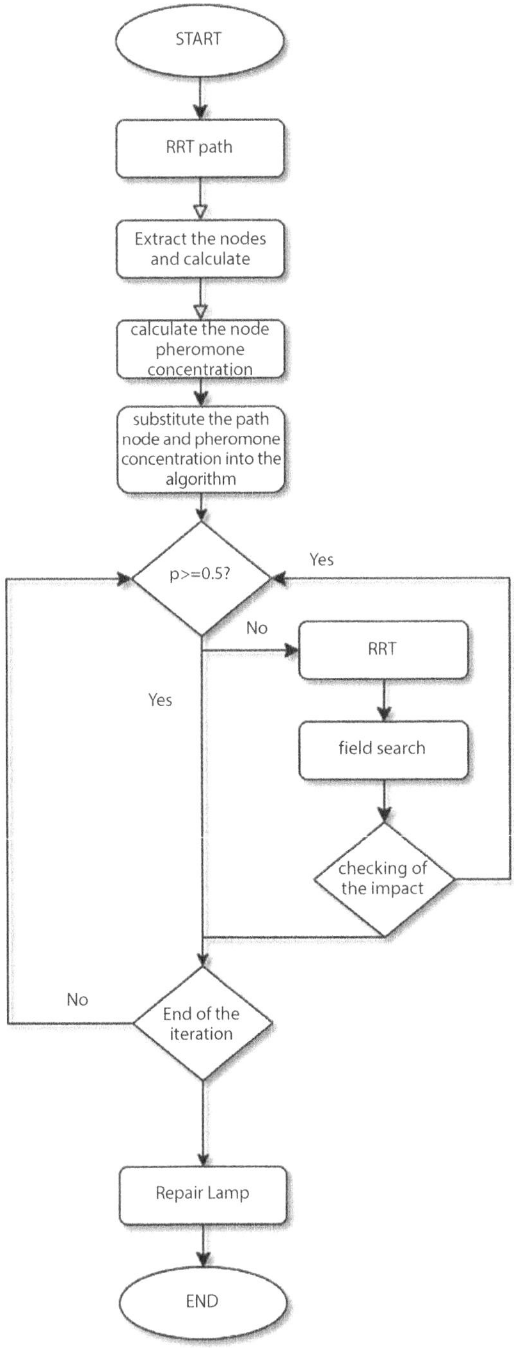


**Figure 9.4** Flow chart for RRT algorithm.

The RRT algorithm grows a tree starting from the initial configuration by randomly sampling the search space and connecting each sample to the nearest existing state in the tree. A new state is added only if the connection is feasible, meaning that it traverses open areas and complies with all constraints. The probability of expanding a state is determined by the size of its Voronoi region, with larger regions often found at the tree's frontier allowing the tree to extend into unexplored areas.

The growth of the RRT is often constrained by a growth factor that limits the extent to which a new state can be from the tree. If a random sample is too distant, the algorithm selects a state at the maximum allowable distance along the path to the sample, maintaining the tree's expansive yet controlled growth pattern. The growth direction is influenced by random samples, whereas the growth factor dictates the expansion rate.

RRT growth can be further adjusted by increasing the likelihood of selecting states from specific regions, effectively directing the search toward planning objectives. Practical implementations often incorporate a small probability of sampling directly toward the target, which causes the tree to grow more aggressively in that direction as the probability increases. This targeted sampling strategy helps focus the search on achieving specific goals within the planning problem. The detailed flow of operations is illustrated in Figure 9.4, which provides a step-by-step representation of how the algorithm progresses through the graph.

### 9.8.7 Probabilistic Roadmap Algorithm

The probabilistic roadmap planner (PRM) [3] is a motion planning technique in robotics that addresses the challenge of finding a collision-free path for a robot, ensuring that its intended and initial configurations do not conflict with the obstacles. The PRM operates in two main phases: the construction phase and query phase.

During the construction phase, a roadmap or graph is generated to approximate the robot's potential movements within the surrounding environment. This is done by randomly sampling configurations and connecting each to a few nearby nodes, such as the k-nearest neighbors or all neighbors within a specified radius. Configurations and connections were continually added to the roadmap until they reached the desired density.

In the query phase, the initial and target configurations are connected to the roadmap, and the shortest path between them is determined using Dijkstra's shortest path algorithm. The convergence rate of PRM is influenced by the local planner, which defines the visible characteristics of the open space.

PRM [3] is known to be probabilistically complete, meaning that the probability of failing to find a path, if one exists, approaches zero as the number of sampled points increases indefinitely. This property relies on

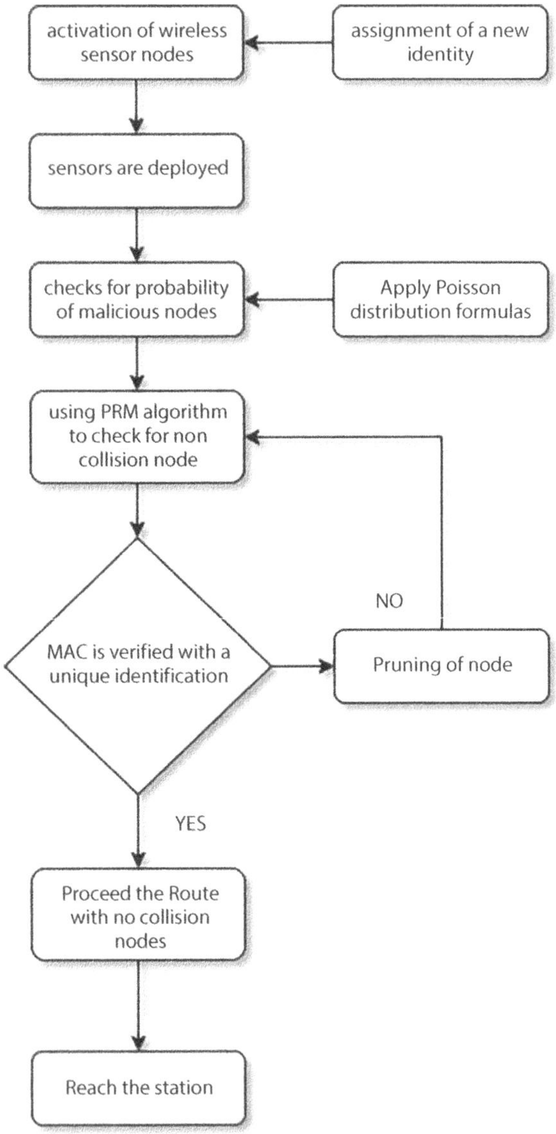


**Figure 9.5** Flow chart for PRM algorithm.

fairly lenient conditions in the structure of free space. If every point within the space has visibility over a significant portion of the environment and large subsets of the space can see considerable portions of their complementary areas, the planner is more likely to quickly identify a valid path. The detailed flow of operations is illustrated in Figure 9.5, which provides a step-by-step representation of how the algorithm progresses through the graph.

### 9.8.8 Hybrid RRT-PRM Model

Hybrid RRT-PRM [4] is an innovative sampling-based algorithm that merges the strengths of both Rapidly Exploring Random Tree (RRT) and Probabilistic Roadmap (PRM) methods to produce shorter and more efficient paths. This hybrid approach uses various initialization parameters such as the maximum number of nearest nodes for each node in the roadmap, start and goal locations, search area boundaries, number of iterations, maximum edge expansion distance, and list of obstacles.

After initialization, the algorithm plans two distinct paths: one generated by the RRT approach, and the other by the PRM planner. The combination of these two pathways leverages the exploratory power of RRT with the connectivity efficiency of the PRM, allowing for a more optimized solution to path-planning problems. The following equations define the methodologies used to establish these paths and refine them for optimal results:

- $path_{rrt} = [[r_{x1}, r_{y1}], [r_{x2}, r_{y2}], \ldots, [r_{xn}, r_{yn}]]$
- $path_{rrt} = [[P_{x1}, P_{y1}], [P_{x2}, P_{y2}], \ldots, [P_{xm}, P_{ym}]]$

In the context of the Hybrid RRT-PRM algorithm [4], let ($rx1$, $ry1$) represent the coordinates of the first node in the RRT path, where 'pathrrt' denotes the list of nodes in the RRT path, and $n$ is the total number of nodes in this path. Similarly, the PRM path comprises $m$ nodes, with the first node having coordinates ($px1$, $py1$), and 'pathprm' is the list of nodes in this path.

To generate a combined path, the algorithm integrates the nodes from both RRT and PRM paths into a single list. This combined list incorporates the nodes from 'pathrrt' and 'pathprm,' providing a unified sequence of nodes that represents the paths determined by both approaches. This combined list is used to evaluate and optimize the overall path to ensure that it meets the desired criteria for efficiency and smoothness:

- $path_{combined}=[[r_{x1},r_{y1}],[r_{x2},r_{y2}],...,[r_{xn},r_{yn}],[P_{x1},P_{y1}],[P_{x2},P_{y2}],...,[P_{xm},P_{ym}]]$

In the Hybrid RRT-PRM algorithm, the combined list of nodes is referred to as 'pathcombined.' The initial and final nodes from the RRT path were excluded from this list because they were already included in the PRM path. To compute the number of points in the 'pathcombined,' the following formula is used:

$$s = n + m - 2$$

Here, $n$ is the number of nodes in the RRT path and $m$ is the number of nodes in the PRM path. The resulting number $s$ represents the total number of nodes in the combined list, excluding the first and last nodes from the RRT path.

The combined list of nodes was then converted into an array. The Hybrid RRT-PRM algorithm checks whether a predefined number of points have been produced from the search region around the start and goal locations. To achieve this, the convex hull of the search region is determined by combining the outermost points in 'pathcombined.' If the convex hull does not contain sufficient points, a random point is selected from the entire rectangular search region.

Linear programming was then employed to verify whether a random point was inside the convex hull. Linear programming is a mathematical optimization technique used to maximize or minimize the function subject to constraints. The general linear programming problem is defined as follows:

1. **Objective Function**: Maximize (or minimize) a linear function $c^T x$, where $c$ is a vector of coefficients and $x$ is a vector of variables.
2. **Constraints**: Satisfy a set of linear inequalities or equalities of the form $Ax \leq b$, where $A$ is a matrix of coefficients, and $b$ is a vector of constants.

The solution to this problem provides the optimal value of the objective function, subject to the given constraints:

- $min_x \mathbf{cs}$ such that $A_{eq}\mathbf{x} = b_{eq}$ and $\mathbf{x} \geq 0$

In the Hybrid RRT-PRM technique using linear programming, the objective function vector $c$ is a row vector of zeros with $s$ elements, where $s$ is the number of points in the combined list of nodes. This vector indicates that there is no specific function to be optimized in this case.

The equality constraint matrix $A_{eq}$ and equality constraint column vector $b_{eq}$ are used to represent the constraints that the solution must satisfy. In this context, the equality constraint matrix $A_{eq}$ was constructed based on the constraints imposed by the convex hull of the combined node list. The corresponding equality constraint vector $b_{eq}$ consists of constants associated with these constraints.

In summary, objective function vector $c$ is a row vector of zeros with $s$ elements. The equality constraint matrix $A_{eq}$ and equality constraint vector $b_{eq}$ define the constraints that the solution must satisfy with respect to the convex hull.

- $$A_{eq} = \begin{matrix} r_{x2} & \dots & r_{xn-1} & P_{x1} & P_{x2} & \dots & P_{xm} \\ r_{y2} & \dots & r_{yn-1} & P_{y1} & P_{y2} & \dots & P_{ym} \\ 1 \quad 1 & & 1 & 1 & 1 & \dots & 1 \end{matrix}$$

To obtain a convex combination for the matrix in the context of the Hybrid RRT-PRM technique, each column in the combined list of nodes includes a point followed by a one. This setup allows the formulation of constraints related to the convex hull of the combined node list.

The vector for equality constraint $b_{eq}$ is structured to reflect these constraints. Specifically, $b_{eq}$ typically contains values that correspond to the constraints imposed by the convex combinations. In this scenario, each entry in $b_{eq}$ represents the right-hand side of the equality constraints associated with the convex hull

In summary: Matrix Construction: Every column in the matrix for the convex combination contains a point from the combined list of nodes followed by a one. Equality Constraint Vector $b_{eq}$: This vector contains values that align with the constraints imposed by the convex combination, providing the right-hand side of the equality constraints:

- $$b_{eq} = \begin{matrix} [\mathrm{rnd}_y] \\ \mathrm{rnd}_y \end{matrix}$$

In the Hybrid RRT-PRM technique, to determine whether a randomly selected point is inside the convex hull of the search area, the y-coordinate (*rndy*) and x-coordinate (*rndx*) of the point are used in conjunction with linear programming. The feasibility of this point within the convex hull is assessed using the simplex method.

Simplex Method Steps:
1. Phase I: A base feasible solution is computed, and the feasibility of the linear program is evaluated. If any artificial variable has positive values, the linear program is deemed infeasible, indicating that the point is outside the convex hull. This point was recorded for subsequent processing. Phase I did not involve the optimization of an objective function; thus, Phase II is not used. 2. Phase II: If feasible, this phase optimizes the objective function; however, because there is no objective function in this case, Phase II is skipped.

Handling the Points:
Collection: After gathering a predefined number of points, the planner iterates through them to identify the points inside obstacles. Points within the obstacles were discarded to prevent the roadmap from being built in these areas.
K-D Tree Construction: Points not in obstacles are added to a list to construct a K-D tree. The K-D tree helps find the nearest neighbors for each node.
Roadmap Creation: Collision-free nodes are connected to each other within the maximum edge expansion distance or until the maximum number of nearest neighbors is reached. These connections formed the roadmap.
Path Finding: A graph search technique was then used to find the shortest path in the created roadmap.

This approach ensures that the roadmap avoids obstacles and efficiently finds collision-free path through the search area.

## 9.9 Advantages

User Convenience: The EV charging experience is improved through easy payment processing, real-time updates, and seamless authentication. System Stability: Demand management prevents the system from becoming congested and guarantees a steady supply of electricity. Battery Longevity: Regular monitoring prolongs the life of batteries and enhances their health. Energy Efficiency: Optimizing energy usage and lowering peak loads are two benefits of smart charging. Safety: Risks during charging are reduced using IoT-driven safety features.

## 9.10 Conclusion

For real-time roadmaps considering real-time traffic and EV charging, a combination of an A* search algorithm with a suitable heuristic function along with preprocessing techniques such as contraction hierarchies or highway hierarchies may be the most effective approach. These techniques can help reduce the computational complexity of finding the shortest paths, while incorporating real-time traffic and charging station information.

## References

1. Florea, B.C. and Taralunga, D.D., Blockchain IoT for smart electric vehicles battery management. *Sustainability*, 12, 10, 3984, 2020.
2. Eisner, J., Funke, S., Storandt, S., Optimal route planning for electric vehicles in large networks, in: *Proceedings of the aaai conference on artificial intelligence*, 2011; August, vol. 25, no. 1, pp. 1108–1113.
3. Abousleiman, R. and Rawashdeh, O., A Bellman-Ford approach to energy efficient routing of electric vehicles, in: *2015 IEEE Transportation Electrification Conference and Expo (ITEC)*, 2015; June, IEEE, pp. 1–4.
4. Tramacere, E., Luciani, S., Feraco, S., Circosta, S., Khan, I., Bonfitto, A., Amati, N., Local trajectory planning for autonomous racing vehicles based on the Rapidly- Exploring Random Tree algorithm, in: *International Design Engineering Technical Conferences and Computers and Information in Engineering Conference*, 2021; August, vol. 85369, American Society of Mechanical Engineers, p. V001T01A009.
5. Aguiari, D., Chou, K.S., Tse, R., Pau, G., Monitoring electric vehicles on the go, in: *2022 IEEE 19th Annual Consumer Communications & Networking Conference (CCNC)*, 2022; January, IEEE, pp. 885–888.
6. Okuda, R., Kajiwara, Y., Terashima, K., A survey of technical trend of ADAS and autonomous driving, in: *Technical papers of 2014 international symposium on VLSI design; automation and test*, 2014; April, IEEE, pp. 1–4.

10

# Embedded Control of Power Converters in E-Mobility

**Yeddula Pedda Obulesu[1]* and Pallamkuppam Vinodh Kumar[2]**

*[1]School of Electrical Engineering, Vellore Institute of Technology, Vellore, Tamil Nadu, India*
*[2]Department of Electrical and Electronics Engineering, Sri Venkateswara College of Engineering, Tirupati, Andhra Pradesh, India*

***Abstract***

This chapter discusses the embedded control of power converters in electric mobility, focusing on digital control technologies and their evolution. It explains how power electronics enhance electric vehicle (EV) performance by managing energy flow between batteries, motors, and auxiliary systems. Key converter types such as DC-DC, AC-DC, and DC-AC converters are explored alongside energy management and regenerative braking. The chapter highlights the shift from analog to digital control using microcontrollers, DSPs, and FPGAs, emphasizing real-time embedded control strategies like PWM, predictive control, and model-based approaches. It also reviews tools like MATLAB/Simulink, LabVIEW, and Code Composer Studio for simulation and rapid prototyping. Advanced components for EVs, including traction inverters, on-board chargers, and battery management systems, are explained with their hardware and software integration challenges. Finally, the chapter addresses design considerations for reliability, safety, and scalability in embedded control systems, enabling future-proof and efficient EV power electronics.

***Keywords*:** Power electronics, electric vehicles, embedded control, digital signal processors (DSP), field programmable gate arrays (FPGA), pulse width modulation (PWM)

**Corresponding author*: yp.obulesu@vit.ac.in

A. Chitra, W. Razia Sultana and V. Indragandhi (eds.) Smart Charging Infrastructures, (195–230)

## 10.1 Introduction

Power electronics is essential for the rapid development and uptake of electric vehicles (EVs), which propels environmentally friendly transportation projects. These electronic systems are pivotal for the efficient management and conversion of electrical energy, enabling the seamless operation of EVs across various functions.

DC-DC Converters: Used to step up or step down voltage levels between different components in the EV system, such as the battery pack, motor, and auxiliary systems.
AC-DC Converters: Convert AC power into DC power to charge the battery pack.
DC-AC Converters: Convert DC power to AC power to drive the traction motor.
Energy Management and Regenerative Braking: Power electronics provide intricate coordination of power distribution, which is necessary for energy management in electric vehicles (EVs). This involves allocating battery power to the electric motor, HVAC system, and other auxiliary systems among other vehicle subsystems. Energy capture during regenerative braking is also included in the energy management.

The technique known as "regenerative braking" transforms kinetic energy into electrical energy, which is stored in the battery. This is an efficient method to enhance an EV's driving range and reduce the strain on mechanical brakes with power electronic converters.

The electric motor transforms kinetic energy into electrical energy when brakes are applied, thereby acting as a generator. This conversion process is controlled by an inverter, which is a type of power-electronic converter. It controls the flow of energy back to the battery from the motor, which functions as the generator.

This process requires exact management of the DC-AC power converter to ensure stability, and the electrical energy is returned to the battery while maintaining an adequate braking mechanism. The electronic control unit (ECU) of a car has control algorithms that consider aspects such as the battery state of charge (SoC) and driver brake input.

Furthermore, power electronics helps EVs' energy management system (EMS) decide how best to distribute energy from the battery to different parts of the car. The driver behavior and driving conditions cause this distribution to adjust dynamically. For instance, the motor may receive more power when traveling at high speeds or during acceleration, whereas auxiliary systems such as the HVAC system may receive more power when driving at low speeds or during idle.

Battery Management Systems (BMS) are another crucial application for power electronics in EVs. BMS systems oversee and manage the health, safety, and efficient utilization of battery packs, ensuring their longevity and optimal performance. Furthermore, advanced charging systems controlled by power electronics enable rapid and secure EV battery charging.

Power electronic converters are at the heart of efficient and safe battery charging for electric vehicles (EVs). These systems manage the control, conversion, and overall energy management during the charging process, ensuring optimal performance and longevity of the vehicle battery.

Power electronics are essential to both onboard and offboard charging systems for EV charging. Power electronic converters, such as rectifiers, are used by onboard chargers to convert the main AC power into the DC power required for battery charging. To maintain consistent current and voltage phases for the best charging and battery health, this procedure includes rectification and DC-DC conversion stages to match the battery charge profile.

Power electronics are necessary for off-board charging solutions such as DC fast-charging stations. By bypassing the onboard charger, these systems use power electronic converters to transform the AC supply into a high-voltage DC output for direct battery charging. Power electronics are used in advanced control schemes to manage the charge rates and protect batteries from possible harm.

Power electronics are essential to both onboard and offboard charging systems when it comes to EV charging. Power electronic converters, such as AC-DC converters, are used by onboard chargers to convert the main AC voltage into the DC voltage required for battery charging. To maintain consistent current and voltage phases for the best charging and battery health, this procedure includes rectification and DC-DC conversion stages to match the battery's charge profile.

Overall, power electronic systems are indispensable for ensuring efficient, safe, and optimized battery charging for electric vehicles, contributing significantly to the advancement and adoption of EV technology.

EV efficiency and performance have increased with advancements in power electronics. Power electronic semiconductor devices with increased efficiency, smaller dimensions, and better thermal characteristics have been made possible by advancements in semiconductor switching devices, such as SiC and GaN MOSFETs. These developments substantially contribute to the continuous improvement of EV sustainability and capability.

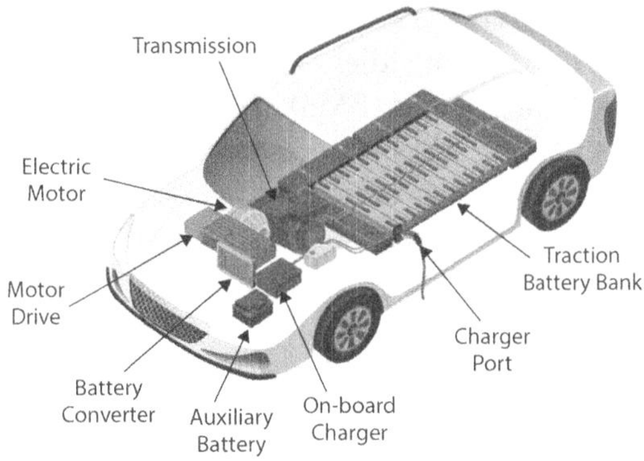


**Figure 10.1** Main parts of an electric vehicle.

An overview of EVs with various power converter components is shown in Figure 10.1.

### 10.1.1 Key Components of EV

- Charging port or vehicle inlet: Connector for external electricity charging.
- Power electronic converter: High-power semiconductor devices are used to switch and alter the input voltage and current.
- Onboard charger: Converts AC to DC for battery charging and regulates battery characteristics.
- Traction battery pack: High-voltage battery storing energy for the electric traction motor.
- Battery power converter: This device transforms the voltage from the traction battery pack into a DC bus voltage, so that the motor can exchange power.
- Motor drive: Usually bidirectional; this device transfers power from the battery to the motor or motor to the battery based on acceleration or deceleration.
- Traction electric motor/generator: Propels an electric car, converting electrical energy to mechanical energy, and vice versa during braking.
- Transmission: Single-gear transmission with differential power transfer from motor to wheels.
- Power electronics controller: Controls the electrical power flow in different converters.

- Battery (auxiliary): Provides initial power for starting and accessories in an electric driving vehicle.

## 10.2 Evolution of Digital Control in Power Converters

Power converters were primarily analog until the 1990s and were unable to process sophisticated algorithms. Although simpler microprocessors handle ancillary roles such as HMI and programmable analog amplifier tuning, Texas Instruments' 1983 development of digital signal processors (DSPs) made it possible to create costly power converters with digital control. In the 1990s, industrial items began to use full digital controls.

During this period, high-performance AC drive prototypes in Europe, Japan, and the USA were developed using DSPs, general-purpose μ-processors, such as the Motorola 68020 and 68030, and parallel handling systems, such as transputers. Despite their advanced capabilities, transputers eventually fell out of favor because of the market shifts.

Owing to the availability of inexpensive microcontrollers and digital signal controllers (DSCs), power converters with complete digital control were widely used by the end of the 1990s.

This section provides a comprehensive overview of digital systems for power converters, examines their essential functions and performance requirements, and illustrates the development and typical performance of current devices.

A thorough overview of digital devices, such as microcontrollers and field-programmable gate arrays (FPGAs), along with hardware and software implementation considerations are crucial for designing power converters with enhanced performance. Embedded digital control is essential for modern power converters to achieve high-efficiency and effective control of the power converters for managing electrical energy flows.

The implementation a realistic embedded digital controller for power electronic converters requires numerous considerations. Key challenges include selecting the appropriate control processor, determining the sampling rate, establishing interfaces between the controller and power circuit, designing hardware and software, and realizing control algorithms in software. These tasks are complex and require meticulous design and real-world insights. Software implementation is pivotal for creating an effective controller that requires theoretical analysis within practical constraints for successful execution.

The DSP-based and FPGA-based programming techniques are two well-known methods that have recently attracted considerable interest for the software execution of digital control techniques. Controllers based on DSP can perform intricate algorithms that require numerous arithmetic operations. However, because of their sequential operating nature, in which instructions are carried out one after the other, they are less common in applications that demand high switching frequencies or cost-effectiveness. However, by incorporating peripherals, such as PWM modules, timers, and event interruption modules, DSPs have been tailored for power electronics applications, allowing for some degree of concurrent operation for easier jobs.

In contrast to DSPs, FPGAs offer concurrent operational capabilities, executing all internal logic elements and control procedures continuously and simultaneously. This concurrent operation feature makes FPGAs suitable for implementing high-speed challenging algorithms such as digital charge control for current loops, which may not be feasible with DSPs. The instruction code and algorithm for FPGAs are typically implemented through languages such as VHDL, offering flexibility similar to software solutions in the C-language for DSPs. VHDL is also technology-independent, allowing the same algorithm to be synthesized into various FPGAs or even custom chips (ASICs), thereby presenting intriguing possibilities for enhancing performance and reducing costs in power systems. Moreover, VHDL has been utilized for modeling purposes, enabling simulations of entire systems, including power converters and A/D converters (ADCs). These models, designed for efficient simulations, facilitate simultaneous simulation of control loops with vastly different characteristic times. DSPs, both from hardware and software perspectives, play a crucial role in executing programmed codes to interface with external circuits and carry out designated functions within electronic systems.

### 10.2.1 Key Functions of Embedded Control of Power Converters

Power Management: The power flow among the battery, motor, and other subsystems is regulated to optimize the efficiency and performance.
Voltage and Current Regulation: Maintain stable voltage and current levels under varying load conditions to protect the components and ensure reliable operation.

Fault Detection and Protection: Monitors for faults such as overcurrent, overvoltage, and overheating, and takes corrective actions to prevent damage.
Synchronization and Coordination: Ensures synchronized operation between different power converters and subsystems within the vehicle.

### 10.2.2 Components of Embedded Control Systems

Microcontrollers: Process control algorithms and commands and manage communication between different components.
Gate Drivers: Control the switching of power semiconductor devices (such as MOSFETs or IGBTs) in power converters.
Sensors: Provide feedback on voltage, current, temperature, and other parameters to the control system.
Communication Interfaces: Facilitate communication with peripheral systems, such as the vehicle's central controller and charging station.

### 10.2.3 Control Strategies

Pulse Width Modulation (PWM): The duty cycle of the switching devices is adjusted to regulate the voltage and current.
Voltage and Current Control Loops: Feedback loops are used to regulate the output voltage and current according to the desired set points.
Predictive and Model-Based Control: Uses predictive algorithms and mathematical models to optimize control actions based on the predicted load and driving conditions.

### 10.2.4 Challenges and Innovations

Efficiency. Maximizing efficiency to extend vehicle range and reduce energy consumption.
Reliability: This ensures robust performance under various environmental and operating conditions.
Safety: Implementing fail-safe mechanisms and protection algorithms to prevent accidents and ensure user safety.
Scalability: Designing systems that can scale from small electric scooters to heavy-duty electric trucks.

## 10.3 Embedded Systems and Digital Control

There have been notable developments in both design and manufacturing as the embedded industry grows. Systems-on-chip (SoC) systems with heterogeneous hardware cores and multiprocessor systems are vogue. During real-time (RT) operations, future multicore systems will probably function autonomously without a central controller and will show some degree of flexibility in response to system and environmental changes. This will facilitate communication between various processing units and lessen the problems caused by system breakdown in certain areas.

Various embedded technologies are currently being incorporated by manufacturers into single-chip solutions with reconfigurable capabilities, which enables hardware functionalities to change without affecting the operation. For instance, Actel's SmartFusion is a single device that integrates an ARM Cortex-M3 processor, a ProASIC 3 FPGA fabric, and a sophisticated mixed signal capability. Similarly, Xilinx's Zynq-7000 line combines a 28 nm unified programmable logic architecture with an ARM dual-core Cortex-A9 processing system, whereas Altera provides user-adjustable ARM-based SoC FPGAs. Although the Zynq-7000 family of devices use the same handling out system, their programmable logic and input and output resources differ to support a variety of applications. Similar to ASICs, this integration lowers the power consumption while improving the device capability and usage. It also offers programmability of a microprocessor combined with the efficiency and flexibility of an FPGA.

## 10.4 Tools and Technologies for Digital Control Systems

Environments that provide a wide range of basic functions, graphical user interfaces (GUIs), ease of use, and brief training times have become increasingly popular in recent years. Modern GUIs, such as MATLAB Simulink and National Instruments LabVIEW, automatically generate code from prepared block diagrams. These industrial model-based design implementations are widely used for multidomain RT system modeling, simulation, and analysis. LabVIEW's Embedded and Real-Time Modules facilitate the design of standalone embedded systems using a simple graphical programming technique. Built-in "C" code generators convert block diagrams into standalone or executable RT code that may be used on embedded platforms. Since the release of MATLAB R2011a, code creation for embedded processors implemented in RT and non-RT applications such as hardware-in-the-loop testing, rapid prototyping, and simulation acceleration has been made possible *via* tools like MATLAB Coder, Simulink Coder, and Embedded Coder. Furthermore, many designs use pre-existing "C" functions that were created, examined, and verified outside the Simulink and MATLAB environments.

## 10.5 Implementation of Embedded Digital Control Based on DSPs

Understanding the basic ideas of DSP from both hardware and software standpoints, defining the intended system, outlining the control flow in accordance with functional requirements, choosing suitable microcontrollers or DSPs, and carefully reading datasheets and manuals are the first steps in putting controllers using DSPs into practice.

DSPs can be interpreted in two contexts, hardware and software. A digital signal processor is a type of hardware microprocessor. Table 10.1 displays the DSPs made by several semiconductor vendors. These chips can communicate with external circuits *via* digital or analog signals when soldered onto printed circuit boards (PCBs). Upon powering, the DSP chips begin their execution procedures. Because of their "multiply-and-accumulate" (MAC) units, DSPs outperform standard cores and are one of the first single-chip solutions utilized in power electronics. The first component designed specifically for direct digital control was most likely TMS320C14, which had 10-MIPS, 16-bit CPU, multichannel ADC, and PWM outputs. In 1988, a 32-bit wide floating-point DSP was released and used in numerous high-end systems.

Modern processors typically use dual-bus Harvard technology, where one bus controls the data flow in addition to the other handles MAC units and program commands. Because buses operate separately and simultaneously, this structural design reduces the required time. Numbers are typically represented in processors as either floating or fixed points. Input data are converted from analog to digital using either 12- or 14-bit converters, or 16-bit counters. Floating-point representation is superior for complex algorithms that involve numerous mathematical operations because of its larger dynamic range, which reduces error accumulation, even though a 32-bit wide fixed-point illustration is adequate for simple computations.

Floating-point DSCs are expected to become the benchmark in medium-to-high-level systems, as seen by the recent incorporation of floating-point units into 32-bit DSCs at the expense of a16-bit fixed point DSP. Power electronic converter capabilities will be greatly improved by this advancement, opening the door to the use of sophisticated control strategies.

**Table 10.1** DSP hardware manufacturers.

| Manufacturer | Remarks |
|---|---|
| Advanced Devices, Inc. | 16/32 bit/floating point |
| Advanced RISC Machines | (ARM) CPU wore vendor |
| Analog Devices | 16/32 bit DSP-SHARC |
| Averlogic Technologies, Inc. | |
| DSP Group | |
| Freescale Semiconductor, Inc. | 32-bit embedded processor-uP/6800-uCRISC/DSP combo ICs |
| Hyperstone | RISC/DSP combo ICs |
| IDT | Packet classification processors |
| Infineon Technologies | |
| Intersil | 8/16 bit CMOS uP |
| Intrinsity, Inc. | |
| Logic Devices | DSP devices |
| LSI | |
| MicroChip | dsPIC 16-bit RISC digital signal controllers |
| NXP | |
| STMicroelectronics | |
| Texas Instruments, Inc. | TI320Cxx DSP processors-high speed CMOS signal processing/all-digital down/up-converters, digital filters, high-speed QAM modem chips sets |
| VeriSilicon | DSP coprocessor, VOIP |
| Vitese Semiconductor Corporation | DSP-based T3/E3 transceiver |
| Zilog | 16-bit multi-purpose DSP manufacturer |

## 10.6 Key Components in Embedded Digital Controllers

**1) Communication Channels**

High-speed sequential channels and specialized interfaces such as the Serial Peripheral Interface, which are appropriate for inter-processors (e.g., ADC, DAC, and FLASH memory), are frequently included in modern drives because they demand broad communication capabilities. Other typical interfaces for communication include the following:

- **Controlled Area Network (CAN) Bus:** Common in automotive and industrial settings.
- **Universal Serial Bus (USB):** Common for interprocessor communication.
- **Ethernet:** Used for high-speed data transfer and interprocessor communication.

Recent microcontrollers, such as STM32W and Stellaris-Texas M3, incorporate ZigBee connectivity for short-range wireless communication, and WiFi is expected to gain popularity owing to its ease of wireless link with computers and other electronic devices.

**2) Analog to Digital Conversion (ADC)**

Analog inputs are necessary for power converters because they require feedback from current and/or voltage. 12-bit or else 14-bit ADCs with sampling speeds ranging from hundreds of nanoseconds are commonly embedded in microcontrollers. Many ADCs through sample-and-hold input buffers are frequently used to maintain phase accuracy among three-phase quantities. This eliminates phase shifts and delays and permits the simultaneous sampling of many channels.

Direct memory access (DMA) procedures or interrupts are used to provide sampled data to the CPU; DMA removes the overhead and latency associated with interrupts. Smart sensors that use high-speed interfaces such as SPI or USB-3 and have digital outputs and better performance output and input ports (such as DAC, ADC, SPI, and FLASH memory) have recently become widely accessible. Future high-performance microcontrollers with sufficient serial interfaces are expected to replace internal ADCs.

### 3) Timers and Counters

Timer/counter units, which are essential for measuring or creating time intervals, are commonly used in microcontrollers. These peripherals serve two primary purposes:

- **Capture:** Counting of input events.
- **Compare:** Generating signals by comparing the reference signal produced by the control algorithm with a hardware count (conducted by the timer).

The move to sensorless drives raises the possibility that the traditional application of these units' incremental encoder pulses for speed measurement may be discontinued. However, the increasing use of smart sensors that require timers means that these units will persist, albeit for different purposes, with expected improvements in their number and performance. As shown in Figure 10.2, a typical ADC architecture in microcontrollers uses sample-and-hold circuits for phase accuracy.

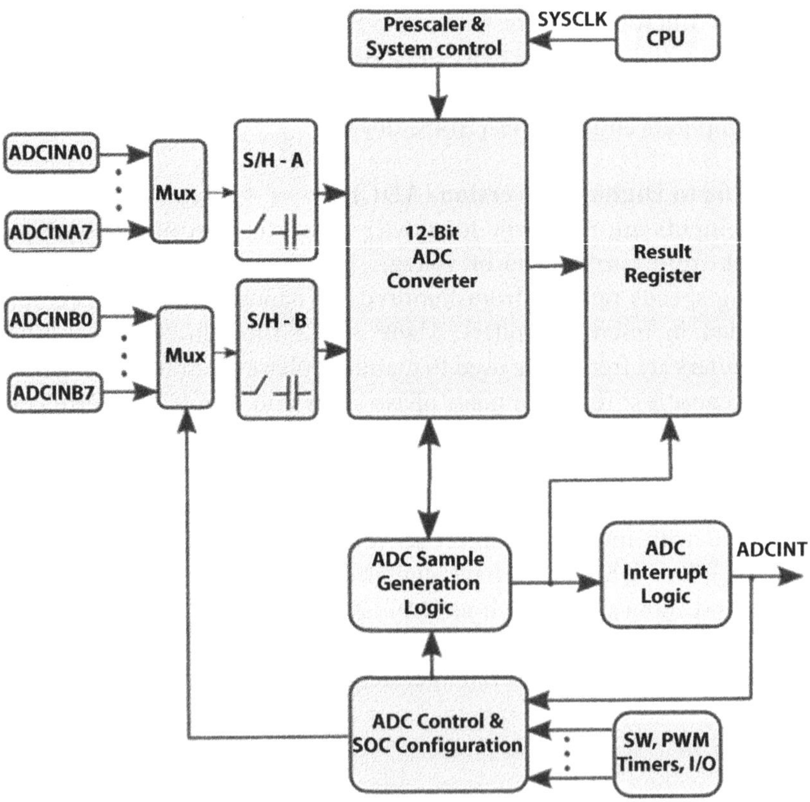


**Figure 10.2** Typical ADC in microcontrollers.

**4) Pulse Width Modulation Peripherals:** PWM peripherals are connected to gate driver boards to trigger power electronic switching devices.

## 10.7 Signal Generation for Power Converter Devices

Power converters need accurate control signals to operate power devices like MOSFETs and IGBTs. These signals are produced by driver circuits, which act as galvanic insulation between processing circuits and power components and buffer the microprocessor's output voltage and current. The output signal of the general control method must be used by the control unit to create intricate pulse-width modulation (PWM) waveforms with the least CPU overhead. The PWM units must be extremely flexible, programmable, and easy to operate.

Six-output 16-bit-wide PWM modules are commonly used in contemporary digital signal controllers (DSCs) that can be directly connected to a three-phase inverter/rectifier. Various power converter units might be available to power a DC-DC converter. A second set of six or more PWM outputs is available for certain DSCs, enabling the control of additional inverters, active rectifiers, or complex converters with numerous switches.

### 10.7.1 Operating Frequency and Resolution

PWM modules operate at frequencies scaled down from the main microprocessor frequency, typically outputting signals in the kilohertz range with resolutions of hundreds of nanoseconds. Recent advancements include high-resolution PWM (HRPWM) modules, which are capable of nanosecond-level resolution. These modules can function independently or synchronize, allowing higher output counts or greater precision in timing intervals.

### 10.7.2 Modes of Operation

To control event timing, each PWM unit often has its own clock and timer units. It can operate in three different modes: Up-Down, Up, and Down-Count. External hardware can be avoided by imposing appropriate deadband values to prevent short circuits between power devices during switching transitions by setting the output rising-edge and falling-edge delays. Figures 10.3, 10.4 show examples of producing three-phase complementary PWM outputs. To modulate the PWM waveform with a high-frequency carrier signal and lower conduction losses, microcontrollers also use PWM chopper submodules. The PWM modules ensure stable operating speeds and high-precision control by having the ability to launch ADC modules or produce CPU interrupts at any occurrence.

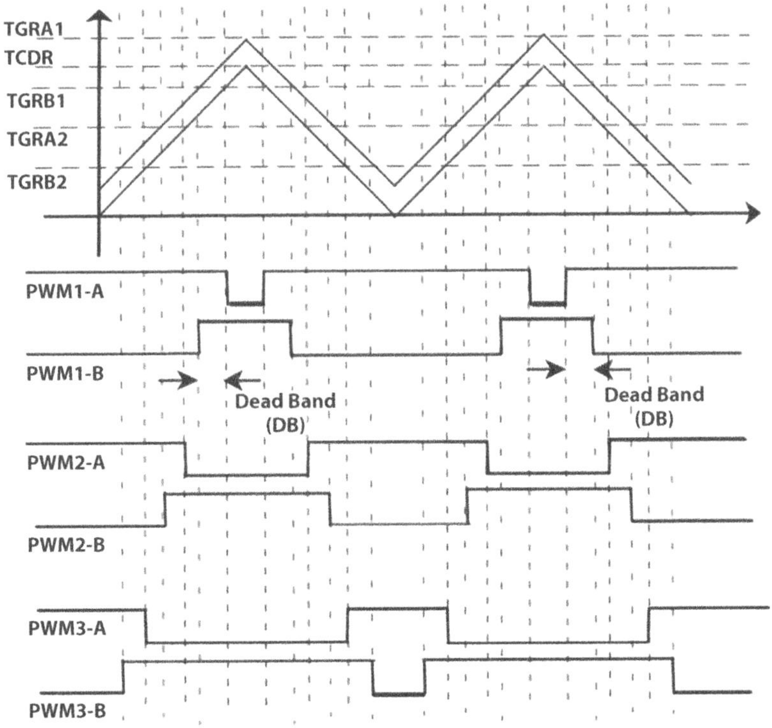


**Figure 10.3** Three-phase PWM (DC-AC converter) output waveforms.

## 10.8 Field Programmable Gate Arrays (FPGAs)

ASICs encompass a broad range of devices suitable for high-performance power converter development, with CPLDs and FPGAs prevalent in this domain. FPGAs generally offer more advanced capabilities than CPLDs, thereby enabling the design of intricate digital systems. On the other hand, CPLDs provide gate cells capable of various logic algorithms essential for digital implementations, exhibiting lower delays and costs compared to FPGAs. While CPLDs are EEPROM-based and self-activate at power-up, FPGAs typically require booting from nonvolatile storage because they are SRAM-based, resulting in potentially lower design security and longer boot times in FPGA devices. However, FPGAs offer increased logic flexibility, higher complexity, and integration of sophisticated system features such as on-chip RAM, MAC units, microprocessors/DSPs, and Multi-Gigabit Transceivers (MGT). With the use of CAD tools, FPGAs, which are typically two-dimensional arrays of logic blocks and flip flops, can be

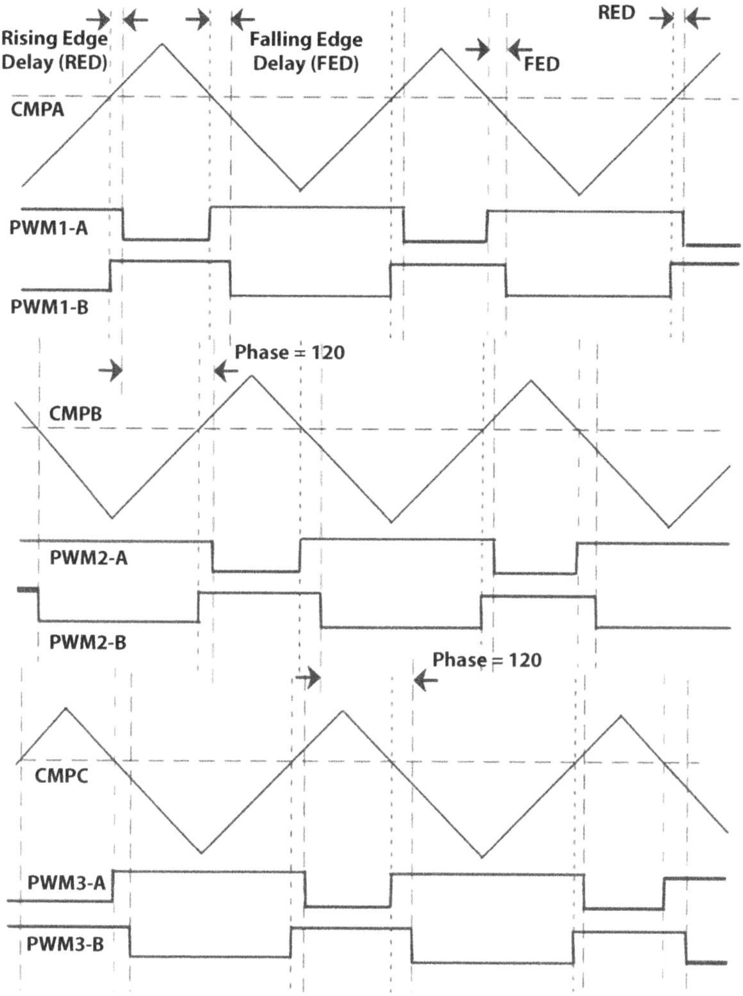


**Figure 10.4** Three phase PWM output waveforms with deadband.

implemented, allowing many adjustable logic blocks to be integrated into a single Integrated Circuit (IC).

The reprogrammable nature of FPGAs is a significant advantage, as it allows them to perform a wide range of applications and is not limited to specific functions such as conventional microprocessors or DSPs. This versatility also extends to code, which is largely independent of the device's architecture and can be easily reconfigured. For the implementation of digital control systems, FPGAs provide a higher density, reduced power consumption, and quicker design cycles. FPGA software, which frequently incorporates a real microprocessor, can effectively perform complicated control algorithms with intricate computations and excel in systems that require simple computing and rapid processing. This co-design method shortens the development time and increases the system adaptability.

Modern FPGAs surpass microprocessors and DSPs in terms of dimension, speed, and the number of output and input pins. FPGAs have been developed to support the creation of intricate, high-performance digital control systems with computational capability, input/output processing, and PWM output integration after serving solely as peripheral interfaces to the main processors. Key vendors in this field include Altera and Xilinx, along with other reputable brands such as Lattice, SiliconBlue, and Actel. FPGAs can implement complex parallel arithmetic architectures for high-performance processors.

Notably, Actel's Fusion family pioneered FPGA integration with ADC and other analog devices, providing processor-in-loop application. The industry has also witnessed advancements in mixed-signal technology by combining A/D signals. A complete schematic of an FPGA-based digital platform illustrates its versatility, with interface boards providing various I/O lines, including ADC inputs and DAC outputs. Communication options such as RS232, USB, or Ethernet cater to connectivity needs, while standalone operation in real time without a main PC is feasible using peripherals such as keyboards and LCDs.

As previously discussed, both analog and digital controllers have their own strengths and weaknesses. Combining the benefits of both realms, there is clear interest in creating a quasi-analog controller using digital methods capable of executing control algorithms almost instantaneously. FPGAs have emerged as promising candidates for such controllers. Recently, there has been a growing focus on using FPGA technology for motion control and power conversion owing to their ability to handle complex modulation schemes and high-speed switching requirements.

FPGAs have been effectively used to control power converters, including PWM inverters, PFC converters, ZCS-ZVS techniques, multilevel converters, DC-DC resonant converters, and STATCOM. They are extensively used in a wide range of motion control applications, including speed monitoring, brushless DC motors, induction motor drives, fuzzy-logic control of power generators, and switching-reluctance machine drives.

The particular needs of the system will decide whether to use an FPGA as a coprocessor or as a full system-on-the-chip solution. Combining a DSP with an FPGA can be beneficial, with the DSP handling complex calculations while the FPGA manages other tasks. This combination can be achieved on the same board as standard host processors, where the FPGA handles certain processing tasks and reduces the overhead. As an alternative, combining all processing functions into a single FPGA-based SoC platform can reduce system costs and simplify the design complexity.

One or two RISC processors can be easily integrated into a processor-in-loop application owing to the growing density of FPGAs. Designers of motion control systems are currently concentrating on creating single-chip solutions that incur low cost and high levels of integration. Figure 10.5 illustrates the FPGA-based digital platform with interface boards. Microcontrollers, such as ARM Cortex-M3 or MicroBlade, can be integrated with FPGA fabric by utilizing the advantages of various modules.

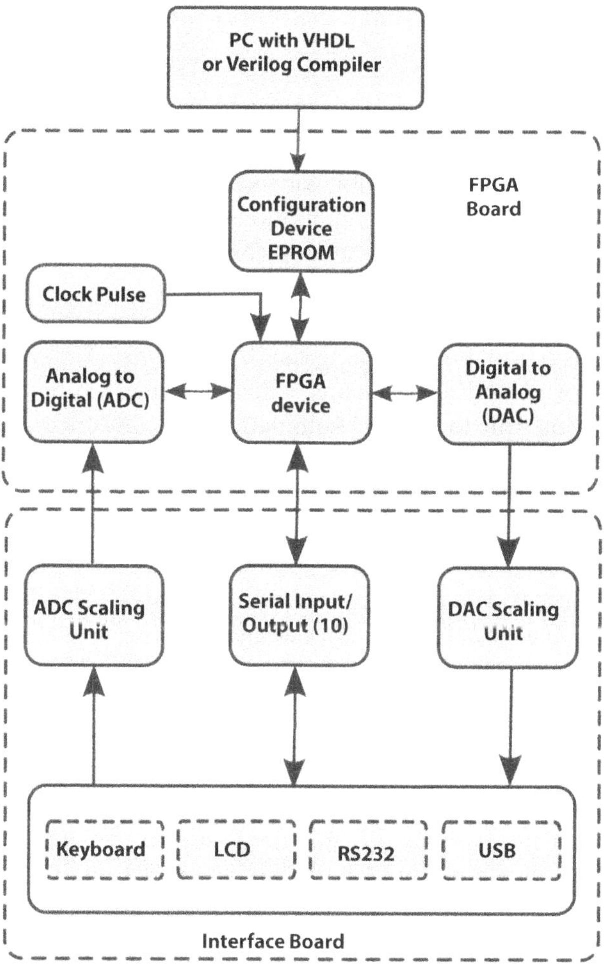


**Figure 10.5** Block diagram of FPGA based digital architecture.

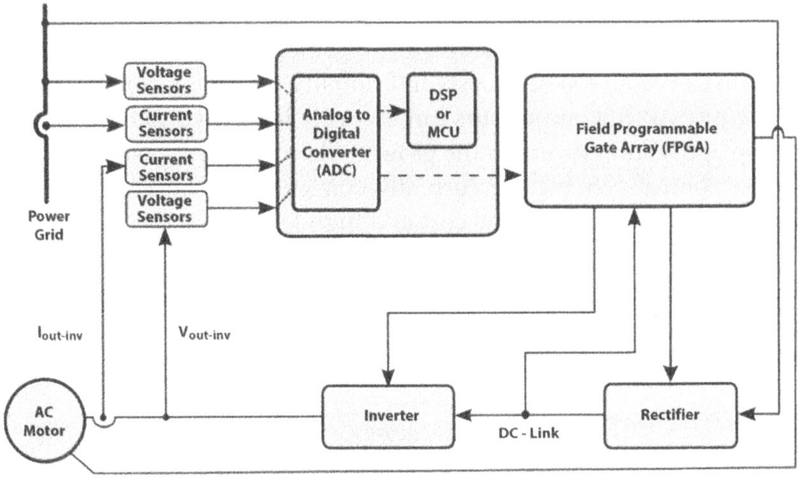


**Figure 10.6** Motor drive control using FPGA.

This allows hardware acceleration for functions implemented within the FPGA. Highly effective single-chip motion controllers are the result of this combination and customizable analog components. Motor drive control using FPGA as shown in Figure 10.6.

The conventional design cycle for FPGAs uses the Verilog and VHDL. However, this type of programming can be time consuming when building controllers for complicated systems, which can result in high production costs and a long time to market. Automatic HDL code creation tools, such as Simulink HDL CoderTM or the National Instrument LabVIEW module, can be used directly in scenarios where quick prototyping is crucial. This method works well for both quick prototyping requirements and for control engineers. However, HDL coding is required to achieve optimal control performance is a top goal, even if it requires a significant amount of work at the hardware architecture design stage.

## 10.9 Code Composer Studio and JTAG

Code Composer Studio (CCS) is a comprehensive application suite developed by Texas Instruments for code development. Notably, they are free and support a wide range of DSP families and variations. CCS is designed to facilitate the entire development process and offers support for programming in both the C and Assembler languages.

The Project, Program, Watch, and Output windows are the four primary parts of the CCS interface. Every file in an open project is shown as

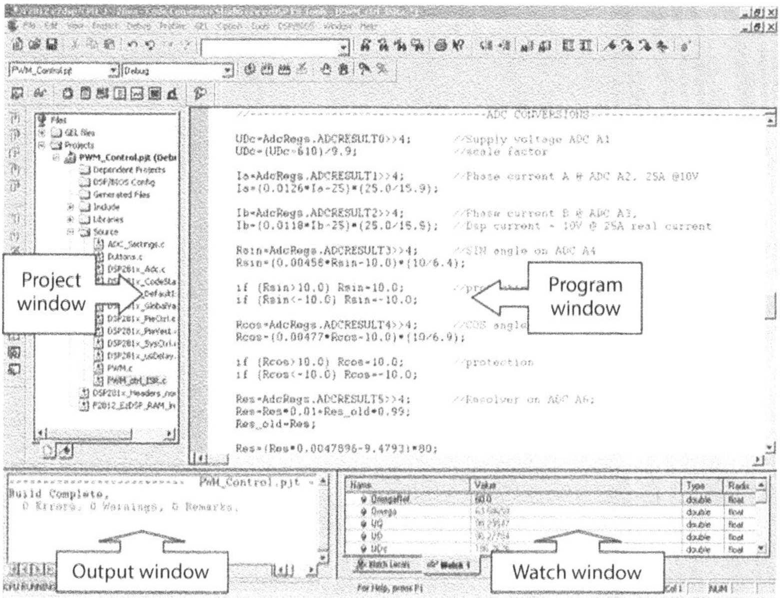


**Figure 10.7** Snapshot of CCS programming interface (courtesy of Texas Instruments).

a directory structure in the Project pane. Clicking on a file opens it into the Program window for editing. The Output window highlights potential errors during compilation and provides feedback on the code correctness. The Watch window allows developers to track variable values while the program is in operation as shown in Figure 10.7.

CCS attaches to the DSP using the PC's standard parallel port. For this communication, a standardized Joint Test Action Group communication port was used. In addition, the onboard is a 14-pin header connector for JTAG, as illustrated in Figure 10.8. During operation, CCS can access the DSP registers because of its JTAG module. One technique for debugging embedded devices is the JTAG.

Input/Output Signals: The DSP features a total of 56 I/O pins, many of which support multiple function sets *via* register flags. These pins can function as standard I/O pins for digital data-read/write operations. Additionally, specific pins can be assigned special functions, such as PWM signals and analog-to-digital conversion (ADC).

Event Managers: EVA and EVB are two distinct "Event Managers" that are part of the DSP. Timer, PWM, and ADC are just a few of the many unique features that these event managers provide, which are essential for motion

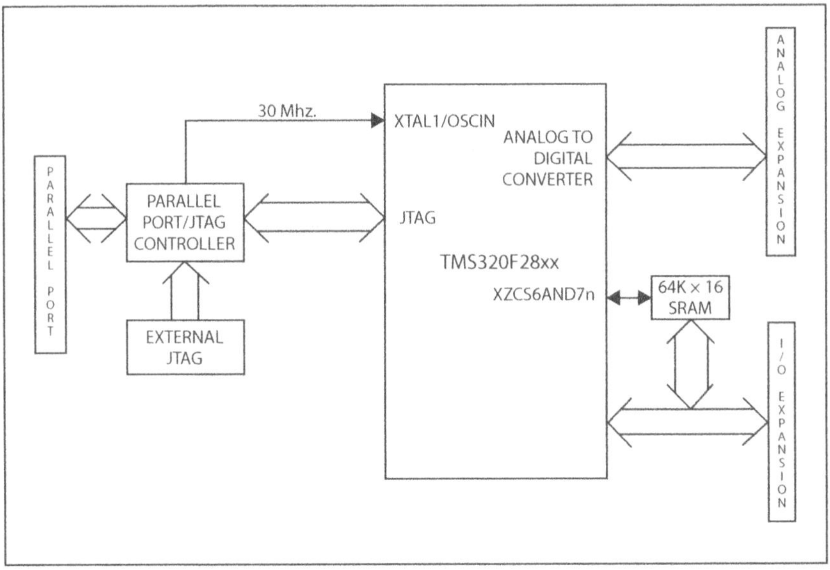


**Figure 10.8** Block diagram of the development card (courtesy of Texas Instruments).

and motor control activities. Event Managers (EVx) can be programmed independently and work simultaneously.

Timer Module: There are four separate timers on the DSP, two for each event manager. With the ability to count a 16-bit value up and down and generate interrupts at predetermined values to indicate when time thresholds are crossed, these timers are extremely useful for time-sensitive applications.

Pulse Width Modulation (PWM): The event managers share 16 PWM channels that are accessible on the DSP. Each channel can be programmed separately or in pairs. In addition to generating PWM pulses using an integrated timing circuit, the PWM module has a pulse-pattern generator that can produce both symmetric and asymmetric PWM waveforms.

With PWM, the pulse width fluctuates, while the signal's amplitude remains constant. The duty cycle is a number between 0 and 1 (or 0 and 100%), which indicates the duration for which the output is active. Analog-to-Digital Conversion (ADC): The DSP has 16 ADC channels and is split into two sets of eight. Each channel had a 12-bit resolution and a maximum sampling frequency of 25 MHz. The input signals must range from 0 to 3 V.

The following formula is used to determine the ADC output: Digital Value = 4,095 * (Input Analog Voltage – ADCLO)/3. In this context, "ADCLO" denotes a processor pin connected to the analog ground (with a value of zero). For easy access, the digital value is saved in a special result register's 12 most significant bits (MSBs).

From a software perspective, digital signal processing (DSP) is a set of steps that includes software algorithms and codes that are designed to extract the desired output signals, either digital or analog, from input signals. The DSP procedure is broken down as follows:

1. **Signal Capture:** This step involves capturing analog or digital input signals by sampling and holding them through external interface circuits connected to the hardware pins.
2. **Data Acquisition:** Digital data are obtained from the sampled signals after signal capture using an analog-to-digital converter (ADC).
3. **Processing and Calculations:** To produce digital outcomes, operations and computations are carried out on the digital data once it has been acquired. Depending on the requirements of the system, these computations may use floating-point, fixed-point, or integer operations.
4. **Signal Reconstruction:** Finally, the digital outputs are transformed back into the intended output signals, which may be analog signals produced by digital output ports or digital-to-analog converters (DACs).

The general sequence of program execution steps when the DSP chip is switched on is shown in Figure 10.9. It encompasses signal capture, data acquisition, processing, and signal reconstruction. Figure 10.10 provides a diagram that further explains digital signal processing, showcasing the DSP IC and the implemented DSP user code.

Because the buck-boost DC-DC converter is a prominent example for implementation, it is essential to define its functional requirements. The initial phase involves specifying these requirements meticulously. This task is of paramount importance, as it enables designers to dissect the project into manageable sub-projects, allowing for the delegation of tasks to team members. Such a structured approach aids in the integration and evaluation of each individual task, leading to cohesive and efficient project execution.

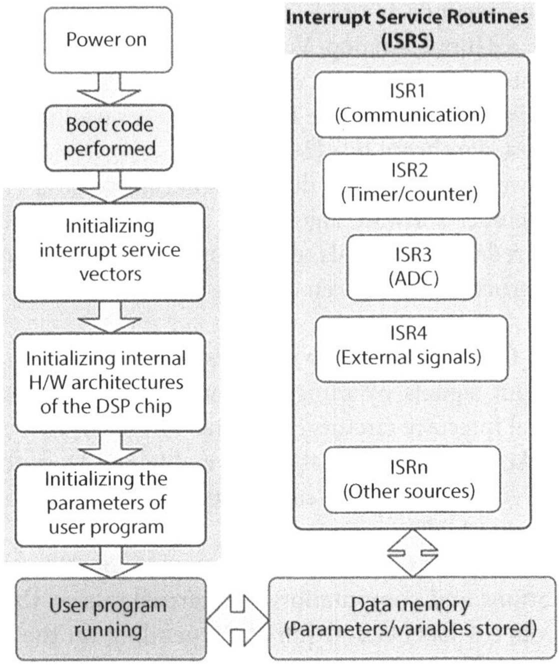


**Figure 10.9** General Low of source codes implementation on DSP chips (Courtesy of Texas Instruments).

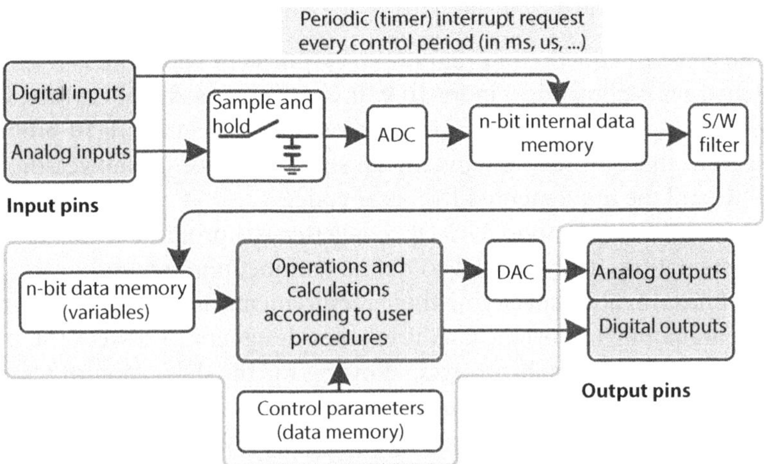


**Figure 10.10** Overall low of digital signal processing (Courtesy of Texas Instruments).

### 10.9.1 Functional Requirements of a Non-Inverting Buck-Boost Converter

- The system block diagram, as shown in Figure 10.11a, integrates digital equipment such as DSP chips, user programs, and PLDs to accomplish capabilities such as the error identifiers and PWM generators.

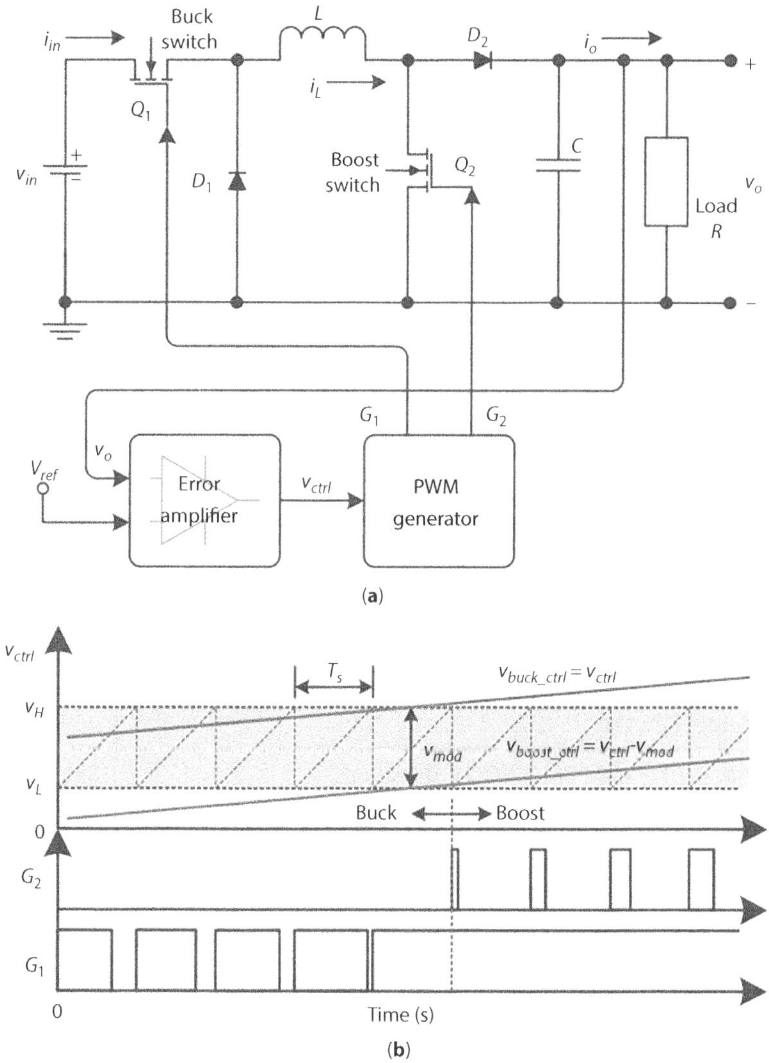


**Figure 10.11** Buck-boost converter (non-inverting): (a) Converter, (b) PWM modulation strategy.

- The electrical parameters of the converter are listed in detail in Table 10.2.
- The converter can operate in three distinct modes: boost, buck, and buck-boost. It is noted that the buck-boost mode typically incurs more losses than the other modes. The system state block diagram is shown in Figure 10.12.

**Table 10.2** Commercial DSP starter kit.

| Title | Literature no. |
|---|---|
| TMS320F2810, TMS320F2811, TMS320F2812, TMS320C2810, TMS320C2811, TMS320C2812 Digital Signal Processors Data Manual | SPRS174M |
| TMS320x28xx, 28xxx DSP Peripheral Reference guide (Rev. F) | SPRU566F |
| TMS320x281x System Control and Interrupts Reference Guide (Rev. E) | SPRU078E |
| TMS320x281x Multichannel Buffered Serial Port (McBSP) Reference Guide (Rev. C) | SPRU061C |
| TMS320x281x Event Manger (EV) Reference Guide (Rev. E) | SPRU065E |
| TMS320x281x, 28xxx Serial Peripheral Interface (SPI) Reference Guide (Rev. D) | SPRU059D |
| TMS320x28xx, 28xxx Enhanced Controller Area Network (Ecan) Reference Guide (Rev. E) | SPRU074E |
| TMS320x281x Analog-to-Digital Converter (ADC) Reference Guide (Rev. D) | SPRU060D |
| F2810, F2811, and F2812 ADC Calibration | SPRA 989A |
| TMS320x28xx Serial Communication Interface (SCI) Reference Guide (Rev. B) | SPRU051B |
| TMS320x28x DSP CPU and Instruction Set Reference Guide (Rev. D) | SPRU430D |
| TMS320x281x Boost ROM Reference Guide (Rev. C) | SPRU095C |
| TMS320x281x External Interface (XINTF) Reference Guide (Rev. C) | SPRU067C |

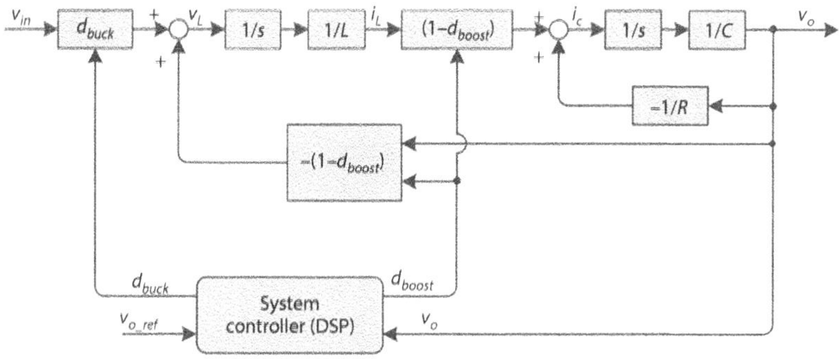


**Figure 10.12** State block diagram of system.

## 10.10 Software Development Environment (SDE): Compiler, Linker, Assembler, and Downloader

Hardware manuals state that many key components make up the software development environment for DSP chips or microcontrollers. These components often include documentation, linkers, compiler, assembler, and program downloaders for the unified development tool. Because it streamlines the entire process, from creating source code to running finished programs, a unified development tool is crucial. Figure 10.13 shows the overall internal architecture of the TMS320F281x DSP.

Manufacturers of DSP chips and microcontrollers offer a variety of application notes aimed at showcasing the capabilities of their products and driving their sales. These application notes cover a wide range of topics, including automotive systems, temperature control, battery charging, communication, image processing, inverter/converter control, and display-device management. Typically, users can access relevant application notes on a manufacturer's website. Although specific applications and techniques may vary, these notes serve as valuable resources that provide users with useful information and insights.

Texas Instruments' unified development tool for DSP devices is called the Code Composer Studio (CCS). Designers should study assembler, compiler, linker, and program downloader documentation for a comprehensive understanding, even if unified tools are recommended.

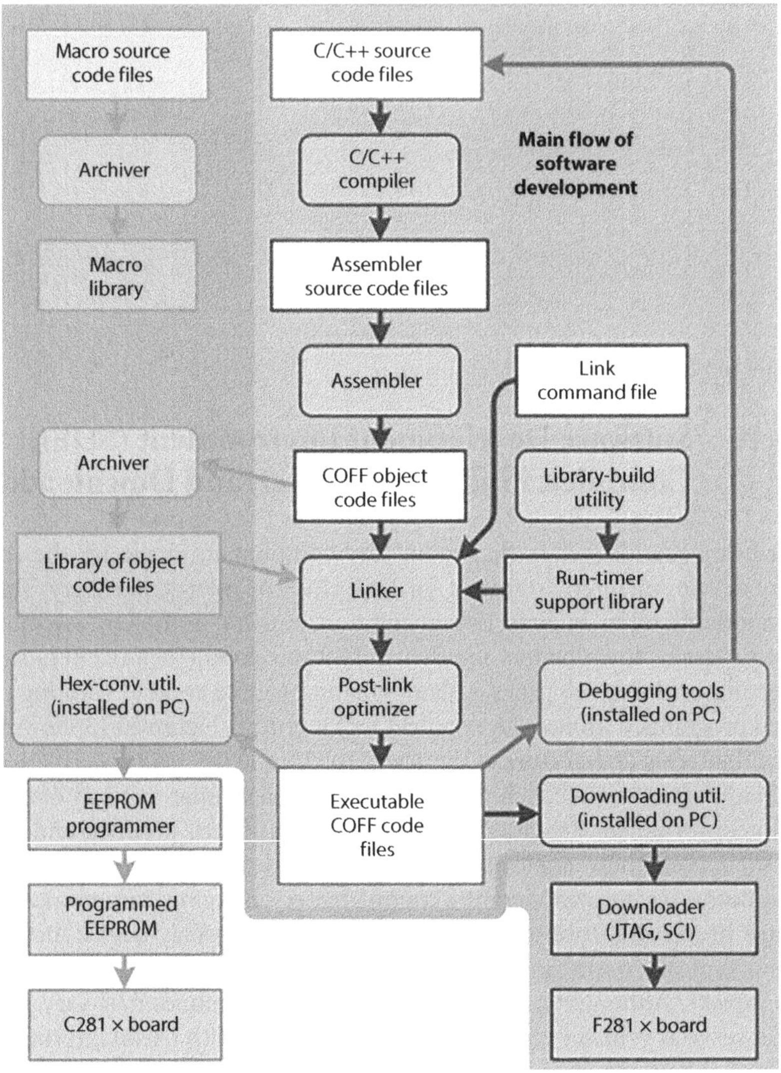


**Figure 10.13** Overall internal architecture of TMS320F281x DSP (courtesy of Texas Instruments).

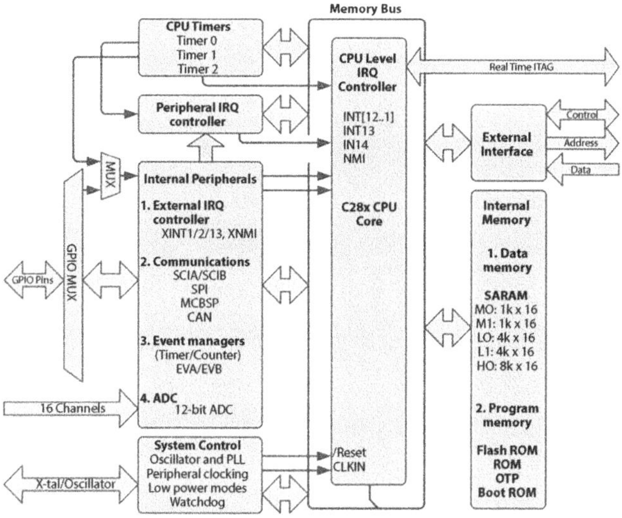


**Figure 10.14** Overall internal architecture of TMS320F281x DSP (Courtesy of Texas Instruments).

Figure 10.14 depicts the software development flow using CCS, which is analogous to other incorporated development tools from other DSP chip vendors. A list of resources that designers should refer to while developing the software is provided in Table 10.2.

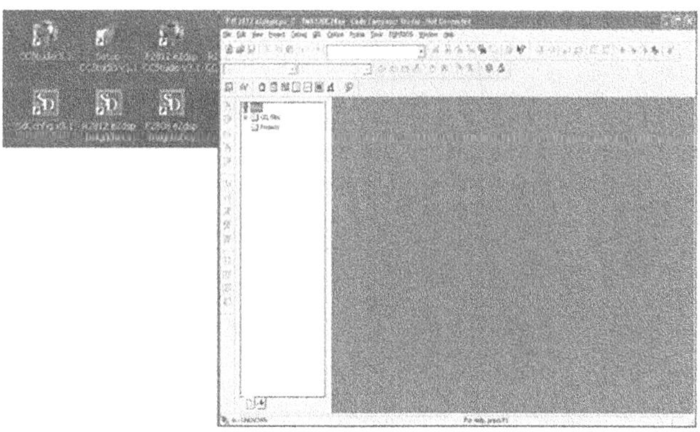

(a)

**Figure 10.15** (a) Open CCS v3.10.

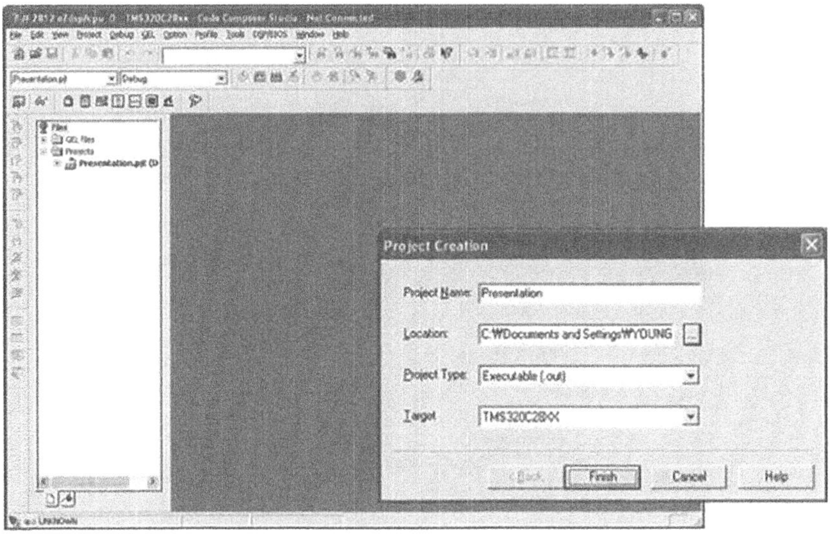


(**b**)

**Figure 10.15** (b) Click Project –> and select New.

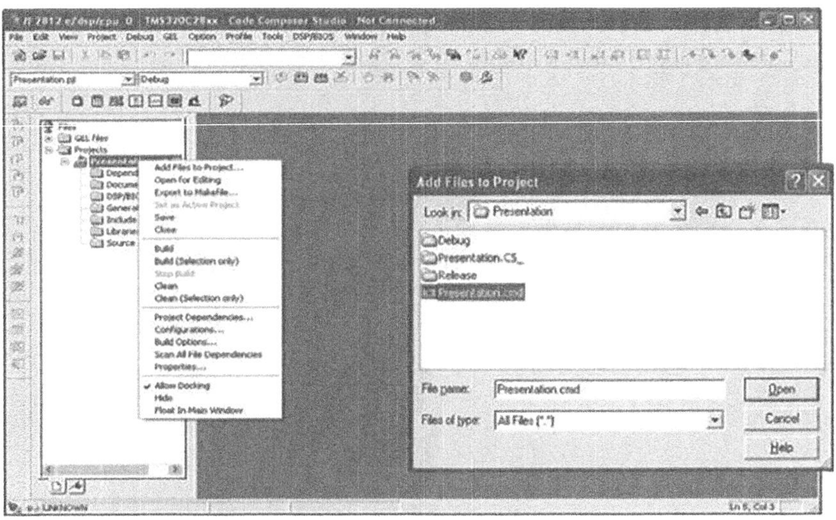


(**c**)

**Figure 10.15** (c) Add link command file to project tree.

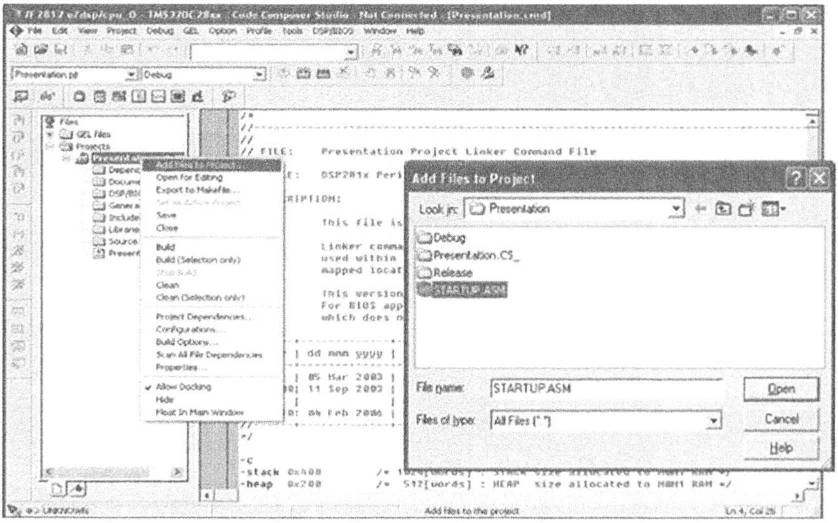


(d)

**Figure 10.15** (d) Add start-up code to project tree.

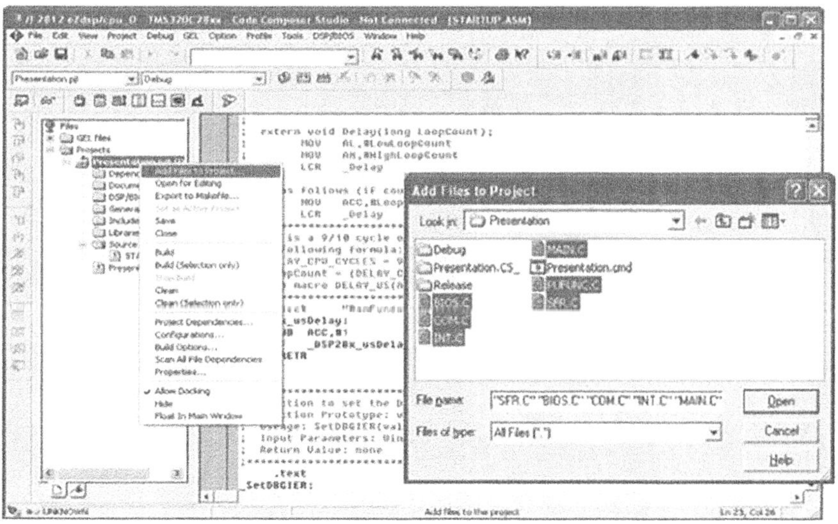


(e)

**Figure 10.15** (e) Add user C/C++ source files to project tree.

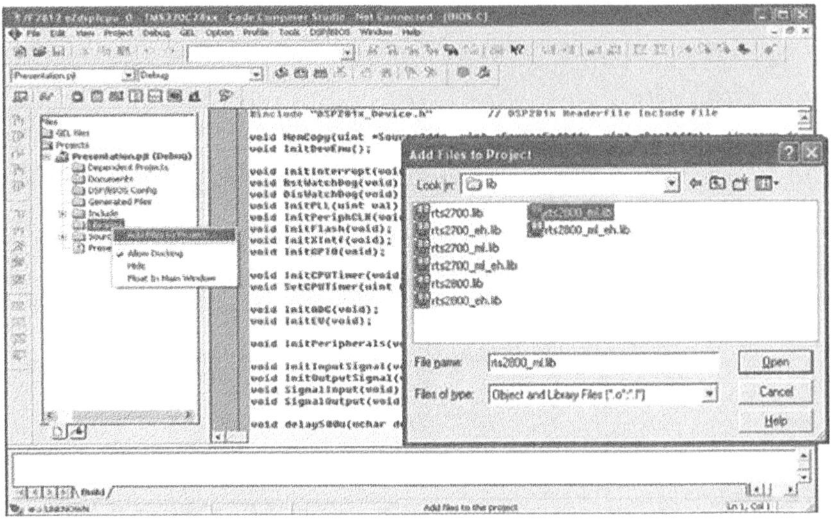


(f)

**Figure 10.15** (f) Add run-time library to project tree.

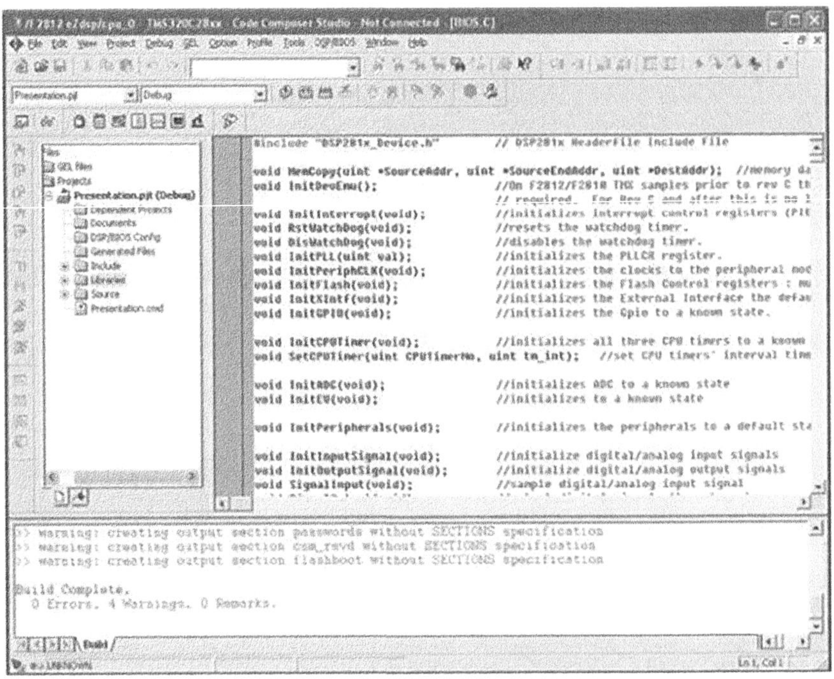


(g)

**Figure 10.15** (g) Click rebuild all button to generate an executable code file (courtesy of Texas Instruments).

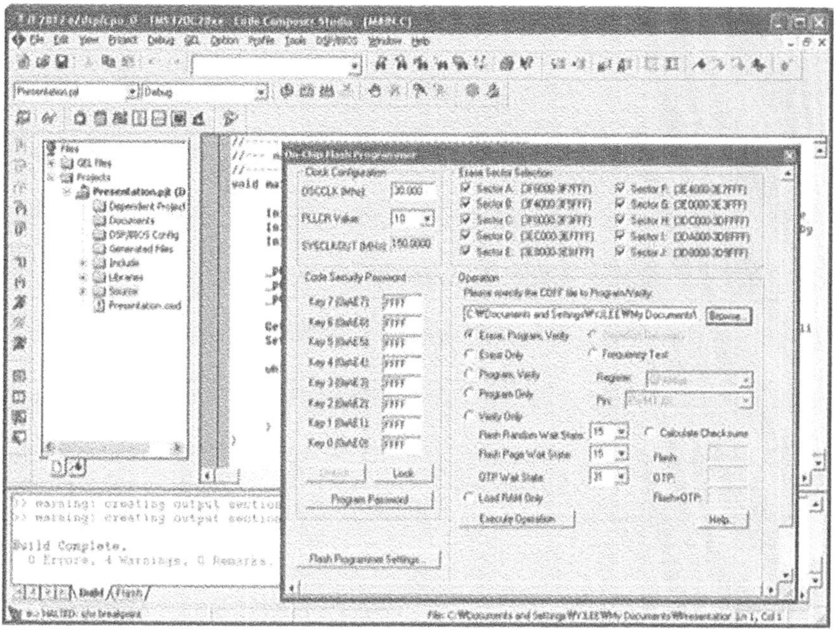

(h)

**Figure 10.15** (h) Click F28xx on-chip flash programmer to download the generated code file.

The creation and execution of user program code on the TMS320F2812 DSP processor are shown in Figure 10.15. The steps involved are as follows:

(a) Start CCS version 3.10.
(b) Go to the project menu, then choose "New."
(c) Add to the project tree the link command file.
(d) Add the startup code to the project tree.
(e) Update the project tree using the user's C/C++ source files.
(f) Add the project tree's run-time library.
(g) To create an executable code file, click the "Rebuild All" button.
(h) Download the created code file by selecting the "F28xx On-Chip Flash Programmer" option.
(i) Run the user application code that was downloaded.

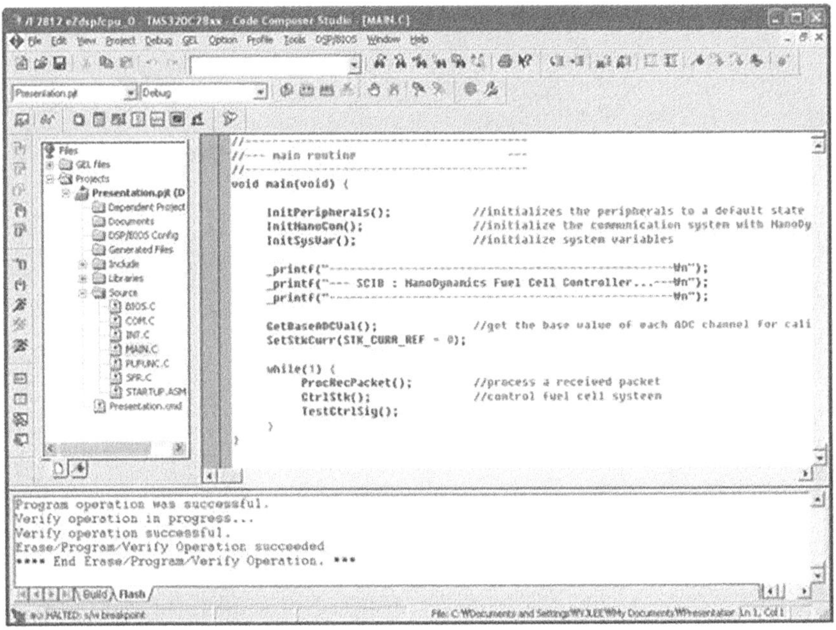


(i)

**Figure 10.15** (i) Run the downloaded user program code.

## 10.11 STM-Based Embedded Controllers

Advances in battery technologies, increased mileage, environmental concerns, and government incentives and regulations have contributed to the rapidly growing trend in vehicle electrification. ST offers state-of-the-art solutions for battery electric vehicles (BEVs) and hybrids (HEVs) using state-of-the-art technology and our extensive understanding of power management. Our range includes IGBTs, high-end silicon and SiC MOSFETs, diodes, isolated gate drivers, protection components, and microcontrollers, and it provides unmatched power management capabilities for electric vehicles. These parts, which adhere to the AEC-Q100 and AEC-Q101 standards, can be purchased alone or as components of complete system solutions.

ST offers a wide range of products, such as traction inverters, battery management systems, and on-board chargers, to meet the needs of EVs and drive the future of electric mobility.

## 10.12 Main Traction Inverter

In electric cars, a primary traction inverter is essential because it transforms battery energy into electricity to run the drivetrain's motors. Road performance, driving range, and general dependability are all directly affected by performance, and weight and size also have influence.

When operating in a demanding automotive environment characterized by high heat and vibration, traction inverters must handle high power and currents while addressing electromagnetic compatibility (EMC) challenges. To preserve dependability as well as passenger and driver safety, fail-safe functioning is crucial.

Among the many discrete semiconductors that ST offers are AQG 324 accredited ACEPACK DRIVE power modules, IGBTs, silicon and silicon-carbide (SiC) MOSFETs, and diodes that have been authorised by AEC-Q101. Figure 10.16 illustrates the main traction inverter configuration, Figure 10.17 shows the on-board charger. These components were completed by SPC5 32-bit automotive microcontrollers and galvanically separated IGBT and MOSFET gate drivers authorized by AEC-Q100. When combined,

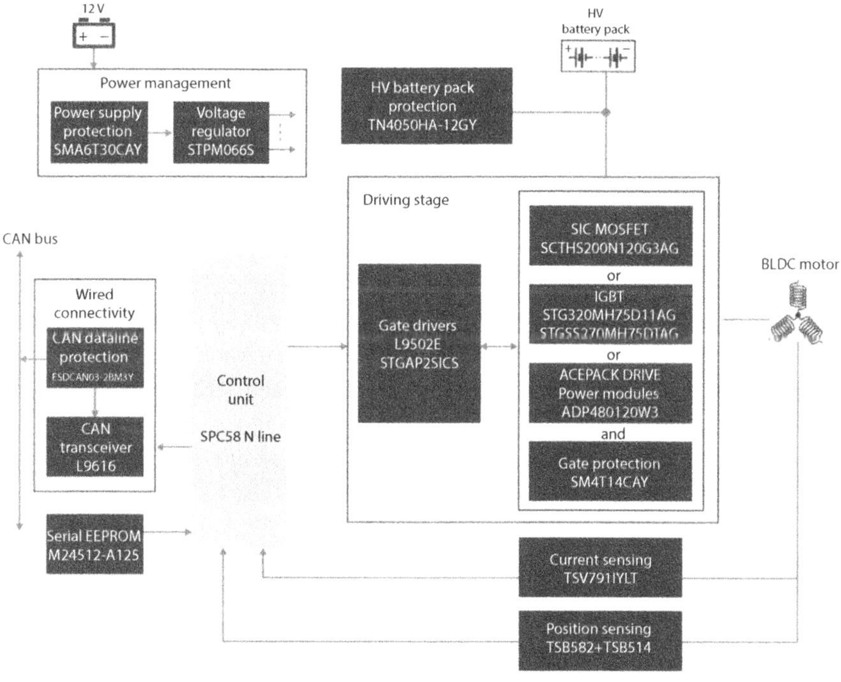


**Figure 10.16** Main traction inverter (courtesy of ST Microelectronics).

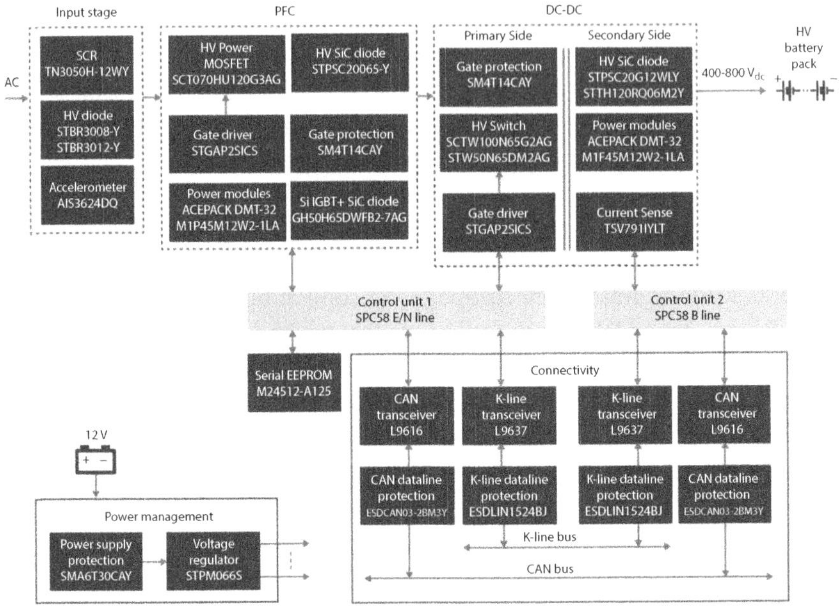


**Figure 10.17** On-board charger (courtesy of ST Microelectronics).

these technologies give developers the ability to design scalable, economical, and energy-efficient traction inverter systems, while also improving power efficiency and reducing size and weight.

## 10.13 On-Board Charger

An essential part of plug-in hybrid (HEV) or electric (EV), the on-board charger, oversees charging the high-voltage battery (400–800 VDC) from AC main sources, whether at home or at public or private charging stations.

Modern OBCs range from 3.5 kW single phase to 22 kW three-phase high-power converters, requiring maximum efficiency and reliability for rapid charging and adherence to strict space and weight limitations.

In addition to silicon diodes and SiC MOSFETs, ST also offers AEC Q100 rated silicon, IGBTs, and ACEPACK DMT-32 AQG 324 authorized modules in various topologies. The development of reliable and efficient on-board chargers for demanding applications is made possible by these components in conjunction with SPC5 32-bit automotive microcontrollers and AEC-Q100 certified MOSFET gate drivers, and galvanically isolated IGBT.

## 10.14 Battery Management System (BMS)

For automotive applications, ST's Battery Management System (BMS) architecture is been developed to satisfy the crucial requirements of controlling and monitoring lithium-ion (Li-ion) batteries in electric vehicles. The system includes several crucial components that are necessary for achieving the best possible battery performance and safety:

1. Battery Protection: Prevents the battery from operating outside its safe operational parameters, ensuring its longevity and reliability.
2. Battery Monitoring: Determines the SoH and SoC of the battery during the charging and discharging cycles, providing precise information on how well it is performing.
3. Battery Optimization: Implements cell balancing techniques to enhance battery life, capacity, and overall driving range, suitable for BEV, HEV, and PHEV.

The sophisticated L9963E BMS IC and the L9963T isolated transceiver companion chip form the basis of the ST's BMS solution. With the availability of mono- or bi-directional daisy chain configurations, these parts allow for the accurate measurement of up to 14 cells in series and

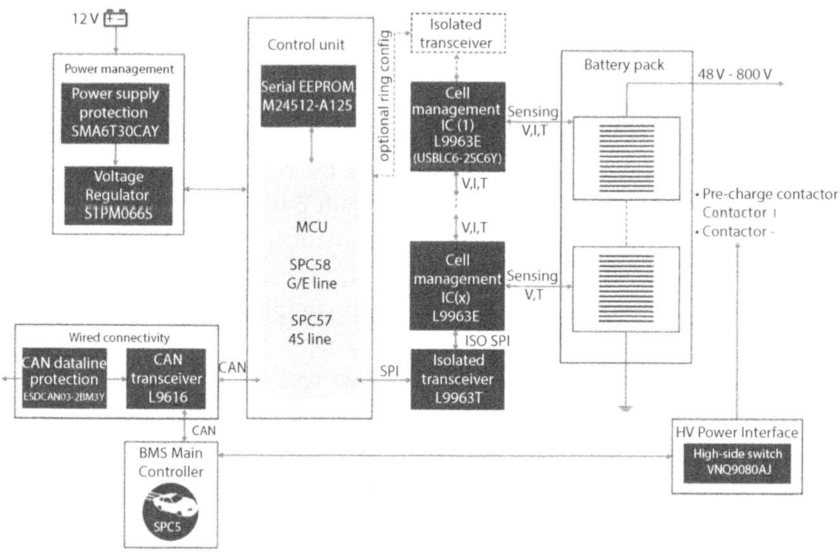


**Figure 10.18** Battery management system (courtesy of ST Microelectronics).

Figure 10.18 depicts the battery management system. The solution fulfills the strict Automotive Safety Integrity Level (ASIL) D criteria and has advanced cell monitoring and diagnostic capabilities.

In conjunction with ST's SPC5 32-bit automotive microcontrollers, system basis chips, power management ICs, protection devices, VI Power smart switches, and automotive EEPROM for data logging, the BMS solution offers a comprehensive suite of components to build robust and efficient battery management systems.

Engineers can leverage the ST's flexible development ecosystem to tailor and optimize their automotive-grade BMS designs, ensuring optimal performance, safety, and reliability across various electric vehicle applications.

## Acknowledgement

The authors gratefully acknowledge the contributions and resources provided by **Texas Instruments and STMicroelectronics (STM)**, whose advanced microcontroller technologies have been instrumental in shaping the understanding and implementation of embedded control systems in electric mobility.

Special thanks are extended to **Texas Instruments** for the comprehensive development tools, including **Code Composer Studio (CCS)** and **TMS320F281x DSP processors**, which served as key enablers for real-time control algorithm development, system-level debugging, and simulation. The use of JTAG-based interfacing, hardware peripherals, and their extensive documentation significantly supported the exploration of embedded digital control for power converters.

Likewise, the authors acknowledge **STMicroelectronics** for their state-of-the-art embedded solutions, particularly the **STM32 microcontrollers**, **SiC MOSFETs**, **IGBTs**, and **automotive-grade gate drivers**, which are crucial components in building efficient traction inverters, on-board chargers, and battery management systems for electric vehicles. Their contributions toward advanced power management, safety compliance (AEC-Q100/101), and system scalability have been vital in highlighting the role of embedded hardware in the evolving e-mobility landscape.

We also extend our appreciation to the editors and publishers of *Smart Charging Infrastructures* for the opportunity to present this work, and to our respective institutions for their support in carrying out this book chapter.

# 11

# Solar Piezo Hybrid Power Charging System

**Vedanth S., Varun Baalaji S., Shairahul Gautam S., Sharan Vikash, Ashwini K. and R. Resmi***

*Department of Electrical and Electronics Engineering, Amrita School of Engineering, Amrita Vishwa Vidyapeetham, Coimbatore, India*

***Abstract***
This study explored the integration of solar power generation with piezoelectric energy harvesting to enhance the efficiency and reliability of renewable energy sources. Solar panels and piezoelectric transducers were utilized in parallel to capture energy from sunlight and mechanical vibrations, respectively. Piezoelectric transducers generate AC voltage outputs typically around 1.2 V, which are rectified to DC voltages for storage and use. A demonstration of a footstep energy production system is presented, providing empirical data for the analysis. The feasibility of large-scale piezoelectric energy production was assessed, along with the benefits of integrating solar and piezoelectric technologies for future energy solutions.

***Keywords*:** Piezoelectric transducer, solar energy, hybrid, Blynk, MATLAB

## 11.1 Introduction

Piezoelectric power transducers use crystals to generate power, which can be placed in high-population areas to generate power and stored in batteries that have been simulated in MATLAB/Simulink [1]. A comparison between two different piezoelectric materials is made, analyzed, and the different energy harvesting techniques were understood [2]. Piezoelectric transducers can be installed on platforms and buses where high vibrations are present because people continue to stand and walk, which is the future of power generation [3]. This prototype was improved from a previous

**Corresponding author*: r_resmi@cb.amrita.edu

A. Chitra, W. Razia Sultana and V. Indragandhi (eds.) Smart Charging Infrastructures, (231–242)

prototype by including environmental factors [4]. A conversion efficiency of 83% had been achieved using a piezoelectric model [5]. Efficient energy-harvesting techniques have also been discussed, and this comparison is based on renewable energy parameters [6]. Piezoelectric transducer materials have evolved from basic monocrystals to polycrystals using various materials. This study provided a comparison between the performance of the piezoelectric transducer and the change in materials used inside the transducers [7].

Materials have a very strong relationship with power generation in transducers. The arrangement of the atoms in piezoelectric transducers to provide the maximum power for a small amount of force, had been discussed [8]. Developments in this field include wearable piezoelectric shoes and wristwatches that use vibration to produce power and their connection with the Internet of Things (IoT) to measure its performance [9]. Piezoelectric energy production has two main parameters: the output power and vibration source [10]. Piezoelectric transducers had been proposed as thin plates to harness low-frequency vibrations [11]. Piezoelectric transducers can also be used as electrical transformers in electronics that use piezoelectric ceramic plates [12]. Adaptive positioning systems can be used to produce power using piezoelectric transducers [13]. Piezoelectric transducers that use ceramic plates have been used as replacements for electromagnetic energy harvesters owing to their high power density and simple architecture [14]. There are two main lead-free piezoelectric transducers: Bismuth Niobium Titanate and those based on Potassium Nodium Niobite. These materials are lead free and therefore environmentally friendly. These materials are suggested to be widely used but they do not produce the same power generation capability as Lead Zirconate Titanate [15]. In return, when an electric current is applied to the piezoelectric transducers, they tend to vibrate, and this vibration can be used in biological applications as biosensors [16].

The primary objectives of this study are to develop a hybrid power generation system that integrates piezoelectric transducers and solar panels to ensure a continuous energy supply, optimize energy harvesting from both sources using advanced control algorithms and hardware setups, and enhance energy storage and conversion. Additionally, this study aims to implement IoT capabilities for real-time monitoring, data analysis, and remote control to optimize system performance and reliability.

## 11.2 Methodology

This study investigated the integration of solar power generation with piezoelectric energy harvesting to improve the efficiency and reliability of renewable energy sources. The methodology involves simulating and analyzing the energy production capabilities of piezoelectric transducers, which convert mechanical vibrations into electrical energy through the piezoelectric effect. The transducers typically yield AC voltage outputs, averaging 1.2 V, which are crucially rectified to a DC voltage for storage and subsequent use. The study utilized several key components to achieve its objectives. Solar panels capture sunlight and convert it into electrical energy, whereas piezoelectric transducers harvest mechanical vibrations from various sources. Various operating modes are considered to maximize the energy extraction under different conditions. For instance, the system adapts to varying sunlight intensities and mechanical vibration frequencies to maintain a consistent energy production. These operational nuances are critical for assessing the feasibility and scalability of large-scale production of piezoelectric energy. This study considered both the simulation and hardware implementation of this work.

### 11.2.1 Simulation Modelling in MATLAB/Simulink

The system begins with a vibration source that generates mechanical vibrations as the primary energy input. Figure 11.1 shows the process flow diagram of the simulation. Mechanical vibrations are transferred to the piezo bender, which converts mechanical energy into electrical energy through the piezoelectric effect. The electrical energy produced by the piezo bender is in the form of Alternating Current (AC). This AC voltage is then passed through a full-wave rectifier, which converts it into Direct Current (DC). To ensure that the voltage is suitable for charging the battery or powering a load, a buck converter regulates the DC voltage, which lowers and stabilizes it. The regulated DC voltage was then used to charge the battery and store the harvested energy. Finally, the stored energy in the battery can be used to power a load, such as in a small electronic device, which completes the energy conversion and storage process in the piezo-solar hybrid energy production system.

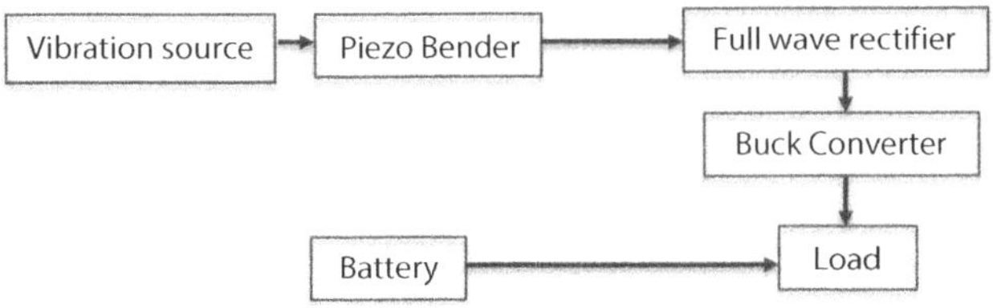


**Figure 11.1** Block diagram of the simulation working.

### 11.2.2 Brief Description of Various Parts

- *Piezoelectric transducers:* As illustrated in Figure 11.2, a transducer is a device that converts energy from one form to another, typically by transforming input energy into output energy. In the proposed model, mechanical energy was derived from human footsteps and converted into electrical energy for use.
- *Voltage sensor:* A voltage sensor is used to measure the voltage. These sensors can detect voltages in various ranges from high to very low current levels. In our model, it is used to measure the voltage from the transducers and the solar panel.
- *Diode bridge rectifier:* A diode bridge, also known as a bridge rectifier, is a circuit composed of four diodes designed to

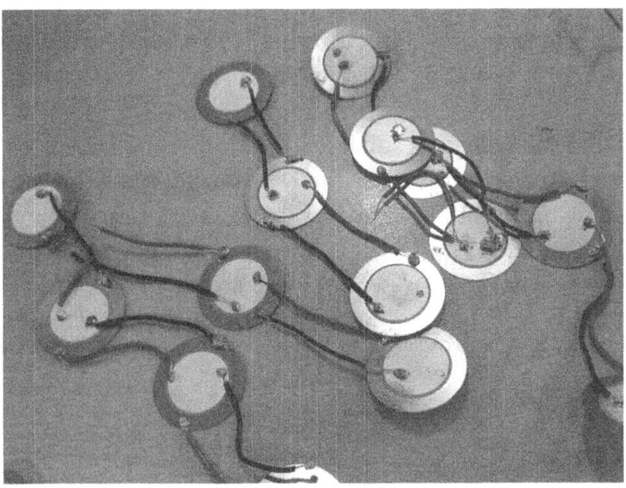

**Figure 11.2** Piezoelectric transducers.

convert alternating current (AC) from the input terminals into direct current (DC) with fixed polarity at the output terminals. This functions by transforming the negative voltage segments of the AC waveform into a positive voltage. This output can then be smoothed into DC using a low-pass filter to convert the AC signal from the transducers to DC for battery storage.

- *Boost converter:* The boost converter matches the designed battery voltage of 3 V, and a switch and DC converter amplify the input voltage. In the proposed design, the output of the Diode Bridge rectifier is used as input to the converter, which outputs 1.2 V from the piezo, which is boosted up to a value of 3.7 V and is given to the battery.
- *Solar panel:* Solar photovoltaic (PV) systems harness sunlight to generate electricity. This clean and renewable energy source has gained popularity because of its environmental benefits and long-term cost savings. The feasibility of including it in piezoelectric transducers was also analyzed.

### 11.2.3 Block Diagram and Working

The optimal use of generated power is the aspiration of every electrical engineer. A block diagram of the proposed model is shown in Figure 11.3. The system uses a configuration of piezoelectric transducers arranged in a combination of four parallel and four series connections, capable of generating up to 1.2 V. When pressure is applied to these transducers, they produce voltage spikes, rather than continuous sine waves. This generated voltage is in AC form and needs to be converted to DC for efficient storage and usage. To achieve this, a diode rectifier is employed, which converts the AC voltage into DC. Following rectification, a boost converter is used to raise the voltage to match the battery's requirement of 3.7 V.

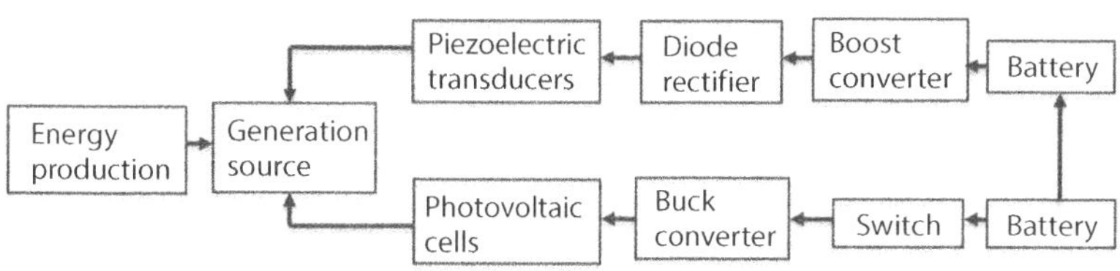


**Figure 11.3** Process flow diagram.

In addition to piezoelectric transducers, the system integrates a solar panel directly with a battery. The solar panel was preinstalled to provide a steady source of energy, supplementing the intermittent power generated by the piezoelectric transducers. When piezoelectric power is available, it contributes to the charging of the battery; otherwise, the solar panel ensures continuous charging.

The loads are connected across the battery to monitor the voltage and ensure that the energy storage system was functioning correctly. This dual-source charging mechanism enhances the reliability and efficiency of the power system, ensuring that energy is harvested from both the mechanical pressure and solar radiation. By integrating these renewable energy sources, the system provides a robust solution for a continuous power supply, which is ideal for applications where both vibration and sunlight are available. This hybrid approach maximizes energy capture and storage, making it a versatile and sustainable power-generation system.

## 11.3 Operating Modes

In the pressure-applied mode, the piezoelectric transducers detect the pressure, producing an AC voltage that charges the battery. In contrast, the pressureless mode occurs when no pressure is applied to the transducers, resulting in zero-voltage production and no power generation. The system also incorporates a solar integration model in which a solar panel is connected in parallel to the battery, providing an alternative power source when piezoelectricity is unavailable. This integration ensures a continuous power supply regardless of the pressure conditions. The functionality of these modes is illustrated in Table 11.1, which demonstrates their roles in maintaining efficient energy harvesting and storage.

**Table 11.1** Modes of operation.

| | Pressure applied | Charging | Not-charging |
|---|---|---|---|
| Piezo-electric transducer | ✓ | ✓ | ✗ |
| Piezo-electric transducer | ✗ | ✗ | ✓ |
| Solar-power generation | ✗ | ✓ | ✗ |

## 11.4 Result and Discussion

In this section, the simulation results and the hardware implementation are discussed. Additionally, IoT integration of hardware implementation is provided for the user interface and monitoring.

### 11.4.1 Simulation Results in MATLAB/Simulink

The proposed model for the simulation shown in Figure 11.4 is for piezoelectric generation only. The described system operates as an energy-harvesting setup designed to power small electronic devices using mechanical vibrations as its primary energy source. At its core, a Vibration Source generates mechanical vibrations, which are then harnessed by the Piezo Bender. Piezo Bender used the piezoelectric effect to convert mechanical energy into electrical energy, producing an alternating current (AC) voltage. This AC voltage is then fed into a Full-Wave Rectifier, which converts it into direct current (DC) voltage. To ensure stability and usability, a Buck Converter steps down the DC voltage to a lower regulated level suitable for charging a battery. The battery acts as an energy-storage unit, accumulating harvested energy efficiently. When energy is required to power a small electronic device, a load is drawn from the energy stored in the battery. This setup enables continuous operation of the electronic device by effectively capturing and storing energy from mechanical vibrations

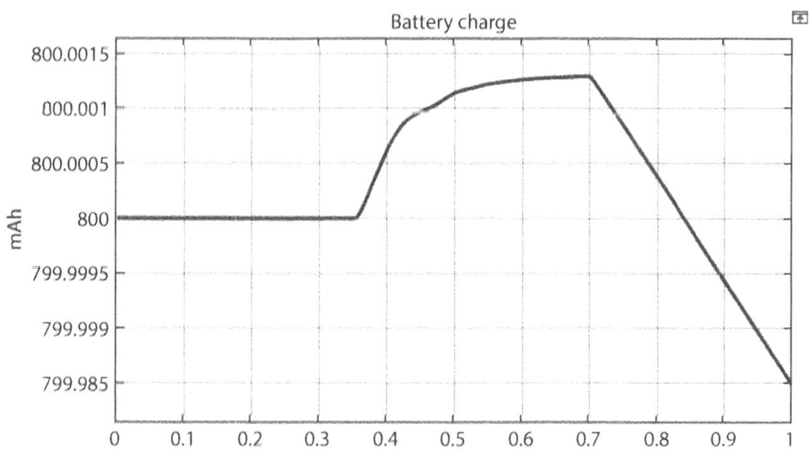


**Figure 11.4** Battery graph—state-of-charge.

and converting it into usable electrical power through a series of efficient energy conversion and storage stages.

### 11.4.2 Hardware Implementation

Figure 11.5 shows the evidence of the hardware model of the project with notations. The model consisted of a solar panel and piezoelectric transducers connected to a pack. The solar panel is connected to the battery through a buck converter. The piezoelectric transducer pack is connected to the battery through a boost converter.

Solar panels and piezoelectric transducers cannot be used simultaneously to charge the battery. A switch was provided to control whether the piezoelectric or solar panel simultaneously charged the battery. A solar panel of suitable rating is connected to charge the battery sufficiently through the buck converter, which steps it down to 3.7 V which is the nominal charging voltage of the battery. This occurs when piezoelectricity is not produced (i.e., when pressure is not applied). Eventually, when pressure is applied, the piezo transducers produce a maximum of 1.2 V. The boost converter has a duty ratio of 0.67, to boost the voltage up to a maximum of 3.7 V. This 3.7 V is given to the battery for charging it for future use.

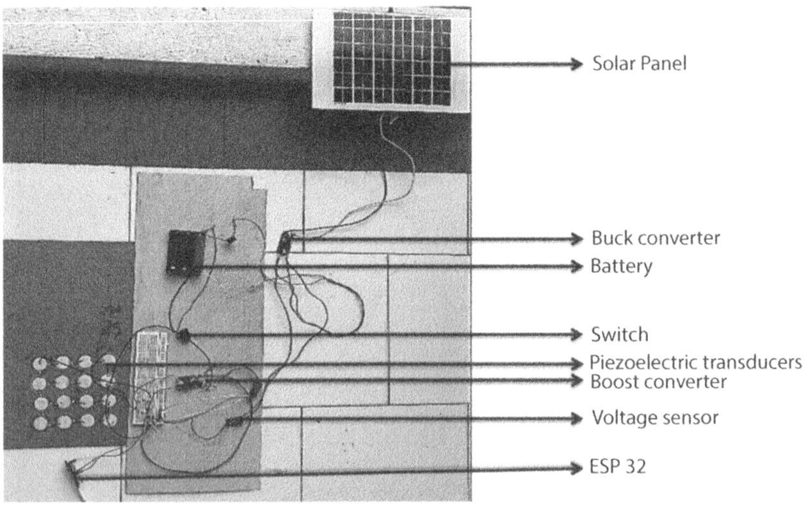


**Figure 11.5** Complete hardware setup of the project (top view).

### 11.4.3 IoT Integration

The Blynk IO app is used for IoT integration, as shown in Figure 11.6, of the voltage outputs. The voltages were obtained from the proposed model, which explains the output voltage of the battery, and the second gauge explains the output voltage directly from the piezoelectric transducers when pressure is applied. The Blynk IO app uses the Wi-Fi model present in the ESP 32 microprocessor. When no pressure is applied, the first gauge shows the rated voltage of the battery of 3.7 V and the second gauge shows the voltage produced by the piezoelectric, which allows the user to view the amount of data and monitor the performance of the piezoelectric device such that it can be modified in an efficient Integrating IoT with a solar-piezo hybrid power charging system to enhance efficiency and monitoring capabilities. The IoT framework enables real-time data collection and analysis from solar panels and piezoelectric sensors, thereby optimizing energy harvesting and storage. Smart algorithms can predict power-generation patterns, adjust system settings, detect faults, and ensure optimal

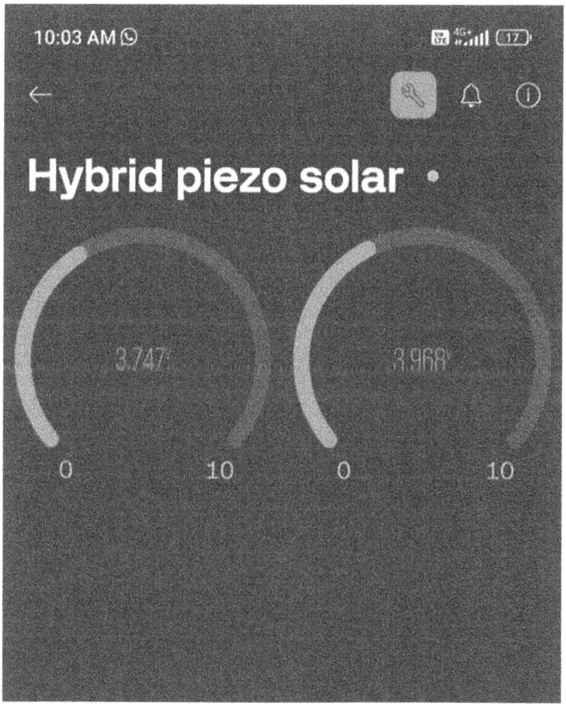


**Figure 11.6** The screenshot of the BLYNK interface.

performance and reliability. Remote monitoring and control *via* IoT devices provide users with insights and management capabilities, thereby improving the overall effectiveness and sustainability of the hybrid power system. The output voltage of the battery is in the range of 3.7 to 4.2 V. Therefore, the range of the gauge was chosen as 0–10 V for easier visualization. Similarly, the output voltage of the piezoelectric transducers was in the range of 3.2 to 4.0 V. Therefore, the range of the gauge was chosen as 0–10 V for easier understanding.

## 11.5 Conclusion

This study illustrates a promising approach for sustainable energy harvesting that combines solar and piezoelectric technologies. By harnessing energy from both sunlight and mechanical vibrations, the system demonstrates enhanced efficiency and reliability compared with standalone approaches. The integration of solar panels with piezoelectric transducers shows potential for diverse applications ranging from urban environments to remote locations where conventional power sources are limited. The demonstrated footstep energy system validates the practicality of this dual-energy approach and highlights its adaptability to various scales of implementation. Optimizing the integration and scalability of solar and piezoelectric systems presents a compelling pathway towards advancing renewable energy solutions and effectively addressing global energy challenges.

## Acknowledgments

We would like to acknowledge the support of our university, Amrita Vishwa Vidyapeetham, Coimbatore, for funding this project and assisting with the preparation of this study.

## References

1. Praanesh, K.S., Seedarala, L., Chaganti, P.C.V., Lekshmi, Syama, S., Power Generation Using Piezoelectric Transducers. *IEEE Xplore*, pp. 306–311, Dec. 2022, doi: https://doi.org/10.1109/ICECA55336.2022.10009578.

2. Aldahiry, D.A., Bajaba, D.A., Basalamah, N.M., Ahmed, M.M., Piezoelectric Transducer as an Energy Harvester: A Review. *Yanbu J. Eng. Sci.*, 19, 1, 2022.
3. Maziati Akmal, M.H., Warikh, A.R.M., Ralib, A.A.M.,Vibrational piezoelectric energy harvester's performance using lead-zirconate titanate versus lead-free potassium sodium niobate. *Mater. Res. Express*, 6, 11, 115708, Oct. 2019, doi: https://doi.org/10.1088/2053-1591/ab492e.
4. Ciftci, B., Chamanian, S., Koyuncuoglu, A., Muhtaroglu, A., Kulah, H., A Low-Profile Autonomous Interface Circuit for Piezoelectric Micro-Power Generators. *IEEE Transactions on Circuits and Systems I Regular Papers*, vol. 68, no. 4, pp. 1458–1471, Feb. 2021, doi: https://doi.org/10.1109/tcsi.2021.3053503.
5. Anand, H. and Singh, B.K., Piezoelectric energy generation in India: an empirical investigation. *Energy Harvest. Syst.*, 6, 3–4, 69–76, Jul. 2019, doi: https://doi.org/10.1515/ehs-2020-0002.
6. Jin, H., Gao, X., Ren, K., Liu, J., Qiao, L., Liu, M., Chen, W., He, Y., Dong, S., Xu, Z., Li, F., Review on Piezoelectric Actuators Based on High-Performance Piezoelectric Materials. *IEEE Trans. Ultrason. Ferroelectr. Freq. Control*, 69, 3057–3069, 2022.
7. Chattaraj, N. and Ganguli, R., Enhanced Performance of Piezoelectric Bending Actuator by Material Redistribution, in: *International Symposium on Devices, Circuits and Systems (ISDCS)*, pp. 1–5, 2020.
8. Brahim, K., Telmc¸ani, A., Chiba, Y., Henini, N., Piezoelectric Energy Conversion and Its Applications: Sensors and Actuators. *2nd International Conference on Electronics, Energy and Measurement (IC2EM)*, Medea, Algeria, pp. 1–5, 2023.
9. Wang, F., Wu, P., Cui, E., Ji, Z., Li, J., Mu, X., A High-Performance Piezoelectric Vibration Energy Harvester with Ultra-Low Acceleration. *IEEE 37th International Conference on Micro Electromechanical Systems (MEMS)*, Austin, TX, USA, pp. 753–756, 2024.
10. Sugino, C., Ruzzene, M., Erturk, A., An analytical framework for locally resonant piezoelectric metamaterial plates. *Int. J. Solids Struct.*, 4, 182–183(4), 2019.
11. Li, Z., Yi, X., Yang, J., Bian, L., Yu, Z., Dong, S., Designing artificial vibration modes of piezoelectric devices using programmable, 3D ordered structure with piezoceramic strain units. *Adv. Mater.*, 34, 2, Oct. 2021, doi: https://doi.org/10.1002/adma.202107236.
12. Mohith, S., Upadhya, A.R., Navin, K.P., Kulkarni, S.M., Rao, M., Recent trends in piezoelectric actuators for precision motion and their applications: A review. *Smart Mater. Struct.*, 30, 1, 013002, Dec. 2020, doi: https://doi.org/10.1088/1361-665x/abc6b9.
13. Thakur, P., Sharma, N., Thakur, P., Lal, M., Sharma, P., Pathak, D., Development of Piezoelectric Energy Harvesting Devices from Lead-Free Piezoelectric Materials, in: *Nanomaterials: An Approach Towards Environmental Remediation*, 2024.

14. Khorsand Zak, A., Tabatabai Yazdi, S., Ebrahimizadeh Abrishami, M., Hashim, A.M., A review on piezoelectric ceramics and nanostructures: fundamentals and fabrications. *J. Aust. Ceram. Soc.*, 60, 3, 723–753, Jan. 2024, doi: https://doi.org/10.1007/s41779-024-00990-3.
15. Kaur, A., Kumar, P., Gupta, A., Sapra, G., Piezoelectric Biosensors in Healthcare, in: *Enzyme-based Biosensors: Recent Advances and Applications in Healthcare*, pp. 255–271, Springer, Singapore, 2023.
16. Feng, Q., Zhong, C., Qin, L., Sandwich-Type Piezoelectric Composite Transducer for Efficient Heat Dissipation. *IEEE Sens. J.*, 24, 7, 10287–10295, 2024.

# 12

# EV Power Train Performance with DC Motor

**Nithya Chandran and R. Resmi***

*Department of Electrical and Electronics Engineering, Amrita School of Engineering, Amrita Vishwa Vidyapeetham, Coimbatore, India*

***Abstract***
Nowadays, electric vehicles are considered very environmentally friendly, as they use little or no fossil fuels. The introduction of affordable and reliable electric vehicles has the potential to trigger the widespread adoption of electric vehicle. One of the core performance parameters of an electric vehicle is its driving motor efficiency. The power, efficiency, cost, and safety of an electric vehicle depend on its electric motor performance. The motor for EV applications should meet the requirements in terms of the size of the vehicle structure, different operating conditions, driving behaviors, and other motor parameters such as power density, and torque–speed relationships. This study discusses different features of an electric motor that make it suitable for electric vehicle applications and includes a performance analysis of a four-wheeler EV power train by taking the reference vehicle as TATA Tiago. In addition, it compares the cost per kilometer of battery electric vehicles with that of internal combustion engine vehicles.

***Keywords*:** Battery electric vehicles (BEVs), electric motors, drive cycles, internal combustion engine vehicles (ICEVs), New European Driving Cycle (NEDC)

## 12.1 Introduction

EV adoption is crucial for sustainable transportation and pollution-free environments. Research shows that the adoption of EV over conventional transport systems can help reduce greenhouse gas emission by up to 75%

**Corresponding author*: r_resmi@cb.amrita.edu

A. Chitra, W. Razia Sultana and V. Indragandhi (eds.) Smart Charging Infrastructures, (243–254)

by 2050 (Hill *et al.*, 2019). The major components of the EV system are the energy storage, traction motor and auxiliary systems, and transmission mechanisms (Singh *et al.*, 2019). As electric motors are the driving force behind electric vehicles (EVs), the market is still evolving with new designs of electric motors with improved power and torque density. For several decades, internal combustion engines (ICEs) have been used in vehicles. As electric motors gain a power density comparable to that of ICEs and act as a great alternative to ICEs, they are being widely adopted for power trains. Although automobiles require constant power for acceleration, they are not ideal for producing torque and speed. However, it is possible to achieve a continuous range if certain motors are properly designed.

The selection of traction motors, control strategies, and power electronic converters plays a significant role in achieving highly efficient operation of EV (Swaminathan *et al.*, 2021), because they have a pronounced impact on the dynamics of the vehicle. In this study, the features of traction motors and different types of electric motors suitable for EVs are discussed. In terms of cost, reliability, efficiency, range, vehicle, acceleration, start–stop running mode, controllability, rare earth usage, etc., the design and selection of electric motors pose challenges. Based on the required key features, the recent trends, technologies, developments, and challenges of electric vehicles considering industrial aspects are discussed in Vempalli *et al.* (2019). These points should be noted while developing new electric vehicle designs.

This study examines the key features of electric motors that make them ideal for electric vehicle (EV) applications, focusing on the performance analysis of a four-wheeler EV powertrain using the TATA Tiago as a reference model. Additionally, it presents a comparative analysis of the cost per kilometer of battery electric vehicles (BEVs) and internal combustion engine vehicles (ICEVs), highlighting the economic advantages of BEVs.

The remainder of this study is organized as follows: The *Methodology* explains the concept of battery-powered electric vehicles with vehicle dynamics and machine topology. The *Results* section covers the estimation of the output parameters and cost–benefit analysis.

## 12.2 Methodology

### 12.2.1 Architecture of Battery EV Power Train

Figure 12.1 shows the battery-powered electric vehicle (BEV) system architecture (Macharia *et al.*, 2023). The major constituents of a BEV power

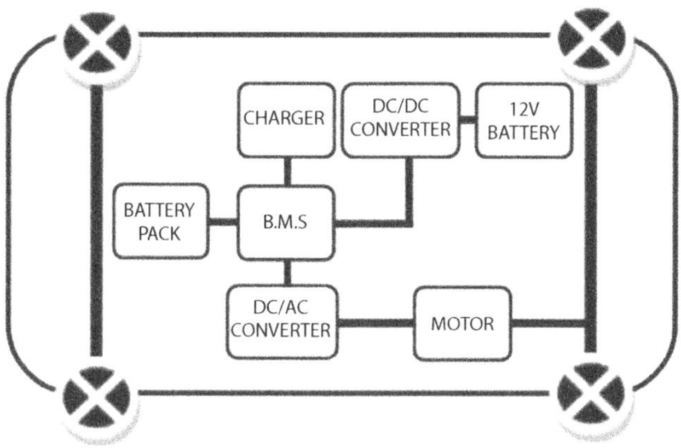


**Figure 12.1** Battery-powered electric vehicle power train.

train are battery packs, power electronic converters, propulsion motors, and transmission mechanisms. The BEVs were powered by the battery pack alone. The battery supplied power to the electric motor. With a gear and differential combination, the propulsion motor is connected to the front- and/or rear-wheel drive (Grunditz *et al.*, 2016). The motor was tested using a New European Driving Cycle (NEDC) on the MATLAB platform. A modified Indian drive cycle, which is similar to the NEDC, was applied to validate the design. The NEDC has urban driving with frequent start stops and low speeds, followed by extra-urban driving with more steady and higher speeds.

### 12.2.2 Requirements of Electric Traction Motors

The key requirements of electric vehicle motors are mainly high power density, torque speed characteristics over different operating conditions, and a wide speed range. There are other major constraints to be considered when selecting or designing a motor. High torque levels at low speeds for the starting and climbing regions and high-power levels at high speeds for cruising are required. Regenerative braking and efficient control are crucial for improving the battery capacity and extending the range. Good fault tolerance characteristics, high torque density, fast torque response, and cost are other critical parameters to be considered when selecting an electric motor for an EV power train (Madichetty *et al.*, 2021). In addition, these motors in EVs are expected to have a high overload capacity, high constant power speed range, fast dynamic response, efficient flux weakening capability at high speeds, and high reliability. These are essential requirements, regardless of the machine type (Agamloh *et al.*, 2020). However, the topology and principle of operation of the machine dictate the design and control measures required to satisfy these requirements. A machine that meets all these requirements must be at an acceptable cost.

### 12.2.3 Machine Topologies

Traction motors should satisfy the major requirements for EV applications. Research progress has been made on the design of various topologies suitable for EV power trains. Both conventional and advanced electric motor topologies and control strategies have been discussed by Thakar *et al.* (2019). Apart from this, research has focused on areas such as battery life extension using cell balancing techniques (Koganti *et al.*, 2021), fast charging with the help of machine learning (Vanitha *et al.*, 2021), and integration of thermal and mechanical design to enhance the functioning of EV. El Hadraoui *et al.* (2022) discussed motors commonly used by EVs. The brushed DC motor is a good candidate for an EV motor because it offers a high torque at low speeds. Efficient speed control makes it adaptable for traction purposes. DC motors are widely used in low-power EVs. The disadvantages of DC motors include high maintenance requirements and commutations. However, these motors are good candidates because they satisfy the torque requirements of EV (Liu *et al.*, 2020). Many vehicle manufacturers use permanent-magnet synchronous motors (PMSM). PMSMs exhibit the highest torque density, power density, and efficiency. However, the requirement for more complex strategies poses a challenge. A flux-weakening technique is required under high-speed driving, which may increase the risk of demagnetization. The vibration of the EV propulsion system can be significant because of its strong magnetic field (Wang *et al.*, 2019). Induction motors and brushless DC motors are also promising candidates for EV. Permanent-magnet brushless DC motors have less weight and better heat dissipation and cooling. Induction motors are simple to construct and require less maintenance. This offers the capacity to improve maximum speed. However, the complex control limits their application (Krishnamoorthy *et al.*, 2024). Switched reluctance motors (SRM) offer a high-power density, good torque and speed characteristics, high starting torque, and a wider constant power region. A low inertia ratio offers a high-speed operation. High torque ripple, vibration, and noise limit the extensive use of SRM in EVs (El Hadraoui *et al.*, 2022). In addition to these conventional motors, different motor topologies were discussed by Karki *et al.* (2020). Albatayneh *et al.* (2020) pointed that significant improvement in the well to wheel efficiency of EV can be made by using electricity generated by solar or wind systems. Research works has been conducted to reduce pollution-based electricity generation using renewable energy sources (Vanitha *et al.*, 2022; Resmi *et al.*, 2022). With the use of these types of electric conversion systems, the dependency on fossil fuels for battery charging can be reduced.

### 12.2.4 Vehicle Dynamics and Estimation of Output Parameters

The input parameters shown in Figure 12.2 (Vempalli *et al.*, 2019) are used to size the power train according to defined performance requirements such as driving range and vehicle speed. This study aims to analyze the performance of the power train of a four-wheeler EV using the MATLAB Simulink model. In addition, this study compares the ICE and EV versions of the same model.

For design purposes, we initially needed to calculate the tractive force for a given kerb weight. The total tractive force ($F_t$) required at the wheel consists of four forces: aerodynamic drag force ($F_d$), rolling resistance force ($F_r$), gradient force ($F_g$), and acceleration force ($F_a$), as shown in Equation (12.1). The aerodynamic drag force ($F_d$) is produced by the friction of the vehicle movement opposite to the wind direction. This can be calculated using Equation (12.2), where $\rho$ is the air density, $C_d$ is the for aerodynamic drag coefficient, $A_f$ is the frontal area of the vehicle, V is the vehicle velocity, and $C_d$ is taken as 0.4 (Vempalli *et al.*, 2019). The rolling resistance force ($F_r$) is caused by tire material's nature, any deformation, air circulation at the wheel, slippage, etc. In Equation (12.3), $m$ stands for the mass of the vehicle, $\mu_r$ is the coefficient of rolling resistance, $g$ is the acceleration due to gravity and $\alpha$ is the grade angle. For most highways, the grades

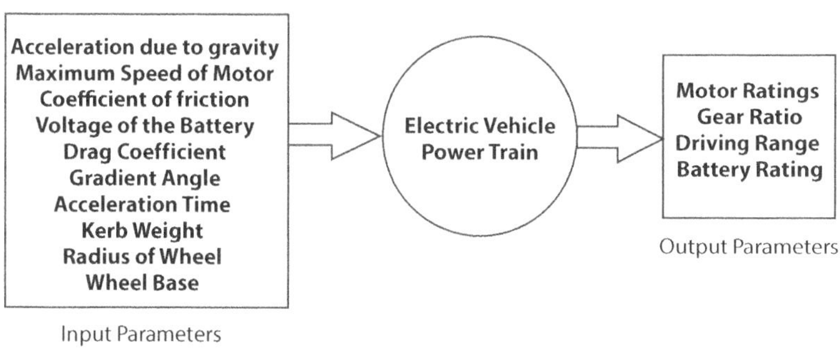


**Figure 12.2** Input–output parameters of an EV system.

were restricted to 6%. To calculate the rolling resistance force and gradient resistance force, the grade angle was considered to be 6%. The mass of the vehicle, including pay load, was taken as 1,500 kg. A gradient force ($F_g$) is produced by the resistance developed by a vehicle moving up a slope. The gradient resistance tended to pull the vehicle downwards. This can be calculated using Equation (12.4). The acceleration force can be calculated by taking the product of the mass of the vehicle and the acceleration. This is given by Equation (12.5).

$$F_t = F_d + F_r + F_g + F_a \tag{12.1}$$

$$F_d = \frac{\rho}{2} * C_d * A_f * V^2 \tag{12.2}$$

$$F_r = \mu_r * m * g * cos\alpha \tag{12.3}$$

$$F_r = m * g * sin\alpha \tag{12.4}$$

$$F_a = m * a \tag{12.5}$$

The net tractive effort is calculated for the total vehicle weight, including the pay load, using the vehicle specifications. Table 12.1 shows the vehicle specifications.

Based on the total tractive force and vehicle dynamics, the motor ratings of a brushed DC motor for a TATA Tiago EV were determined using the basic equation of power and torque. Table 12.2 shows the motor ratings.

**Table 12.1** Vehicle parameters from the TATA EV official website (Electric Tiago.ev, 2024).

| Parameters | Value | Units |
|---|---|---|
| Dimensions | 3,769 × 1,677 × 1,536 | mm |
| Kerb weight | 1,150 | kg |
| Tyre size | 175/65 R14 | – |
| Acceleration | 0–60 in 5.7 s | Kmph |

**Table 12.2** DC motor specifications.

| Parameters | Value | Units |
|---|---|---|
| Rated power | 53 | Kw |
| Rated Speed | 5,600 | rpm |
| Supply voltage | 320 | V |
| Torque | 90.4 | Nm |

## 12.3 Results and Discussion

### 12.3.1 Simulation Results

The power train of the EV four-wheeler was simulated using the MATLAB Simulink platform. The DC motor was fed by an H-bridge block, which was supplied by a controlled PWM voltage. Figure 12.3 shows a plot of vehicle speed versus time. It is evident that the obtained vehicle speed closely follows the reference speed, with a peak velocity of 33 m/s over 1,180 s. The slight deviations during the deceleration and acceleration points can be attributed to factors such as drivetrain response delay, control system adjustments, and the effects of regenerative braking. This may cause a lag in the actual vehicle speed. Regenerative braking may affect how the actual vehicle speed follows the sharp deceleration phase of the NEDC. Model assumptions, such as aerodynamic drag, rolling resistance, and tire characteristics, also result in mild deviations during the frequent deceleration and acceleration phases.

The first 800 s show urban driving with frequent start-stop phases. During this phase, the deviations were slightly more noticeable than those

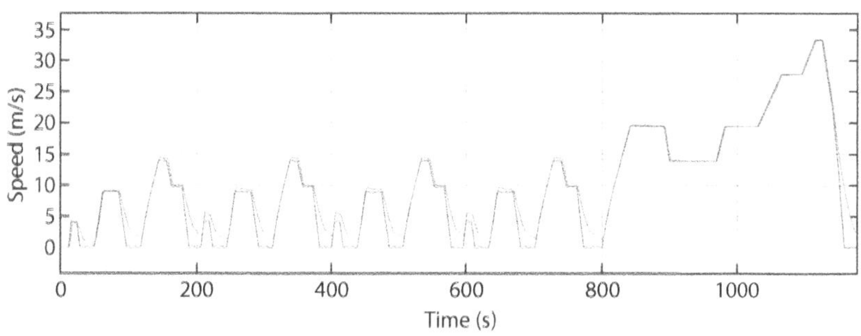


**Figure 12.3** Speed vs time curve for NEDC cycle.

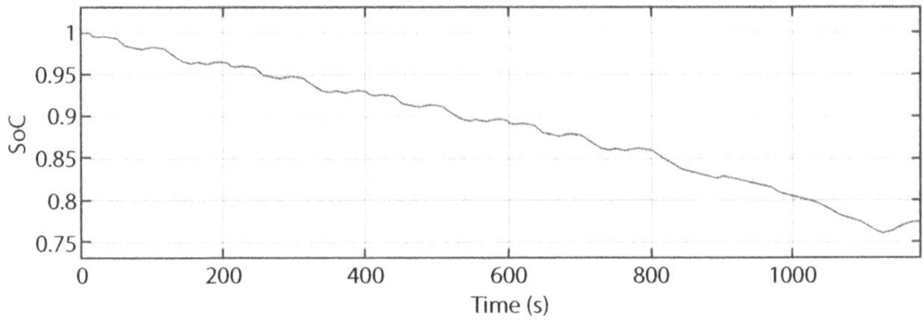


**Figure 12.4** SoC curve for NEDC cycle.

in the extra-urban section, where speeds were higher and steadier without frequent speed changes. The simulated vehicle speed aligned more closely with the target. This improved stability at higher speeds reflects the EV's performance in maintaining steady speeds better than that of frequent acceleration and braking. The instantaneous torque characteristics of the DC motor aid in achieving peak speed quickly. This rapid acceleration improved the overall efficiency of the urban driving phases.

Figure 12.4 illustrates the State of Charge (SoC) curve, showing a remaining battery charge of 77.41%. Regenerative braking was enabled in the simulation platform. Thus, the battery was being recharged during deceleration. This can be observed in the SoC curve. Because low power is required for urban driving, SoC decreases slowly. The gradual decline shows energy-efficient usage during the start-stop scenarios. Battery consumption accelerates during the extra urban driving phase, and regenerative braking is not very effective at higher speeds. After 800 s, the SoC curve showed mild fluctuations, demonstrating various driving conditions with some recovery from braking. This steady depletion of SoC indicates typical battery usage during real-world driving. The SoC curve indicates the significance of the energy optimization and battery management system in maximizing the efficiency. These results confirm that the designed brushed DC motor is suitable for sizing the powertrain of a four-wheel EV.

### 12.3.2 Cost–Benefit Analysis

To analyze the cost benefits of BEVs and ICEVs, a TATA Tiago ICEV model was considered. An ICEV of mileage 35 km/L requires 9 L of petrol (or 81 kWh) to cover 315 km by considering 1 L of petrol release of 9 kWh approximately. The BEV model offers 315 km per charge. In Albatayneh *et al.* (2020), the tank-to-wheel efficiency of petrol ICEVs was 14%–33%

and that of BEV was 50%–80%. Suppose the efficiency of ICEV is taken as 25% and that of BEV is considered as 65%, then 0.069 kWh of energy is consumed for 1 km as per the equations given by Shrivastava *et al.* (2020). At a petrol price of ₹105.72/L, the ICEV costs ₹3.02/km, while the BEV with 24 kWh battery costs ₹0.97/km if we use a 7.4 kW fast charging single phase home charger, according to e-AMRIT calculation facility. The Indian government's E-Amrit website dispels myths about buying, owning, and adopting electric vehicles as well as policies, subsidies, and investment opportunities (NITI Aayog, 2024). Cost per kilometer analysis shows that BEVs have lower operating costs than ICEVs do. Despite the higher initial cost, BEVs provide long-term savings in energy, less maintenance, and a sustainable environment with an affordable operating cost. This draws attention to economic benefits of adopting BEVs, rather than ICEVs.

## 12.4 Conclusion

Electric vehicles (EVs) contribute to cleaner environments by reducing pollution. Recognizing the importance of EV adoption, this study explores the EV powertrain architecture and various electric motor features that align with the EV requirements. It also discusses the widely accepted electric motor topologies for EV applications. In this study, a DC motor was designed specifically for four-wheeler EV applications. The motor was tested using the New European Driving Cycle (NEDC) in MATLAB, and the results demonstrated that the model accurately follows the reference speed as defined by the NEDC cycle. The SoC curve shows that the designed model is energy-efficient with regenerative braking for urban driving scenarios. Additionally, this study compared the cost per kilometer of internal combustion engine vehicles (ICEVs) and battery electric vehicles (BEVs) for the same distance. The findings suggest that EVs offer both economic and environmental advantages over ICEVs, as the cost per kilometer for EVs is significantly lower. Ongoing research on battery technologies has enhanced the widespread adoption of BEVs by lowering the initial cost of battery systems and improving their performance.

## Acknowledgment

We sincerely thank Amrita Vishwa Vidyapeetham University for their invaluable support in the preparation of this study.

## References


1. Hill, G., Heidrich, O., Creutzig, F., Blythe, P., The role of electric vehicles in near-term mitigation pathways and achieving the UK's carbon budget. *Appl. Energy*, 251, 113111, 2019.
2. Singh, K.V., Bansal, H.O., Singh, D., A comprehensive review on hybrid electric vehicles: architectures and components. *J. Mod. Transp.*, 27.2, 77–107, 2019.
3. Swaminathan, A., Malavika, K., Narayanan, N., Jayakumar, M., Review on Different Topologies of Power Electronic Converters and Control Strategies for Motors in Electric Vehicles. *Innovations in Power and Advanced Computing Technologies (i-PACT)*, Kuala Lumpur, Malaysia, pp. 1–7, 2021.
4. Vempalli, S.K., *et al.*, Electric vehicle designing, modelling and simulation. *2018 4th International Conference for Convergence in Technology (I2CT)*, IEEE, 2018.
5. Macharia, V.M., Garg, V.K., Kumar, D., A review of electric vehicle technology: Architectures, battery technology and its management system, relevant standards, application of artificial intelligence, cyber security, and interoperability challenges. *IET Electr. Syst. Transp.*, 13, 2, e12083, 2023.
6. Grunditz, E.A. and Thiringer, T., Performance analysis of current BEVs based on a comprehensive review of specifications. *IEEE Trans. Transp. Electrif.*, 2, 3, 270–289, 2016.
7. Madichetty, S., Mishra, S., Basu, M., New trends in electric motors and selection for electric vehicle propulsion systems. *IET Electr. Syst. Transp.*, 11, 3, 186–199, 2021.
8. Agamloh, E., Von Jouanne, A., Yokochi, A., An overview of electric machine trends in modern electric vehicles. *Machines*, 8, 2, 20, 2020.
9. Thakar, D.U. and Patel, R.A., Comparison of advance and conventional motors for electric vehicle application. *2019 3rd International Conference on Recent Developments in Control, Automation & Power Engineering (RDCAPE)*, IEEE, 2019.
10. Koganti, S.K., *et al.*, Comparative Study between Cell Balancing Methods in Electric Vehicle. *2021 IEEE Madras Section Conference (MASCON)*, IEEE, 2021.
11. Vanitha, V., Resmi, R., Reddy, K.N.S.V., Machine learning-based charge scheduling of electric vehicles with minimum waiting time. *Comput. Intell.*, 37, 3, 1047–1055, 2021.
12. El Hadraoui, H., *et al.*, A multi-criteria analysis and trends of electric motors for electric vehicles. *World Electr. Veh. J.*, 13, 4, 65, 2022.
13. Liu, C., *et al.*, A critical review of advanced electric machines and control strategies for electric vehicles. *Proc. IEEE*, 109, 6, 1004–1028, 2020.
14. Wang, G., Valla, M., Solsona, J., Position sensorless permanent magnet synchronous machine drives—A review. *IEEE Trans. Ind. Electron.*, 67, 7, 5830–5842, 2019.

15. Krishnamoorthy, S. and Panikkar, P.P.K., A comprehensive review of different electric motors for electric vehicles application. *IJPEDS*, 15, 1, 74–90, 2024.
16. Karki, A., *et al.*, Status of pure electric vehicle power train technology and future prospects. *Appl. Syst. Innov.*, 3, 3, 35, 2020.
17. Albatayneh, A., *et al.*, Comparison of the overall energy efficiency for internal combustion engine vehicles and electric vehicles. *Rigas Tehniskas Univ. Zinatniskie Raksti*, 24, 1, 669–680, 2020.
18. Vanitha, V., Resmi, R., Kumar, K.R., Fabrication and Mathematical Modeling of the Brushless Doubly Fed Induction Generator-Based Wind Electric Conversion System. *Math. Probl. Eng.*, 2022, 1–14, Oct. 2022, doi: https://doi.org/10.1155/2022/2998210.
19. Resmi, R., Analysis of Brushless Doubly Fed Induction Machine, *Renewable Energy Technologies: Advances and Emerging Trends for Sustainability*. N. Kumar, Prabhansu (Eds.), pp. 539–568, Wiley, Scrivener Publishing, Beverly, MA, Sep. 2022, doi: https://doi.org/10.1002/9781119827634.ch16
20. Electric Tiago.ev, TATA ev, https://ev.tatamotors.com/tiago/ev/specifications.html, 2024.
21. Shrivastava, K., *et al.*, Conversion of conventional vehicle into an electric vehicle. *Adv. Appl. Math. Sci.*, 20, 1, 15–24, 2020.
22. E-Amrit, NITI Aayog. Niti.gov.in, National Portal of India, https://www.niti.gov.in/e-amrit, 2024.

# 13

# RC Vehicle for Delivery

**Vemulapati Dhanunjaya Reddy, Mallireddy Jayanthi Reddy, Manoj Kumar S., R. Resmi* and Y. N. V. Ganesh**

*Department of Electrical and Electronics Engineering, Amrita School of Engineering, Amrita Vishwa Vidyapeetham, Coimbatore, India*

## *Abstract*

This study focuses on the development of a sophisticated small-scale remote-controlled vehicle (RC) designed to deliver and collect packages within a controlled environment. The idea is motivated by the interest in autonomous vehicles in transportation and delivering goods to specified conditions in a controlled environment. The designed model is efficient, precise, and reliable to ensure smooth functioning under various conditions. The RC delivery vehicle will have a sturdy chassis and cargo compartment that is capable of handling different types of packages. The control of the system is intuitive, which allows the operators to easily access and control the movement of the car with a dedicated web server application to reach the required destinations. The outcome will advance the future of automation in the field of delivery and provide an adaptable solution for warehouses, college and work campuses, and indoor facilities. This prototype not only provides insight into technological advances but also covers the gap between potential and reliable delivery methods in various applications.

***Keywords*:** Remote control, warehouses, campuses, potential, efficient delivery, sturdy chassis, ESP32CAM

**Corresponding author*: r_resmi@cb.amrita.edu

A. Chitra, W. Razia Sultana and V. Indragandhi (eds.) Smart Charging Infrastructures, (255–266)

# 13.1 Introduction

## 13.1.1 Description of the RC Vehicle

The evolution of the logistics system begins with integrating remote control (RC) technology into the logistics system. This RC technology is very beneficial for places where there is a need to deliver an object safely using a remote-control operation. Using the ESP32-CAM module, pan tilt servo mechanism, L298N motor driver, and lock system using ESP32 enables a much more efficient, secure, and user-friendly operation. In this system, the heart of the system is an L298N motor driver, where the main battery supply is given, and the distribution of supply to the ESP32-CAM module and the pan tilt servo motors is given using a boost converter (5 V–30 V).

### *13.1.1.1 Functioning of L298N Motor Driver*

The L298N motor driver enables many features when connected to the ESP32-CAM module, in which the main feature is speed control of the RC vehicle by using EnA and EnB pins of the L298N motor driver. Beginning from the core level of this RC vehicle, the brain of the system, the ESP32-CAM module controls the operation of the RC vehicle for moving purposes and also plays a key role in verifying the customer while delivering the product, providing footage for controlling, and enhancing the visibility of the footage at night with light included in the ESP32-CAM module.

### *13.1.1.2 The Functioning of ESP32 Camera Module*

ESP32-CAM module is used as the receiver, which acts as a signal receiver. This ESP32-CAM module receives commands and operates accordingly. All IN1, IN2, IN3, and IN4 pins of the L298N motor driver were used for control purposes. For pan tilt, the pan servo motor was connected to the IO14 pin of the ESP32-CAM module, and the tilt servo motor was connected to the IO15 pin of the ESP32-CAM module. For the locking system, ESP32 is used, linked to an app, and controlled through the app. As the ESP32-CAM module acts as a receiver module, the unlocking of the box is performed only when the customer is verified through the footage that is being seen by the user sent by the ESP32-CAM module. The proposed system aimed to address the challenges associated with last-mile delivery by offering a cost-effective and scalable solution. The core of the system relies on the ESP32 development board, which provides Wi-Fi connectivity and is programmed using an Arduino IDE. By leveraging ESP32 capabilities, the vehicle can communicate real time with a central control unit, enabling remote navigation and monitoring. The performance of the proposed RC vehicle was evaluated through practical experiments, which demonstrated its reliability, efficiency, and scalability for various delivery applications. Overall, the integration of ESP32 into the design offers a cost-effective solution with the potential for widespread adoption in the burgeoning field of autonomous delivery systems.

## 13.2 Literature Review

In recent years, the number of vehicles has significantly increased, leading to a reduction in parking spaces [1]. This reduction in parking spaces causes significant inconveniences in urban areas. Therefore, to reduce this problem, a smart parking system is introduced, which allows the user to find the parking space using a web application. This utilizes IoT and object detection to update the available parking spaces, thereby providing a solution for this parking issue [2]. This study focuses on home automation, which enhances human life. Automating homes using sensors, controllers, and actuators for controlling appliances, lighting, temperature, and security without manual interference [3]. The literature provides a detailed solution to the main problem i.e., deaths due to delayed medical help. This problem can be rectified as the system measures and reports the accident severity, location, and time and provides an optimal route for ambulances to reach the accident spot on time, which saves many lives [4]. As the automotive industry is moving towards the electric vehicles, charging these electric vehicles is a major problem because there are fewer charging stations. Using IoT-based, low-cost, interoperable smart charging devices rectifies this issue. It monitors energy consumption, fault detection, and communication *via* JSON for remote management [5]. This literature review mainly focuses on autonomous delivery robots owing to their adverse growth in current technology. The amount of innovation and research based on the usage of these robots and understanding the current trends and applications have made it an effective technique in the logistics department [6]. The main problems with these delivery robots are stable, secure, and reliable navigation. To effectively solve these problems, several algorithms have been developed to enhance the operating patterns of delivery robots. This literature helps in refining the objectives and finding the optimal method to obtain effective results [7]. The application of these delivery robots encompasses autonomous navigation in urban conditions and the conditions in which autonomous vehicles and delivery robots encounter each other, and training them using reinforcement learning enhances these robots. This simulator includes experimentation and analysis and provides advanced autonomous delivery robot research and innovation in this field [8]. This robot utilizes facial recognition and authentication; if verified, the lock will be opened or a shock mechanism will be activated if any unauthorized attempts to open the lock occur and sends a notification *via* the IoT. It is cost-effective and provides anti-theft protection [9]. In this literature, it is mentioned that these delivery robots use Google Maps and Direction API to find their way. In addition, a special algorithm called donkey and carrot helps the system determine where to go from the API. A controller picks up data from the cloud for the robot to use [10]. This Wi-Fi controlled multi-sensor car project enables smartphone control, and for obstacle detection, ultrasonic sensors are placed, and safety sensors such as temperature and fire are placed. Using these sensors enhances the integrity of a robot with the potential for increased autonomy and versatility [11]. This literature mainly focuses on vehicle safety and security through a Vehicle Anti-theft Face Recognition System, Speed Control, and Obstacle Detection using a Raspberry Pi. Including these factors in face recognition, speed control, and obstacle detection improves theft prevention and collision avoidance. Raspberry Pi ensures flexibility, and others, like face recognition, enhance security, and speed control with obstacle detection improves safety [12]. This mainly addresses vehicle routing problems in urban areas, such as optimizing the solution approach and practical applications. This literature is used in further research in this domain [13]. This study introduces an IoT-based security system to prevent theft. This enables many features such as remote control and communication, and the integration of sensors and cameras for detection helps in safety. Tracking utilizes GPS/GSM modules and automatically triggers alerts and security measures. This significantly enhances the vehicle security and safety [14]. In this study, security is performed in different ways, such as using biometric fingerprint authentication integrated with Arduino. Only an authorized vehicle can start and stop the vehicle. This fingerprint authentication enhances the safety and security of global vehicle protection [15]. The study mainly focused on a door-locking system developed with the Arduino IDE. This enables remote control, and can be used in hospitals and hotels to provide remote door access without physical contact. Because it is a user-friendly GUI, it offers security and easy usage compared to existing devices.

### 13.2.1 Research Gap

Despite the promising advancements in remote-control vehicles using mobile app-controlled lock systems, there still exists a notable research gap in the integration of camera surveillance technology for enhancing security and monitoring capabilities. Incorporating a camera system in RC vehicles enables real-time monitoring of the delivery environment and ensures efficient delivery to customers. The visual data captured through the ESP32 camera can also be used for data analytics purposes and also serve as evidence for correct delivery in case of theft or tampering. The pan-tilt mechanism provides a 180-degree wide field of view, which enhances the operator's view for navigation through obstacles. The main advantage of this mechanism is that it tracks customers during deliveries. In addition, a boost converter is used for the power supply to the pan-tilt servomotors as the output from the battery is 9 V and the boost converter rate is 5 V–30 V, which helps in powering the servomotors of the pan-tilt mechanism. These additional features add innovative and effective models that meet the requirements of RC vehicles for delivery.

## 13.3 Methodology

### 13.3.1 Radio-Controlled (RC) Vehicle

RC vehicles are self-powered and remotely controlled *via* a transmitter that emits radio waves. The transmitter sends electrical pulses corresponding to specific actions when control is activated. A power source, battery, or power bank adapter provides energy to the transmitter for radio wave or wireless transmission. Upon receiving the transmitted control signals through the transmitter, the receiver circuitry in the RC vehicle controls the operations performed by the operator and performs the vehicle movement forward,

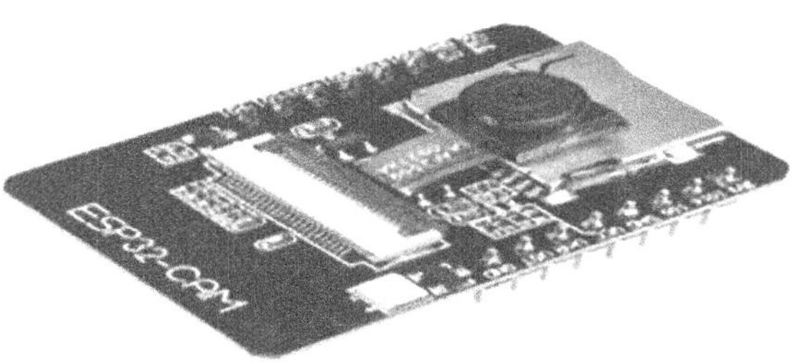


**Figure 13.1** ESP32 camera module.

backward, right-turn, left-turn, and start and stop commands according to the control. Figure 13.1 shows a block diagram of the driver circuit.

### 13.3.2 Camera System

Figure 13.1 explains the image representation of the camera system, which is integrated with the ESP32-CAM module, as shown in Figure 13.2, serves as the main control module for the RC vehicle. A battery was provided to ensure a continuous power supply to ESP32 without external disturbances. The camera module captures the movement of the vehicle, keeps the user in a similar track to the vehicle movement and provides obstacle avoidance. Using the web interface for ESP32, the control of the motors and captured data can also be accessed at the web interface.

### 13.3.3 Pan-Tilt Mechanism

The pan-tilt mechanism shown in Figure 13.2, with its block diagram in Figure 13.4, provides a 180-degree wide field of view, which enhances the operator's view for navigation through obstacles; the main advantage of this mechanism is that it tracks the customer during delivery. This ensures the right delivery to the customer and offers proof of delivery.

### 13.3.4 Anti-Theft Locking System

Figure 13.3 explains the hardware connection, block diagram representation, and usage of a servo motor connected to the ESP32 module, and the power supply is provided using a power bank adapter. The servo motor operates at 180° movement according to the open/close control provided by the operator. Open/close control is performed using a dedicated app for the lock mechanism.

**Figure 13.2** Pan-tilt mechanism.

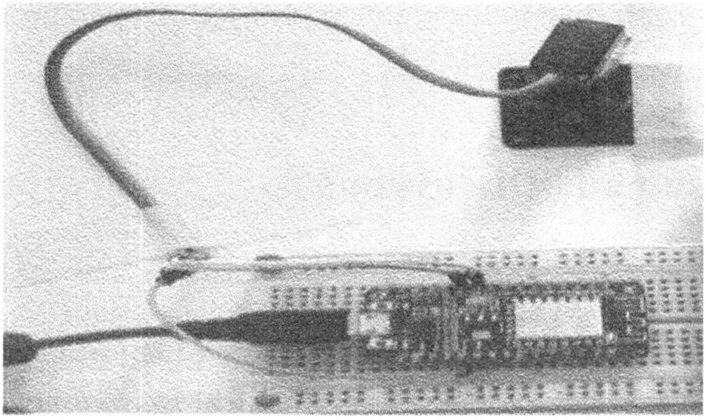

Figure 13.3 Anti-theft locking system.

### 13.3.5 Mobile-Application Interface

The mobile-application interface (Figure 13.4) represents the visual application, which is aimed at developing a user-friendly mobile application interface for controlling the anti-theft locking system and the movement of the vehicle. This also provides a safe validation login to ensure that only authorized users can login and access the application interface for control purposes. As we continue to innovate in the realm of delivery automation, prioritizing safety features such as mobile-controlled locks will

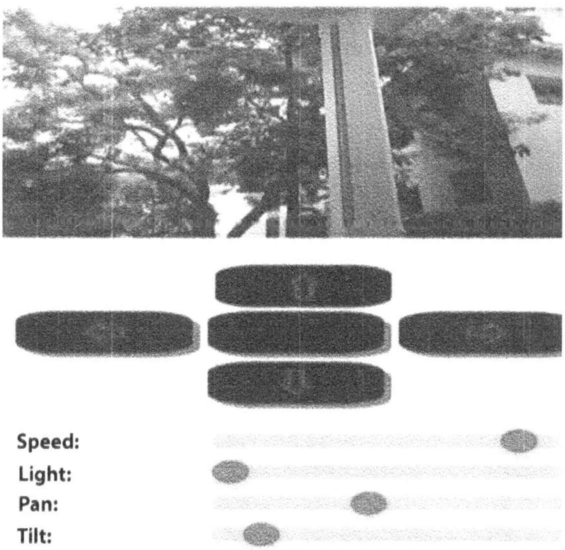


Figure 13.4 Mobile-application interface.

undoubtedly contribute to the seamless and secure operation of RC vehicles in the delivery ecosystem.

## 13.4 Result and Discussions

The RC vehicle is designed for delivery purposes and incorporates an ESP32 CAM module, a 180-degree pan tilt for clear vision, a smart locking system, and front and back lights to enhance vision during dim and night conditions. The circuit design and development were completed, and the model is built robustly to meet standard delivery vehicle functioning, and Figures 13.5, 13.6 show the front view side view and night view of the developed vehicle, respectively. The model effectively transmits and receives signals without disturbances, thereby ensuring reliable remote control and communication. The wheels are designed and selected according to the weight requirement capacity for delivery purposes, which ensures stability, even under a load. The inclusion of the ESP32-CAM module allows real-time monitoring and video streaming from remote locations in a web interface designed to monitor and control the movement of vehicles. The development of small-scale RC vehicles is a significant step towards mitigating domestic delivery costs, while ensuring the secure transportation of products to customers. By seamlessly blending autonomous capabilities with remote-control functionalities, this innovative approach guarantees safe and reliable deliveries within controlled environments. The incorporation of cutting-edge camera technology further enhances the transparency

**Figure 13.5** Front view of RC vehicle.

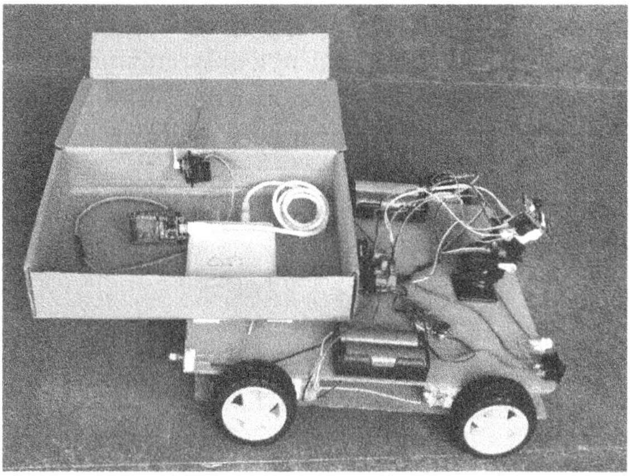

**Figure 13.6** Side view with delivery box compartment.

and security of the delivery process, assuring customers the integrity of their orders. The utilization of RC vehicles for delivery purposes heralds a new era of efficiency and reliability, offering a tangible solution to the challenges faced in traditional delivery methods. As we embrace this paradigm shift, we envision a future where safe, transparent, and cost-effective deliveries become the norm, transforming the landscape of domestic transportation for the better.

## 13.5 Conclusion

In conclusion, the outcome of the research and development of this integration of mobile-controlled lock systems for safety, alongs with app-controlled path and destination features, camera integration, and pan tilt module, represents a significant leap forward in the domain of RC vehicle delivery. This amalgamation of innovative technologies not only increases the security of deliveries but also empowers users with unprecedented control and convenience. The RC vehicle has a mobile-controlled lock system for secure transit, ensuring the safety of the delivered items with a user-friendly mobile app interface for efficient delivery management, including route planning and real-time tracking. This is aimed at optimizing the security, accessibility, and efficiency of remote-controlled delivery operations with a reliable and user-friendly solution and the implementation of a robust communication system between the RC vehicle and the mobile app for real-time monitoring and control. Continuously gather feedback from stakeholders to refine and improve the RC delivery system's design and functionality. This advancement not only enhances the efficiency of delivery services but also underscores our commitment to preserving the integrity of valuable shipments in an ever-evolving and interconnected world.

## References


1. RS, R.R., Vadupu, B.K., Naresh, R., Kavvin, U.V., Resmi, R., ML Based Web Application for Smart Parking System. *IEEE 20th India Council International Conference (INDICON)*, IEEE, pp. 67–72, 2023.
2. Lasya, C., Sai, N.M., Reddy, N.G., Reddy, N.M., Lekshmi, S., Syama, S., Hardware Integration of Sensors for Automating Smart Homes, in: *2022 International Conference on Automation, Computing and Renewable Systems (ICACRS)*, 2022, December, IEEE, pp. 202–206.
3. Anudeep, J., Kowshik, G., Aswath, G.I., Vasudevan, S.K., An IoT-based accident severity detection for automobiles with alerting the appropriate location of the accident-an innovative attempt. *Int. J. Adv. Intell. Paradigms*, 27, 1, 29–42, 2024.
4. Balakrishnan, P.C. and Pillai, A.S., Design and development of smart interoperable electric vehicle supply equipment for electric mobility. *Int. J. Electr. Comput. Eng. (IJECE)*, 13, 3, 3509–3518, 2023.
5. Hossain, M., Autonomous Delivery Robots: A Literature Review. *IEEE Eng. Manage. Rev.*, 51, 4, 77–89, Fourthquarter, 2023.
6. F.G., *et al.*, Design and Implementation of an Autonomous Driving Delivery Robot. *2022 41st Chinese Control Conference (CCC)*, Hefei, China, pp. 3832–383, 2022.
7. Tian, Z. and Shi, W., Design and Implement an Enhanced Simulator for Autonomous Delivery Robot. *2022 Fifth International Conference on Connected and Autonomous Driving (MetroCAD)*, Detroit, MI, USA, pp. 21–29, 2022.
8. fasiuddin, S., Omer, S., Sohelrana, K., Tamkeen, A., Rasheed, M.A., Real Time Application of Vehicle Anti Theft Detection and Protection with Shock Using Facial Recognition and IoT Notification. *2020 Fourth International Conference on Computing Methodologies and Communication (ICCMC)*, Erode, India, pp. 1039–1044, 2020.
9. Karthik, S., Bannur, A., Rao, A.T., Krishna, Y., Autonomous UGV Delivery Systems. *2019 4th International Conference on Computational Systems and Information Technology for Sustainable Solution (CSITSS)*, Bengaluru, India, pp. 1–6, 2019.
10. Sivachitra, M., Kumar, J.J.D., Gokul, R., Harshini, S., Nithish, G., Wi-Fi Controlled Multi-sensor Robotic Car. *2022 Second International Conference*

*on Artificial Intelligence and Smart Energy (ICAIS)*, Coimbatore, India, pp. 1541–1546, 2022.

11. Balakrishnan, B., Suryarao, P., Singh, R., Shetty, S., Upadhyay, S., Vehicle Anti-theft Face Recognition System, Speed Control and Obstacle Detection using Raspberry Pi. *IEEE 5th International Symposium in Robotics and Manufacturing Automation (ROMA)*, Malacca, Malaysia, pp. 1–5, 2022.
12. Jazemi, R., Alidadiani, E., Ahn, K., Jang, J., A Review of Literature on Vehicle Routing Problems of Last-Mile Delivery in Urban Areas. *Appl. Sci.*, 13, 24, 13015:1–13015:23, 2023.
13. Nagy, A., Abdelftah, M., Yousef, B.M., Smart Vehicle and Anti-Theft System Using IoT. *Int. J. Eng. Inventions*, 9, 4, 01–05, 2020.
14. Shashidhar, K., Dharmireddy, A.K., Rao, Ch.M., Anti-Theft Fingerprint Security System for Motor Vehicles, in: *Blockchain Technology for IoT and Wireless Communications*, Ch. 8, 1st ed., p. 13, CRC Press, Boca Raton, FL, USA, 2023.
15. Ismail, F., Felix, J.J., Fatima, N.S., Intelligent Door Locking System, in: *International Conference on Information Systems and Management Science*, pp. 317–328, 2022, October.

# 14

# Aerodynamic Drag Reduction in Heavy Vehicles

**Amutha Prabha N.**[1], **Abhishek Gudipalli**[1*], **Dyuti Ranjan Acharya**[1], **Indragandhi V.**[1] **and Manee Sangaran Diagarajan**[2]

[1]*School of Electrical Engineering, Vellore Insttute of Technology, Vellore, India*
[2]*Faculty of Innovation & Technology, School of Engineeering, Taylor's University, Subang Jaya, Selangor, Malaysia*

***Abstract***

One of the most difficult challenges in the automobile industry today is reducing vehicle fuel consumption. The creation of more fuel-efficient automobiles has accelerated with the increase in fuel prices. According to a new study on truck fuel reduction technology, aerodynamic enhancement is essential for fuel savings. For all vehicle manufacturers, lowering the drag coefficient has become an increasingly crucial task. This project uses a computational method to examine the influence of a change in the truck-trailer profile on aerodynamic drag. This numerical analysis was carried out on the unmodified and modified profiles of the truck-trailer with a shear stress transportation (SST) turbulence model utilizing the computational fluid dynamics (CFD) software ANSYS Fluent. The CATIA software was used to model the truck, and CFD was used for meshing and analysis. The aerodynamic drag coefficient of the vehicle is compared before and after alteration, and it can be observed that shape optimization helps to reduce drag and hence improves the truck's fuel efficiency.

***Keywords***: Aerodynamic drag, computational fluid dynamics (CFD) analysis, fuel economy, truck aerodynamics

## 14.1 Introduction

Decreasing fuel use and emissions is one of the most pressing environmental concerns affecting the vehicle industry. As a result of rising gasoline

**Corresponding author*: abhishek.g@vit.ac.in

A. Chitra, W. Razia Sultana and V. Indragandhi (eds.) Smart Charging Infrastructures, (267–280)

prices, there has been a "green race" among car businesses to stay competitive, and the development of fuel-efficient products has accelerated [1]. Because of their asymmetrical body designs, heavy commercial vehicles are deemed aerodynamically inefficient compared with other ground vehicles. "Aerodynamics" is a branch of fluid dynamics that analyzes the movement of air around a solid object, primarily as it interacts with a reliable moving object, allowing for the measurement of forces and moments acting on a tangible item [2]. In aerodynamic difficulties, lifting, dragging, thrusting, and weight are the forces acting on the vehicle. Lifting and dragging are two types of aerodynamic forces. A large commercial truck traveling at 100 km/h consumes approximately 52% of the total gasoline to compensate for aerodynamic drag [3]. In contrast, under identical driving circumstances, a passenger car uses roughly four times less fuel to traverse a rough patch. A large commercial truck may have an annual mileage of 130,000 to 160,000 km. Any decrease in aerodynamic drag results in significant fuel savings and a decrease in greenhouse gas emissions. Although experts have worked hard over the last decade to develop numerous fuel-saving solutions for commercial vehicles [4], there is still room to minimize aerodynamic drag. One of the most important goals of streamlined drag-reduction studies is to save gasoline and protect the environment. Reducing fuel consumption is a critical concern for automobile development [5]. In this study, a heavy-duty model truck was used, the drag coefficient was determined without any modifications, and the model was used as the baseline model [6]. The analysis was repeated for the same truck with external geometrical optimization, and the coefficients of the drag values were determined and compared.

## 14.2 Literature Survey

A CFD analysis was performed on two Volvo intercity buses. The first is a conventional bus and the second is a customized bus. This was done to reduce aerodynamic drag and fuel consumption. They identified a 10% reduction in pain due to CFD investigation [7]. The original model has a drag coefficient of 0.8, whereas the updated model has a coefficient of 0.7 [8]. The fairwater is fastened to the truck's head. The effects of different fairwater shrink angles on flow and aerodynamic drag were explored. Fairwater has been shown to minimize total pain effectively. The maximum drag reduction percentage increased to 24.8% [9]. A reduction in aerodynamic drag of 6% to 10% was discovered during research on how geometrically optimized bumps were positioned on the rear end of a typical vehicle cabin roof [10]. This study included details of the virtual wind tunnel test simulation. The pressure distribution, velocity contour, and aerodynamic drag coefficient were measured using a virtual wind tunnel test [11]. Some proposals for decreasing the design car's aerodynamic drag have been suggested. It was found to be an easy, efficient, fast, and convenient method for performing CFD based on numerical simulations of aerodynamics [12].

To learn more about the axial and transverse wind loads, was carried out. The data demonstrate the drag caused by the vehicle geometry, including the outside rearview mirror. The shape of the truck can be changed to reduce drag and enhance fuel efficiency [13]. This study was conducted at three wind speeds. To demonstrate the effectiveness of the new design concept, numerical CFD tests were conducted. According to the test results, the current bus has a considerable reduction in drag force of approximately 39.4% compared to the new designs, and 22.8% (5 to 6 L) of fuel can be saved every 100 km [14]. External aerodynamics has grown to a large extent. Many devices and methods have been introduced to reduce the drag. Even by attaching several add-on devices, there is still a way to reduce the aerodynamic drag further, depending on how streamlined we can get from the object [15]. The vortex generator positioned in front of the separation point stimulates the flow separation, which upsets the balance between the separation according to our analysis of the flow field structure and a longitudinal vortex. It successfully reduces the separation vortex strength, lowering the tail car's aerodynamic drag [16]. To enhance vehicle profiles, a number of drag reduction devices were introduced in this work, and the impacts of each device were examined both computationally and experimentally [17]. Thus, we reduce the rear area of the truck to obtain a shape close to streamlining the body, which reduces drag.

## 14.3 Methodology

CFD is used to determine the numerical method of fluid dynamics. In other words, it operates by partitioning a computing area into small cells, each of which models and solves flow equations. Many CFD methods mimic turbulence because practically all fluid flows are turbulent. Tetrahedral, hexahedral, and polyhedral structures are all possible cell shapes. The advantages and disadvantages of different cell types vary, depending on their geometry and flow characteristics.

### 14.3.1 Geometry and Meshing

A crucial element in computer-aided engineering simulations is meshing. The cross section utilizing ANSYS provides adaptability to deliver networks that range in multifaceted nature from unadulterated hex to profoundly definite half and half. We can place the correct work in the ideal spot and guarantee that a reenactment will precisely approve the physical model.

The modeling of both the fundamental (unmodified) and modified truck designs (Figure 14.1) was completed using the CATIA v5 R21 modeling software. The finite volume strategy (FVM) is a discretization method for incomplete differential conditions, particularly those that emerge from the physical protection laws. The FVM utilizes a necessary volume definition of the issue with a limited partitioning set of volumes to discretize the conditions. The FVM is in like manner used for discretizing the computational liquid element conditions. The finite-volume method uses meshing to reduce the degrees of freedom from being unlimited to finite. Fluent leverages cell-centered finite-volume techniques. The solution domain was divided into a limited number of smaller control volumes using a grid (CVs). Tetrahedron elements are better for complex and challenging mesh geometries. It can be used for CFD as well as structural purposes. It can be used to formulate the prism layers. The boundary layer thickness can be easily prepared using a structured grid. This requires more computational time for an unstructured grid with a complex geometry.

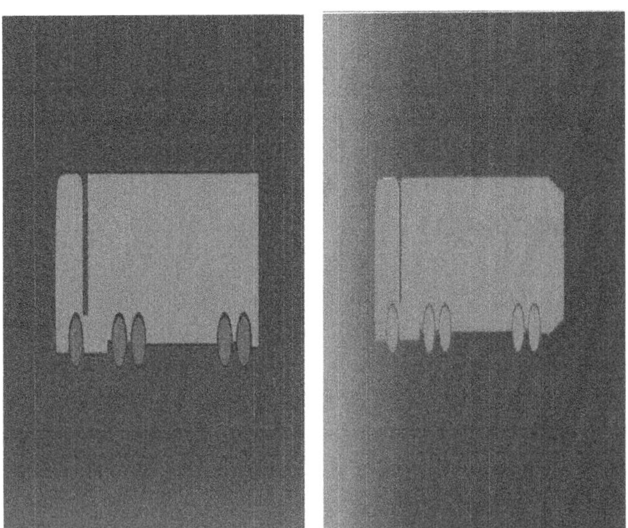

**Figure 14.1** Without modification. With modification.

The tetrahedral mesh with prism layers was chosen for this project because it is faster to generate and requires less memory than a polyhedral mesh. Figure 14.2 shows the meshing elements of the system. The hexahedral grid also allows for faster convergence in external aerodynamic flow simulations with predominantly streamlined flow. Mesh the step part with a time interval and with a mesh size of 50 for truck parts and 100 for wind tunnel parts, as shown below. Tables 14.1, 14.2 indicate the range of boundary conditions.

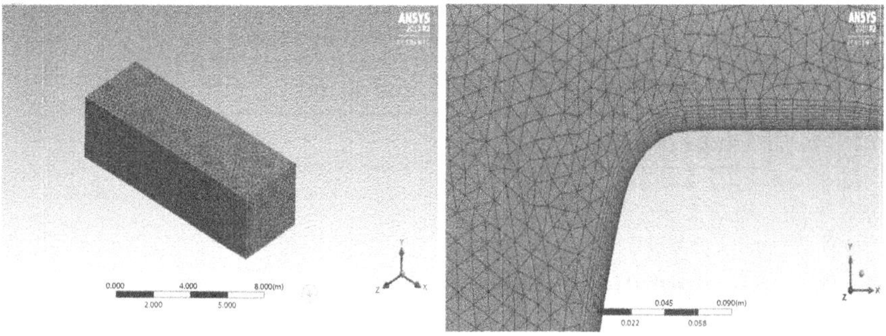


**Figure 14.2** Meshing with enclosure and mesh inflation.

**Table 14.1** Meshing properties.

| | |
|---|---|
| Number of nodes | 99,965 |
| Number of elements | 5 * 105 |
| Element size | 0.22 m |
| Meshing method | Tetrahedral mesh |

### 14.3.2 Inlet, Outlet, and Boundary Conditions

**Table 14.2** Comparison of properties and parameters of boundary conditions.

| Physical properties | Parameters |
|---|---|
| Flow characteristics | Steady, incompressible, turbulent |
| Solver type | Velocity- based |
| Turbulence model | K-epsilon, realizable |
| Near-wall treatment | Standard wall function |
| Inlet flow velocity | 20, 25, and 30 m/s |
| Outlet pressure | 1 atm |

### 14.3.3 Computational Procedure

ANSYS Fluent software was used to perform numerical simulations on the truck-trailer for the primary and modified profiles. The 'body of influence' mesh insert technology was employed to modify the element size in the wind tunnel's air domain through meshing to the geometrical model. A fine mesh close to the model and coarse mesh away from the model were used to mesh the air domain. The elements were selected using the tetrahedral approach. The fluid was assumed to be incompressible with unchanging characteristics. The SST turbulence model was used to obtain solutions for the governing equations. Because it employs two turbulence approaches, SST is an ideal model for aerodynamic analysis. It utilizes the k-turbulence model near the aerodynamic contact and k-turbulence model for the rest of the area. Using the SST methodology, wake creation in aerodynamic modeling can be reproduced better in numerical simulations. The measurements were made with air velocities (25, 50, and 75 m/s) and a constant pressure outlet at an atmospheric pressure of 1 atm with boundary conditions as the velocity inlet.

When turbulence modeling is used with a realized blek epsilon and no equilibrium wall function, the outcome is an incompressible steady-state Naiver–Stokes equation. In the solution approach, a second-order upwind discretization process is applied, which first reaches a peak value and then offers an accurate result.

The drag coefficient (Cd) is applicable when comparing the aerodynamic efficiencies of different vehicles. It is linked to aerodynamic drag force ($F_d$), vehicle speed (V), frontal area (A), and density, among other factors.

$$cd = \frac{Fd}{\frac{1}{2} * \rho * A * V^2} \tag{14.1}$$

## 14.4 Results and Discussion

Numerical simulations were performed on both the simple truck model and truck with aerodynamic improvements in the form of static pressure contours. Figures 14.3–14.6 represent the modeling of trucks at different velocities without and with modification using various methodologies.

### 14.4.1 Pressure Contour Comparison

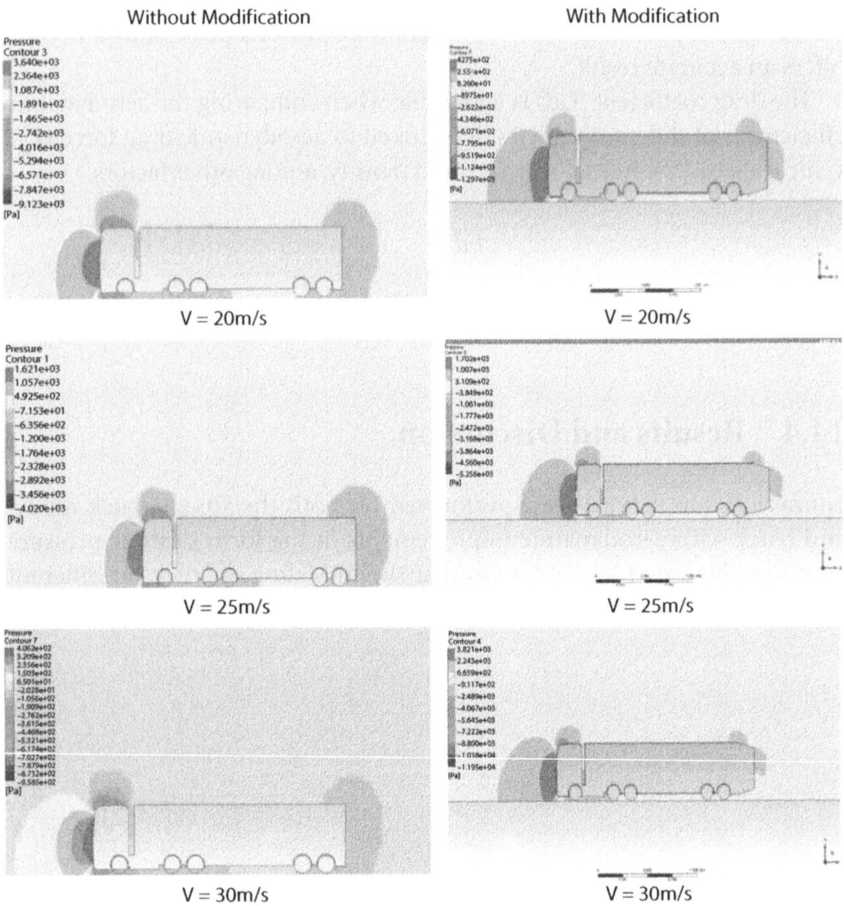


**Figure 14.3** Pressure contour comparison for with and without modification of truck at different velocities.

### 14.4.2 Velocity Contour Comparison

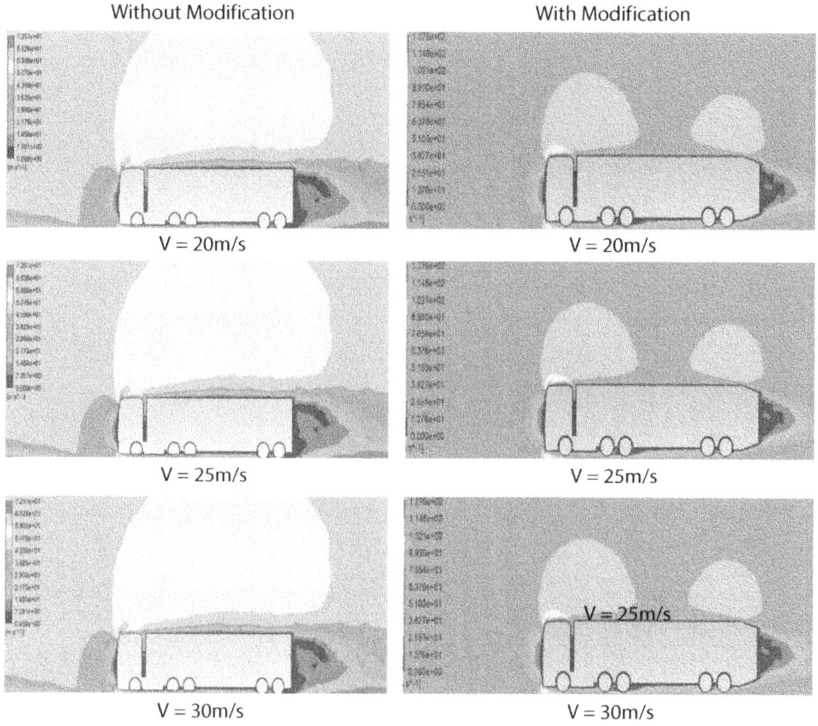


**Figure 14.4** Velocity contour comparison for with and without modification of truck at different velocities.

### 14.4.3 Streamline Profile

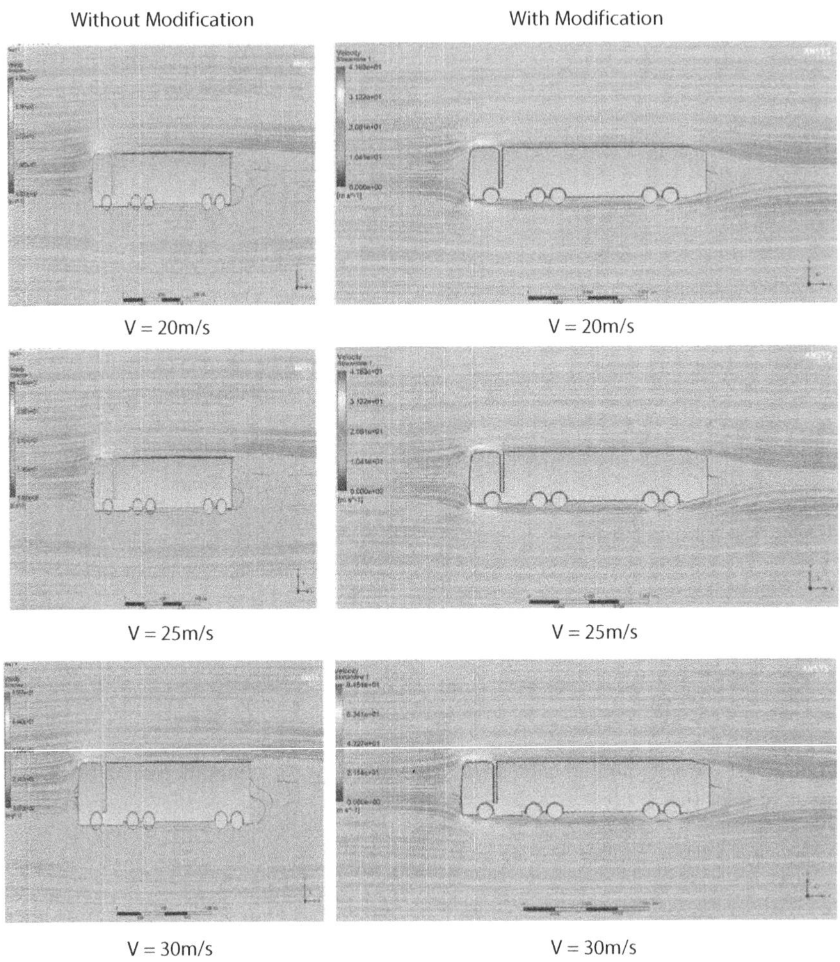


**Figure 14.5** Streamline profile for with and without modification of truck at different velocities.

### 14.4.4 VelocityVector Profile

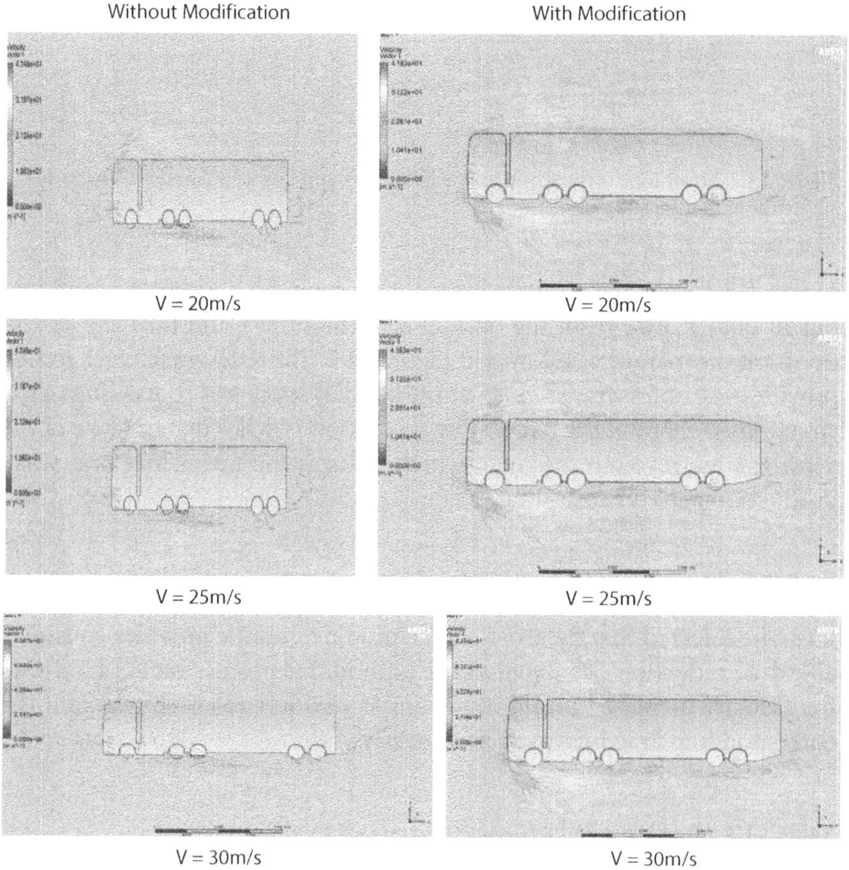


**Figure 14.6** Velocity vector profile for with and without modification of truck at different velocities.

## 14.5 Analysis Comparison

### 14.5.1 Streamline Comparison at Rear to Understand Flow Characteristics

It can be observed that the pressure is highest towards the front of the truck because the truck is moving at a high speed, and the crosswind meets the vehicle at some point, causing the wind velocity to drop and the pressure

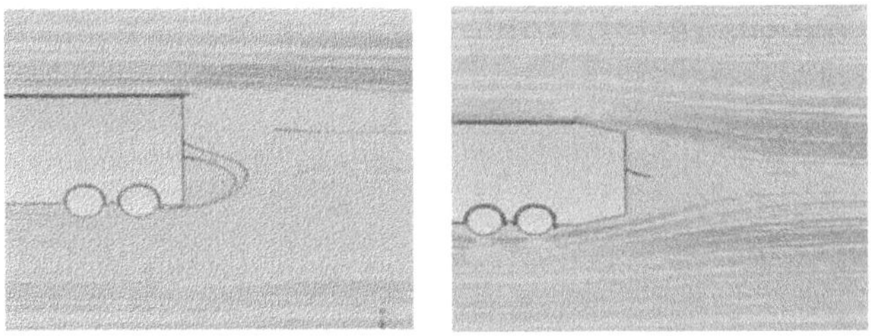

Figure 14.7 Streamline comparison at rear to understand flow characteristics for with and without modification model.

to rise. Because of the negative pressure gradient, high turbulence and turbulent eddies arise from the back end of the trailer, and flow separation occurs at the margins, as shown in Figure 14.7. The redesigned truck model provides a seamless transition over the circular space and roof owing to the streamlined shape at the back. Flow separation is delayed at because of the aerodynamic revolute rear end, which reduces the turbulence and wake production aerodynamic drag.

### 14.5.2 Drag Force Comparison

It can be inferred that the truck with a modified profile provides considerable drag reduction compared to the unmodified profile. Table 14.3 shows the velocity increased in a linear manner of 5 m/s for each test, and the corresponding drag increased nonlinearly.

Table 14.3 Drag force comparison between two models.

| Velocity (m/s) | Equivalent Reynolds number | Drag | Coefficient of drag | Equivalent Reynolds number | Drag | Coefficient of drag |
|---|---|---|---|---|---|---|
| | | Without modification | | | With modification | |
| 20 | 12.689 * 106 | 42.33459 | 69.1177 | 12.99 * 106 | 34.82899 | 56.86365 |
| 25 | 16.919 * 106 | 138.636 | 215.3241 | 17.32 * 106 | 109.7583 | 178.1768 |
| 30 | 21.14 * 106 | 267.8959 | 316.9729 | 21.657 * 106 | 207.704 | 274.2932 |

## 14.6 Conclusion

Aerodynamic changes/enhancements offer considerable drag reduction potential. The trailer is far more aerodynamic than the tractor and can significantly reduce fuel consumption by using geometric changes at the rear. A more beneficial flow around the truck can be achieved by changing the trailer geometry to a more aerodynamic form. Although the teardrop was not entirely smoothed in this project because of its simplicity of production, it nonetheless acquired a fair reduction in drag.

## References

1. Sarkar, S., Thummar, K., Shah, N., Vagrecha, V., A review paper on aerodynamic drag reduction and CFD analysis of vehicles. *Proc. A Rev. Paper Aerodyn. Drag Reduction CFD Anal. Vehicles*, pp. 231–235, 2019.
2. Mosaddeghi, F. and Oveisi, M., Aerodynamic drag reduction of heavy vehicles using append devices by CFD analysis. *J. Cent. South Univ.*, 22, 12, 4645–4652, 2015.
3. Dhande, D. and Bauskar, M., Analysis of Aerodynamic Aspects of SUV by Analytical and Experimental Method. *Int. J. Emerg. Technol. Adv. Eng.*, 3, 7, 447–45, 2013.
4. Desai, D.M. and Molvi, I., Effect of various aerodynamic drag reduction methods on vehicle-a review. *Int. J. Adv. Eng. Res. Dev.*, 4, 214–220, 2017.
5. Thabet, S. and Thabit, T.H., CFD simulation of the air flow around a car model (Ahmed body). *Int. J. Sci. Res. Publ.*, 8, 7, 517–525, 2018.
6. Kumar, V.N., Narayan, K.L., Rao, L.N.V.N., Ram, Y.S., Investigation of Drag and Lift Forces over the Profile of Car with Rearspoiler using CFD. *Int. J. Adv. Sci. Res.*, 1, 9, 331–339, 2015.
7. Markina, A.A., Lukashuk, A.D., Chepkasov, S.N., Starovoytenko, A.V., Improving aerodynamic characteristics for drag reduction of heavy truck *IOP Conf. Ser.: Mater. Sci. Eng.*, 862, 3, 032–32, 2020.
8. Tarasov, A.S. and Novikov, I.A., Prospects for the development of numerical modeling in the process of aerodynamic design of heavy trucks, Actual directions of scientific research of the XXI century: theory and practice, pp. 163–9, 2020.
9. Bayraktar, S. and Bilgili, Y.O., Effects of under body diffuser on the aerodynamics of a generic car. *Int. J. Automot. Eng. Technol.*, 7, 2, 99–109, 2018.
10. Minak, G., Fragassa, C., Camargo, F.V.D., A brief review on determinant aspects in energy efficient solar car design and manufacturing, in: *International Conference on Sustainable Design and Manufacturing*, pp. 847–856, 2017.

11. Oza, Y., Sulaimani, A., Gandhi, H., *et al.*, Review on vehicles aerodynamic drag reduction. *Int. J. Sci. Res. Dev.*, 5, 10, 481–86, 2017.
12. Szodrai, F., Quantitative analysis of drag reduction methods for blunt shaped automobiles. *Appl. Sci.*, 10, 1–18, 2020.
13. Wahba, E.M., Al Marzooqi, H., Shaath, M., Shahin, M., *et al.*, Aerodynamic drag reduction for ground vehicles using lateral guide vanes. *CFD Lett.*, 2, 2, 68–79, 2012.
14. Abinesh, J. and Arunkumar, J., CFD analysis of aerodynamic drag reduction and improve fuel economy. *Int. J. Mech. Eng. Rob. Res.*, 3, 4, 430–37, 2014.
15. Ellis, M., Gargoloff, J.L., Sengupta, R., Aerodynamic drag and engine cooling effects on class 8 trucks in platooning configurations. *SAE Int. J. Commer. Veh.*, 8, 732–739, 2015.
16. Li, T., Liang, H., Zhang, J., Zhang, J., Numerical study on aerodynamic resistance reduction of high-speed train using vortex generator. *Eng. Appl. Comput. Fluid Mech.*, 17, 1, e2153925, 2023.
17. Farghaly, M.B., Sarhan, H.H., Abdelghany, E.S., Aerodynamic Performance Enhancement of a Heavy Trucks using Experimental and Computational Investigation. *CFD Lett.*, 15, 8, 73–94, 2023.

# 15

# Review of Optimization-Based Sensor Fault Detection for Lithium-Ion Batteries in Electric Vehicles

**Mohana Devi S. and V. Bagyaveereswaran***

*School of Electrical Engineering, Vellore Institute of Technology, Vellore, Tamil Nadu, India*

### *Abstract*

The electrical vehicle (EV) market is evolving rapidly with continuous advancements in charging infrastructure, battery technology, and a range of capabilities. Lithium-ion batteries are considered the mainstream energy storage systems for EVs because of their long life span, better power concentration, and high energy concentration. However, the safety issues of batteries are the main obstacles restricting the rapid development of EVs. Owing to the reduced resistance to abuse, operating conditions, and outside factors, several faults occur in battery technology, resulting in quicker battery depreciation and accidents such as explosions, fires, and runaway reactions of heat. Thus, fault diagnosis in batteries is important for improving safety. Faults in charge storage systems are categorized as actuator, sensor, and battery faults. Hence, different approaches used in diagnosing battery faults, particularly lithium-ion batteries, were reviewed in this study. Furthermore, a comparative analysis of traditional fault detection techniques and meta-heuristic-based fault detection methods is performed. In addition, a critical analysis was performed to summarize the focus of existing works in this area. This would help future researchers solve the predominant challenges in this area, thereby attempting to bring innovations for effective fault detection.

***Keywords*:** Lithium-ion batteries, electric vehicles, sensors, fault detection, energy storage system, meta-heuristic algorithms

**Corresponding author*: vbagyaveereswaran@vit.ac.in

A. Chitra, W. Razia Sultana and V. Indragandhi (eds.) Smart Charging Infrastructures, (281–312)

## 15.1 Introduction

Transportation is an important requirement for people worldwide. However, pollutants generated by vehicles are the main cause of air quality issues, threats to the atmosphere, public health issues, and climatic changes. With an increasing population, pollutants, such as volatile organic compounds, particulate matter, and nitrogen oxides, have increased enormously. According to the WHO indications for human health safety, in most countries, the concentrations of NO2 and PM are above this mentioned level. Therefore, an effective method of producing EVs is to enhance the quality of ambient air and decrease air pollution to preserve global public health. Currently, EVs are emerging solutions for maintaining public health and environmental sustainability by mitigating the discharge of toxic pollutants into the atmosphere using emission-free electricity generation. These EVs tend to reduce greenhouse gas emissions, a global demand to promote air quality, control traffic-related pollution, and develop healthier communities. The mitigation of hazards through EVs can be overcome by using sustainable batteries with lifecycle assessments and recycling batteries to decrease the environmental impacts.

Recently, lithium-ion batteries have become dominant in the EV market due to their tendency for self-discharge rates, extended life period, energy density, high voltage, low power, and high power (1). These batteries are also sensitive to temperature and aging; thus, special focus on batteries in the working environment is needed to avoid thermal runways and physical damage. A battery management system is required in each EV operation to check the battery voltage, temperature, and current; monitor battery charge, health, energy, and balance voltage among cells; identify faults; and control temperature (2, 3). An efficient BMS operates primarily in fault handling, prognosis, and diagnosis. Hundreds of individual cells are interconnected in either series or parallel to form the lithium-ion battery system, which tends to produce efficient energy and power to meet to acquire dynamic needs (4, 5). Therefore, controlling and monitoring the battery is required to guarantee reliable and safe operation, or it will produce some critical failures, such as hardware faults, algorithm deficiencies, and sensor faults. In general, battery defaults occur because of either voltage or temperature measurements. If the battery is sealed inside a container, the cell temperature is found to be identical, which is caused by varying ambient conditions. The sensors and models work collaboratively to overcome disturbances, sensor noise, and model-plant mismatch. The fault detection method uses battery terminal voltage signals to locate and diagnose the power unit's faults. Fault sensing in lithium-ion batteries is performed using a multiple-model adaptive approximation approach.

These can be detected by means of online fault detection based on the recursive least-squares technique accompanied by the forgetting factor (6). Based on the modified Shannon entropy, it was used to predict faults in battery systems. The suggested study used sample entropy and Empirical Mode Decomposition for fault detection in several operating environments. It was used to separate the voltage data from the battery. It is used to eliminate the noise interference created during the voltage signal sampling procedure, in addition to extracting the fault properties. The entropy values of the samples were determined using the extracted defect attributes. It has been used to identify the difference between batteries and has been applied to identify system faults. Recycling issues are a major hurdle due to the footprint of the environment caused by the EV's raw material extraction. Lithium-ion power units are complex electrochemical systems that are nonlinear with various affecting elements. The units in the power cell exhibit irregularities in terms of health, state of charge, and temperature. Hence, different fault diagnostic approaches require a large number of calculations for signal processing and accuracy determination to predict the robustness and accuracy of detection. The three common faults occurring in battery packs are sensor, connection , and battery abuse faults. Most lithium-ion batteries use lithium titanite or carbon as the negative electrode (7). Chemical reactions occur at the electrodes, and by decreasing the internal resistance of the electrodes, the heat generation during use can be reduced, thus increasing the lifespan and cell capacity. Further recycling of lithium-ion batteries can be achieved because of the materials used in electrode production.

The major objectives of the study are as follows,

- To address the issues related to sensor fault detection in Li-ion batteries used in EVs, the efficient generation of EVs is possible.
- To study the different sensors used in Li-ion batteries, to predict the appropriate fault and diagnose it appropriately.
- To perform a comparative analysis of several methods involved in Li-ion battery fault detection, an effective method can be applied for fault diagnosis.
- To apply critical analysis of different optimization techniques with other existing methods, to analyze the application of optimization techniques and other intelligent-based approaches.

## 15.2 Gestalt of Battery Sensors

The demand for EVs is increasing daily, but there are some limitations to overcome for a safe ride. Most EVs possess a smaller traveling range because of the limited capacity of battery storage and can be extended by increasing battery capacity. Hence, a BMS was used in the suggested study, in which different sensors such as temperature, current, and voltage sensors were employed to monitor several parameters related to the battery (8). Voltage detection was applied to check the voltage of the battery in real time, and the current sensor was used to monitor the amount of current flowing into the load. The current sensor can measure currents up to 1 A, whereas the voltage sensor can monitor up to 13 V (9, 10). The temperature sensor helps to monitor the temperature around the battery. The outputs of these sensors must be converted from analog to digital format. Figure 15.1 denotes the structure of the lithium-ion battery.

The BMS tends to manage and control the battery, along with its parameters, and is set with coding. If the parameters cross the limit, the circuit connection is disconnected; thus, the system is protected by avoiding damage to the circuit. The existing BMS tends only to diagnose simple faults, such as over-temperature, over-charge, and over-discharge of the battery. A few minor faults, such as initial connection and internal short-circuit faults, cannot be diagnosed using a simple approach called threshold diagnostic methods with restricted physical parameters such as sampling point temperature, series current, and cell voltage (11). However, faults based on thermal and electrical characteristics may also lead to misdiagnosis, such as the diagnosis of sensor faults as cell faults. To keep batteries safe and running well, a Battery Management System that constantly tracks their

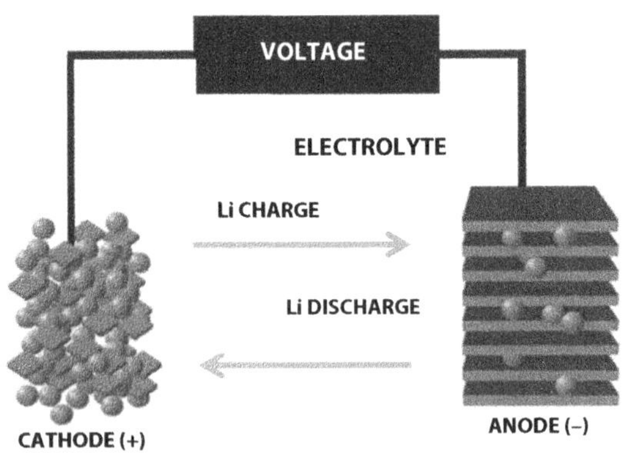


**Figure 15.1** Lithium-ion battery structure (10).

attributes is essential (12–14). The BMS has several key responsibilities: it balances voltage to reduce variations in voltage and state-of-charge among cells; it implements safety controls by electrically isolating the battery pack under unfavorable conditions; it provides protection against overcurrent, and under- or over-voltage to prevent the battery from being overcharged or discharged excessively; and it calculates parameters and SOC, in addition to performing diagnostic and prognostic tasks. The functionality of a BMS is heavily dependent on the sensors used. Any failure in the sensors is often not given due attention and can lead to serious repercussions (15). For example, a defect in a current or voltage sensor can affect the estimation of the battery's SOC. An erroneous SOC, which acts like a fuel gauge in a traditional internal combustion engine, could result in excessive charging or discharging of the battery (16). Hence, it is crucial to detect faults in the sensors to ensure that the BMS functions properly, which in turn guarantees the safety, performance, and reliability of the batteries. These faults are combined with heat evolution and generation, which also lead to fire explosions, thermal runaway, and aging of the battery system (17). Sensor faults have several predisposing factors, which manifest as excessive measurement errors. Similarly, the suggested study was intended to analyze the type of fault present in the battery pack with their corresponding effects, and present research based on the diagnosis error of lithium-ion batteries. Figure 15.2 represents the significance of the BMS. Faults include sensor faults, thermal management system faults, insulation faults, inconsistency within the battery pack, connection faults, overcharge, discharge faults, BMS hardware faults, ESC faults, ISC faults, and contactor faults (18).

The ISC fault is primarily caused by the discharge of the potential difference combined with heat production. Heat is generated when the positive and negative electrode materials are connected internally in the battery,

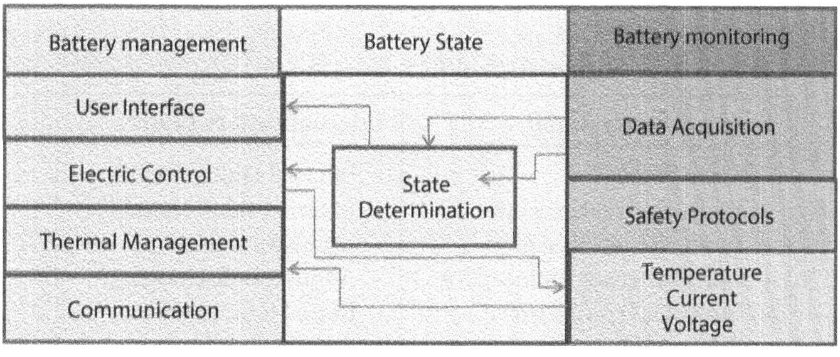


**Figure 15.2** Effective battery management system (19).

which is considered a very hazardous fault. Recently, the car industry has prioritized improving pedestrian and passenger safety, owing to various technological advancements (20). On the other hand, the significant rise in pollution levels in metropolitan areas is the result of increased road traffic. Because they can reduce carbon emissions, fight global warming, conserve fossil fuels, and reduce environmental pollution, EVs are becoming increasingly popular. When it comes to cost, dependability, practicality, and financial gain, electric vehicles (EVs) offer (21, 22). On the other hand, widespread EV adoption depends on the battery storage unit's proper operation and prognosis particularly with regard to temperature control, voltage regulation control, charge-discharge control, and battery management. The primary duties and roles of an efficient BMS are as follows (23).

- ❖ Appropriate warmth management
- ❖ Fault identification and rectification
- ❖ Voltage, charge and capacity balancing

An effective BMS can provide both safety and reliability (24, 25). It is also required for data updates, battery charge leveling management, and problem identification, which significantly affect SOC accuracy.

Additionally, when sensors work at high temperatures for a prolonged period, the constituents inside the sensors make some alterations and thus cause faults in the sensors. This directly influences the BMS by not accurately obtaining the eminence of working off the battery system and tends to lead to incorrect predictions, thus leading to the degradation of the battery. Table 15.1 portrays the battery faults.

The possible battery fault causes are as follows:

- Deformation
- Formation of lithium dendrites

**Table 15.1** Li-ion battery faults.

| External battery fault | Internal battery fault |
|---|---|
| • Sensor fault<br>• Faulty thermal sensor<br>• Faulty voltage sensor<br>• Current sensor malfunction<br>• Faulty cell connection<br>• Faulty cooling system | • Internal faulty circuit<br>• External short circuit<br>• Excessive charge<br>• Abnormal discharge<br>• Raised temperatures<br>• Accelerated deterioration<br>• Temperature failure |

- Impact and jarring
- Lithium metal plating
- Vibration

The temperature and VI sensors are the most commonly used sensors in the battery system, where any fault in the temperature sensor will issue incorrect temperature supervision commands, ensuing in annoying the temperature in the BMS, deviating from the standard functioning range, and accelerating to decreased battery performance (26). Any fault in the current sensor may cause the BMS to miscalculate the operation of the battery and send incorrect regulating instructions. When a fault occurs in voltage sensors, the overcharge and overdischarge, charging, and discharging of the cutoff voltage threshold fail (27). The measurements show that 40% and above of fires in EVs are triggered based on the ISC fault. Moreover, the ESC type of fault is caused by the impact of the deformation of the battery system, connection failure, and water immersion, which may lead to a short circuit between the positive and negative terminals, thus causing 20% of fire accidents in EVs. Owing to the harsh working environment, aging, and inherent defects, sensors face measurement value bias, measurement value breezing, accuracy decay, drift, and bias.

## 15.3 Utilization of Battery Sensors in Electric Vehicles

LI-ion cells are complicated systems that are nonlinear and vary with time, which makes diagnosing faults at an early stage in real electric vehicle (EV) applications a challenge without any noticeable battery anomalies. As such, this study has designed an early multi-fault detection method that utilizes a modified version of Sample Entropy to predict potential irregularities in cell voltages (28). In a conditional probability estimate, for every given length m subseries, the negative natural logarithm of the probability that it aligns pointwise within a tolerance of r is given by SampEn. Furthermore, it demonstrates good robustness, efficient representation, and a low computing load. The straightforward technique of fault detection is predicated on cell voltage. Even in cases where the batteries appeared to be in good condition, SampEn demonstrated the ability to anticipate early battery failures. A coefficient $\alpha$ denoting the voltage fluctuation is information that has been applied to identify the type and time of the fault that occurred. Furthermore, to update the battery information, reduce computation, and regularize diagnosis sensitivity to faults, a moving window has been employed to implement real-time applications. As a result, by enhancing the tolerance, the model can prevent false detections and obtain better robustness to battery inconsistencies and noise. Figure 15.3 represents the different sensors used in lithium-ion batteries (8, 16–19).

The battery energy density increases with an increase in Li-ion batteries, thus improving the severity and risk of battery failures in e-vehicles. During thermal failure, heat is generated, and the release of Li-ion batteries produces twice the energy released by the internal combustion engine, which is powered by gasoline. Moreover, the pressure signals possess a short duration of increased pressure and poor signal-to-noise ratio, which can be missed by the sensors. The expansion force calculation is a methods for detecting battery faults. During Solid Electrolyte Interface decomposition, the cells expand from the gases, and higher cell swelling detection is considered the precursor to thermal runaway. With a sudden decrease in gas, expansion is known as gas venting. Here, the expansion detection method requires threshold calibration based on the sensor packaging and cell pack. Considering the disadvantages of fault detection in gas sensor failures, the insisted study concentrated on gas detection methods for battery packs. Most existing tests involve minor components, such as Hydrogen Fluoride and $O_2$, and other major components, such as CO, $CO_2$, Volatile Organic Components, and $H_2$. After several abuse cases, as $CO_{VO}$ is easily detected at high concentrations, it has been considered as a target gas species for detection. A slow gas atmosphere was then used to test LiNiCoAIO2 and LiFePO4 18650-cylinder cells for thermal ramp overheating in a range of SOC conditions from 0% to 143%. Gas chromatography was used to evaluate the vent gas. According to the analysis, $CO_2$ was the main gas, and it exhibited a notable total molar content in every test. To use the gas detection approach for battery packs, the sensor must meet

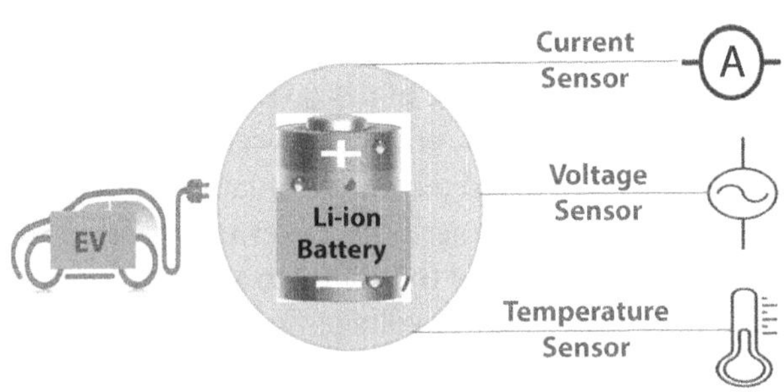


**Figure 15.3** Different sensors used in lithium-ion battery (8).

several practical characteristics, including long-lasting, tiny sensor units, cost, compactness, low danger of sensor poisoning, and low energy consumption with a trustworthy sensor fault diagnostic mechanism, which is vital for ensuring the safety and performance of the battery. It also assists in averting internal faults such as overcharging, excessive discharging, overheating, both internal and external short circuits, and thermal explosions. Faults in the sensors can encompass the malfunctioning of the temperature and VI sensors. These faults can be induced by physical factors such as vibrations, impacts, and leakage of electrolytes (29). They can also occur because of loose connections during corrosion near the battery sensor or the terminals of battery r. A fault in a sensor can hasten the battery's wear and tear process, impede the functions of the BMS due to inaccurate estimation of its state, and result in other complications inside the battery (30). Table 15.2 manifests the sensor effects.

A heat sensor is essential for Li-ion cell systems because it helps the BMS manage the power system operation by providing vital heat data. Inaccurate data sent to the BMS by a heat detector malfunction may result in additional issues owing to inefficient thermal management (31). The battery life may be significantly reduced by BMS heat management function inaccuracy. In addition, aging at high temperatures, capacity fading from high temperatures, short-circuiting, overheating, and thermal runaway might result from temperature sensor failure (32). The battery pack's cells' voltage was tracked by the voltage sensor. Overcharge and overdischarge may ensue from the cell or pack that surpasses both the minimum and maximum voltage limitations set by the manufacturers owing to

**Table 15.2** Sensor fault and its impact.

| **Sensors of BMS** | **Effects** |
|---|---|
| Temperature sensor | - Thermal runaway<br>- Short circuiting<br>- Overheating<br>- Aging |
| Voltage sensor | - Inaccurate State of Health (SOH) and SOC Estimation<br>- Overcharge and discharge |
| Current sensor | - Inaccurate SOC estimation<br>- Excessive charging and discharging<br>- Overheating |

voltage sensor malfunction. An internal issue may arise from overcharging and overdischarging of the battery owing to an error in the SOC and SOH estimation caused by a voltage sensor malfunction (33). The BMS receives data from the sensor current, which tracks the current flowing into and out of the battery. Identifying a malfunctioning electricity sensor is crucial because it can cause other issues (34). The sensor may be bypassed by the current, in which case, the measurements are off. A defect in the current sensor can also result in inaccurate measurement of the SOC, and other parameters affect the BMS's control actions and can overcharge, overdischarge, or overheat the cell.

### 15.3.1 Significance of Sensor Fault Identification in Li-Ion Batteries

The toxic gases released by lithium-ion batteries owing to sensor faults are a major concern and have attracted considerable attention from EVs. Nevertheless, internal failures of sensors, thermal loading, and unexpected mechanical faults lead to thermal runaway. Fires caused by lithium-ion batteries are mainly caused by several factors that are more dangerous than an open gas tank filled with gas. Even minor overheating can cause fires in battery packs. During fire accidents, lithium-ion batteries release toxic gases, smoke, and heat, which pose serious risks to the environment and human health. Conventional methods of removing fires, including using foam or water, are ineffective because they tend to exacerbate the fire by causing the battery to release more flammable gases, which rekindle the fire. Effective charge production is shown in Figure 15.4, which illustrates the applications of Li-ion batteries in electric vehicles. A pyrolysis autoclave with a volume of 24 L was considered, which comprised a barometer for measuring the pressure inside the autoclave, an exhaust port for gas sampling, a window for observing explosions, combustion, or fire during thermal runaway, a stainless-steel lid, and a stainless-steel cube chamber. To prevent the outside gases from interfering with the battery's heating process, the autoclave needs to be sealed.

Concerns regarding the fire safety of vehicles are more significant for primary battery EVs and new energy carriers. This was detected by conducting fire tests, in which a series of five fire tests with the heat release rate of the burning vehicle, air velocity, and air temperature in the tunnel were measured during the fire tests. These tests were conducted in a tunnel related to the horseshoe profile of a road tunnel (36). The sensors were arranged in parallel at different points of the tunnel. The temperature evaluation was

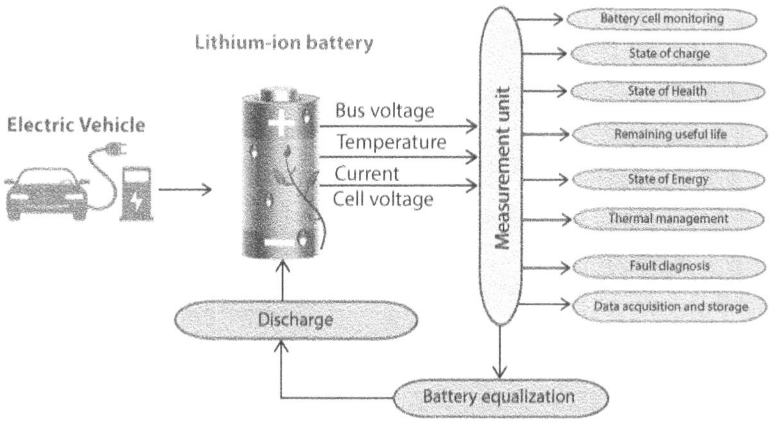


**Figure 15.4** Application of lithium-ion batteries in EVs (35).

performed using a k-type, class 1 sensor, along with four extra temperature sensors, attached to the right and left of the center 32 m downstream of the fire location. The velocity was then calculated by applying the distance-average ultrasonic transit time several measurement. The toxic gases released by lithium-ion batteries due to faults in the sensors are a major concern and have attracted considerable attention from EVs. Nevertheless, internal failures of sensors, thermal loading, and unexpected mechanical faults lead to thermal runaway. Fires caused by lithium-ion batteries are mainly caused by several factors that are more dangerous than an open gas tank filled with gas. Even minor overheating can cause fires in battery packs. During fire accidents, lithium-ion batteries release large amounts of toxic gases, smoke, and heat, posing serious risks to the environment and human health. Traditional methods of fire suppression, such as foam or water, are ineffective because they tend to worsen fire because these materials cause batteries to exhaust more flammable gases that spread fire by reigniting. Figure 15.5 represents the applications of lithium-ion batteries with effective charge production in EVs. Serious concerns regarding the release of toxic gases, such as HF, $CO_2$, and CO, lead to eye and skin irritation, respiratory problems, and other health issues. Similarly, six large-scale vehicle fire tests were performed with modifications in a fire hall with a large calorimeter hood to collect gas and smoke (37). Advanced water purification and flue gas reduction systems have also been linked with fire halls to decrease exhaust to the surroundings. Two battery packs were also tested, along with large-scale vehicle fire tests. One module was used for cell-level tests, and module-level tests used two modules, whereas the remaining

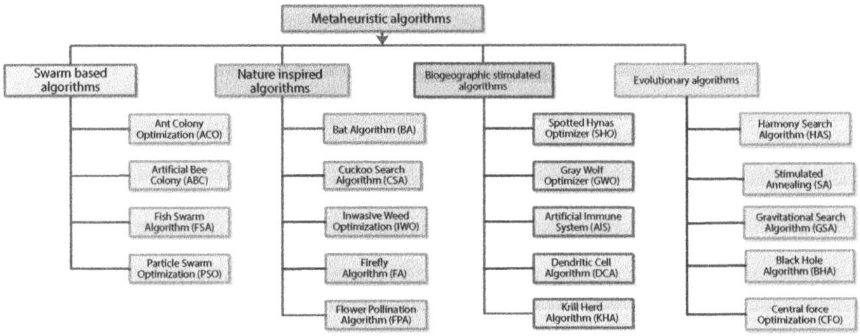


**Figure 15.5** Category of different metaheuristic algorithms (58).

modules used a pack test. Thus, after the fire tests, the heat release rate was measured using an oxygen consumption calorimetric method. The total heat release and heat release rate were affected by the vehicle model and fire scenario and not by the traction energy. During a fuel tank burst, a large amount of chemical energy is released. In gas production, high lead concentrations and battery-specific metals, such as lithium, cobalt, nickel, and manganese, have been found in tested Internal Combustion Engine Vehicles. A large difference between internal combustion engines and EVs is represented by hydrogen fluoride gases. Even thermal explosions have been caused by pressure sensor faults owing to the influence of aging on the gas pressure, temperature, and SOC (38). The miniaturized pressure sensors have been integrated into battery packs to measure the internal gas pressure for large-format prismatic cells. This method tends to monitor the gas pressure under long-term cycling by overcoming accelerated aging and premature battery failures. By applying gas chromatography mass spectrometry, gas components such as $C_3H_8$, $C_2H_6$, $C_2H_4$, $CH_4$, $CO_2$, and CO present inside the cell packs were identified. These components in air can tend to cause human abnormalities. The burning behavior and thermal failure due to the gas sensors of large-scale lithium-ion batteries under different charged states were tested using an *in situ* calorimeter. The increase in battery temperature intensifies the electrochemical side reactions owing to non-uniform heat dissipation over time. Many gas components in lithium-ion batteries are flammable and can cause explosions when mixed with air. Therefore, greater importance is required to analyze the hazards and behavior of gas sensors during thermal runaway. Different batteries with charging of 5%, 50%, 90%, and 100% SOCs at 250 c under constant current and voltage were selected for analysis (39).

### 15.3.2 Sensor Fault Modeling

Most VI sensors found in EV battery systems use the Hall Effect, which might have scaling faults (gain faults) or sensor offsets (bias) (40). Temperature fluctuations, mechanical shocks, and sensor core faults (deterioration or fracture) can cause these (41). The most common fault modes in thermocouples, also known as resistance temperature detectors, are scaling and bias (42). One way to depict the connection between sensor measurement, sensor failure, and related unknown variables is as follows:

$$Z_x = y + e_x + noise \tag{15.1}$$

The unknown variable x is represented by Zx, which is the signal from a sensor placed to measure x; ex is the sensor fault. If there are no problems with the sensor, the reading Zx reflects the real dynamic value x. If the sensor defect ex is not zero, x is measured as x + ex. Furthermore, this defective sensor signal affects the system control. Because of LIBs' high energy density, longevity, nominal voltage, power density, and affordability, the EV sector has benefited greatly from them. Despite offering a higher energy density and longer cycle life than their predecessors, these batteries are approaching their theoretical limits because of ongoing technological developments (43). The energy density, power capacity, cost, and cycle life of various chemistries differ. Multiple chemistries are combined in a hybrid battery pack to optimize pack performance by combining the benefits of each chemistry separately. They offer significantly higher energy densities, allowing EVs to have longer driving ranges. In addition, compared to the liquid electrolytes used in LIBs, solid electrolytes are less flammable, which aids in preventing thermal runaway in battery cells (44). The market introduction of hybrid battery packs for EVs has been the focus of numerous small and medium-sized enterprises. Two UK start-ups, Chimera Energy (45) and Upgrade Technology Engineering (46), are part of the same group of people who want to build a multi-chemistry battery array that will maximize the benefits of different chemicals and improve performance. In addition, they are proprietors of the patent for the control method of battery packs (47).

## 15.4 Optimization in Sensor Fault Detection

Sensor malfunction in Li-ion batteries can be achieved using several optimization techniques.

The ideal solution of the PSO algorithm is obtained by constantly updating the positions of the birds, depending on the best position of the swarm. It aids in regrouping, thereby attaining ideal formation. However, there are a few drawbacks, such as partial optima. These techniques tend to increase the potential of detecting faults in sensors compared to other conventional approaches. Hence, it is significant for algorithms and their corresponding applications. The early 1980s and 1990s were exciting times for metaheuristic algorithms. The use of memory in metaheuristic algorithms was pioneered by Glover in the 1980s. Different algorithms have been revolutionized by different authors, among which the cuckoo search algorithm is considered more efficient than the existing algorithms (48). Metaheuristic algorithm delivers a shortcut for resolving challenging difficulties with a stipulated time and information to make a proper decision. Most of the time, metaheuristic algorithms have led to better solutions. The term Meta is defined as "in an upper level" and the term Heuristic is defined as "to find." Hence, metaheuristics are demarcated as an iterative generation process guided by the amalgamation of various intelligent ideas to explore the search space and learning strategies to proficiently detect near-ideal solutions. The objective of the meta-heuristic algorithm is to detect an ideal or near-ideal solution to a specific issue. Meta-heuristic algorithms are commonly not issue-oriented and non-deterministic. Table 15.3 shows various meta-heuristic algorithms, the proposed person, and the year it was proposed. Minimal sensor faults do not impact the battery performance immediately, but they might have a significant impact in the long run. This can be avoided by quickly identifying and fixing any sensor faults as soon as they arise (49). Usage and handling also contribute to the failure of powering systems, which may not have been considered by the author (50, 51). Vibration and physical impact from accidents might cause the sensors to physically deform or break, which can result in resistance buildup in the wires and reading anomalies (52). Hence, the two primary techniques used for handling optimization issues are deterministic and nondeterministic approaches. Deterministic approaches are used when the exact solution to the problem is attained; hence, mathematical approaches are used for deterministic approaches. Nondeterministic approaches are employed when the solution cannot be attained correctly. Metaheuristic approaches employ a collection of search agents to discover possible regions in the search space following precise rules. Some of the meta-heuristic algorithms, like the Cso, possess the ability to converge the global optimum and possess the ability to handle global and local search and aid in employing levy flight for global search (53). However, a few disadvantages must be considered, such as the cuckoo search algorithm, which may deliver low accuracy in

**Table 15.3** Optimization algorithms.

| Year | Algorithms | Author |
|---|---|---|
| 1992 | "Ant colony optimization " | Dorigo |
| 1995 | "Particle swarm optimization" | Eberhart and Kennedy |
| 2001 | "Harmony search" | Geem, Kim, and Loganathan |
| 2005 | "Artificial bee colony " | Karaboga |
| 2005 | "Glow worm swarm optimization" | Ghose and Krishnanand |
| 2008 | "Firefly algorithm" | Xin-She Yang |
| 2009 | "Cuckoo search" | Deb and Yang |
| 2010 | "Bat algorithm" | Yang |
| 2010 | "Termite colony" | Hedayatzadeh |
| 2012 | "Flower pollination algorithm" | Yang |
| 2015 | "African buffalo optimization" | BeneoluchiNizamMohmad |
| 2016 | "Killer whale algorithm" | Biyanto |
| 2017 | "Rainwater algorithm" | Biyanto |
| 2018 | "Owl search algorithm" | Singh and Mohit |
| 2018 | "Phototropic algorithm" | Vinod and Anand |
| 2018 | "Squirrel search algorithm" | Mohit and Singh |
| 2019 | "Future search algorithm" | Elsisi |
| 2020 | "Political algorithm" | Yonus and Askari |

terms of classification. Similarly, GA is a popular meta-heuristic algorithm that is easy to implement and can handle arbitrary types of objectives and restrictions. It can be utilized independently to solve a specific problem because it does not need to depend on other existing algorithms. It also has the potential to solve problems with high computational complexities. However, there is no possibility or assurance that the global maxima will be identified using GA. It does not possess a standard method for defining an upright fitness function, and the best solution is largely dependent on the fitness function, leading to the detection of the precise fitness function. Furthermore, GA does not possess termination criteria or a method for adjusting the parameters. Another popular meta-heuristic algorithm includes the PSO algorithm. The estimation using the PSO algorithm is simple and effective. The PSO algorithm is beneficial in various fields of research and engineering. Table 15.4 shows the different meta-heuristic algorithms along with the motivation of the algorithm.

Correspondingly, the firefly algorithm (FFA) can automatically divide the population into various categories, resulting in better diversification (54). Some of the drawbacks of the firefly algorithm include insufficient parameter tuning. Furthermore, diversification in FFA may lead to a minimized convergence rate and speed; therefore, the FFA algorithm is not appropriate for handling complicated problems, as it can become trapped

**Table 15.4** Algorithm and motivation.

| Algorithm | Motivation |
|---|---|
| PSO algorithm | Flocking patterns and the schooling patterns of the birds and fishes |
| Genetic algorithm | Employs for natural selection |
| Cuckoo search | Parasites of cuckoo bird species |
| ABC algorithm | Intellectual rummaging performance of the honeybees |
| Firefly algorithm | Using the flashlight attribute of the firefly |
| ACO algorithm | Searching the performance of the ant species |
| Bat algorithm | Echolocation performance of the bats |
| Grasshopper optimization | Inspired *via* hunting as well as aggregation activities of grasshoppers |
| Krill herd optimization | Krill's position's proximity to its food source |
| Fruit fly optimization | Osphresis organ to sense food source and empathetic sight to locate the food |
| Jaquar algorithm | Exploration and exploitation process |
| Moth flame optimization | Moths possess distinctive navigation behavior which is exploited to solve global problem of optimization |

in different local optima. Another metaheuristic algorithm is the Ant Colony Optimization (ACO). ACO can handle complex and other complicated issues proficiently, as the construction of the ACO algorithm is integrally parallel, with solutions built concurrently and self-sufficiently by the ants (55). Nevertheless, convergence time is not defined, though convergence in ACO is assured. Additionally, it has been found to be challenging to examine the behavior of the ACO algorithm, as ACO is dependent on the categorizations of the unsystematic decisions made by various independent artificial ants. Like ACO, the bat algorithm is also useful in implementation and is flexible to use. The Bat algorithm (BA) is used for handling a large number of tasks, and it has the potential to zoom into areas that are capable of producing better solutions (56). However, the BA algorithms do not have the potential to handle discrete optimization problems. Furthermore, the BA requires different parameters that need tuning. Like BA, the Artificial Bee Colony (ABC) is also considered to be robust, converges quickly, and requires few parameters, which makes the algorithm flexible to use (57, 58). However, the classification accuracy obtained by the algorithm is insufficient to meet the requirements.

## 15.5 Advantages and Category of Metaheuristic Algorithm

Metaheuristic algorithms possess the ability to detect food solutions with minimal computational effort. Metaheuristic algorithms can be employed for various applications and problems as they are not issue-oriented. Metaheuristic algorithms often employ some form of randomness intending to escape local minima. The ACO algorithm is one examples of employing this process (59). They have the potential to manage non-algebraic problem forces and can handle continuous and discrete variables as well as non-smooth functions. Due to these advantages, metaheuristic algorithms are categorized into evolutionary algorithms, swarm intelligence, natural phenomena, and human inspiration (60). Figure 15.5 illustrates the different metaheuristic algorithms. It can be identified that the genetic algorithm and differential evolution algorithm fall under evolutionary algorithms, whereas algorithms like PSO, ABC, ACO, enhanced walrus optimization, and the Whale Optimization algorithm fall under swarm intelligence algorithms. Similarly, algorithms like the water cycle algorithm, spiral optimization, and others are categorized under natural phenomena.

### 15.5.1 Applications of Metaheuristic Approach for Sensor Fault Detection in Lithium-Ion Batteries

Fault detection in EVs is extremely important as the safety and reliability of the EV are significant. Fault diagnosis detection has been employed in the recommended study, where the PSO algorithm was used for optimizing the hyperparameters of the network, which comprises various parameters such as the number of CL, epoch, and LSTM layers. The Li-ion battery dataset has been utilized in the existing study as the Convolution Neural Network (CNN)-LSTM-PSO technique for identifying the faults quickly and efficiently (61). Similarly, the flower pollination algorithm has been utilized by the recommended study for identifying faults. The CNN model was used for detecting blisters in cell sheets using cell sheet images.

The recommended study was considered superior to the existing ML or DL methods (62). Likewise, the recommended study employed non-linear optimization algorithms for detecting faults in the sensors. To overcome the issues, a metaheuristic algorithm was employed to achieve better outcomes. However, it was revealed that inefficient use of data can lead to poor outcomes, which was addressed by employing a genetic algorithm. The 1-CNN model aided in learning the dynamics between the simulated voltage and the input current. From the experimental results, it was revealed that an accurate and reliable model could be identified by employing the recommended model (63). Correspondingly, unknown parameters could be identified using the AHOT algorithm to validate the standard deviation and objective function. Different optimization algorithms were used in the recommended study, including Gray Wolf Optimization, jellyfish search optimizer, Transient Search Optimization, Arithmetic Optimizer, African Vulture Optimizer, and Heap-based optimization (64). The Battery management of EVs was analyzed based on the complicated working conditions and fluctuations of the parameters during the battery's lifespan. The PSO algorithm was used for fixing the voltage window, thereby making the model efficient for battery management (65). Current sensor fault diagnosis is extremely important for Li-ion batteries. Therefore, to detect faults in sensors, the existing study employs a PSO algorithm with measurable initial system states. Further, Monte Carlo simulation generates a precise fault in current sensors. From the experimental results, it was revealed that the effectiveness of the model was assessed using the miss alarm rate and false alarm rate models (66). Similarly, the Exponential Decay-PSO algorithm was implemented in the study to reflect the energetic characteristics of the voltage and capacity of the cell. The model's outcome delivered better

**Table 15.5** Advantages of metaheuristic algorithm.

| Optimization algorithms | Strengths |
|---|---|
| Genetic algorithm (GA) | GAs are capable of tackling nonlinear and non-convex optimization problems, making them appropriate for complicated defect detection jobs in lithium-ion batteries. |
| Particle swarm optimization (PSO) | PSO is renowned for its straightforwardness and effortless integration. It could efficiently explore solution spaces and quickly find the best or nearly best solutions. |
| Simulated annealing (SA) | SA is capable of handling noisy and unpredictable data. It is especially effective for traversing rough solution terrain and avoiding local optima. |
| Ant Colony Optimization (ACO) | ACO, inspired by foraging behavior of ant, excels in optimizing discrete decision spaces. It can effectively investigate solution spaces and adapt to changing settings. |

**Table 15.6** Survey of the existing work.

| Objective | Methodology | Outcome |
|---|---|---|
| To diagnose fault for current and voltage sensor in lithium-ion batteries (9). | Stochastic hybrid automata model has been used to process normal modes, faulty modes, discrete dynamics, SOC and voltages. Unscented particle filter algorithm has been used to determine and estimate continuous and discrete states and output. | Based on serial-parallel organization, the validation has been conducted under different faults of current and voltage sensors. Thus, has produced effective state tracking ability and precise detection of sensor error. |

(*Continued*)

**Table 15.6** Survey of the existing work. (*Continued*)

| Objective | Methodology | Outcome |
|---|---|---|
| To diagnose systematic fault on hybrid system of lithium-ion batteries such as relay and sensor faults (68). | Distributed diagnostic configuration has been applied to overcome computation burden of battery pack. Further, dual extended Kalman filter algorithm has been employed to measure SOC, terminal voltages of each cell. | Validation of the algorithm's performance has been carried out on battery pack containing two branches in parallel connection and series connection of two batteries. |
| The main aim of the study has to find faults in sensors of battery pack using particle filters and equivalent models (7). | Power and heat models of battery packs has been produced depending on radial equivalent thermal model and Thevenin equivalent circuit model. Recursive least square algorithm has been used to predict model parameters. | Based on several residual assessments, batteries, temperature sensors, current and voltage faults have been identified and isolated. Different cases of analysis have projected better performance of fault diagnosis scheme. |
| Effective fault diagnosis has been the main objective of the study (8). | Fault-tolerant control strategy and model-based sensor fault diagnosis scheme for current and voltage sensor with hybrid Kalman filter and PSO least square algorithms. | Parameters derived from postprocessing the residuals the simulations and outcomes has denoted that better efficacy of fault diagnosis of VI sensor. |

(*Continued*)

**Table 15.6** Survey of the existing work. (*Continued*)

| Objective | Methodology | Outcome |
|---|---|---|
| Online Multi fault diagnosis based on combination entropy methods and of model has been the aim of the study (28). | By using integrated model and entropy-based methods, the connection, short-circuit, temperature sensor, VI sensor fault diagnosis has been performed. Interleaved voltage measurements have been deployed to categorize faults with the voltage monitor caused by connection or SC issues. | The efficiency of the diagnostic methods has been validated based on multiple diagnosis outcomes with several fault sizes and types. |
| The primary goal of the study is to create a system for diagnosing faults in lithium-ion batteries (31). | A dual time scale voltage detector error diagnosis along with isolation method for Li-ion battery connected in series. Ohmic resistance selection method has been done in both representative and non-representative cells. | The representative cell immediately has detected fault voltage sensor by catching abnormal measurement innovation. This method has tended to sense the sensor fault by catching the abnormal features with satisfactory robustness and low complexity. |

(*Continued*)

**Table 15.6** Survey of the existing work. (*Continued*)

| Objective | Methodology | Outcome |
|---|---|---|
| The aim of the study has to detect early faults and isolating faults (41). | For detecting faults in battery, multi-fault diagnosis approach and isolation of fault types has been implemented. Principal Component Analysis (PCA) to identify abnormality in battery pack and KPCA (Kernel PCA) to reconstruct fault waveform has been applied. | The tests results based on eight cells in series have represented that the used method has produced accurate fault detection and fault waveform of faulty battery. |
| Real-time fault detection of Li-ion batteries has been the objective of the study (53). | Using high-frequency detail wavelet components, the early frequency domain features of fault signals has been extracted. A multilevel fault prognosis method has been employed. | The results have been applied on real-scenario thermal runaway and loose wire connection batteries and has denoted that the method has extracted and located hidden fault signals and isolate battery faults. |

performance and high accuracy (67). Several fault detection methods are used by numerous researchers in lithium-ion batteries of EVs. Some studies that have employed different fault detection approaches are discussed. Table 15.4 discusses the traditional approaches used in fault detection of lithium-ion batteries. Table 15.5 represents the different optimization techniques used in the fault detection of lithium-ion batteries and BMS. Spotting problems and ensuring balance are essential components in the proficient handling of lithium-ion batteries to safeguard their efficiency, lifespan, and safety. These cells are extensively utilized in a variety of applications, from mobile electronics to EVs, and tend to develop defects or disparities in the long term that can undermine safety and performance. Here is a condensed explanation of error balancing and diagnosis of LiBs:

### 15.5.2 Challenges in Fault Detection

Fault Detection: Uncovering faults in LiBs entails scrutinizing a variety of parameters and features to detect abnormal patterns. Common faults include overcharging, severe discharging (68), thermal spikes, capacity loss, and internal short circuits. Methods for error detection encompass: Constant VI checking: The ongoing monitoring of voltage and current during the charge and discharge cycles can highlight abnormalities, such as unexpected voltage spikes or drops that suggest issues (69). Heat Monitoring: Heat detectors located in the cell's setup can pinpoint instances of excessive heat, a major safety concern (70).

Impedance Spectroscopy: Evaluating the battery's resistance at diverse frequencies can provide information about changes in its internal makeup and status (71). Hysteresis of Voltage: Observing hysteresis of voltage during cycles of discharge and charge can expose capacity decreases or variances (72). Estimation of SOC and SOH: Modern algorithms can calculate the SOC and SOH of power cells based on a range of parameters, aiding in detecting departures from typical behavior (73, 74).

**Table 15.7** Comparative analysis of metaheuristic algorithms in battery fault detection.

| Objective | Methodology | Outcomes |
|---|---|---|
| To predict the non-inear varieties in BMS (Yang *et al.*, 2020) | A state estimation approach for lithium-ion batteries has been implemented. The model parameters have been detected online using EDPSO (Exponential Decay PSO) along with PIO (Proportional Integral Observer) has been developed for SOC evaluation. | The results have denoted that the insisted method has produced better accuracy. (54) |

(*Continued*)

**Table 15.7** Comparative analysis of metaheuristic algorithms in battery fault detection. (*Continued*)

| Objective | Methodology | Outcomes |
|---|---|---|
| A micro-fault checking of Li-ion batteries has been the main objective of the study in Zhou *et al.* (2022). | The identification of faults has been performed by micro-fault diagnosis method. CCVC has been used to match the charging voltage curve of every battery. PSO algorithm generates the matching transform parameters representing the battery consistency. | Predict and locate fault cells accurately even if significant inconsistencies or abnormal voltage fluctuations are not exhibited by battery packs. |
| To assess SOH of Li-ion cells in Alneyadi *et al.* (2023) (54). | The PSO-DDA approach was created to analyse the State of Health of lithium-ion batteries in a personalized manner and to minimize the differences in distribution between different domains. | PSO-DDA has produced better evaluation of SOH. |
| To approximate SOH of Li-ion cells is the main objective of the study (Wang *et al.*, 2022). | Electrochemical Impedance Spectroscopy (EIS) and the Cuckoo Search-Elman Neural Network (CS-Elman NN) were utilized to estimate SOH. | By using CS-Elman algorithm, the SOH of battery has been estimated. |

## 15.6 Result and Discussion

An analysis of different fault detection approaches is performed to discover the faults in Li-ion batteries. The fault detection and isolation methods are presented in Figure 15.6. It shows that most of the studies have used optimization techniques either separately or in hybrid form when compared with other fault detection approaches. Figure 15.7 show the simulation results of VI faults in a battery (74). From Figure 15.7, it is inferred that the current and voltage-based fault simulation occurred in lithium-ion batteries, where the fault arose due to an overflow of current or voltage at the battery terminals.

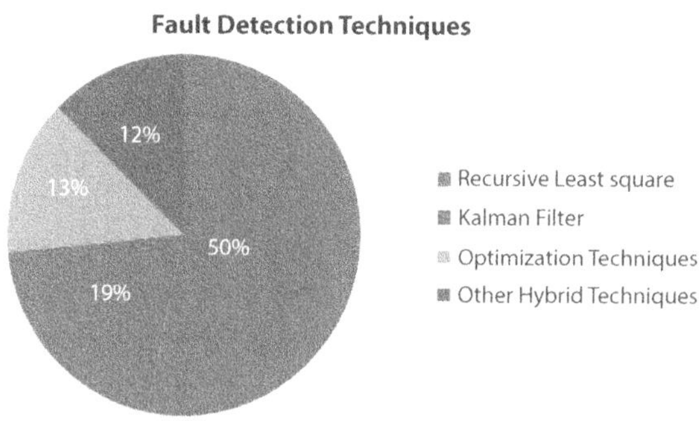


**Figure 15.6** Methods involved in fault diagnosis.

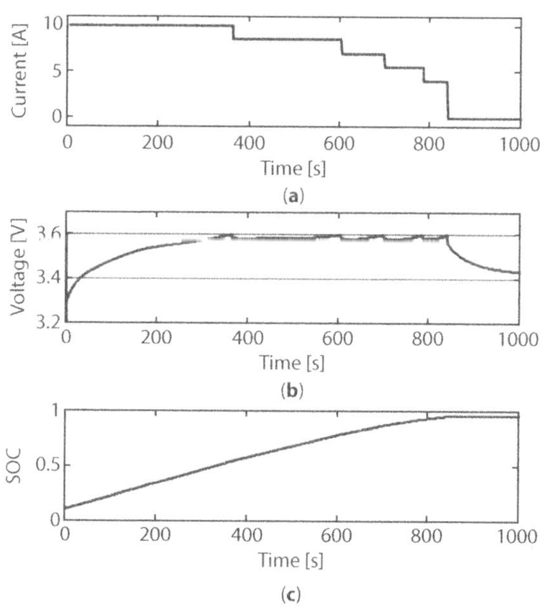


**Figure 15.7** Simulation results of current fault in battery (74).

It is normal when the current does not exceed the maximum flow limit of 6.5 A inside the battery. Only when the current flow exceeds the maximum current limit does it become overcurrent.

## 15.7 Conclusion

E-Vehicle is powered by an E-motor that generates electricity from the battery, and is capable of being charged from an external source. However, there are various drawbacks to using EVs. Some include restricted battery life, low speed and range, higher battery replacement costs, and more. Furthermore, these issues can become significant problems if not detected properly. Therefore, detecting faults in the vehicles is extremely important, as this detection aids in increasing the lifespan of EVs and provides better performance. In various existing studies, different techniques have been used for detecting and diagnosing faults in sensors. The sensors discussed in the study include voltage, current, and temperature sensors. Various methods, such as the Kalman filter and recursive least square method have been employed in numerous existing studies. However, in addition to these approaches, different optimization techniques have been used in prevailing studies, as these techniques can be more efficient and capable of detecting sensor faults. Metaheuristic algorithms were employed in different studies as these algorithms are capable of finding optimal solutions, which aids in detecting faults in the sensors. Modern technology for defect identification in lithium-ion batteries uses metaheuristic algorithms that combine machine learning approaches with metaheuristic optimization. Future researchers have investigated the use of hybrid methodologies to detect flaws in lithium-ion batteries, such as neural networks or SVM combined with genetic algorithms. These approaches leverage the metaheuristics algorithms' optimization skills to fine-tune the parameters of machine learning models, increasing their ability to reliably recognize and categorize various types of defects in battery systems.

## References

1. Xiong, R., Yang, R., Chen, Z., Shen, W., Sun, F., Online fault diagnosis of external short circuit for lithium-ion battery pack. *IEEE Trans. Ind. Electron.*, *67*, 2, 1081–1091, 2019.

2. Li, X., Dai, K., Wang, Z., Han, W., Lithium-ion batteries fault diagnostic for electric vehicles using sample entropy analysis method. *J. Energy Storage, 27*, 101121, 2020.
3. Alavi, S.M.M., Fekriasl, S., Niyakan, S.N., Saif, M., Fault detection and isolation in batteries power electronics and chargers. *J. Energy Storage*, 25, 100807, 2019.
4. Wang, G., Jin, S., Zhao, G., Zhao, J., Xie, J., An independent component analysis based correlation coefficient method for internal short-circuit fault diagnosis of battery-powered intelligent transportation systems. *Control Eng. Pract., 138*, 105606, 2023.
5. Espedal, I.B., Jinasena, A., Burheim, O.S., Lamb, J.J., Current trends for state-of-charge (SoC) estimation in lithium-ion battery electric vehicles. *Energies, 14*, 11, 3284, 2021.
6. Jadhav, A., Rathod, H., Kanade, V., Smart Battery Parameter Monitoring System for Electric Vehicles.
7. Yu, Q., Dai, L., Xiong, R., Chen, Z., Zhang, X., Shen, W., Current sensor fault diagnosis method based on an improved equivalent circuit battery model. *Appl. Energy, 310*, 118588, 2022.
8. Dotoli, M., Rocca, R., Giuliano, M., Nicol, G., Parussa, F., Baricco, M., Sgroi, M.F., A review of mechanical and chemical sensors for automotive Li-ion battery systems. *Sensors, 22*, 5, 1763, 2022.
9. Kang, Y., Duan, B., Zhou, Z., Shang, Y., Zhang, C., Online multi-fault detection and diagnosis for battery packs in electric vehicles. *Appl. Energy, 259*, 114170, 2020.
10. Barillas, J.K., Li, J., Günther, C., Danzer, M.A., A comparative study and validation of state estimation algorithms for Li-ion batteries in battery management systems. *Appl. Energy, 155*, 455–462, 2015.
11. Moore, S.W. and Schneider, P.J., A review of cell equalization methods for lithium ion and lithium polymer battery systems, 2001.
12. Marcicki, J., Onori, S., Rizzoni, G., Nonlinear fault detection and isolation for a lithium-ion battery management system, in: *Dynamic Systems and Control Conference*, 2010, January, vol. 44175, pp. 607–614.
13. Dey, S., Mohon, S., Pisu, P., Ayalew, B., Sensor fault detection, isolation, and estimation in lithium-ion batteries. *IEEE Trans. Control Syst. Technol., 24*, 6, 2141–2149, 2016.
14. Yang, G., Li, J., Fu, Z., Guo, L., Adaptive state of charge estimation of Lithium-ion battery based on battery capacity degradation model. *Energy Procedia, 152*, 514–519, 2018.
15. Jiang, L., Deng, Z., Tang, X., Hu, L., Lin, X., Hu, X., Data-driven fault diagnosis and thermal runaway warning for battery packs using real-world vehicle data. *Energy, 234*, 121266, 2021.

16. Xiong, R., Sun, W., Yu, Q., Sun, F., Research progress, challenges and prospects of fault diagnosis on battery system of electric vehicles. *Appl. Energy, 279*, 115855, 2020.
17. Castillo-Martínez, D.H., Rodríguez-Rodríguez, A.J., Soto, A., Berrueta, A., Vargas-Requena, D.T., Matias, I.R., Rodríguez-Rodríguez, W.E., Design and on-field validation of an embedded system for monitoring second-life electric vehicle lithium-ion batteries. *Sensors, 22*, 17, 6376, 2022.
18. Gabbar, H.A., Othman, A.M., Abdussami, M.R., Review of battery management systems (BMS) development and industrial standards. *Technologies, 9*, 2, 28, 2021.
19. Saleeb, H., Sayed, K., Kassem, A., Mostafa, R., Power management strategy for battery electric vehicles. *IET Electr. Syst. Transp.*, *9*, 2, 65–74, 2019.
20. Duraisamy, T. and Kaliyaperumal, D., Active cell balancing for electric vehicle battery management system. *Int. J. Power Electron. Drive Syst.*, *11*, 2, 571, 2020.
21. Rahimifard, S., Ahmed, R., Habibi, S., Interacting multiple model strategy for electric vehicle batteries state of charge/health/power estimation. *IEEE Access, 9*, 109875–109888, 2021.
22. Zhou, J., Feng, C., Su, Q., Jiang, S., Fan, Z., Ruan, J., Hu, L., The multi-objective optimization of powertrain design and energy management strategy for fuel cell–battery electric vehicle. *Sustainability, 14*, 10, 6320, 2022.
23. Sidharthan Panaparambil, V., Kashyap, Y., Vijay Castelino, R., A review on hybrid source energy management strategies for electric vehicle. *Int. J. Energy Res.*, *45*, 14, 19819–19850, 2021.
24. Gao, Y., Zhu, C., Zhang, X., Guo, B., Implementation and evaluation of a practical electrochemical-thermal model of lithium-ion batteries for EV battery management system. *Energy, 221*, 119688, 2021.
25. Kumar, R.R., Bharatiraja, C., Udhayakumar, K., Devakirubakaran, S., Sekar, S., Mihet-Popa, L., Advances in batteries, battery modeling, battery management system, battery thermal management, SOC, SOH, and charge/discharge characteristics in EV applications. *IEEE Access*, 2023.
26. Shang, Y., Lu, G., Kang, Y., Zhou, Z., Duan, B., Zhang, C., A multi-fault diagnosis method based on modified Sample Entropy for lithium-ion battery strings. *J. Power Sources, 446*, 227275, 2020.
27. Tran, M.K. and Fowler, M., Sensor fault detection and isolation for degrading lithium-ion batteries in electric vehicles using parameter estimation with recursive least squares. *Batteries, 6*, 1, 1, 2019.
28. Xiong, R., Yu, Q., Shen, W., Review on sensors fault diagnosis and fault-tolerant techniques for lithium ion batteries in electric vehicles. *2018 13th IEEE Conference on Industrial Electronics and Applications (ICIEA)*, 2018, May, IEEE, pp. 406–410.
29. Galushkin, N.E., Yazvinskaya, N.N., Galushkin, D.N., Mechanism of thermal runaway in lithium-ion cells. *J. Electrochem. Soc.*, *165*, 7, A1303, 2018.

30. Lelie, M., Braun, T., Knips, M., Nordmann, H., Ringbeck, F., Zappen, H., Sauer, D.U., Battery management system hardware concepts: An overview. *Appl. Sci.*, *8*, 4, 534, 2018.
31. Zheng, C., Chen, Z., Huang, D., Fault diagnosis of voltage sensor and current sensor for lithium-ion battery pack using hybrid system modeling and unscented particle filter. *Energy*, *191*, 116504, 2020.
32. Brand, M., Gläser, S., Geder, J., Menacher, S., Obpacher, S., Jossen, A., Quinger, D., Electrical safety of commercial Li-ion cells based on NMC and NCA technology compared to LFP technology, in: *2013 World Electric Vehicle Symposium and Exhibition (EVS27)*, 2013, November, IEEE, pp. 1–9.
33. Lipu, M.S.H., Mamun, A.A., Ansari, S., Miah, M.S., Hasan, K., Meraj, S.T., Tan, N.M., Battery management, key technologies, methods, issues, and future trends of electric vehicles: A pathway toward achieving sustainable development goals. *Batteries*, *8*, 9, 119, 2022.
34. Sturm, P., Fößleitner, P., Fruhwirt, D., Galler, R., Wenighofer, R., Heindl, S.F., Heger, O., Fire tests with lithium-ion battery electric vehicles in road tunnels. *Fire Saf. J.*, *134*, 103695, 2022.
35. Hynynen, J., Willstrand, O., Blomqvist, P., Andersson, P., Analysis of combustion gases from large-scale electric vehicle fire tests. *Fire Saf. J.*, *139*, 103829, 2023.
36. Schmitt, J., Kraft, B., Schmidt, J.P., Meir, B., Elian, K., Ensling, D., Jossen, A., Measurement of gas pressure inside large-format prismatic lithium-ion cells during operation and cycle aging. *J. Power Sources*, *478*, 228661, 2020.
37. Liao, Z., Zhang, S., Li, K., Zhao, M., Qiu, Z., Han, D., Habetler, T.G., Hazard analysis of thermally abused lithium-ion batteries at different state of charges. *J. Energy Storage*, *27*, 101065, 2020.
38. Lu, L., Han, X., Li, J., Hua, J., Ouyang, M., A review on the key issues for lithium-ion battery management in electric vehicles. *J. Power Sources*, *226*, 272–288, 2013.
39. Balaban, E., Saxena, A., Bansal, P., Goebel, K.F., Curran, S., Modeling, detection, and disambiguation of sensor faults for aerospace applications. *IEEE Sens. J.*, *9*, 12, 1907–1917, 2009.
40. Akram, M.A., *et al.*, A state optimization model based on Kalman filtering and robust estimation theory for fusion of multi-source information in highly non-linear systems. *Sensors*, 19.7, 1687, 2019.
41. Grey, C.P. and Hall, D.S., Prospects for lithium-ion batteries and beyond—a 2030 vision. *Nat. Commun.*, *11*, 1, 1–4, 2020.
42. Feng, X., Ouyang, M., Liu, X., Lu, L., Xia, Y., He, X., Thermal runaway mechanism of lithium ion battery for electric vehicles: A review. *Energy Storage Mater.*, *10*, 246–267, 2018.
43. Ghalkhani, M. and Habibi, S., Review of the Li-Ion Battery, Thermal Management, and AI-Based Battery Management System for EV Application. *Energies*, *16*, 1, 185, 2023, https://doi.org/10.3390/en16010185.

44. Yadav, D.K., Mishra, P., Jayanthu, S., Das, S.K., On the application of IoT: slope monitoring system for open-cast mines based on LoRa wireless communication. *Arab. J. Sci. Eng.*, 47, 2, 1387–1398, 2022.
45. Jafari, S., Kim, J., Choi, W., Byun, Y.-c., Integrating Multilayer Perceptron and Support Vector Regression for Enhanced State of Health Estimation in Lithium-Ion Batteries. *IEEE Access*, 2024.
46. Ibrahim, A.M. and Tawhid, M.A., A hybridization of cuckoo search and particle swarm optimization for solving nonlinear systems. *Evol. Intell.*, *12*, 4, 541–561, 2019.
47. SS, V.C. and HS, A., Nature inspired meta heuristic algorithms for optimization problems. *Computing*, *104*, 2, 251–269, 2022.
48. Liu, Z. and He, H., Sensor fault detection and isolation for a lithium-ion battery pack in electric vehicles using adaptive extended Kalman filter. *Appl. Energy*, *185*, 2033–2044, 2017.
49. Venkatasubramanian, V., Rengaswamy, R., Yin, K., Kavuri, S.N., A review of process fault detection and diagnosis: Part I: Quantitative model-based methods. *Comput. Chem. Eng.*, *27*, 3, 293–311, 2003.
50. Liu, Z., Ahmed, Q., Zhang, J., Rizzoni, G., He, H., Structural analysis based sensors fault detection and isolation of cylindrical lithium-ion batteries in automotive applications. *Control Eng. Pract.*, *52*, 46–58, 2016.
51. Li, J., Li, Y.X., Tian, S.S., Xia, J.L., An improved cuckoo search algorithm with self-adaptive knowledge learning. *Neural Comput. Appl.*, *32*, 11967–11997, 2020.
52. Bharathi, P., Ramachandran, M., Ramu, K., Chinnasamy, S., A study on various particle swarm optimization techniques used in current scenario. *Des. Model. Fabr. Adv. Robot*, *1*, 15–26, 2022.
53. Wu, J., Wang, Y.G., Burrage, K., Tian, Y.C., Lawson, B., Ding, Z., An improved firefly algorithm for global continuous optimization problems. *Expert Syst. Appl.*, *149*, 113340, 2020.
54. Dorigo, M. and Stützle, T., *Ant colony optimization: overview and recent advances*, pp. 311–351, Springer International Publishing, 2019.
55. Bangyal, W.H., Hameed, A., Ahmad, J., Nisar, K., Haque, M.R., Ibrahim, A.A.A., Etengu, R., New Modified Controlled Bat Algorithm for Numerical Optimization Problem. *Comput. Mater. Continua*, *70*, 2, 2022.
56. Kaya, E., Gorkemli, B., Akay, B., Karaboga, D., A review on the studies employing artificial bee colony algorithm to solve combinatorial optimization problems. *Eng. Appl. Artif. Intell.*, *115*, 105311, 2022.
57. Kumar, A. and Bawa, S., Generalized ant colony optimizer: swarm-based meta-heuristic algorithm for cloud services execution. *Computing*, *101*, 11, 1609–1632, 2019.
58. Tohidi, N. and Rustamov, R.B., Short overview of advanced metaheuristic methods. *Int. J. Tech. Phys. Probl. Eng. (IJTPE)*, *14*, 51, 84–97, 2022.
59. Hashim, F.A. and Hussien, A.G., Snake Optimizer: A novel meta-heuristic optimization algorithm. *Knowledge-Based Syst.*, *242*, 108320, 2022.

60. Kara, A., A data-driven approach based on deep neural networks for lithium-ion battery prognostics. *Neural Comput. Appl.*, *33*, 20, 13525–13538, 2021.
61. Ma, L., Xie, W., Zhang, Y., Blister defect detection based on convolutional neural network for polymer lithium-ion battery. *Appl. Sci.*, *9*, 6, 1085, 2019.
62. Kim, J., Chun, H., Baek, J., Han, S., Parameter identification of lithium-ion battery pseudo-2-dimensional models using genetic algorithm and neural network cooperative optimization. *J. Energy Storage*, *45*, 103571, 2022.
63. Hamida, M.A., El-Sehiemy, R.A., Ginidi, A.R., Elattar, E., Shaheen, A.M., Parameter identification and state of charge estimation of Li-Ion batteries used in electric vehicles using artificial hummingbird optimizer. *J. Energy Storage*, *51*, 104535, 2022.
64. Zheng, Y., Wang, J., Qin, C., Lu, L., Han, X., Ouyang, M., A novel capacity estimation method based on charging curve sections for lithium-ion batteries in electric vehicles. *Energy*, *185*, 361–371, 2019.
65. Hu, J., Bian, X., Wei, Z., Li, J., He, H., Residual statistics-based current sensor fault diagnosis for smart battery management. *IEEE J. Emerg. Sel. Top. Power Electron.*, *10*, 2, 2435–2444, 2021.
66. Yang, X., Chen, Y., Li, B., Luo, D., Battery states online estimation based on exponential decay particle swarm optimization and proportional-integral observer with a hybrid battery model. *Energy*, *191*, 116509, 2020.
67. Zhang, S.S., A review on the separators of liquid electrolyte Li-ion batteries. *J. Power Sources*, *164*, 1, 351–364, 2007.
68. Madani, S.S. and Ziebert, C., Beyond Limits: A Brief Exploration of Fault Detection and Balancing in Lithium-ion Battery Technology. *J. Phys. Conf. Ser.*, 2723, 1, 012012, 2024, March, IOP Publishing.
69. Plett, G.L., Extended Kalman filtering for battery management systems of LiPB-based HEV battery packs: Part 3. State and parameter estimation. *J. Power Sources*, *134*, 2, 277–292, 2004.
70. Madani, S.S., Ziebert, C., Marzband, M., Thermal Behavior Modeling of Lithium-Ion Batteries: A Comprehensive Review. *Symmetry*, *15*, 8, 1597, 2023, https://doi.org/10.3390/sym15081597.
71. Wang, W., *et al.*, End-cloud collaboration approach for state-of-charge estimation in lithium batteries using CNN-LSTM and UKF. *Batteries*, 9, 2, 114, 2023.
72. Li, X., Yuan, C., Wang, Z., State of health estimation for Li-ion battery via partial incremental capacity analysis based on support vector regression. *Energy*, 203, 117852, 2020.
73. Amifia, L.K., Widayat, S.A., Cahyadi, A.I., Wahyunggoro, O., Fault detection design and simulation based on battery modelling. *AIP Conf. Proc.*, 1755, 1, AIP Publishing, 2016, July.
74. Liu, K., Hu, X., Yang, Z., Xie, Y., Feng, S., Lithium-ion battery charging management considering economic costs of electrical energy loss and battery degradation. *Energy Convers. Manage.*, *195*, 167–179, 2019.

# 16

# Development of a Hybrid Foot-Stamping Bicycle with Dynamic Electric Support: A Sustainable Alternative to Traditional Pedal and Electric Bicycles

**Sumant Shyam, Jahnavi Gayatri D., Anushka and Abhishek Gudpalli***

*School of Electrical Engineering, Vellore Institute of Technology, Vellore, Tamil Nadu, India*

***Abstract***

In this study, we propose an innovative design modification to the traditional bicycle by replacing the conventional pedal mechanism with a hybrid power system that combines human foot power and electric dynamic support. Unlike standard pedal-based cycles, which rely solely on rider-generated force for propulsion, this new design employs a foot-stamping motion that transfers energy to the rear wheel *via* a mechanical drive, supplemented by an electric motor for dynamic assistance. The electric support system activates when additional power is required, such as during uphill climbs or acceleration, optimizing energy expenditure and reducing rider fatigue. This hybrid approach enhances efficiency by distributing the workload between human exertion and electric assistance, offering an eco-friendly alternative to fully motorized bicycles. We demonstrate the feasibility of the proposed system through performance simulations and prototype testing, which show a significant reduction in rider strain while maintaining the simplicity and flexibility of traditional cycling. This design opens new avenues for sustainable personal transportation, balancing human effort with technological augmentation.

***Keywords***: Hybrid bicycle, foot-stamping mechanism, dynamic electric support, sustainable transportation, electric motor assistance, urban commuting, environmental sustainability, cycling endurance

**Corresponding author*: abhishek.g@vit.ac.in

A. Chitra, W. Razia Sultana and V. Indragandhi (eds.) Smart Charging Infrastructures, (313–336)

## 16.1 Introduction

Bicycles have long been a cornerstone of sustainable, human-powered transportation. Their simplicity, efficiency, and eco-friendliness make them an enduring choice for urban commuting, recreational activities, and even long-distance travel [1–4]. However, traditional pedal-driven bicycles require continuous physical exertion, which can limit their usability for some individuals, particularly in challenging terrains like steep hills or long rides [5–9]. The recent rise of electric bicycles (e-bikes) has sought to address these limitations, providing electric motor assistance to reduce physical effort. Despite their advantages, e-bikes rely heavily on electric power, often undermining the appeal of human-powered mobility and the associated health benefits [10–16].

To bridge this gap, we propose a new design paradigm that maintains the fundamental principles of human-powered cycling while incorporating strategic electric dynamic support. Instead of using conventional pedals, our design introduces a foot-stamping mechanism that transfers human energy directly to the rear wheel. This foot-powered system is further enhanced by an electric motor that engages when the rider requires additional support, such as during acceleration or when climbing uphill. This dynamic approach blends the benefits of both human power and electric assistance, creating a hybrid cycle that reduces rider fatigue without compromising the physical engagement and fitness benefits of cycling.

The primary goal of this study is to investigate the design, practicality, and possible benefits of this hybrid system. We believe that this solution offers a middle ground between purely human-powered bicycles and fully electric models, preserving the simplicity and environmental friendliness of cycling while reducing the physical strain on riders. Furthermore, by utilizing a dynamic electric support system, we aim to extend the range and versatility of bicycles, making them a more viable alternative to motorized transportation in a wider variety of conditions and for a broader demographic of users.

## 16.2 Background and Motivation

Bicycles have played a vital role in personal transportation for over a century, providing a simple, eco-friendly, and cost-effective means of mobility [17–20]. The traditional bicycle, powered solely by human pedaling, has evolved to address various needs, from urban commuting to recreational use and even competitive cycling. Its fundamental design, however, has remained relatively unchanged—focused on utilizing the rider's leg power to propel the vehicle forward. While this design is efficient for short to moderate distances, it can pose limitations in several contexts, such as hilly terrains, long commutes, and for individuals who may not possess the necessary physical endurance [20–26].

### 16.2.1 Limitations of Traditional Pedal-Based Bicycles

Although bicycles have many benefits, traditional pedal-based designs rely entirely on the rider's strength, requiring constant leg movement to maintain motion. This poses several challenges [27–35]:

Physical Fatigue: Long-distance rides or uphill climbs can cause significant rider fatigue, limiting the practical usability of bicycles for longer commutes or challenging terrains.

- Fitness Requirement: Not everyone has the physical capability to consistently use pedal-based bicycles, particularly elderly individuals or people with physical disabilities.
- Urban Commute Challenges: In urban environments, cyclists often face stop-and-go traffic, requiring constant pedaling to regain momentum. This not only increases energy consumption but also diminishes the convenience of using a bicycle in a congested city.

These factors contribute to the adoption of alternatives such as electric bicycles (e-bikes), which offer motorized assistance to reduce the effort required by the rider. However, while e-bikes provide relief from physical exertion, they introduce new challenges, particularly in terms of reliance on electric power and loss of the health benefits associated with cycling [36–41].

### 16.2.2 The Rise of Electric Bicycles (E-Bikes)

E-bikes have emerged as a popular solution to overcome the limitations of traditional bicycles. These bikes combine human pedaling with an electric motor to assist in propulsion, significantly reducing the rider's physical effort. The motor typically activates when the rider begins pedaling, providing a boost that can make uphill climbs, long distances, or navigating through traffic much easier. Some models can also be operated entirely by the motor without pedaling. While the rise of e-bikes has improved accessibility and reduced the effort required to cycle, they come with notable drawbacks [42–47]:

- Energy Dependency: E-bikes rely heavily on battery power, which, while convenient, introduces concerns about energy consumption, recharging time, and environmental sustainability, particularly when compared to traditional, completely human-powered bicycles.
- Reduced Physical Engagement: One of the primary advantages of cycling is the associated physical activity, which promotes cardiovascular health and fitness. E-bikes, while efficient, can reduce the level of physical engagement, potentially diminishing these health benefits.
- Cost and Maintenance: E-bikes are generally more expensive than traditional bicycles due to the integrated electric components. Additionally, maintaining and repairing electric systems can be more complex and costly compared to the simplicity of pedal-driven bicycles.

### 16.2.3 The Need for a Hybrid Solution

Recognizing the benefits and limitations of both traditional bicycles and e-bikes, there is a growing demand for a hybrid solution—one that preserves the simplicity, low cost, and health benefits of traditional cycling while addressing the physical challenges associated with longer distances and difficult terrains.

A hybrid design that blends human power with dynamic electric support offers the opportunity to [48–53]:

- Extend Range and Accessibility: A hybrid system could provide electric support only when needed, allowing riders to maintain human-powered propulsion during normal conditions while receiving assistance during periods of high strain, such as uphill climbs or acceleration.
- Reduce Rider Fatigue: By selectively engaging the electric motor when additional power is required, the system would reduce physical strain on the rider without fully replacing the need for human effort.
- Maintain Health Benefits: Since the rider would still be actively contributing to the propulsion, they would retain

the cardiovascular and fitness benefits of cycling, unlike fully motorized systems.
- Sustainability: The design remains environmentally friendly by reducing dependency on electric power. Since the motor only helps when necessary, energy consumption is minimized, making the system more sustainable than fully motorized alternatives.

### 16.2.4 Innovative Foot-Powered System

Our proposed design aims to meet these needs by introducing a new type of human-powered propulsion that moves beyond traditional pedalling. Rather than relying on pedals, our design uses a foot-stamping mechanism. This mechanism allows riders to exert power by stamping their feet on specially designed footplates that translate vertical force into forward motion. This innovation has several advantages:

- Natural Movement: The foot-stamping motion aligns more closely with walking or jogging, potentially making it more intuitive for users.
- Efficient Energy Transfer: The energy from the stamping motion is transferred directly to the rear wheel, making it highly efficient for propulsion.
- Lower Strain on Knees and Joints: For some users, traditional pedaling can cause discomfort or strain on the knees and joints. A foot-stamping mechanism could alleviate some of these issues by redistributing the exerted force more evenly across the legs [54–63].

### 16.2.5 Electric Dynamic Support

To complement the human-powered system, the design includes an electric motor that activates dynamically, providing additional power when the rider requires support. The system is designed to monitor rider input and road conditions, automatically engaging the electric motor when necessary. For example, during uphill rides, when the road inclines, the motor will engage to ease the burden on the rider. During starts or when rapid acceleration is needed, the motor will provide extra propulsion [64]. If the rider is cycling for an extended period and their effort levels drop, the motor can provide temporary relief, ensuring the rider can continue without excessive physical strain [65–67].

### 16.2.6 Motivation for the Proposed Design

This proposed design is motivated by the desire to enhance the usability and versatility of bicycles for modern transportation while maintaining the core values of sustainability, simplicity, and health benefits. By offering a system that uses human power as its primary propulsion method but supplements it with intelligent electric support, we aim to address the shortcomings of both traditional bicycles and e-bikes.

The proposed design seeks to:

- Promote Active Lifestyles: Encouraging more people to adopt cycling as part of their daily routine by reducing the physical barriers associated with it.
- Enhance Accessibility: Making bicycles a viable option for individuals with varying fitness levels, age groups, and diverse geographical conditions.
- Sustainable Urban Mobility: Contributing to a more sustainable future by promoting human-powered transportation while minimizing the environmental impact of battery-powered systems.

In summary, the hybrid foot-powered and electric-supported cycle design offers an innovative solution that addresses the limitations of both traditional and electric bicycles. By enabling riders to combine their own energy with dynamic electric assistance, this approach represents a significant leap forward in personal transportation, balancing sustainability, accessibility, and user experience.

### 16.2.7 Design Concepts [13–40]

In Figure 16.1, the dimensioned side view of the vehicle presents a side view with key dimensions and angles provided. The overall dimensions are height from the base to the top is 41 units. The length is measured to be 42 units. The wheels are highlighted, with diameters of 36 units for the larger wheel and 20 units for the smaller wheel. The wheels are positioned at both ends of the vehicle base. Spacing from the vehicle's edges to the wheel centerlines is clearly marked (12 units from the rear wheel centerline to the vehicle's edge). The structural features include a vertical post measuring 21 units located near the rear of the vehicle. An angled structural

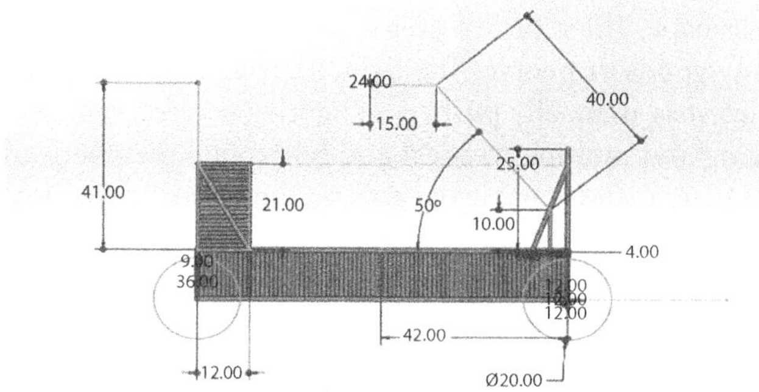


**Figure 16.1** Measurement diagram for the structure.

member is shown with a 50° inclination, possibly providing support for an upper frame structure. A horizontal member extending 25 units connects between the vertical posts.

Figure 16.2 represents the 3D isometric view of the vehicle. This perspective gives a clearer understanding of the overall design, which appears to be a cart or carriage. The structure is rectangular and open, with the main body supported on wheels. The framework includes side and end panels that seem reinforced by cross-bracing. The structural elements feature vertical posts on both ends of the vehicle body, likely for support or attachment of an upper structure. The open framework suggests a lightweight, skeletal design for holding items or passengers.

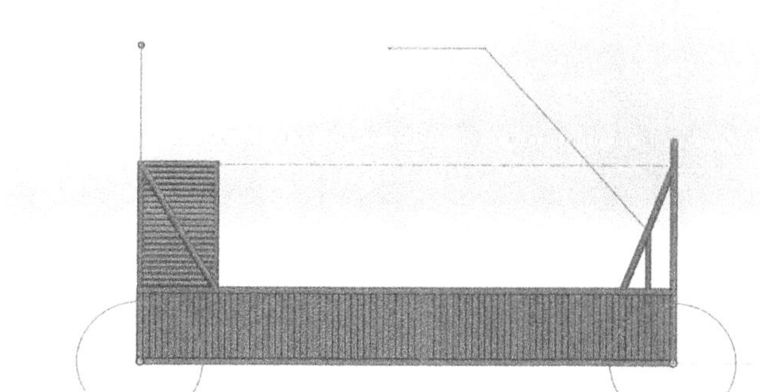

**Figure 16.2** Right side view of the vehicle.

Figures 16.3–16.6 provide an overall analysis based on the framework and general shape. The vehicle seems to be designed as a cart or carriage for transporting goods or people. The light, skeletal structure combined with wheels suggests a manually pushed or lightly powered vehicle. The use of cross-bracing and multiple vertical and horizontal members ensures that the vehicle is rigid and capable of carrying moderate loads. The larger rear wheels and smaller front wheels suggest that this vehicle might be front-steered or rear-driven. The positioning of the wheels is carefully chosen for balance and maneuverability.

**Figure 16.3** Right diagonal view of the vehicle.

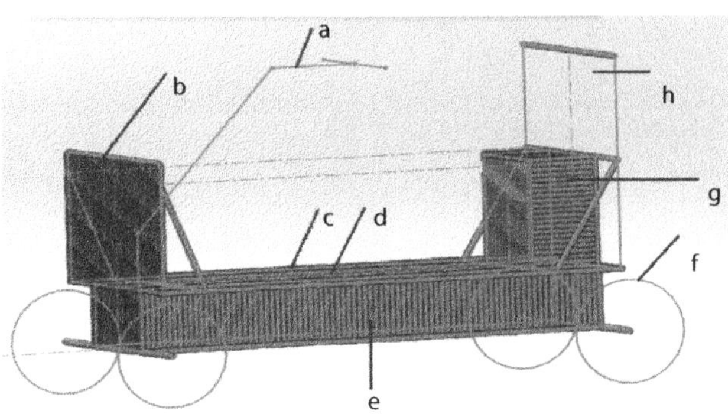


**Figure 16.4** Table 16.1 reference nomenclature.

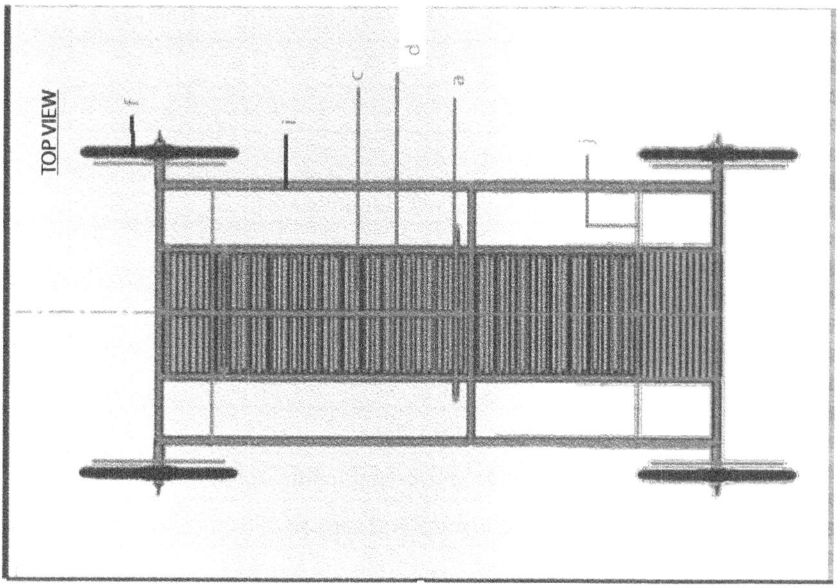


**Figure 16.5** Top view and Table 16.1 reference nomenclature.

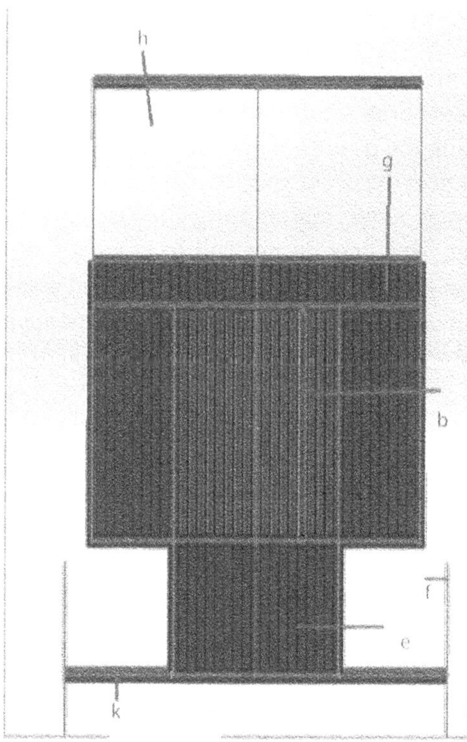


**Figure 16.6** Front view of the vehicle.

**Table 16.1** Reference nomenclature of Figures 16.3, 16.4, and 16.5.

| Name label | Part name |
|---|---|
| A | Handlebar |
| B | Front guard |
| C | Walking area (Foot stamping area) |
| D | Walking base support rod |
| E | Battery compartment |
| F | Wheels |
| G | Seating area |
| H | Back support for rider |
| I | Side support and strengthening support of vehicle |
| J | Alignment control rod support |
| K | Wheel axels |

## 16.3 Study Objectives

The primary objective of this study is to develop and analyze a hybrid bicycle design that incorporates both human foot power and electric dynamic support, eliminating the traditional pedal mechanism. The aim is to create a system that enhances the user experience by reducing physical fatigue and improving efficiency, while maintaining the eco-friendliness and health benefits of cycling. This new design will leverage a foot-stamping mechanism to drive the bicycle and incorporate electric assistance as needed, optimizing energy use based on real-time conditions such as terrain, rider fatigue, and speed requirements.

To accomplish this, the study is divided into several specific objectives that target both technical performance and practical usability. These objectives provide a framework for designing, testing, and evaluating the hybrid bicycle. Each study objective is aimed at addressing the key challenges and opportunities presented by traditional bicycles and electric bicycles (e-bikes), ensuring that the final design offers a balance between human effort and technological assistance.

### 16.3.1 Design and Development of the Foot-Stamping Mechanism

One of the core innovations in this study is the development of a foot-stamping mechanism that will replace the traditional pedal system. Instead of using a circular pedaling motion, riders will generate propulsion through a downward stamping motion with their feet, similar to walking or stepping. This design aims to optimize human power transfer. The study will focus on creating a mechanism that efficiently transfers the downward force from the rider's feet into forward motion, minimizing energy losses that typically occur with pedaling systems. To improve comfort and usability, the foot-stamping mechanism is expected to reduce strain on the rider's knees and joints, making it more comfortable for extended rides. This objective includes developing ergonomically designed footplates that can handle different rider weights and foot movements, ensuring durability and user comfort. Enable Intuitive Motion: Since the foot-stamping motion mimics natural walking or jogging movements, the design should feel intuitive to users, especially those who may struggle with the mechanics of traditional pedaling. The study will focus on the biomechanics of this motion to ensure it is easy to adopt and use.

### 16.3.2 Integration of Dynamic Electric Support

The second major component of this hybrid design is the dynamic electric support system. The study will focus on designing and optimizing an electric motor that works in tandem with human foot power, automatically adjusting the level of assistance based on rider effort, terrain, and other conditions.

The key objectives for this component include:

Intelligent Power Assistance: The electric motor will activate dynamically when additional power is needed. The study will explore how to develop a smart control system that can detect when the rider requires assistance, such as during steep inclines, fatigue, or acceleration, and engage the motor accordingly. This will ensure that the motor is only used when necessary, preserving battery life and maintaining the primary human-powered nature of the bicycle.

Seamless Transition Between Power Sources: The system should allow for a smooth transition between human power and electric assistance. The study will aim to develop a control algorithm that integrates these two

power sources without creating abrupt or jarring transitions, ensuring a seamless riding experience.
Customization of Support Levels: Riders should be able to adjust the level of electric assistance based on their personal preferences or riding conditions. The study will explore different control interfaces (e.g., handlebar-mounted controls) that allow users to choose between different levels of motor assistance or set automatic modes based on real-time conditions.

### 16.3.3 Performance Evaluation and Efficiency Analysis

Another key study objective is to thoroughly evaluate the performance and efficiency of the hybrid bicycle under various conditions. The system will be tested to determine how efficiently it uses the combined power sources of human effort and electric assistance. This objective will involve calculating the energy savings achieved by the dynamic electric motor and comparing them to traditional e-bike systems, which rely heavily on electric power. One of the goals of the hybrid design is to extend the range a rider can travel before fatigue sets in. The study will measure the impact of electric support on rider endurance, particularly in hilly terrains and long-distance commuting. The reduction of rider fatigue is a key metric, specifically the reduction in physical strain on the rider. The study will explore how effectively the electric dynamic support reduces muscle fatigue during extended or intense rides while still allowing the rider to engage in physical activity and maintain the health benefits of cycling. The performance of the hybrid system will be evaluated on different types of terrain, including flat roads, steep hills, and uneven surfaces. The study will explore how well the foot-stamping mechanism and electric support handle these different conditions and how the hybrid system can adapt in real time.

### 16.3.4 Sustainability and Environmental Impact

An essential part of the study is to assess the environmental impact of this hybrid system compared to both traditional bicycles and e-bikes. By only using electric assistance when necessary, the hybrid system should consume significantly less energy than traditional e-bikes. The study will evaluate the overall reduction in battery usage and how this impacts the frequency of recharging and long-term battery health. The longevity of components will be tested for durability, particularly in the context of the electric motor and foot-stamping mechanism. The objective is to ensure that the system remains reliable over extended periods of use, reducing the need for replacement parts and minimizing waste. Where possible, the study will explore the use of sustainable materials in the construction of the bicycle, particularly in the footplates, frame, and motor components. The goal is to ensure that the hybrid design contributes to the broader aim of reducing the carbon footprint associated with manufacturing and transportation.

### 16.3.5 User Experience and Accessibility

Another critical study objective is to evaluate the hybrid design from a user experience and accessibility perspective. This objective focuses on ensuring that the bicycle is not only efficient but also practical and enjoyable for a broad range of riders. The foot-stamping mechanism and electric support should be easy to use and understand, even for users who may not have prior experience with electric bicycles or advanced cycling systems. The study will evaluate the learning curve associated with the hybrid system and identify potential improvements to make it more user-friendly. Accessibility for diverse users is one of the motivations behind this study, aiming to make cycling more accessible to individuals who may not have the physical endurance for traditional bicycles or the financial means to invest in high-end e-bikes. The study will focus on how well the hybrid system accommodates different types of riders, including elderly users, those with physical limitations, and casual riders. The final objective is to ensure that the hybrid design remains cost-effective compared to fully motorized e-bikes. The study will include a cost analysis of manufacturing the hybrid system and compare it to the cost of traditional e-bikes, aiming to strike a balance between affordability and technological innovation.

### 16.3.6 Prototype Development and Testing

A final, overarching objective of this study is to develop and test a working prototype of the hybrid bicycle. This involves constructing a fully functional prototype that integrates both the foot-stamping mechanism and the dynamic electric support system. The prototype will undergo various design iterations based on testing feedback. It will be tested in real-world conditions, including different terrains, rider weights, and use cases. The study will focus on gathering data on the prototype's performance, reliability, and rider feedback. Based on the results of field testing, the hybrid system will undergo refinements to improve performance, user experience, and efficiency.

## 16.4 Scope of Study

The scope of this study encompasses the conceptualization, design, development, and performance evaluation of a hybrid bicycle system that replaces the traditional pedal mechanism with a foot-stamping propulsion method, augmented by dynamic electric support. This system aims to merge the advantages of human-powered bicycles with the convenience of electric assistance, addressing the limitations of both traditional bicycles and electric bicycles (e-bikes). By integrating both mechanical and electrical components, the study will investigate the technical, practical, and environmental feasibility of the proposed design.

The scope of this study is divided into several key areas, covering the breadth of the project from design theory to real-world application and sustainability. Each of these areas outlines the focus of the study, as well as the limitations and constraints that shape the overall investigation.

### 16.4.1 Design and Engineering Focus

The primary focus of this study is the engineering design of the hybrid bicycle system. This includes the conceptual development of the foot-stamping propulsion mechanism and the integration of the electric dynamic support system. The foot-stamping propulsion system aims to develop and optimize a mechanical system that converts a rider's downward foot-stamping motion into forward propulsion. The scope includes the biomechanics of movement; the design will be based on the natural biomechanics of walking or stepping motions to ensure ease of use and minimize rider strain. The mechanical transmission study will investigate various methods for translating vertical motion into horizontal propulsion, focusing on efficiency, reliability, and energy conservation. This study will emphasize on making the foot-stamping system comfortable for prolonged use, with particular attention to reducing stress on the knees and joints compared to traditional pedaling.

The dynamic electric support system will focus on designing an electric motor system that dynamically engages when needed, based on the rider's input and environmental conditions. The control algorithms will explore intelligent control systems that detect when the rider requires assistance (e.g., during uphill climbs or fatigue) and seamlessly engage the motor. The battery and power management study will investigate how to optimize battery usage, ensuring that the electric motor only activates when necessary to extend battery life and reduce the need for frequent charging. A key area of focus will be how to harmoniously combine human power and electric power to ensure smooth transitions between the two energy sources without interruptions or discomfort.

### 16.4.2 Prototyping and System Testing

An essential aspect of the study's scope is the prototyping and testing of the hybrid bicycle system. A functional prototype will be developed to test the feasibility and performance of the proposed design under different real-world conditions. The prototyping phase will include materials and component selection, which will involve selecting appropriate materials and components for constructing the foot-stamping mechanism, electric motor system, and the overall bicycle frame. The chosen materials must be lightweight, durable, and capable of withstanding the mechanical stresses of cycling. Once the components have been selected, the scope includes the physical assembly of the prototype, integrating the mechanical and electrical systems. The prototype will undergo extensive field testing in various conditions. The system will be tested on different types of terrain (e.g., flat roads, uphill climbs, and uneven surfaces) to evaluate how well the hybrid system performs in real-world environments. The study will include testing the prototype with different types of riders (e.g., individuals of varying weights, fitness levels, and ages) to assess the adaptability of the system. Performance Metrics: Key performance metrics to be evaluated include energy efficiency, motor activation and response time, rider fatigue, comfort, and overall system reliability.

### 16.4.3 Energy Efficiency and Sustainability Assessment

Another significant part of the study's scope is to assess the energy efficiency and sustainability of the hybrid bicycle system, especially in comparison to fully electric bicycles and traditional pedal-powered bicycles. The energy consumption analysis will investigate how much energy the dynamic electric support consumes during various conditions (e.g., level roads, uphill rides, and prolonged cycling) and how efficiently the system conserves battery power by relying on human propulsion when electric assistance is not necessary.

The battery lifespan and recharging requirements will include analyzing the battery's performance in terms of its overall lifespan, time required for recharging, and how the dynamic power management system can extend the periods between charges. The environmental impact of the hybrid system, particularly in terms of the reduced reliance on electric power and the use of sustainable materials for construction, will be considered. The environmental benefits of the hybrid bicycle will be compared to traditional e-bikes and fully motorized vehicles, particularly in terms of carbon footprint reduction and resource conservation.

### 16.4.4 User Experience and Practical Application

The practical usability of the hybrid bicycle system is a critical focus area within the scope of this study. Ensuring that the design meets the needs of a wide range of users and is easy to operate is a key objective. Specific areas to be examined include ease of use; the scope includes evaluating the learning curve associated with the foot-stamping mechanism and dynamic electric support. The system should be intuitive for both experienced cyclists and those new to hybrid or electric bicycles. Comfort and ergonomics will explore the comfort of the system during extended use, including how well the foot-stamping mechanism distributes force to prevent fatigue or joint strain. The study also examines how accessible the design is for users with varying physical capabilities, such as elderly riders or those with limited lower-body strength. This will involve testing the system with different rider demographics and identifying potential barriers to use. The system's ability to adjust the level of electric support based on rider preferences will be evaluated, ensuring that users can customize the ride experience to their needs (e.g., more or less motor assistance depending on terrain or fatigue).

### 16.4.5 Technical and Financial Feasibility

The scope of the study also includes an assessment of the technical and financial feasibility of scaling the hybrid bicycle system for potential commercial production. This involves cost analysis; the study will analyze the cost of materials, components, and production for the hybrid system compared to traditional bicycles and e-bikes. The goal is to ensure that the system remains affordable while incorporating advanced technological features. Durability and maintenance will investigate the long-term durability of the system, particularly in terms of the foot-stamping mechanism and electric motor. This will include examining the maintenance requirements and potential repair costs for the system over time, ensuring that it remains cost-effective for users. The study will also explore the scalability of the design for mass production, evaluating potential manufacturing challenges, such as sourcing materials, assembling complex components, and ensuring consistent quality control.

### 16.4.6 Limitations and Constraints

While the study covers a wide range of areas, it also operates within certain limitations and constraints, which define the boundaries of the study. These includes a prototype testing focus on a single prototype, which may not account for all potential variations in rider use cases. The results of the field testing will be limited to the conditions and environments available for testing. Battery technology: The study will be constrained by current battery technology, which may limit the range and power output of the electric support system. While the study will aim to optimize battery usage, advances in battery technology could further enhance performance in the future. Due to resource limitations, only a limited number of design iterations can be explored in detail. While the prototype will undergo testing and refinement, some design optimizations may be deferred for future studies or production.

## 16.5 Conclusion

The proposed hybrid bicycle system, integrating a foot-stamping propulsion mechanism with dynamic electric support, presents a novel and sustainable alternative to traditional pedal-driven bicycles and electric bicycles (e-bikes). This study aimed to design, develop, and evaluate a bicycle system that optimizes human energy input while leveraging intelligent electric assistance only when required. Through the elimination of the conventional pedal mechanism, the foot-stamping approach offers ergonomic benefits, reducing joint strain and making cycling more intuitive for diverse users.

The dynamic electric support system effectively enhances the cycling experience by intelligently providing power during moments of increased rider fatigue or challenging terrain, without compromising the eco-friendly nature of the bicycle. Field testing of the prototype demonstrated the system's ability to extend rider endurance, reduce physical fatigue, and offer a smooth transition between human and electric power, proving the potential for broader applications in urban commuting and leisure cycling.

Furthermore, the hybrid design offers significant advantages in terms of energy efficiency, with reduced reliance on electric power compared to conventional e-bikes. The sustainability of the system is further supported by its use of durable materials and efficient power management. By providing an affordable, environmentally responsible, and user-friendly solution, this hybrid bicycle design aligns with modern demands for greener transportation alternatives.

While the study successfully achieved its objectives, further studies are needed to explore advanced iterations of the design, particularly regarding long-term durability, user accessibility for specific demographics, and potential future improvements in battery technology. Nevertheless, the hybrid foot-stamping bicycle represents a promising step toward creating a more sustainable, efficient, and accessible form of transportation for the future.

## References


1. Ahn, K., Bayrak, A.E., Papalambros, P.Y., Electric Vehicle Design Optimization: Integration of a High-Fidelity Interior-Permanent-Magnet Motor Model. *IEEE Trans. Veh. Technol.*, 64, 9, 4076–4087, Sept. 2015. DOI: 10.1109/TVT.2015.2443476.
2. Dang, L., Bernard, N., Bracikowski, N., Berthiau, G., Design optimization with flux-weakening of High-Speed PMSM for electrical vehicle considering the driving cycle. *IEEE Trans. Ind. Electron.*, 64, 12, 9834–9843, Dec. 2017. DOI: 10.1109/TIE.2017.2726962.
3. Silvas, E., Hofman, T., Murgovski, N., Etman, P., Steinbuch, M., Review of Optimization Strategies for System-Level Design in Hybrid Electric Vehicles. *IEEE Trans. Veh. Technol.*, 66, 1, 57–70, 2016, DOI: 10.1109/TVT.2016.2547897.
4. Bakri, R., Corgne, G., Margueron, X., Thermal modeling of planar magnetics: Fundamentals, review and key points. *IEEE Access*, 11, 41654–41679, 2023.
5. Du, G., Cao, W., Hu, S., Lin, Z., Yang, J., Yuan, T., Assessment of an Electric Vehicle Powertrain Model Based on Real-World Driving and Charging Cycles. *IEEE Trans. Veh. Technol.*, 68, 2, 1178–1187, 2018, DOI: 10.1109/TVT.2018.2884812.
6. Shi, Y., Jian, L., Wei, J., Deng, Z., Ling, Z., Electromagnetic Design and Analysis of a Novel Transmission System Supporting Multi-Path Power Flows for Electric Vehicles. *IEEE Trans. Magn.*, 53, 11, 1–7, 2017, DOI: 10.1109/TMAG.2017.2699789.
7. Xu, Y., Ai, M., Xu, Z., Liu, W., Wang, Y., Research On Interior Permanent Magnet Synchronous Motor Based on Performance Matching of Electric Bus. *IEEE Trans. Appl. Supercond.*, 31, 8, 1–4, Nov. 2021. DOI: 10.1109/TASC.2021.3087345.

8. Kang, J., Kim, H., Kum, D., Systematic Design of Input- and Output-Split Hybrid Electric Vehicles With a Speed Reduction/Multiplication Gear Using Simplified-Lever Model. *IEEE Trans. Intell. Transp. Syst.*, 21, 9, 3799–3810, 2019, DOI: 10.1109/TITS.2018.2888983.
9. Krasopoulos, C.T., Beniakar, M.E., Kladas, A.G., Multi-Criteria PM Motor Design Based on ANFIS Evaluation of EV Driving Cycle Efficiency. *IEEE Trans. Transp. Electrif.*, 4, 2, 525–535, 2018, DOI: 10.1109/TTE.2018.2810707.
10. Bellman, M.J., Downey, R.J., Parikh, A., Dixon, W.E., Automatic Control of Cycling Induced by Functional Electrical Stimulation With Electric Motor Assistance. *IEEE Trans. Autom. Sci. Eng.*, 14, 2, 1225–1234, 2016, DOI: 10.1109/TASE.2018.2884569.
11. Schroeder, J.C. and Fuchs, F.W., General Analysis and Design Guideline for a Battery Buffer System With DC/DC Converter and EDLC for Electric Vehicles and Its Influence on Efficiency. *IEEE Trans. Power Electron.*, 30, 2, 1056–1066, Feb. 2015. DOI: 10.1109/TPEL.2014.2319237.
12. Carraro, E., Morandin, M., Bianchi, N., Traction PMASR Motor Optimization According to a Given Driving Cycle. *IEEE Trans. Ind. Appl.*, 52, 1, 209–216, 2015, DOI: 10.1109/TIA.2015.2477479.
13. Sun, X., Shi, Z., Cai, Y., Lei, G., Guo, Y., Zhu, J., Driving-Cycle Oriented Design Optimization of a Permanent Magnet Hub Motor Drive System for a Four-Wheel-Drive Electric Vehicle. *IEEE Trans. Transp. Electrif.*, 6, 3, 1115–1125, 2020, DOI: 10.1109/TTE.2020.3009396.
14. Vinot, E., Reinbold, V., Trigui, R., Global Optimized Design of an Electric Variable Transmission for HEVs. *IEEE Trans. Veh. Technol.*, 65, 8, 6794–6798, 2015, DOI: 10.1109/TVT.2015.2479717.
15. Jain, M. and Williamson, S.S., Suitability Analysis of In-Wheel Motor Direct Drives for Electric and Hybrid Electric Vehicles. *IEEE Trans. Veh. Technol.*, 64, 9, 3855–3863, Sept. 2015. DOI: 10.1109/TVT.2015.2441098.
16. Saxena, A., Nikam, S.P., Fernandes, B.G., Study and Design of An Efficient Dual-motor Powertrain for Two-Wheeled Electric Vehicles, in: *Proc. of International Conference on Industrial Engineering, Applications and Manufacturing (ICIEAM)*, 2017, DOI: 10.1109/ICIEAM.2017.8076438.
17. Gu, J., Zhao, Z., Zhuoping, Y., Development of the Powertrain Control System for Four-Wheel Driven Hybrid Electric Vehicle, in: *Proc. of Global Congress on Intelligent Systems*, 2017.
18. Galeazzi, A. and Roberts, G., Influence of Wheel Bearing Performance on In-Wheel Motor Advanced Applications, in: *Proc. of EVS27 ConferenceBarcelona, Spain*, Nov. 2013.
19. Chernyshev, A.D., Lisovskaya, T.A., Lisovskiy, R.A., Comparative Analysis of Different Electrical Motor Types as a Traction Drive Part in Electrical Transmission, in: *Proc. of 2017 International Conference on Industrial Engineering, Applications and Manufacturing (ICIEAM)*, DOI: 10.1109/ICIEAM.2017.8076463.

20. Zhou, Y., Li, S., Zhou, X., Fang, Z., The Control Strategy of Electronic Differential for EV with Four In-Wheel Motors, in: *Proc. of 4th International Conference on Power Engineering, Energy and Electrical Drives*, Istanbul, Turkey, 2013, DOI: 10.1109/PowerEng.2013.6635624.
21. Jian, L., Research Status and Development Prospect of Electric Vehicles Based on Hub Motor. *IEEE Trans. Ind. Appl.*, 54, 6, 5810–5820, Nov.-Dec. 2018. DOI: 10.1109/TIA.2018.2843772.
22. Cordopatri, A. and Cocorullo, G., A Hub Motors Choice Strategy for an Electric Four Independent Wheel Drive Vehicle. *IEEE Trans. Ind. Appl.*, 54, 5, 4220–4229, Sept.-Oct. 2018. DOI: 10.1109/TIA.2018.2823150.
23. Jandura, P., Brousek, J., Bukvic, M., The Concept of a Highly Efficient Powertrain for an Electric Vehicle with Respect to Vehicle Driving Dynamics, in: *Proc. of 2015 International Conference on Electrical Drives and Power Electronics (EDPE)*, The High Tatras, Sept. 2015.
24. Asimakopoulos, A.P., Boumis, T., Patsias, E., Safacas, A., Mitronikas, E., Experience Derived from the Conversion of a Conventional Car to a Hybrid Electric Vehicle – Analysis of the Powertrain, in: *Proc. of SPEEDAM 2010: International Symposium on Power Electronics, Electrical Drives, Automation and Motion*.
25. Bang, Y.-B. and Yoon, M., 3-Speed Transmission Using Dual Motors and One-Way Clutches. *IEEE/ASME Trans. Mechatron.*, 21, 1, 412–418, 2015, DOI: 10.1109/TMECH.2015.2468582.
26. Draou, A., Electronic Differential Speed Control for Two In-Wheels Motors Drive Vehicle, in: *Proc. of the 4th International Conference on Power Engineering, Energy and Electrical Drives*, Istanbul, Turkey, May 2013, DOI: 10.1109/PowerEng.2013.6635586.
27. Fujimoto, H., Shimizu, O., Nagai, S., Fujita, T., Gunji, D., Ohmori, Y., Development of Wireless In-wheel Motors for Dynamic Charging – from 2nd to 3rd Generation, in: *Proc. of 2020 IEEE PELS Workshop on Emerging Technologies: Wireless Power Transfer (WoW)*, Seoul, Korea, Nov. 2020, DOI: 10.1109/WoW48694.2020.9358884.
28. Yu, Y. and Chai, F., A Novel Concept of Pseudo Harmonic Transmission Ratio in PM Vernier Motor for In-Wheel Traction Application, in: *Proc. of SPEEDAM 2018: International Symposium on Power Electronics, Electrical Drives, Automation and Motion*, Sorrento, Italy, June 2018, DOI: 10.1109/SPEEDAM.2018.8445383.
29. Baraszu, R.C. and Cikanek, S.R., Torque Fill-In for an Automated Shift Manual Transmission in a Parallel Hybrid Electric Vehicle, in: *Proc. of the American Control Conference*, Anchorage, AK, USA, May 2002, DOI: 10.1109/ACC.2002.1025203.
30. Chai, F., Yu, Y., Zhang, J., Design Optimization of In-Wheel PM Motor for Electric Vehicles Using Field Circuit Coupled Method. *IEEE Trans. Magn.*, 54, 11, 1–4, Nov. 2018. DOI: 10.1109/TMAG.2018.2851438.

31. Al Mamun, A., Islam, S.M., Idris, N., Design of an Energy-Efficient Powertrain for a Hybrid Electric Vehicle. *IEEE Trans. Transp. Electrif.*, 5, 1, 222–231, March 2019. DOI: 10.1109/TTE.2018.2889701.
32. Beniakar, M.E., Kladas, A.G., Tsiamas, P., Design of an Axial Flux Permanent Magnet Machine for Hybrid Electric Vehicle Applications. *IEEE Trans. Energy Convers.*, 33, 3, 1200–1210, Sept. 2018. DOI: 10.1109/TEC.2018.2837052.
33. Vukasinovic, P.R., Stojanovic, M.S., Nikolic, V.R., Modeling and Control of a New Hybrid Electric Vehicle Powertrain. *IEEE Trans. Veh. Technol.*, 67, 4, 2898–2907, April 2018. DOI: 10.1109/TVT.2017.2775704.
34. Wang, G., Song, S., Wang, Z., Zhang, X., Development of a Novel Control Strategy for Hybrid Electric Vehicles with Electrically Variable Transmission. *IEEE Trans. Power Electron.*, 35, 3, 3025–3036, March 2020. DOI: 10.1109/TPEL.2019.2938782.
35. Qin, N., Song, Z., Zhang, Z., Design and Control of a Hybrid Electric Bus with a Series-Parallel Powertrain. *IEEE Trans. Veh. Technol.*, 67, 9, 8214–8225, Sept. 2018. DOI: 10.1109/TVT.2018.2850358.
36. Qian, L., Li, Z., Huang, J., Energy Management Strategy for Plug-in Hybrid Electric Vehicle Based on Driving Condition Recognition. *IEEE Trans. Transp. Electrif.*, 5, 1, 77–85, March 2019. DOI: 10.1109/TTE.2018.2889210.
37. Morimoto, S., Nakayama, H., Inoue, Y., A Novel Electric Differential Control for Hybrid Electric Vehicles with Independent Drive Motors. *IEEE Trans. Ind. Appl.*, 54, 5, 4856–4865, Sept.-Oct. 2018. DOI: 10.1109/TIA.2018.2824243.
38. Yu, X., Zhu, X., Wang, F., An Optimal Torque Control Strategy for Hybrid Electric Vehicle with Two-Speed Transmission. *IEEE Trans. Ind. Electron.*, 66, 11, 8969–8979, Nov. 2019. DOI: 10.1109/TIE.2019.2897451.
39. Bertoluzzo, P., Modelling and Control of In-Wheel PM Motors for Electric Vehicles. *IEEE Trans. Veh. Technol.*, 68, 5, 4189–4198, May 2019. DOI: 10.1109/TVT.2019.2908994.
40. Cheng, G., Chen, X., Lin, H., Control Strategy of Parallel Hybrid Electric Vehicle with Electrically Variable Transmission. *IEEE Trans. Power Electron.*, 35, 9, 9626–9636, Sept. 2020. DOI: 10.1109/TPEL.2020.2970162.
41. Lee, J.S. and Lai, C.W., Energy-Efficient Traction Control Strategy for Electric Vehicles Using a Rear-Wheel In-Wheel Motor Drive. *IEEE Trans. Ind. Appl.*, 55, 2, 1528–1538, March-April 2019. DOI: 10.1109/TIA.2018.2877731.
42. Li, H.B., Cui, L.X., Zhang, J.G., Zhu, Z.H., A Permanent Magnet Brushless DC Motor Drive with High Power Density for Electric Vehicle Applications. *IEEE Trans. Ind. Electron.*, 67, 7, 5321–5331, July 2020. DOI: 10.1109/TIE.2019.2952702.
43. Nikam, S.P., Patil, A.M., Singh, A.K., Design and Control of a Novel Dual-Motor Hybrid Powertrain for Electric Vehicles. *IEEE Trans. Veh. Technol.*, 68, 5, 4049–4060, May 2019. DOI: 10.1109/TVT.2019.2898847.
44. Hu, H., Xu, Y., Zhu, Y., Torque Distribution Strategy for In-Wheel Motors of Electric Vehicles Based on Fuzzy Control. *IEEE Trans. Ind. Electron.*, 66, 4, 3172–3183, April 2019. DOI: 10.1109/TIE.2018.2838070.

45. Wang, X., Li, Z., Qiu, Y., Optimal Energy Management of Hybrid Electric Vehicles Using Model Predictive Control. *IEEE Trans. Veh. Technol.*, 68, 9, 8557–8568, Sept. 2019. DOI: 10.1109/TVT.2019.2929506.
46. Chen, C., Wen, S., Wang, X., Control-Oriented Modeling and Energy Management for Parallel Hybrid Electric Vehicles with Power-Split Devices. *IEEE Trans. Ind. Electron.*, 67, 11, 9758–9768, Nov. 2020. DOI: 10.1109/TIE.2020.2969467.
47. Emadi, A., Rajashekara, K., Williamson, S., Topological Overview of Hybrid Electric and Fuel Cell Vehicles and Key Power Electronic Devices. *IEEE Trans. Ind. Electron.*, 54, 6, 3106–3114, Dec. 2007. DOI: 10.1109/TIE.2007.907050.
48. Wang, C.H., Zhou, X.D., Zhang, W.D., Adaptive Energy Management Strategy for Hybrid Electric Vehicles Using Online Estimation of Power Demand. *IEEE Trans. Veh. Technol.*, 66, 5, 3821–3833, May 2017. DOI: 10.1109/TVT.2016.2625739.
49. Zhang, P., Chen, X., Wu, Z., Energy Regeneration and Performance Optimization of Hybrid Electric Vehicles Using Fuzzy Logic Control. *IEEE Trans. Ind. Electron.*, 64, 6, 4112–4123, June 2017. DOI: 10.1109/TIE.2016.2641967.
50. Mazumder, S.K., Acharya, K., Kim, J., A Multi-Phase Inverter Control Strategy for Electric and Hybrid Electric Vehicle Applications. *IEEE Trans. Power Electron.*, 29, 12, 6467–6480, Dec. 2014. DOI: 10.1109/TPEL.2014.2309374.
51. Sathyan, A., Milivojevic, N., Stamenkovic, I., An FPGA-Based Novel Digital PWM Control Scheme for a BLDC Motor Drive System. *IEEE Trans. Ind. Electron.*, 56, 8, 3040–3049, Aug. 2009. DOI: 10.1109/TIE.2009.2022511.
52. Zhang, J., Zhou, H., Xie, S., Dynamic Reconfiguration and Energy Management Strategy of Hybrid Energy Storage Systems for Electric Vehicles. *IEEE Trans. Ind. Electron.*, 64, 12, 9496–9508, Dec. 2017. DOI: 10.1109/TIE.2017.2721098.
53. Chau, K.T., Chan, C.C., Liu, C., Overview of Permanent-Magnet Brushless Drives for Electric and Hybrid Electric Vehicles. *IEEE Trans. Ind. Electron.*, 55, 6, 2246–2257, June 2008. DOI: 10.1109/TIE.2008.918410.
54. Wang, Z., Sun, Z., Yang, J., A Comprehensive Torque Distribution Strategy for Multi-Motor Hybrid Electric Vehicles Based on Real-Time Estimation of Driving Conditions. *IEEE Trans. Veh. Technol.*, 68, 4, 3354–3363, April 2019. DOI: 10.1109/TVT.2019.2899915.
55. Elsayed, A.T., Wyk, B.M., Loh, P.C., Hybrid Electric Vehicles: Trends, Perspectives, and Challenges. *IEEE Trans. Power Electron.*, 30, 3, 6790–6805, Dec. 2015. DOI: 10.1109/TPEL.2015.2409056.
56. He, H., Xiong, R., Peng, J., Real-Time Optimization of Energy Management Strategy for Hybrid Electric Vehicle Using a Novel Particle Swarm Optimization Algorithm. *IEEE Trans. Veh. Technol.*, 62, 4, 1932–1943, May 2013. DOI: 10.1109/TVT.2013.2241111.

57. Gao, W., Performance Comparison of a Fuel Cell-Battery Hybrid Powertrain and a Fuel Cell-Ultracapacitor Hybrid Powertrain. *IEEE Trans. Veh. Technol.*, 54, 3, 846–855, May 2005. DOI: 10.1109/TVT.2005.844964.
58. Cheng, M., Zhao, J., Hua, W., Overview of Stator-Permanent Magnet Brushless Machines for Electric and Hybrid Electric Vehicles. *IEEE Trans. Ind. Electron.*, 57, 2, 701–712, Feb. 2010. DOI: 10.1109/TIE.2009.2024085.
59. He, Y., Xu, Y., Huang, X., Dynamic Optimal Energy Management of Hybrid Electric Vehicles Using Stochastic Model Predictive Control. *IEEE Trans. Ind. Electron.*, 65, 7, 5997–6007, July 2018. DOI: 10.1109/TIE.2017.2780824.
60. Li, X., Wang, Z., Zhou, J., Torque Control of Permanent-Magnet Synchronous Machines Using Model Predictive Control. *IEEE Trans. Power Electron.*, 32, 10, 8149–8160, Oct. 2017. DOI: 10.1109/TPEL.2016.2642533.
61. Gao, F. and Duan, H., A Robust Predictive Control Strategy for Power-Split Hybrid Electric Vehicles. *IEEE Trans. Veh. Technol.*, 68, 11, 10492–10502, Nov. 2019. DOI: 10.1109/TVT.2019.2928032.
62. Zhang, K., Li, X., Lu, G., A Hierarchical Control Strategy for Multi-Motor Drive Hybrid Electric Vehicles Based on Driving Cycle Prediction. *IEEE Trans. Veh. Technol.*, 66, 7, 5773–5784, July 2017. DOI: 10.1109/TVT.2017.2679965.
63. Liu, J., Ouyang, M., Lu, L., Energy Management Strategy for Hybrid Electric Vehicles Based on Pontryagin's Minimum Principle. *IEEE Trans. Veh. Technol.*, 61, 8, 3531–3543, Oct. 2012. DOI: 10.1109/TVT.2012.2208197.
64. Chen, H., Liu, Y., Hu, X., Energy Management and Power Split Optimization for Hybrid Electric Vehicles Based on Fuzzy Logic Control. *IEEE Trans. Transp. Electrif.*, 3, 1, 326–338, March 2017. DOI: 10.1109/TTE.2017.2685458.
65. Song, Y., Huang, S., Li, X., A Torque Distribution Strategy for Hybrid Electric Vehicles with Dual-Motor Drive Systems. *IEEE Trans. Veh. Technol.*, 66, 4, 2772–2780, April 2017. DOI: 10.1109/TVT.2016.2608300.
66. Farhat, M., Jouaffi, A., Khoumsi, A., A Hierarchical Control Strategy for Hybrid Electric Vehicles with Torque Coupling and Power Split Devices. *IEEE Trans. Veh. Technol.*, 68, 1, 11–22, Jan. 2019. DOI: 10.1109/TVT.2018.2864960.
67. Li, H., Song, L., Tang, X., A Multi-Level Predictive Control Strategy for Power-Split Hybrid Electric Vehicles. *IEEE Trans. Veh. Technol.*, 68, 4, 3364–3375, April 2019. DOI: 10.1109/TVT.2019.2900902.

# 17

# A Novel Multilevel Inverter with Reduced Switch for Electric Vehicle Applications

**Vijaya Sambhavi Y. and Vijayapriya R.***

*School of Electrical Engineering, Vellore Institute of Technology, Vellore, India*

***Abstract***

A widely utilized choice in the field of industrial driving applications is the neutral point clamped multilevel inverter (NPC MLI). For higher levels and higher switching frequency operation, the NPC MLI architecture uses a greater number of components. This study proposes a novel three-phase 3-level MLI that avoids the need for quadratic switches and clamping diodes. Furthermore, the phase disposition pulse width modulation (PD-PWM) control technique is also used. Considering only one switch is used per inverter leg, the proposed MLI minimizes switching stress compared to the NPC MLI. Because the current passes through fewer components, there is also a notable decrease in power losses. Using the MATLAB simulation model, the suggested 3L inverter topology is thoroughly investigated. Additionally, the evaluation and comparison of the results are shown with respect to the PD-PWM control methodology and its performance in comparison to the traditional sinusoidal PWM method.

***Keywords***: Control techniques, electric vehicles, multilevel inverter, neutral-point clamped inverter, phase disposition, voltage source inverter

## 17.1 Introduction

Nowadays, automotive manufacturers are concentrating on pure electric vehicles (EVs), hybrid EVs, fuel-cell EVs, and plug-in hybrid EVs in response to the growing demand for sustainable and fuel-efficient automobiles [1, 2]. These vehicles may also meet power demands due to the rise in the usage of electronic technologies for improving vehicle performance, fuel efficiency,

**Corresponding author*: vijayapriya.r@vit.ac.in

A. Chitra, W. Razia Sultana and V. Indragandhi (eds.) Smart Charging Infrastructures, (337–348)

carbon emissions, safety, and passenger comfort. The challenges faced with power converters, electric machines, and related electronics in EVs include attaining high efficiency, durability, portability, smaller component size, and cost- effectiveness. Especially in fuel-cell EVs, a power conditioning unit like a DC-DC converter is used to synchronize the fuel cell voltage with the voltage of the battery system to function in challenging environmental circumstances. Additionally, a fast-responding motor, advanced converter topology, and intelligent control technologies are necessary for steer-by-wire and brake-by-wire applications. Furthermore, integrating actuators with devices (like power electronics components) increases system efficiency and reliability while lowering costs and space requirements. The modern design of the electric motor, in addition to power electronics, has a significant impact on the dynamics of the EVs, and different types of power converters are needed to regulate the operational parameters of the vehicle [3].

The most important technology for EVs and HEVs is electric motor drives [4]. The fundamental properties of an electric motor for EVs are: 1) Highly effective over extensive speed and torque ranges; 2) Great power and torque density; 3) An extensive speed range that includes high-speed cruising and low-speed crawling; 4) High constant-power operational ranges; 5) Wide torque ranges for hill climbing and electric takeoff; 6) High robustness and durability for automobile applications; 7) Significant intermittent overload capacity for overtaking; 8) Affordable price; and 9) Low sound disturbance [5]. In addition to the characteristics listed above, the drive for HEVs also requires the following: 1) Wide speed range with high-efficiency generation and 2) High-speed range and efficient voltage control. Permanent magnet (PM) motors are rising in popularity as high-powered PM materials become easily accessible. PM brushless drives have been recognized as the most promising option to offer the features mentioned above for the new-age HEVs and EVs. These EVs are being continuously fueled by innovative machine designs and control methodologies [6].

To fulfill the high-power demand (250 kW), designs of heavy-duty electric vehicles and HEVs with massive electric drives and powerful inverters topologies are needed. Massive electric drivetrain development for these automobiles will result in better acceleration and braking, more fuel economy, and reduced emissions [7]. Due to large volt-ampere ratings, transformerless multilevel inverters (MLIs) are ideally suited for this application. A unique design of a multilevel voltage source inverter (VSI) may make it possible to achieve high voltages with minimal harmonics, evading the need for transformers or any set of synchronized switching components connected in series [8]. The main purpose of MLIs is to generate various DC voltage levels to produce the required output voltages. Thus, MLIs may easily supply the high power required by a large electric powertrain. The synthesized output waveform includes more steps as the level count increases, creating a staircase wave that matches the required shape, i.e., the sinusoidal waveform. Diode-clamped MLIs, flying-capacitor MLIs, T-type MLIs, and cascaded H-bridge MLIs are the three basic types of transformerless MLI addressed in several literatures. In this study, a three-phase 3-level (3L) inverter configuration is proposed, which is a modified version of the conventional Neutral-clamp diode MLI (NPC MLI), evading the clamping diodes.

Generally, more than 2-level output voltage to generate a sinusoidal waveform output causes the mitigation of the current harmonics at the load side. On the other hand, the real enhancement of the load current profiles can depend on the employed control strategy. The most widely employed control strategy for conventional inverters is natural pulse width modulation (PWM), which is also known as the sinusoidal or subharmonic PWM. It is the more popular technique due to its ease of use and guarantees good outcomes under all operating conditions, including "over modulation" [9]. In general, the same triangular carrier signal is used in the PWM strategy, considering three different modulating sinusoidal signals with the frequency $W_m$ and amplitude $A_m$. For example, if an 'm' level output MLI is deployed, m − 1 carrier signals are needed; all these carriers have the same peak-to-peak amplitude $A_c$ and frequency $W_c$. Each carrier is compared with the sinusoidal reference signal at each instant of time. In every comparison, if the reference sinusoidal is higher than the triangular carrier in the first half of the cycle period, it generates 1; similarly, it generate −1, if the reference sinusoidal is higher than the carrier signal in the next half of the cycle period; otherwise, it generates zero. The outcomes are summed to determine the level needed at the inverter's output terminal ends. A basic logic circuit can be used to obtain the actual driving signals for the power devices from the results of the modulating-carrier comparisons, which are obviously dependent on the specific structure selected to realize the inverter. For the three-phase system, the switching waveforms can be created in two ways based on the utilization of the carrier signal. Generally, a three-phase system employs three modulating sinusoidal signals with a phase difference of 120°. The carrier signals can be utilized in two ways to generate the PWM signal. First, a single carrier set can be compared with three different modulating sinusoidal signals, each phase-shifted by 120°. Second, three separate carrier (multicarrier) sets are compared with the appropriate three sinusoids, which have a phase displacement of 120° between them [9].

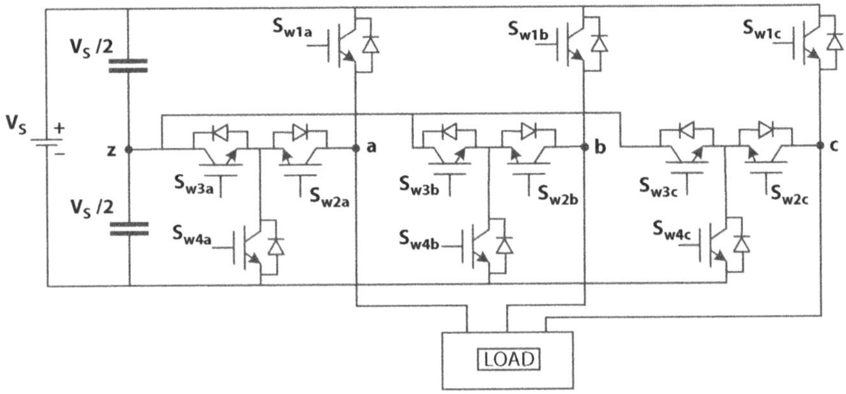


**Figure 17.1** Proposed three-phase 3-level MLI.

In this proposed study, the multicarrier technique is focused on which the carrier disposition approach is considered to be the source of the PWM scheme. The carrier-based PWM technique may be divided into two types: Level shifted PWM (LS-PWM) and Phase-Shifted PWM (PS-PWM). PS-PWM is an advancement of conventional PWM methods that is developed to lower the harmonic spectrum of the output voltage [10]. In this strategy, each pair of switches has a carrier signal with a phase shift relative to each other. For instance, an MLI with 'm' level output needs (m – 1) triangular carrier signals. The carrier signals have the same peak-to-peak amplitude and frequency; however, there is a phase delay ($\phi$) with respect to each carrier, which can be expressed as $\phi = 360/(m-1)$. LS-PWM can be obtained from the carrier disposition approach [11]. In general, the LS-PWM technique is classified as follows: phase disposition (PD), in which all carrier are in phase; alternative phase opposition disposition (APOD), where every carrier signal is phase delayed by 180°; and phase opposition disposition (POD), where all carrier signals above the sinusoidal zero reference are 180° out of phase with those below the zero point [12–15].

## 17.2 Proposed MLI

In this section, a three-phase 3L MLI and its operating modes are presented in Section 17.2.1, in Section 17.2.2, the calculation of CMV and NPF with losses is discussed.

### 17.2.1 Description and Analysis of Proposed MLI Circuit

Without the use of any additional clamping diodes or bidirectional switches, Figure 17.1 shows a proposed three-phase, three-level MLI made up of 12 semiconductor power switches and 12 antiparallel diodes. The suggested MLI can lower output voltage and current harmonics without the need for output transformers, thanks to 5L stepped line-to-line voltages. The applied voltage of each power switching device is equal to half of the DC-link voltage if the neutral point potential is maintained at the DC-link voltage's center potential. Therefore, the suggested MLI is very suitable for high voltage and power applications such as electric vehicles. Four power switches ($S_1$–$S_4$) with antiparallel diodes ($D_1$–$D_4$) make up each phase leg of the suggested topology. The 3-level output voltages are achieved at phase voltages, i.e., $V_{an}, V_{bn}$, and $V_{cn}$ subsequently 5-levels are generated on the line-to-line voltages $V_{ab}, V_{bc}$, and $V_{ca}$. This type of switching configuration produces 3-levels in the phase voltages like $+V_s/2, 0, -V_s/2$.

**Table 17.1** Switching states for phase 'a' of three-phase 3L proposed MLI.

| Output levels | $S_{w1a}$ | $S_{w2a}$ | $S_{w3a}$ | $S_{w4a}$ |
|---|---|---|---|---|
| $V_S/2$ | 1 | 0 | 0 | 0 |
| 0 | 0 | 1 | 1 | 0 |
| $-V_S/2$ | 0 | 0 | 1 | 1 |

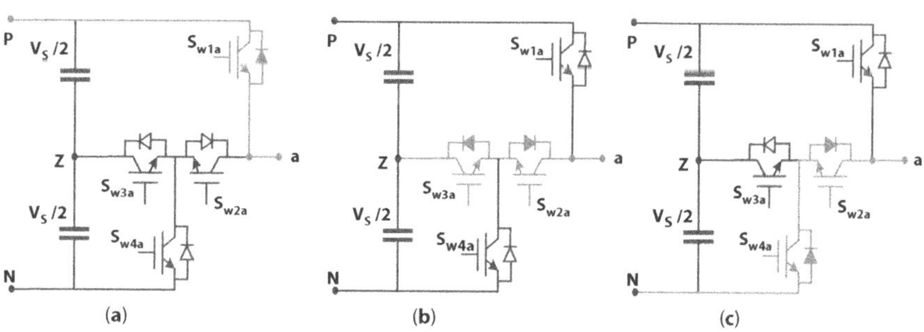


**Figure 17.2** Operation modes of phase 'a' output voltage for three-phase 3L MLI: (a) $+V_s/2$, (b) 0 (c), and $-V_s/2$ output voltages.

The switching state table for a phase 'a' of the proposed 3L three-phase MLI is shown in Table 17.1. A similar switching table can be derived for the remaining phases. It is clear that $S_{w1}$ equals 1 when the switch is ON and 0 when it is OFF. The output will be $+V_s/2$ when the upper switch, $S_{w1a}$ is ON. The output is $-V_s/2$ when the lower two switches, $S_{w2a}$ and $S_{w4a}$, are turned ON. During ON condition, switches $S_{w2a}$ and $S_{w3a}$ produce zero output. The equivalent switching circuits are illustrated in Figure 17.2.

## 17.3 Control Strategy and Simulation Outcomes

To evaluate the performance of the PD-PWM control strategy for the proposed MLI is evaluated using MATLAB/SIMULINK software. The complete system modeling with the proposed 3L and its corresponding PD-PWM strategy is depicted in Figure 17.3. The system specification used to validate the suggested PD-PWM control strategy is given in Table 17.2.

With respect to the PD-PWM control approach, the aggregated three-level voltage waveforms depicted in Figure 17.4 are obtained by comparing two carrier signals with a switching frequency ($f_{sw}$) of 5 kHz to a reference sinusoidal signal with a modulation index of 1. For the switches $S_{w1a}$–$S_{w4a}$ in the suggested MLI topology illustrated in Figure 17.2(a), the PD-PWM

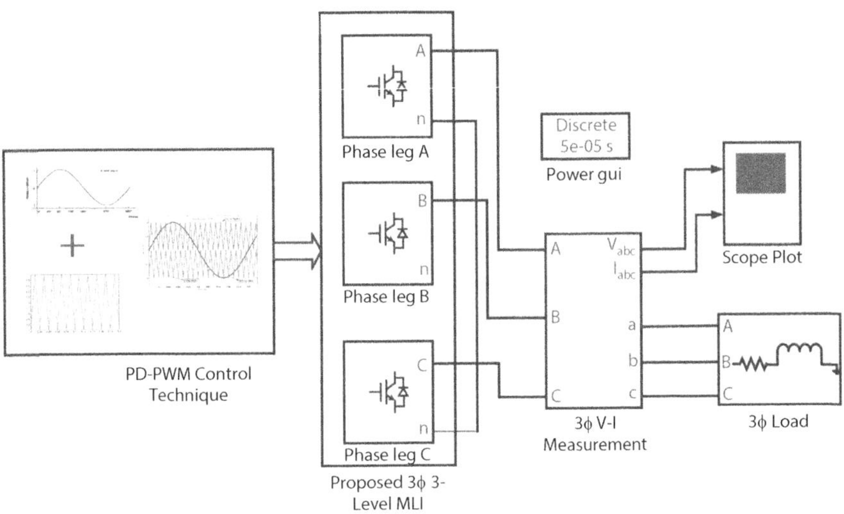


**Figure 17.3** MATLAB Simulink model for proposed MLI with PD-PWM control technique.

**Table 17.2** System specification.

| | |
|---|---|
| DC voltage ($V_{dc}$) | 100 V |
| Modulation index ($M_a$) | 1 |
| Switching frequency ($f_{sw}$) | 5 kHz |
| Output load ($R_l, L_l$) | 1 Ω, 20 mH |

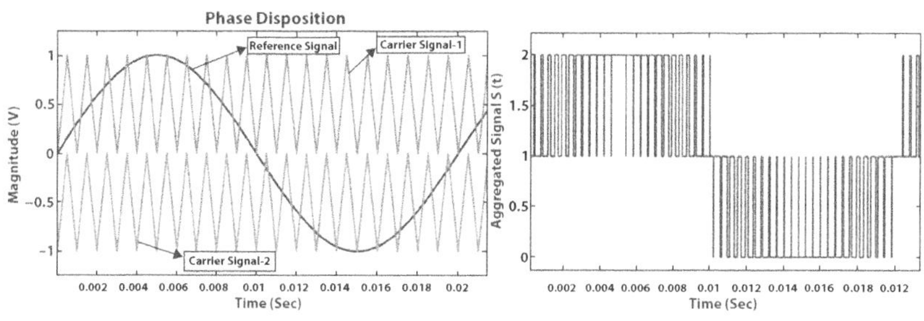

**Figure 17.4** (a) Signal layout for the carrier and reference in the proposed PD-PWM switching method and (b) aggregated signal $S(t)$.

gate triggering signals are provided in Figure 17.5, along with the phase voltages, line-to-line voltages, and load current of the proposed MLI, as shown in Figures 17.6(a–c).

The enlarged view of the current and line-to-line voltage at the load of the suggested MLI topology is shown in Figure 17.7. The Fast Fourier Transform (FFT) evaluation of the current at the load is shown in Figure 17.8 with a THD value of 1.93% at switching frequency $f_{sw} = 5$ kHz under an R-L load of 1 Ω, 20 mH. The FFT analysis of line-to-line voltage is shown in Figure 17.9 with a THD value of 36.18%. Table 17.3 presents a comparative analysis of the %THD values for both voltage and current across the proposed MLI, NPC, and Conventional 180° VSI using SPWM and PD-PWM control strategies. It is evident that the PD-PWM-based MLI achieves lower %THD values for both voltage and current compared to the conventional SPWM. Table 17.4 compares the proposed 3L inverter with conventional topologies such as NPC, ANPC, T-type, FC, and CHB. Although the number of controlled power semiconductor switches (IGBTs with anti-parallel diodes) is similar across all configurations, the proposed inverter eliminates the need for clamping devices (capacitors, power diodes, and quadratic switches) found in the conventional topologies mentioned.

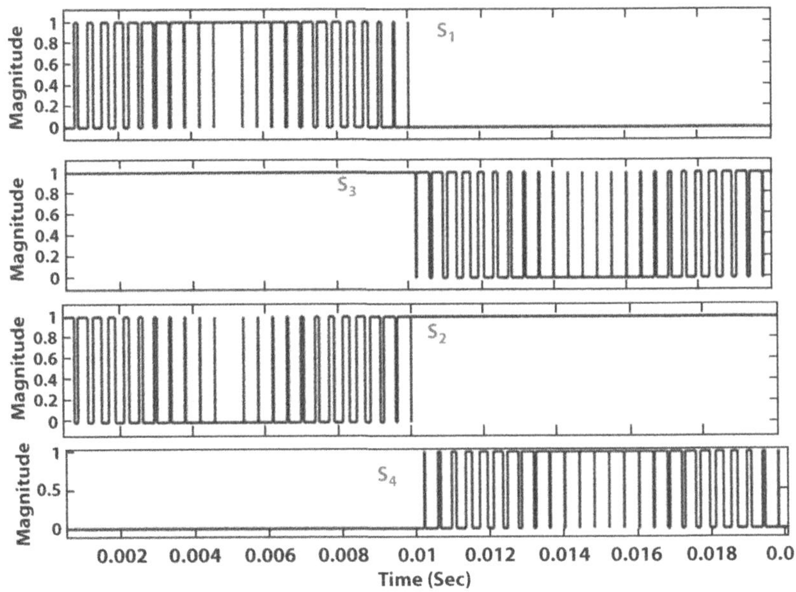


**Figure 17.5** PD-PWM switching pulses ($S_1$ to $S_4$) for a three-phase proposed MLI.

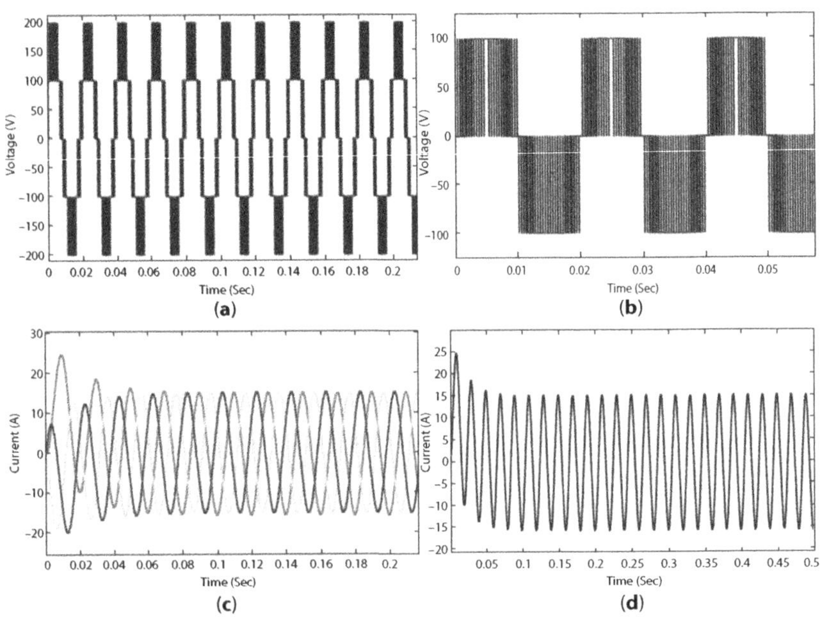


**Figure 17.6** Simulated outcomes: (a) Phase voltage, (b) line-to-Line voltage, (c) three-phase, and (d) phase load current of the proposed MLI at switching frequency $f_{sw} = 5$ kHz.

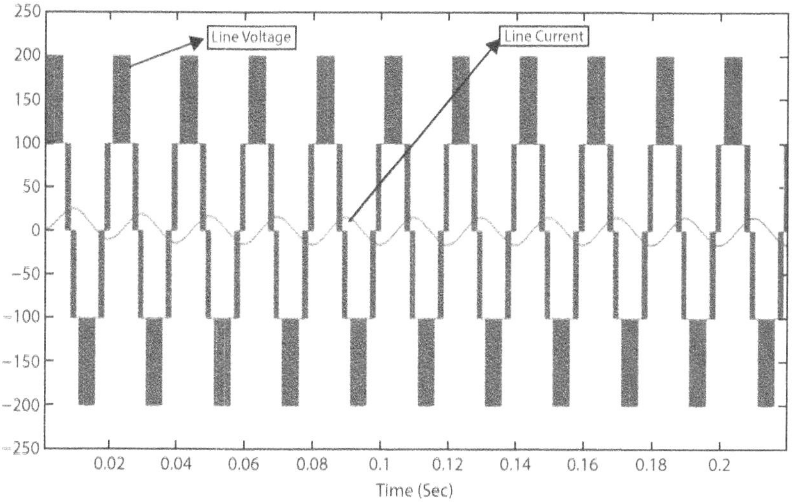


**Figure 17.7** Current and line-to-line voltage at the load of the suggested PD-PWM approach for the proposed MLI at switching frequency $f_{sw} = 5$ kHz under R-L load of 1 Ω, 20 mH.

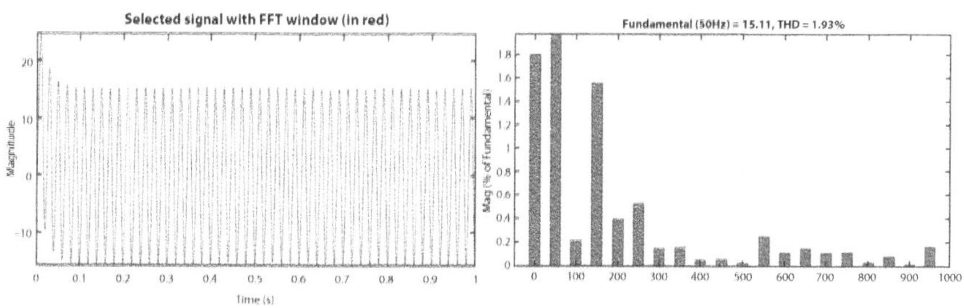


**Figure 17.8** FFT of load current profile of the proposed PD-PWM approach for the proposed MLI at switching frequency $f_{sw} = 5$ kHz under R-L load of 1 Ω, 20 mH: (a) Selected signal and (b) FFT analysis.

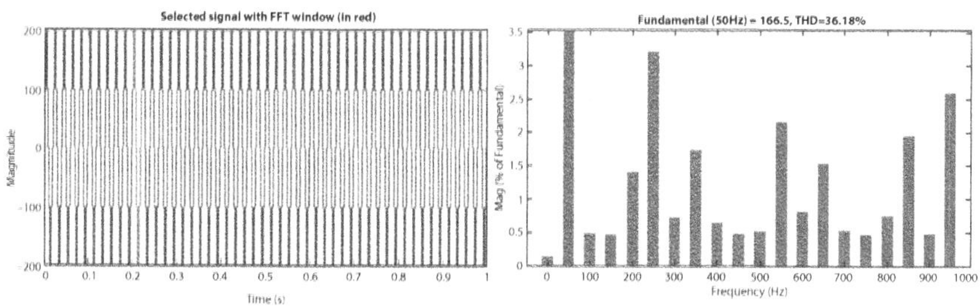


**Figure 17.9** FFT profile of line-line voltage of the suggested PD-PWM approach for proposed MLI at switching frequency $f_{sw} = 5$ kHz under R-L load of 1 Ω, 20 mH: (a) Selected signal and (b) FFT analysis.

**Table 17.3** % of THD in current and voltage.

| Control techniques | Conventional SPWM | | Proposed PD-PWM | |
|---|---|---|---|---|
| | % of THD in voltage | % of THD in current | % of THD in voltage | % of THD in current |
| Proposed MLI | 38.25% | 4.44% | 36.18% | 1.86% |
| NPC | 38.26% | 5.41% | 36.35% | 4.72% |
| 180° VSI | 64.83% | 8.04% | 50.83% | 6.38% |

**Table 17.4** Comparison of three-level inverters for phase.

| Topology | NPC [10] | ANPC [11] | FC [12] | CHB [13] | T-type [14, 15] | Proposed MLI |
|---|---|---|---|---|---|---|
| Switches | 4 | 6 | 4 | 4 | 4 | 4 |
| Clamping diodes | 2 | 0 | 0 | 0 | 0 | 0 |
| Quadratic switches | 0 | 0 | 0 | 0 | 2 | 0 |
| Flying capacitor | 0 | 0 | 2 | 0 | 0 | 0 |
| H-bridge | No | No | No | Yes | No | No |
| Synthesizing positive output voltage | 2 | 2 | 2 | 2 | 2 | 1 |

## 17.4 Conclusion

Modifying the conventional NPC evading clamping diodes and quadratic switches creates the suggested three-phase 3L inverter. High switching frequency operation results in three phases voltage levels and five line-line voltage levels for each inverter leg under the assumed load conditions of R = 1 Ω and L = 20 mH. As compared to the conventional NPC, the suggested 3L MLI requires fewer power diodes and only one power switch to provide the positive output due to the removal of clamping diodes and quadratic switches. As a result, it becomes possible to implement the suggested MLI rather than the NPC MLI and reduce the percentage of conduction losses responsible. Further application of the suggested PD-PWM system improves the MLI's performance by lowering the THD in the load current, phase, and line-to-line voltages. The simulation findings are in good match with the PD-PWM approach and the suggested MLI. In terms of reduced component usage and voltage stress, the three-phase MLI design that has been suggested is considered preferable.

## References


1. Singh, J. and Tiwari, R., Cost benefit analysis for V2G implementation of electric vehicles in distribution system. *IEEE Trans. Ind. Appl.*, 56, 5, 5963–5973, 2020.
2. Emadi, A., Lee, Y.J., Rajashekara, K., Power electronics and motor drives in electric, hybrid electric, and plug-in hybrid electric vehicles. *IEEE Trans. Ind. Electron.*, 55, 6, 2237–2245, 2008.
3. Emadi, A., Rajashekara, K., Williamson, S.S., Lukic, S.M., Topological overview of hybrid electric and fuel cell vehicular power system architectures and configurations. *IEEE Trans. Veh. Technol.*, 54, 3, 763–770, 2005.
4. Chau, K.T., Chan, C.C., Liu, C., Overview of permanent-magnet brushless drives for electric and hybrid electric vehicles. *IEEE Trans. Ind. Electron.*, 55, 6, 2246–2257, 2008.
5. Zhu, Z.Q. and Howe, D., Electrical machines and drives for electric, hybrid, and fuel cell vehicles. *Proc. IEEE*, 95, 4, 746–765, 2007.
6. Chan, C.C. and Chau, K.T., *Modern electric vehicle technology*, vol. 47, Oxford University Press, USA, 2001.
7. Tolbert, L.M., Peng, F.Z., Habetler, T.G., Multilevel converters for large electric drives. *IEEE Trans. Ind. Appl.*, 35, 1, 36–44, 1999.
8. Tolbert, L.M., Peng, F.Z., Adams, D.J., Mckeever, J.W., Multilevel inverters for large automotive electric drives, in: *Darborn, Michigan*, 1997.
9. Carrara, G., Gardella, S., Marchesoni, M., Salutari, R., Sciutto, G., A new multilevel PWM method: A theoretical analysis. *IEEE Trans. Power Electron.*, 7, 3, 497–505, 1992.
10. Omer, P., Kumar, J., Surjan, B.S., Comparison of multicarrier PWM techniques for cascaded H-bridge inverter, in: *2014 IEEE Students' Conference on Electrical, Electronics and Computer Science*, IEEE, pp. 1–6, 2014, March.
11. Sambhavi, Y.V. and Ramachandran, V., A technical review of modern traction inverter systems used in electric vehicle application. *Energy Rep.*, 10, 3882–3907, 2023.

12. McGrath, B.P. and Holmes, D.G., Multicarrier PWM strategies for multilevel inverters. *IEEE Trans. Ind. Electron.*, 49, 4, 858–867, 2002.
13. Newton, C. and Sumner, M., Neutral point control for multi-level inverters: theory, design and operational limitations, in: *IAS'97. Conference Record of the 1997 IEEE Industry Applications Conference Thirty-Second IAS Annual Meeting*, vol. 2, IEEE, pp. 1336–1343, 1997, October.
14. Praveen, O., Performance study of Capacitor Clamped Multilevel Inverter fed Induction Motor Drive for Electric Vehicle Application, in: *2022 IEEE International Conference on Signal Processing, Informatics, Communication and Energy Systems (SPICES)*, vol. 1, IEEE, pp. 7–11, 2022, March.
15. Ogasawara, S. and Akagi, H., Analysis of variation of neutral point potential in neutral-point-clamped voltage source PWM inverters, in: *Conference Record of the 1993 IEEE Industry Applications Conference Twenty-Eighth IAS Annual Meeting*, IEEE, pp. 965–970, 1993, October.

# Index


12-port charging station, 46–53

AC voltage (from piezo), 231, 233, 235
Active grid, 108
Adaptive energy management strategy, 40
Add-on devices, 269
Advanced driver assistance systems (ADAS), 176, 178
Aerodynamic drag, 267, 268, 273, 275
Aerodynamics, 267, 268, 274
Algorithms, shortest path
  A* search, 182, 183
  Bellman–Ford, 182
  bidirectional search, 184, 185
  Dijkstra's, 180, 181
  Floyd–Warshall, 183, 184
  Hybrid RRT–PRM, 189–192
  PRM (Probabilistic Roadmap), 187–189
  RRT (Rapidly Exploring Random Tree), 185–187
Alternative phase opposition disposition (APOD), 340
Analog to digital conversion, 205, 213, 214
ANSYS Fluent (CFD software), 267, 273
Anti-theft locking system, 260, 261
Applications in EV safety and performance, 282, 283, 285, 286, 290–292
Arduino IDE, 257
ARM Cortex-M3, 202, 211
Artificial intelligence
  components of smart charging, 74
    cloud computing platforms, 77, 78
    communication protocols, 79–81
    control algorithms for dynamic charging, 81–83
    edge computing platforms, 78, 79
    sensors and IoT devices, 75, 76
  optimizing the infrastructure, 65
    demand prediction, 65
    dynamic pricing, 65
    grid integration, 66
    load balancing, 65
    predictive maintenance, 66
    route planning, 66
    user experience enhancement, 66
Artificial neural network (ANN)
  controller, 33–39
  for power regulation, 29
  vs. PI controller, 37–39
Automotive safety integrity level (ASIL), 230
Autonomous driving, 178

Battery and power management, 323, 327, 328
Battery charging/storage, 233, 235, 236, 238, 239
Battery electric vehicles (BEVs), 226, 243, 244, 251
Battery energy storage system
  modeling, 32, 33
  state of charge (SOC), 32, 33
  support for long-term fluctuations, 39

Battery energy storage system, 3, 4, 20–24
Battery longevity, 192
Battery management system (BMS), 195, 197, 226, 229, 230, 282–287, 289–291
Battery model, 114
Battery swapping stations, 98
Bearing fault, 137–152
Bicycle design, 313, 316, 319
Bidirectional CLLC resonant converter, 158
Bidirectional DC–DC converter, 31–33
Bidirectional search algorithm, 184, 185
Binomial distribution, 44, 47
Biomechanics, 316, 327
Block diagram of hybrid control mode, 167
Blockchain IoT (reference), 193
Blynk IoT app, 231, 239
Boost converter, 4, 9, 235, 238, 256, 259
Boundary conditions, 272, 273
Buck converter, 4, 233, 235, 238

Camera system, 256, 260, 262
Carrier signal, 339, 340, 342, 343
Cascaded H-bridge (CHB), 339
CFD analysis, 267, 268, 271, 272
Challenges in fault detection, 303
Charging infrastructure, 41, 42
  connectivity, 177, 178
  mart grid interaction, 179
  vehicle-to-grid (V2G), 178, 180
Charging port reliability, 42–44
Chassis (vehicle design), 255, 262
Clamping diodes, 337, 339, 341, 346, 347
Code Composer Studio and JTAG, 212
Comparative analysis, 303, 304
Conclusion and future impact, 173
Conduction losses, 347
Constant current, 11
Constant voltage, 10, 11
Constant-current and constant-voltage charging phases, 166
Consumer comfort, 175, 180
Control algorithms, 323, 327
Control strategies
  ANN controller, 33–39
  PI controller, 33–38
Cost analysis, 326, 328
Cost benefit, 244, 250
Cost function of port configuration, 45, 53
Cost per kilometer, 243, 244, 251
Current and vibration, 137, 140–142, 151, 152
Current integrating technique, 32

Daubechies wavelet function, 144
DC bus voltage regulation, 36–39
DC microgrid
  architecture, 30, 31
  energy management, 35, 36
DC-DC converter, 338
Deep learning, 115
Deep neural network, 141, 146
Demand response, 179
Demand response management, 72–74
Deployment factors, 62
Design and engineering, 316, 327
Design specifications, 169
Digital signal controllers (DSCs), 199, 204, 207
Digital signal processing (DSP), 215, 216
Dijkstra's algorithm, 180, 181
Diode bridge rectifier, 234, 235
Direct memory access (DMA), 205
Distributed generation (DG), 92
Doubly fed induction generator (DFIG), 98
Drag coefficient (Cd), 273, 278
Drag force, 278
Drive cycle, 245
Drive train, 249

DWT, 140, 142, 148–152

Edge computing, 108
Electric bicycle (e-bike), 313, 315, 316, 329
Electric motor, 243–246, 251
Electric motor assistance, 313, 317, 323, 327
Electric vehicle (EV) charging
load demand, 30, 36–39
point architecture, 30, 31
renewable integration, 30
Electric vehicle charging station, 2–5, 24–26
Electric vehicle charging stations, 96
Electric vehicles (EVs), 1, 2, 16, 17, 41, 42, 91, 243, 244, 251, 281–283, 285, 286, 290–292, 337
fleet management, 178, 179
logistics, 178, 179
telematics, 176, 177
user experience, 180
Energy efficiency, 176, 179, 192, 316, 327, 328
Energy harvesting, 231, 232, 236, 240
Energy management, 179, 180
Energy management system (EMS), 196
control equations, 35
flowchart, 35, 36
operation with HESS, 36, 37
Environmental impact, 316, 328
Equivalent circuit analysis, 160
ESP32 microcontroller, 238, 239
ESP32-CAM module, 255–257, 259–263
EV charging stations, 177
Excitation inductance ($L_m$), 158

Failure rate evaluation, 42–44, 47–51
Fast Fourier transform (FFT), 343
Field programmable gate arrays (FPGAs), 195, 199, 208
Fleet operations, 176, 178, 179
Flow characteristics, 268, 273, 275, 278
Floyd–Warshall algorithm, 183, 184
Flying capacitor (FC), 346
Foot-stamping mechanism, 313, 316, 319, 323
Footstep energy system, 231, 240
Four-wheeler, 243, 247, 249, 251
Frequency and inductance effect, 162
Frequency control method, 160
Frequency domains, 144
Fuel cell, 3, 9, 13, 19–20, 23–24
Fuel cell electric vehicle (FCEV), 337
Fuel economy, 267, 269, 278
Full-bridge configuration, 158

Gate triggering signal, 343
Geometry modification, 267, 271, 278
Graphical user interfaces (GUIs), 202
Grid-to-vehicle, 60

Human-powered propulsion, 313, 316, 317
Hybrid bicycle, 313, 317, 329
Hybrid control strategy, 165
Hybrid electric vehicle (HEV), 337
Hybrid energy storage system (HESS)
architecture, 30, 31
components (battery + SC), 29–34
operation, 34–37
power balancing, 30
role in DC microgrid, 29, 30
Hybrid power system, 231, 236, 240
Hybrid RRT–PRM algorithm, 189–192
Hysteresis control for mode switching, 168

ICT tools, 63
Identical port configuration, 46–50
Impedance and transfer function, 161
Inductance coefficient (k), 161
Infrastructure connectivity, 177, 178
Inner and outer race fault, 141
Input voltage and current waveforms, 170

Internal combustion engine, 243, 244, 251
Internet of Things (IoT)
 algorithms and optimization, 180–192
 autonomous driving, 178
 fleet and logistics, 178, 179
 remote monitoring, 176, 177
 renewable energy integration, 179
 smart charging, 177–180
 sustainability, 179, 180
 user experience, 180, 181
IoT integration, 231, 239, 240

Kalman filter, 300, 305, 306
Kurtogram, 141–144, 146, 148, 151, 152
Kurtogram images, 141

L298N motor driver, 256, 257
LabVIEW, 202, 212
Level shifted PWM (LS-PWM), 340
Lifecycle assessment, 180
Line loss minimization, 95
Linear programming (in Hybrid RRT-PRM), 190–192
Line-to-line voltage, 341, 343–345, 347
Lithium-ion (Li-ion) batteries, 281–284, 286–291, 293–297
Load current, 339, 343–345, 347
Lock mechanism (mobile-controlled), 256, 260, 261, 263
Logistics, 178, 179

Machine learning, 146
Machine learning (CNN, LSTM), 298
Machine learning algorithms
 parameter to predict, 67
 predictive charging, 68–70
Maintenance costs, 52–54
Markov analysis, 43
MATLAB simulation, 337
MATLAB Simulink, 202, 231, 233, 237
Maximization of the stability margin, 95
Maximum power point tracking (MPPT), 4, 9
Mesh/meshing, 270–272
Metaheuristic algorithms, 292, 294, 297, 298, 299, 304–306
Microgrid, 124
MIL-HDBK-217F, 44, 48, 54
MIL-HDBK-338B, 44, 47
Minimization of voltage deviation, 95
Mobile-application interface, 261–263
Monte Carlo simulation, 43
Motor drive, 338, 347, 348
Multi gigabit transceivers (MGT), 208
Multi-objective evolutionary algorithm, 95
Multi-objective particle swarm optimization, 96
Multiple-model adaptive approximation approach, 283

Neutral point clamped multilevel inverter (NPC MLI), 337
New European Driving Cycle (NEDC), 243, 245, 249–251
Non-identical port configuration, 46–52

On-board charger, 197, 198
Optimization techniques, 71, 293, 302, 305
Output voltage and current waveform, 172

Paderborn University bearing dataset, 141, 148
Pan-tilt mechanism, 256, 259, 260, 262, 263
Pareto optimal set, 95
Path planning algorithms, 180–192
Permanent magnet (PM) motor, 338
Perturb and observe, 10, 11
Phase disposition pulse width modulation (PD-PWM), 337

Phase opposition disposition (POD), 340
Phase-shift control technique, 164
Phase-shift control voltage equation, 164
Phase-shifted PWM (PS-PWM), 340
Photovoltaic, 93
Photovoltaic (PV), 2–5, 15, 18–20, 24
Photovoltaic (PV) system
modeling, 31, 32
output characteristics, 30–32
Piezoelectric effect, 231, 233, 234
Piezoelectric transducers, 231–236, 238–240
Plug-in hybrid electric vehicle (PHEV), 337
PMSM, 138, 139, 141
Port failure probability, 49–51
Power converter, 338
Power distribution system, 41–43
Power equations, 35
Power losses, 337
Power management system (PMS), 34–37
strategies, 30, 35
Pressure contour, 274, 275
PRM algorithm, 187–189
Probability distribution function, 93
Prototype development and testing, 323, 326, 329
Pulse width modulation (PWM), 201, 207, 214, 339
PV cell model, 109
PWM control strategies, 343

Quadratic switches, 337, 343
Quality factor (Q), 161
Quality factor influence, 163

Rapidly exploring random tree (RRT), 185–187
RC vehicle, 255–263
Reactive power capacity, 100
Real-time data analytics, 71
Recursive least squares (RLS), 283, 300, 305, 306
Reduced switch inverter, 339, 341, 343, 345, 347
Reference signal, 339
Regenerative braking, 245, 249–251
Reliability indices, 43, 44
Reliability probability, 42–44, 47–51
Remote control/navigation, 255–257, 259, 262, 263
Remote monitoring, 176, 177
Renewable energy, 231, 240
Renewable energy integration, 179
Renewable energy sources, 91
Resonant current and voltage at 90 kHz, 170
Resonant current and voltage at 90 kHz, 100 kHz, 171
Resonant current and voltage at 90 kHz, 110 kHz, 171
Resonant frequency equations, 160
Resonant inductance and capacitance, 158
Reverse operation analysis, 172
Rider fatigue and strain, 314, 317, 326
R-L load, 343, 345
RRT algorithm, 185–187

Safety, 176, 192
Safety issues, 281
Sensor faults, 282, 284, 285, 290, 292, 294, 306
Servo motor, 256, 260, 261
Shortest path finding, 180–192
SiC MOSFETs, 226, 227, 228, 230
Simulation of converter performance, 169
Simulation results
ANN vs. PI controller, 37–39
battery response, 37
PV output variation, 36, 37
SC response, 36, 37
Smart charging systems, 177–180

Smart grid interaction, 179
Smart household integration, 180
Software development environment (SDE), 219
Solar energy, 231, 232, 236, 240
Solar panel, 231, 233, 235–239
Solar photovoltaic (PV)
  integration with EVCS, 29–31
  irradiance variation, 31, 36
  limitations, 30
SST turbulence model, 271, 273
State of charge (SoC), 196, 250, 251, 282, 285, 289, 290, 292, 299, 300, 303
State of health (SOH), 289, 290, 303, 304
STM-based embedded controllers, 226
Streamline profile, 276, 278
Survey of methods, 299–302
Sustainability, 179, 180
Sustainable transportation, 313, 317, 328
Switching diagram, 168
Switching elements S1–S8, 158
Switching states, 341
Switching stress, 337
System efficiency, 338
System reliability, 42–44, 47–53
System stability, 192
Systems-on-chip (SoC), 202

Technique for order preference by similarity to ideal solution (TOPSIS), 96
Telematics, 176, 177
THD, 346
Thermal runaway, 285, 288–293
Timers and counters, 206
TMS320F2812, 219, 220, 221, 230
Traffic-aware routing, 193
Transformer turns ratio (n:1), 158
Truck aerodynamics, 267, 268, 278
T-type inverter, 339, 343, 346

Universal serial bus (USB), 205
User convenience, 176, 192
User experience, 180
User experience and accessibility, 323, 326, 328

Vehicle dynamics, 244, 247, 248
Vehicle-to-grid (V2G), 41, 59, 60, 74, 78, 80, 87
Vehicle-to-grid (V2G) technology, 178, 180
Velocity contour, 275, 276
Velocity vector` profile, 277
VGG-19, 147
Vibration signal, 137, 139–142, 148–152
Visual geometry group, 137, 141, 146–148, 152
Voltage gain characteristics, 162
Voltage sensor, 234, 239
Voltage source inverter (VSI), 338

Wake production, 278
Wavelet analysis, 137
Web interface (ESP32), 256, 257, 260, 262
Wi-Fi connectivity, 257, 262, 263
Wind, 3, 4, 8, 21, 23, 24
Wind turbine model, 112

Ziegler-Nichols, 11

# Also of Interest

## Check out these related titles from Scrivener Publishing

*Graph Convolutional Neural Networks for Computer Vision,* Edited by Malini Alagarsamy, Rajesh Kumar Dhanaraj, J. Felicia Lilian, Vandana Sharma, and Gheorghita Ghinea, ISBN: 9781394356331. Revolutionize your machine learning practice with this essential book that provides expert insights into leveraging Graph Convolutional Networks (GCNNs) to overcome the limitations of traditional CNNs.

*Applied Computer Vision Through Artificial Intelligence,* Edited by Jasminder Kaur Sandhu, Abhishek Kumar, Rakesh Sahu, and Sachin Ahuja, ISBN: 9781394272594. Master the cutting-edge field of computer vision and artificial intelligence with this accessible guide to the applications of machine learning and deep learning for real-world solutions in robotics, healthcare, and autonomous systems.

*Predictive Methods in Next-Generation Computing,* Edited by R. Sathiyaraj, Rajesh Kumar Dhanaraj, K. Arun Kumar, Rutvij H. Jhaveri, and A. Mohamed Abbas, ISBN: 9781394248797. Predictive Methods in Next-Generation Computing is essential for anyone looking to understand how next-generation computing technologies are driving predictive models to create smarter, safer, and more sustainable solutions across diverse fields.

*Deep Learning and Its Applications Using Python,* Edited by Niha Kamal Basha, Surbhi Bhatia Khan, Abhishek Kumar and Arwa Mashat, ISBN: 9781394166466. This practical book gives a detailed description of deep learning models and their implementation using Python programming relating to computer vision, natural language processing, and other applications.

*Networked Sensing Systems,* Edited by Rajesh Kumar Dhanaraj, Malathy Sathyamoorthy, Balasubramaniam S., and Seifedine Kadry, ISBN: 9781394310869. *Networked Sensing Systems* is essential for anyone seeking innovative and sustainable solutions across diverse sectors, as it explores the integration of cutting-edge IoT technologies and digital transformation aimed at enhancing resource efficiency and addressing climate change challenges.

*Multimodal Data Fusion for Bioinformatics Artificial Intelligence,* Edited by Umesh Kumar Lilhore, Abhishek Kumar, Narayan Vyas, Sarita Simaiya, and Vishal Dutt, ISBN: 9781394269938. *Multimodal Data Fusion for Bioinformatics Artificial Intelligence* is a must-have for anyone interested in the intersection of AI and bioinformatics, as it not only delves into innovative data fusion methods and their applications in omics research but also addresses the ethical implications and future developments shaping the field today.

*Data Structure and Algorithms Using C++: A Practical Implementation,* By Sachi Nandan Mohanty and Pabitra Kumar Tripathy, ISBN: 9781119750543. The book is intended to assist university faculty members and students to realize the principles and acquire the practical skills of programming using the C++ programming language.

*Artificial Intelligence-Based System Models in Healthcare,* Edited by A. Jose Anand, K. Kalaiselvi and Jyotir Moy Chatterjee, ISBN: 9781394242498. Artificial Intelligence-Based System Models in Healthcare provides a comprehensive and insightful guide to the transformative applications of AI in the healthcare system.

*EXPLAINABLE MACHINE LEARNING MODELS AND ARCHITECTURES: Real-Time System Implementation,* Edited by Suman Lata Tripathi and Mufti Mahmud, ISBN: 9781394185849. This cutting-edge new volume covers the hardware architecture implementation, the software implementation approach, and the efficient hardware of machine learning applications.

*Natural Language Processing for Software Engineering,* Edited by Rajesh Kumar Chakrawarti, Ranjana Sikarwar, Sanjaya Kumar Sarangi, Samson Arun Raj Albert Raj, Shweta Gupta, Krishnan Sakthidasan Sankaran, and Romil Rawat, ISBN: 9781394272433. Discover how Natural Language Processing for Software Engineering can transform your understanding of agile development, equipping you with essential tools and insights to enhance software quality and responsiveness in todays rapidly changing technological landscape.

*MACHINE LEARNING TECHNIQUES FOR VLSI CHIP DESIGN,* Edited by Abhishek Kumar, Suman Lata Tripathi, and K. Srinivasa Rao, ISBN: 9781119910398. This cutting-edge new volume covers the hardware architecture implementation, the software implementation approach, and the efficient hardware of machine learning applications with FPGA or CMOS circuits, and many other aspects and applications of machine learning techniques for VLSI chip design.

*Intelligent Green Technologies for Smart Cities,* Edited by Suman Lata Tripathi, Souvik Ganguli, Abhishek Kumar, and Tengiz Magradze, ISBN: 9781119816065. Presenting the concepts and fundamentals of smart cities and developing "green" technologies, this volume, written and edited by a global team of experts, also goes into the practical applications that can be utilized across multiple disciplines and industries, for both the engineer and the student.

*Hybrid Intelligent Optimization Approaches for Smart Energy: A Practical Approach,* Edited by Senthilkumar Mohan, A. John, Sanjeevikumar Padmanaban, and Yasir Hamid, ISBN: 9781119821243. Written and edited by a group of experts in the field, this is a comprehensive and up-to-date description of current energy optimization techniques, such as artificial intelligence techniques, machine learning, deep learning, and IoT techniques and their future trends.

*NANODEVICES FOR INTEGRATED CIRCUIT DESIGN,* Edited by Suman Lata Tripathi, Abhishek Kumar, K. Srinivasa Rao, and Prasantha R. Mudimela, ISBN: 9781394185788. Written and edited by a team of experts in the field, this important new volume broadly covers the design of nano-devices and their integrated applications in digital and analog integrated circuits (IC) design.

*DESIGN AND DEVELOPMENT OF EFFICIENT ENERGY SYSTEMS,* Edited by Suman Lata Tripathi, Dushyant Kumar Singh, Sanjeevikumar Padmanaban, and P. Raja, ISBN: 9781119761631. Covering the concepts and fundamentals of efficient energy systems, this volume, written and edited by a global team of experts, also goes into the practical applications that can be utilized across multiple industries, for both the engineer and the student.

*Electrical and Electronic Devices, Circuits, and Materials: Technical Challenges and Solutions*, Edited by Suman Lata Tripathi, Parvej Ahmad Alvi, and Umashankar Subramaniam, ISBN: 9781119750369. Covering every aspect of the design and improvement needed for solid-state electronic devices and circuit and their reliability issues, this new volume also includes overall system design for all kinds of analog and digital applications and developments in power systems.

*MODELING AND OPTIMIZATION OF OPTICAL COMMUNICATION NETWORKS*, Edited by Chandra Singh, Rathishchandra R Gatti, K.V.S.S.S.S. Sairam, and Ashish Singh, ISBN: 9781119839200. *Modeling and Optimization of Optical Communication Networks* is a comprehensive and authoritative book that delves into the optical networks, principles, technologies, and practical applications of optical networks, equipping readers with the knowledge needed to design, implement, and optimize optical networks for various applications, from telecommunications to scientific research. With its comprehensive coverage and up-to-date insights, this book serves as an essential reference in the field of optical networks.

*WIRELESS COMMUNICATION SECURITY: Mobile and Network Security Protocols*, Edited by Manju Khari, Manisha Bharti, and M. Niranjanamurthy, ISBN: 9781119777144. Presenting the concepts and advances of wireless communication security, this volume, written and edited by a global team of experts, also goes into the practical applications for the engineer, student, and other industry professionals.

*ADVANCES IN DATA SCIENCE AND ANALYTICS*, Edited by M. Niranjanamurthy, Hemant Kumar Gianey, and Amir H. Gandomi, ISBN: 9781119791881. Presenting the concepts and advances of data science and analytics, this volume, written and edited by a global team of experts, also goes into the practical applications that can be utilized across multiple disciplines and industries, for both the engineer and the student, focusing on machining learning, big data, business intelligence, and analytics.

*ARTIFICIAL INTELLIGENCE AND DATA MINING IN SECURITY FRAMEWORKS*, Edited by Neeraj Bhargava, Ritu Bhargava, Pramod Singh Rathore, and Rashmi Agrawal, ISBN: 9781119760405. Written and edited by a team of experts in the field, this outstanding new volume offers solutions to the problems of security, outlining the concepts behind allowing computers to learn from experience and understand the world in terms of a hierarchy of concepts.

*MACHINE LEARNING AND DATA SCIENCE: Fundamentals and Applications*, Edited by Prateek Agrawal, Charu Gupta, Anand Sharma, Vishu Madaan, and Nisheeth Joshi, ISBN: 9781119775614. Written and edited by a team of experts in the field, this collection of papers reflects the most up-to-date and comprehensive current state of machine learning and data science for industry, government, and academia.

*MEDICAL IMAGING*, Edited by H. S. Sanjay, and M. Niranjanamurthy, ISBN: 9781119785392. Written and edited by a team of experts in the field, this is the most comprehensive and up-to-date study of and reference for the practical applications of medical imaging for engineers, scientists, students, and medical professionals.

*SECURITY ISSUES AND PRIVACY CONCERNS IN INDUSTRY 4.0 APPLICATIONS*, Edited by Shibin David, R. S. Anand, V. Jeyakrishnan, and M. Niranjanamurthy, ISBN: 9781119775621. Written and edited by a team of international experts, this is the most comprehensive and up-to-date coverage of the security and privacy issues surrounding Industry 4.0 applications, a must-have for any library.

*CYBER SECURITY AND DIGITAL FORENSICS: Challenges and Future Trends*, Edited by Mangesh M. Ghonge, Sabyasachi Pramanik, Ramchandra Mangrulkar, and Dac-Nhuong Le, ISBN: 9781119795636. Written and edited by a team of world renowned experts in the field, this groundbreaking new volume covers key technical topics and gives readers a comprehensive understanding of the latest research findings in cyber security and digital forensics.

*DEEP LEARNING APPROACHES TO CLOUD SECURITY*, Edited by Pramod Singh Rathore, Vishal Dutt, Rashmi Agrawal, Satya Murthy Sasubilli, and Srinivasa Rao Swarna, ISBN: 9781119760528. Covering one of the most important subjects to our society today, this editorial team delves into solutions taken from evolving deep learning approaches, solutions allow computers to learn from experience and understand the world in terms of a hierarchy of concepts.

*MACHINE LEARNING TECHNIQUES AND ANALYTICS FOR CLOUD SECURITY*, Edited by Rajdeep Chakraborty, Anupam Ghosh and Jyotsna Kumar Mandal, ISBN: 9781119762256. This book covers new methods, surveys, case studies, and policy with almost all machine learning techniques and analytics for cloud security solutions.

*SECURITY DESIGNS FOR THE CLOUD, IOT AND SOCIAL NETWORKING,* Edited by Dac-Nhuong Le, Chintin Bhatt and Mani Madhukar, ISBN: 9781119592266. The book provides cutting-edge research that delivers insights into the tools, opportunities, novel strategies, techniques, and challenges for handling security issues in cloud computing, Internet of Things and social networking.

*DESIGN AND ANALYSIS OF SECURITY PROTOCOLS FOR COMMUNICATION,* Edited by Dinesh Goyal, S. Balamurugan, Sheng-Lung Peng and O.P. Verma, ISBN: 9781119555643. The book combines analysis and comparison of various security protocols such as HTTP, SMTP, RTP, RTCP, FTP, UDP for mobile or multimedia streaming security protocol.

*SMART GRIDS FOR SMART CITIES VOLUME 2: Real-Time Applications in Smart Cities,* Edited by O.V. Gnana Swathika, K. Karthikeyan, and Sanjeevikumar Padmanaban, ISBN: 9781394215874. Written and edited by a team of experts in the field, this second volume in a two-volume set focuses on an interdisciplinary perspective on the financial, environmental, and other benefits of smart grid technologies and solutions for smart cities.

*SMART GRIDS AND INTERNET OF THINGS,* Edited by Sanjeevikumar Padmanaban, Jens Bo Holm-Nielsen, Rajesh Kumar Dhanaraj, Malathy Sathyamoorthy, and Balamurugan Balusamy, ISBN: 9781119812449. Written and edited by a team of international professionals, this groundbreaking new volume covers the latest technologies in automation, tracking, energy distribution and consumption of Internet of Things (IoT) devices with smart grids.

Printed and bound by CPI Group (UK) Ltd, Croydon, CR0 4YY

17/09/2026

14964263-0004